# contemporary art in texas

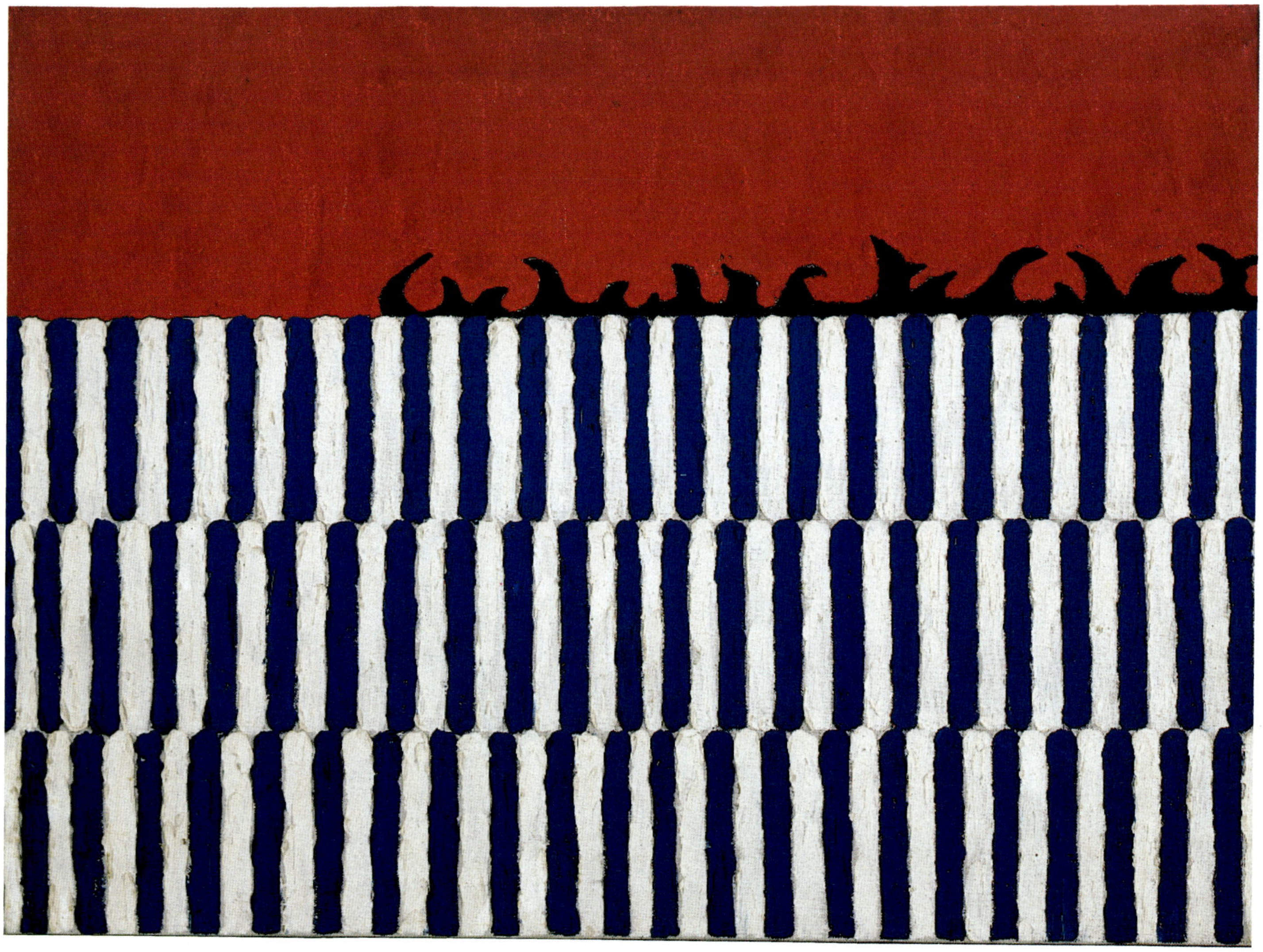

Forrest Bess

**Untitled IIA**

1958, Oil on canvas, $18^{11}/_{16}$" x $24^{3}/_{4}$".
Courtesy of the Museum of Fine Arts, Houston.
Collection of the Museum of Fine Arts, Houston,
Museum purchase with funds provided by
Panhandle Eastern Corporation

# contemporary art in texas

patricia covo johnson

foreword by walter hopps

CRAFTSMAN HOUSE
G+B Arts International

Distributed in Australia by Craftsman House,
20 Barcoo Street, Roseville East, NSW 2069
in association with G+B Arts International:
Australia, Austria, Belgium, China, France, Germany,
Hong Kong, India, Japan, Malaysia, Netherlands,
Russia, Singapore, Switzerland, United Kingdom,
United States of America



ISBN 976 8097 70 1

Design Caroline de Fries
Printer Toppan, Singapore

# Contents

# Acknowledgments

I have brought to this book only one story. It is composed of many others, given graciously and generously by more individuals than can be adequately thanked.

The artists first and foremost, who gave of their time, their insight, their humor, and most of all, their art.

The owners and personnel of galleries who provided photographs, biographies and answered all questions with patience.

The institutions and private collectors who hold the art in trust.

The historians, curators and critics whose work and writings are a crucial resource for us all.

The artists profiled on these pages are Texas' best, but they are not the only ones. Many others could have been selected in their stead.

And a new generation emerges rapidly, with fire and freshness and the desire to change everything — again.

One story never suffices.

# Foreword

**"When I was driving through El Paso**
**That's when I ran out of gaso"**
Robert Frizz Fuller
*Texas Tango*

**1943:** My first encounter with Texas occurred while riding in my father's brand new Cadillac; I rode in the back seat with my grandmother, looking forward to the experience of seeing Texas. The occasion was sparked by my father's desire to try out his new car on a cross-country trip. He had packed up the entire family in Eagle Rock, California, and driven east across the great Southwest, headed for Tampico, Mexico. Unfortunately, my enthusiasm at the prospect of crossing through Texas and going to Mexico was cut short by the onset of a particularly virulent strain of pneumonia which had developed in my eleven-year-old body. Though my parents were both doctors (and atheists), the exigencies of this long trip forced them to rely on the medical services of the Catholic Sisters of Mercy at a small hospital, where I was bedridden within the confines of a Mexican architectural style typical of El Paso's civic buildings. I vividly remember my early appreciation of the healing properties of *menudo*, a tripe soup which I credit with having brought me through this terrible ordeal.

I mention this incident because it was a defining trauma of my young life and also because it was at this time that I first saw the close connection which Texas bears to Mexico. Beyond geographic proximity, the spiritual strain that runs through Mexican culture and art has always been a rich influence on Texas and continues to be an important resource for its artists. The fevered visions which accompanied my first trip to Texas were similar to those that still inhabit some of the haunting imagery populating the work of many Texas imagist and assemblage artists.

**1957:** My involvement with the founding of Ferus Gallery and with the developing art scene in my home base of Los Angeles fed my curiosity about emerging artists in other parts of the country. Naturally, this interest was focused on places like Chicago and New York. It was through two New York exhibitions that I encountered the extraordinary works of both Forrest Bess and Ben L. Culwell. Again, my attention was unexpectedly diverted to Texas.

New York's Museum of Modern Art had been staging exhibitions since 1942 as part of "The Americans" series. In 1957, I ran across Ben L. Culwell's work in a catalogue for the 1946 exhibition "Fourteen Americans". It was at this point that I first became aware of this very important forerunner to a major style that continues to influence, and sometimes to dominate, artists in Texas.

In this same year I first saw the work of visionary Texas artist Forrest Bess at a one-man exhibition at the Betty Parsons Gallery in New York. Bess was certainly not the only Texas artist to have a show in New York by this time, but he was certainly one of the few Texas artists working in an abstract expressionist vein. I was immediately engaged with the high quality of this work; my surprise at the fact that Bess worked in Texas illustrates the great distance then, and still, that existed between much of the art world and the achievements that were taking place simultaneously in that state.

**Mid-1960s:** I met John de Menil. He and his wife Dominique had amassed an important collection of art spanning from antiquities to significant 20th century holdings. John de Menil had been instrumental in placing James Johnson Sweeney as director of the Museum of Fine Arts, Houston, and I had known Sweeney and admired his museum work. Through these associations I had had numerous occasions to encounter the developing art scene in Houston and Texas during the 1960s and into the 1970s.

**1980:** I became founding director of The Menil Collection in Houston and was transplanted to Texas. While assessing The Menil Collection's holdings, I, of course, became aware of the de Menils' extensive holdings of work by Jim Love. Love, Roy Fridge and David McManaway stand as pioneers of the important assemblage strain in Texas art. Their approach to this medium echoes California artists of my generation, such as Wallace Berman, Bruce Conner, and George Herms.

**1993:** Patricia Covo Johnson asked me to write a foreword for a book on Texas artists. This request triggered my reflections on the different experiences which have introduced me to Texas art and affected my understanding and appreciation of its continuing development. Johnson's introductory essay addresses the imagist and expressionist directions in Texas art that have been dominant since the 1950s, when national and international recognition was first afforded this region. Other directions, such as lyrical abstraction and more recent minimalist and conceptual concerns, are also included. The continuing strong affinities with related currents in Latin America, particularly Mexico, are explored as well.

While I have witnessed the burgeoning of native artistic activity and observed the migration of artists to Dallas, Houston, Austin, San Antonio, El Paso and the Rio Grande Valley of south Texas (a phenomenon I readily liken to the early development of contemporary art during my years in Los Angeles in the 1950s and 1960s), I find that Texas art remains little documented in comprehensive publications. It has been recognized chiefly in the successes of certain individual Texas artists and through a number of important solo and group exhibitions with their accompanying catalogues and reviews. This new book is critical to a continuing acknowledgment of Texas's rightful position within, and important contribution to, the development of contemporary art.

*Walter Hopps*

# Introduction

The history of art, critic John Russell wrote, is the history of everything. The history of art in Texas, however, is essentially a history of eccentricity. It could not be otherwise, it seems, given the vastness of the land and its geographic location, the particular political history that gave birth to the state, and in the 20th century, its aura as a mythical place. These conditions have fostered rebellious self-reliance and independence of thought.

The enormous land mass defined by the state lines, spreads across 264,000 square miles of mountains, plains, desert, swamps, 624 miles of coast line, and more than 2,000 miles of the Rio Grande marking the border with Mexico. As recently as the late 1960s, Texas was primarily rural. Its cities and towns, from El Paso on the west to Houston 750 miles to the east, essentially served the needs of the cattle, cotton, timber and oil industries. For the artist, that meant spare opportunities to exhibit work, fewer still to sell it. It also meant the artist worked in virtual isolation, even within his home town. Although art museums were established in Dallas, Fort Worth and Houston in the first decades of this century, they were primarily the efforts of ladies who wanted culture for their families. Collecting art was not a burning interest, and making art was just not regarded as a serious pursuit.

Art in Texas in the 1990s represents the revolutionary changes which occurred within and without the state since mid-century. They began, as most revolutions do, with sparks here and there, ignited in different ways and for different reasons. In Dallas, the match was struck by Douglas MacAgy, hired to direct the Dallas Center for Contemporary Art (since dissolved). In San Antonio, the impetus came from the political Chicano Movement, comprised of artists and activists who sought to involve a disenfranchised Latino population. In Houston, the combination of the visionary exhibitions and events sponsored by John and Dominique de Menil and the sophisticated presence of James Johnson Sweeney as director of the Museum of Fine Arts, fired the imagination of budding collectors.

Since the turn of the century and most rapidly since the 1960s, Texas has become increasingly urban with the resulting concentration of artists and patrons in metropolitan areas. Art galleries more than tripled in number in the largest cities during the 1970s, and some ventured into the smaller ones. Museums developed more aggressive programming to bring larger and more glamorous exhibitions, expanded educational services, and stretched to reach a growing audience.

For the first time now, three generations of artists are working simultaneously and not in isolation. For the first time, too, the fierce independence of their art is being generally recognized. In the age of pluralism, Texas has a tremendous advantage for its art has never been anything but. In that sense, all Texas art is contemporary. And as the rest of the country and mainstream institutions focus on "outsider" art and "multiculturalism" in these last years of the millennium, artists from the Lone Star State appear downright oracular.

Artists in Texas work in multiple modes and frequently with unorthodox materials, away from the theoretical and commercial art world epicenters of New York and Los Angeles. The distance is more psychological than physical. But trying to define art in Texas is like the parable of the five blind wise men who were asked to identify an elephant: Each could only describe the part he could "see". The sheer size of the state suggests a similar difficulty in understanding the complexity of the whole. Like the elephant, art in Texas is greater than the sum of its parts.

The concept of regionalism is anachronistic in this global age, and maybe especially in a state that is home to the cowboy of the range as well as of outer space. And yet, contemporary art in Texas has a nuance that is all its own.

A crucial component is Texas's shared history with Mexico. The Rio Grande, 2,400 miles long as it winds its way from El Paso on the state line with New Mexico, to Brownsville on the Gulf of Mexico, is both a wound and the connecting ribbon between the two countries. It is also part of the psychological landscape that finds artistic expression in apparent and implied ways. It is concrete in Luis Jimenez's imagery, a tacit presence in the iconography of Michael Tracy and Lucas Johnson, and the subject of work as varied as James Drake's sculpture, Terry Allen's songs and assemblages, and Celia Muñoz's photography.

Three other, elusive qualities are discernible in describing Texas art. Foremost among them is a sense of spirit in terms of content as well as motivation. The artists speak about their work in the language of intuition, metaphysics and magic. Rarely do the terms of art history enter into it, not because of ignorance, but because of a fine disregard of prevailing trends and language.

Equally important is the concept of assemblage, a term I use to mean the way a work of art is envisioned, as well as in its traditional meaning of how the work is physically put together. Joe Guy's graphite compositions, for instance, incorporate Christian symbols and Buddhist mysticism, Mark Rothko's abstraction, and Japanese screen making techniques. Melissa Miller's paintings are technically pure painting in oils on canvas, but she integrates a diversity of approaches and subjects ranging from Giotto to Nancy Graves.

Some would call this post-modernism, but the term is inappropriate for the majority of Texas artists. Post-modernism has a cynical edge, and implies a deliberate harvesting of ideas or images. Texans, for the most part, arrive at the complexity through intuitive means. Past literature and interviews conducted for this book consistently reveal the artists' genuine surprise in discovering that what they had been doing in isolation was done by others elsewhere. Conversely, they also express real pleasure at finding such validation for what they discovered on their own. "I felt I was given permission" is the implied and often explicit refrain in many an artist's statement.

Finally, there's irony. Texas exists suspended between its myth, the dream of its heroes, and the reality of the end of the millennium. Which has the greater gravitational pull remains a matter of conjecture. If the state is the subject of jokes and braggadocio, it is also ingrained in the American consciousness as a mythological place, by definition larger than life. It represents the romance of the American dream — independence, courage, and hard-working honesty — symbolized by the cowboy and the wildcatter.

Caught between the past which gave rise to the myth, and anxiously looking to the future, artists in Texas wryly exploit the former to shape visions for the latter. Myths, after all, even personal ones, are a perception of reality. Like the old saw says, you don't need to know where you are to be there.

## The Cities

In Texas, like anywhere else, the relationship between artists and cities is a symbiotic one. Throughout history artists have gravitated to the urban centers where intellectual and economic opportunity concentrate, giving the city its visual definition in the process. Since the turn of the century, museums have displaced the palace and the cathedral as public testimonials to the health of this relationship.

The first art museums in Texas were primarily founded by cultural associations as educational institutions during the first two decades of the 20th century. The encyclopedic mandate of their charters is reflected in the permanent collections, gathered initially in a more or less ad hoc manner, dependent on the individual taste and generosity of patrons. European painting, neoclassical sculpture and the obviously beautiful antiquities from Greece shaped their nucleus. Until mid-century, the onus of contemporary art was on universities and the occasional brave commercial gallery.

In 1948, though, a group of young professionals in Houston founded the Contemporary Art Association with the mandate to collect and exhibit contemporary art. Nine years later, a similar desire prompted a civic group in Dallas to establish the Dallas Museum for Contemporary Art. Both organizations teetered along, with amateur directors and well-meaning, occasionally exciting exhibitions, but remained essentially private clubs until the late fifties. In a remarkable stroke of timing, Jermayne MacAgy was hired by the CAA in Houston in 1955 as its first professional director; four years later, her former husband, Douglas MacAgy, accepted a similar post as director of the DMCA. Between them, they changed the perception of contemporary art and the way the communities would deal with the artists in their midst.

In the decades since, the private passions of visionary collectors, including John and Dominique de Menil in Houston, Kay and Velma Kimbell and Amon Carter in Fort Worth, have become public institutions that greatly enrich and define art's landscape. As the century has grown older, distances shorter, access easier, some differences blur. But each city has its own history and personality and these are reflected in its institutions and by its artists.

### Dallas and Fort Worth: The Metroplex

Dallas and Fort Worth are distinct civic entities, but spoken of in a single breath as the Metroplex. The combined population of 3.9 million shares not only the landmark Trinity River, but also an international airport and the 30-mile asphalt ribbon of Interstate 30 that connects one downtown to the other on an East-West axis.

Dallas, founded in 1841, was a mercantile and banking center even before the railroads arrived in the early 1870s. It is a sophisticated city which many perceive as having more in common with the East Coast than its Western heritage. It is modern and urbane, headquarters for regional and national banking, insurance and petroleum industries, essentially conservative and white collar. Its architecture is classic, if uninspired, modernism with all the austere elegance implied by glass and steel skins.

The Dallas Museum of Art chartered at the beginning of the century, is the major, general institution. It was housed in Fair Park until 1984 when city bond money and private contributions built a new home for it on 8.9 acres in the heart of the city. In 1993, the DMA added the 140,000 square-foot Hamon Building to showcase its permanent collections of non-European art — Pre-Columbian, Native American, and African art — and provided a spacious gallery for temporary exhibitions. Its permanent collections of American art, including a fine selection of work by area artists, is complemented with regularly scheduled exhibitions titled *Visions* which spotlight the most recent works by Texas artists.

Artists remember Douglas MacAgy's tenure as director of the short-lived Dallas Museum for Contemporary Art, for two especially significant things. First, he made them feel welcome in the museum. Secondly, he created a context for them by weaving their work into national traveling exhibitions, and through presentations of landmark events such as Rene Magritte's first exhibit in an American museum (1960) and Claes Oldenburg's first "Happening" (1961), he exposed them to art and concepts which echoed or expanded their own.

Fort Worth, incorporated in 1876, had been a trading and supply depot for cattlemen since the 1850s. It is nicknamed Cowtown, and stockyards are still part of its economy as well as its relaxed social definition. Civic efforts to preserve downtown's 19th century, red brick architecture resulted in one stunning contemporary example when Richard Haas disguised the nondescript concrete federal courthouse with deliciously witty illusion.

Fort Worth is home to three outstanding specialized museums, two of which were built by private philanthropy. The jewel-like Kimbell Art Museum, designed by Louis Kahn, opened to the public in 1972 with a multi-million dollar endowment. It is the gift of Kay and Velma Kimbell who established the Kimbell Foundation in 1936 to acquire world-class Old Masters. The small, but impeccable collection ranges from the Italian Renaissance to the 19th century, from illuminated manuscripts to crucial works by major European masters. The Kimbell also contributes to the contemporary world of art through its enlightened series, *The Artist's Eye*. Initiated in 1982, the occasional program invites an artist, Melissa Miller and Terry Allen have been among them, to select an exhibition from the permanent collection and place his or her own work in context.

The Amon Carter Museum opened in 1961 with a core collection of fine Western art, notably by

Frederic Remington and Charles Russell, acquired by Amon Carter, founder and publisher of the *Fort Worth Star Telegram*. In the years since, the collections have diversified, especially in the area of modern American photography.

The Museum of Modern Art of Fort Worth was chartered in 1892 as the Fort Worth Art Museum and housed in the city's public library. Its collection, which was always intentionally modern and contemporary with a focus on American art, became increasingly so after it moved to its present location in 1954. The museum has expanded twice since then. Under the dynamic directorship of Henry Hopkins (1968–1973), its presence was intensified, doing for the artists in the 1970s what Douglas MacAgy had done a decade earlier in Dallas. The museum's recent history of exhibitions ranges from the raucous 1976 *The Great American Rodeo Show*, which in addition to works by Texans like Terry Allen included Red Grooms' amazing installation *Ruckus Rodeo*, to the elegant wit of the Nancy Graves retrospective in 1987.

The University of North Texas (formerly North Texas State University) in Denton, and the three-year-old Arlington Museum of Art, located about half-way between Dallas and Forth Worth, serve the community as alternative art centers.

## Houston

Houston is the undisputed capital of contemporary art in Texas and the region, touted nationally as the Third Coast (New York and Los Angeles being the other two). It is the fourth largest city and the third busiest port in the United States, this latter thanks to the 50-mile long Intercoastal Canal connecting it to Galveston on the Gulf. Founded in 1836 as a real estate scam by two entrepreneurial brothers from New York, John Kirby and Augustus Allen, Houston is an accommodating multi-ethnic urban sprawl with a population of four million people, that willingly reinvents itself to suit changing moods and needs.

Three major museums provide the backbone of the art community: The Museum of Fine Arts, The Contemporary Arts Museum, and The Menil Collection.

The MFA was founded in 1900 with an encyclopedic mandate and the hopes of donations for its collections. It opened to the public in 1924 with 50 objects. Through most of the century, its acquisition of Texas art was through purchase awards from annual juried exhibitions it sponsored and also occasional gifts. Spurred by the momentum of the exhibition *Fresh Paint: The Houston School* in 1985, the museum has made a concerted effort to increase its holdings of art from Texas and the region. Plans for a new exhibition hall slated to open in the late 1990s, include a gallery where these works would be exhibited on a permanent, rotating basis.

The Contemporary Arts Museum, established in 1948 as a collecting institution, redefined its charter fifteen years later as a *kunsthalle* with no art of its own. As such, its energy and funds are directed towards temporary exhibitions in two galleries. Under the directorship of Linda Cathcart during the 1980s, the CAM instituted a program of alternating exhibitions, many curated in-house, between large theme shows like *Southern Fictions* (1983) and overviews of individual, usually established artists like Robert Rauschenberg in its main gallery. Smaller, focus exhibitions are held in the more intimate space downstairs. Although most of its exhibits since the late 1980s have been curated by other institutions, the mix is pretty much the same today.

The treasure house that is The Menil Collection was five decades in the making as a private affair. Its parent, the Menil Foundation, had organized and sponsored pristine exhibitions over the decades in select venues, including the Rice Institute for the Arts and St. Thomas University. Complemented by scholarly lectures and informal discussions about art and collecting during the MacAgy years especially, the foundation educated and excited its audience. But when the museum opened to the public in 1987, the scope of its world-class holdings in antiquities, African and Oceanic art, Surrealism and modern European and American art, was stunningly revealed. Three or four temporary exhibitions a year reflect the spirit of the permanent collections. Some highlights include tightly focused but generous exhibitions of 20th century luminaries like Marcel Duchamp, Rene Magritte and Joseph Beuys, and equally scholarly and impeccable installations of contemporary art by Texans Michael Tracy and Mel Chin.

One of Houston's strengths is its ability to foster community spirit. It became evident towards the end of the 1970s when the CAM was flirting with the idea of dissolving. The prospect was particularly painful for the artists since just five years earlier, they had felt they finally had a friend in director James Harithas. He presented *12/Texas* in 1974, which acknowledged young Texas artists, including Chicanos, for the first time in the museum. When the museum was devastated by flooding two years later, it was forced to close for nine months. The losses, coupled with ongoing financial distress and animosity between Harithas and some [the more conservative] members of the board, led to his resignation in 1978. With interim directors and no schedule, sculptor James Surls and allies on the board organized *Fire!* in 1979, an embrasive exhibition of 100 Houston artists with a strong point to make about the community's richness.

The weakened CAM was a crucial impetus for the creation of the city's alternative centers. The Lawndale Annex came first, established in 1979 in association with the art department of the University of Houston. Although it has gone through several metamorphoses including changing its name to Lawndale Alternative Art and Performance Center to reflect its restructuring as an independent nonprofit organization, the collaborative spirit which engendered it continues and its presence grows. When it looked like Lawndale might falter, too, another group of artists created DiverseWorks in 1983. Its stated aims are similar, and it has emerged in the 1990s as the city's leading venue for performance art and some of the more experimental visual media.

The Museum's School is not an alternative venue as such, but in recent years has become active in that arena. Founded in 1927, it assumed a new and prominent role when it built its first permanent home and was renamed the Alfred C. Glassell School of Art in 1979. It historically had a strong and loyal faculty, but the fact that it was not accredited was limiting to students seeking a degree. In 1982, however, then director Alan Hacklin initiated the Core Program for art school graduates. Designed to ease their transition from a school environment into the real world of galleries and exhibitions, the Core has become an important channel for a new generation of artists. An important corollary is the program's visiting artist lecture and exhibition series, which, like those at the Sarah Campbell Blaffer Gallery (established in 1973) of the University of Houston, reach a community beyond the academic environment.

## Other cities

Eight million of Texas' 18 million people live in the Metroplex and Houston. Numbers alone suggest the concentration of artists and the institutions they need would exist within those boundaries. But smaller organizations in far-flung municipalities, from the Amarillo Art Center in the Panhandle to the Art Museum of Southeast Texas in Beaumont, have added definition and opportunity as well.

The city of San Antonio is both the geographic and historical heart of Texas. It was founded by Franciscan friars sent by the Spanish viceroy in Mexico City to civilize the territory in the early 1700s. Seven missions along eight miles on the San Antonio River, served the religious and secular needs of the Spanish colonizers and converted the native population. One of the missions, San Antonio de Valero, would become the rallying point of Texas' independence in 1836 and thereafter be known as The Alamo.

But the San Antonio Museum of Art has been marginal in terms of contemporary art. It is housed in the former Lone Star Brewery, a brick structure built in the late 19th century, that the museum redesigned as its permanent home in the mid seventies. Its varied but uneven collection of art of the Americas consists of folk art from Mexico and South America, comprised primarily of a gift from Rockefeller Foundation; and holdings ranging form 19th century American landscapes to a small group of American regionalist and Mexican paintings from the 1930s and 1940s. The museum expanded in the 1990s to house the Gilbert Denham collection of antiquities, and added a wing for its contemporary art. Attention to the latter had been inconsistent at best throughout the museum's history. For a few years in the late 1980s, however, Jim Edwards, curator of 20th century art, transformed the museum into a dynamic player in the field. Accessions in the area increased greatly during his tenure and exhibitions he curated, like *The Poetic Eye*, drew welcome national attention. At the same time, the Blue Star Art Space and the Guadalupe Art Center, emerged in the 1980s to help fill the vacuum.

Austin, the state capital, is home to nearly 800,000 people and the University of Texas. Unlike other major cities in Texas, its art community is centered around the university with its faculty and the collections of the Archer M. Huntington Gallery of Art. Notable among them, is the Mari and James Michener Collection of Twentieth Century American Paintings, major holdings of approximately 8,500 prints and drawings with particular strength in Old Master and especially Latin American art and archives. The university is home as well to the pre-eminent Gernsheim Collection of historical photographs, considered to be among the best in the world.

The Laguna Gloria Art Museum, an intimate Mediterranean style home in the Austin hills, was deeded to the Texas Fine Arts Association. The association had dreams of transforming it into an important regional center for contemporary art and got as far as to commission drawings from Robert Venutri for a downtown location. The economic depression of the mid eighties, however, has put plans on indefinite hold.

El Paso's name means "The Pass". It describes this city on the far western edge of the state, named by Spanish explorers in 1598 to mark the mountain route north for missionaries and soldiers to follow. Although it was not settled until 1827, its counterpart to the south, Ciudad Juarez, was an important supply and rest station. The city, nestled against the Texas-New Mexico state line and the international border with Mexico on the Rio Grande, holds special significance as both the literal and the metaphorical gate where two countries, two cultural and economic psyches, dramatically meet, clash and meld.

The El Paso Museum of Art has been mostly irrelevant to working artists and the vast majority of the population. Only in the last three years has it offered something more than what artist James Magee described as "art for ladies that drink tea". However, The Bridge Center for Contemporary Art, founded in the late 1980s, attempts to address the issues of the city's unique geographical place and the needs of its working artists with small but significant exhibits and lecture series. The Adair Margo Gallery is the only venue of its kind in the area. And a recent project has generated renewed interest in the city's murals. The project was started in 1990 by the city's Junior League which documented more than 100 of these monumental, open air paintings, restored older ones and sponsored the creation of new ones. As defined by the Mexican muralist movement of the 1920s and thirties, the purpose of such work was didactic. In its late 20th century version on the border, the murals are a public celebration of individual artists and their complex heritage.

Many towns and a few medium size cities dot the Rio Grande between El Paso on the west and Brownsville on the Gulf Coast. They exist on both sides of the river, separated by political history but united in almost every other way. Laredo and Nuevo Laredo, El Paso/Juarez, Brownsville/Matamoros are spoken practically in the same breath. Art museums are virtually nonexistent along this route, but since the mid 1980s, non-profit organizations, including the tiny Bridge Center in El Paso and Michael Tracy's River Pierce Foundation in San Ygancio, 50 miles south of Laredo, are visible pioneers.

## The Artists

At the end of the 1960s, a group of artists came together in the Dallas neighborhood of Oak Cliff. The industrial suburb provided the name for the loose association which included Bob Wade, Jim Roche, Jack Mims, and George Green. It was short lived as the artists discovered other interests, found jobs and moved away. But for the brief five years of its existence, "they were linked ... by a willingness to take risks and a determination to make others notice what they were doing. They bucked the hard-edge minimalist styles that were then in vogue, opting instead for art that reflected an emotional response to the world around them."[1] The impact of the group was less in terms of artistic style than in proving it was possible to be an artist in Texas.

"They were all teachers, but it was their presence that was influential," Douglas MacWithey recalled. "They made art and it was out there, not as a project for class, but out in society for a general audience."

The realization was pivotal. Twenty-five years before, an ambitious young artist named Robert Rauschenberg left his East Texas home for New York, with everything to gain and never looking back. Many would follow. Exhibition opportunities were limited to the occasional juried show and commercial galleries were virtually non-existent. Only a few art programs were available and none at the graduate level. Even to date the only doctorate program in art history is the one offered at the University of Texas in Austin. For the artists that stayed, like Forrest Bess (1911–1977), it meant almost complete isolation. Bess created powerful paintings in which he transformed his dreams into abstract symbols of his invention. Although he attained recognition from such influential people as Betty Parsons, who exhibited his work in her New York gallery in the 1950s, and from the revered art historian and critic Meyer Shapiro, the highly original artist remained isolated, essentially unknown, and destitute.

The balance shifted in the 1970s. With a growing economy and a swelling population, opportunity and access to it increased. Artists who had left the state in their pursuit of an art degree, Vernon Fisher, James Drake, Luis Jimenez and Jesse Lott among them, returned, some to teaching positions available in newly formed art departments.

The major institutions expanded, smaller museums blossomed across the state, and several universities opened public galleries. The Contemporary Arts Museum in Houston under the directorship of James Harithas (1974–1978) gave Texas artists a tremendous boost with his genuine personal interest in their art, and also by bringing it into an institutional setting that had seemed all but antagonistic. By the 1980s, alternative exhibition spaces and commercial galleries were also feeling more secure.

The 1976 sesquicentennial celebrations of Texas' independence had made Texans look at themselves, and the economy magnified the state's presence in the national eye. Publications began to talk about Houston as the Third Coast, with New York and Los Angeles as first and second, as if they really believed it. For the artists, an article in *Art in America* in the spring of 1987 confirmed it. In her introduction, Jamey Gambrell wrote that no earth-shattering structural changes had occurred in the state's art scene since the mid seventies. However, she noted that in itself was a change. "Leaving the state is no longer considered a prerequisite for achieving a national or even international reputation. In 1976 an outsider [critic Roberta Smith] wondered whether or not what she saw really constituted a viable art scene. In 1986, the answer is obvious."[2]

The crucial change was in attitude. For the first time, Texas artists could choose to stay home, and while many still gravitated to New York or Los Angeles, the reverse was also true. Artists, including Donald Judd in the early 1970s, Edward and Nancy Kienholz more recently in the nineties, elected to call Texas home. And of great import for the "locals", curators and critics from the east and the west came specifically to look, sometimes buy and often to return with work for inclusion in their essays and exhibitions. The state's institutions began to pay more attention, too. The net result was heightened activity.

The artistic isolation had had its advantages, though, Bess's archetype notwithstanding. Without a history of modernity or a system of support, artists were free to do exactly what they wanted any way they chose. The only expectations were individual ones. As artist Vernon Fisher recalls Henry Hopkins describe the situation in the early 1970s, artists in Texas could be reckless because they didn't have anything to lose.

The "radiance of discovery", to borrow a phrase from philosopher/mythologist Joseph Campbell, and "a propensity for creating and believing fictions — anecdotes, stories, legends, myths — about themselves,"[3] identified by Monroe Spears in a 1983 essay about art in the American south, are the dual anchors of art in Texas. Both are an internal process of intuition or faith, whether drawn from mysticism or abiding humanity. Both, too, are inventions, conceptual and material. They are manifest in as many different ways and for as many reasons as there are artists.

Contemporary art in Texas changes daily, but the bases both ancient and recent provide a sense of continuity. It's true, as many have noted, that the myth of Texas is no longer viable like it was even twenty years ago. The urbanization of the great state has changed the way its people think of themselves and of the larger community within a global society. And yet, a unique sense of place persists in the vastness of the state. Its complex history, its origins fictionalized by Hollywood but historical nonetheless, flavor the collective psyche. From the desolation of the Chihuahua Desert to the cosmopolitan density of Houston, Texas remains a state of mind as much as of place. The artists are the guides.

1. Kutner, Janet, "Four who shared an irreverence for art", *The Dallas Morning News*, March 1993.
2. Cambrell, Jamey, "Art Capital of the Third Coast", *Art in America*, March 1987, p.15.
3. Spears, Monroe, *Southern Fictions*, Contemporary Arts Museum, Houston, 1993, p.16.

# The Aaart Guys: **Galbreth & Massing**

Michael Galbreth and Jack Massing, The Aaart Guys, don't talk about art, they perform it or glue it and even drag it down a highway. Sometimes they tell anecdotes. One, that may well be apocryphal, is nonetheless insightful to their method and artistic madness. They were students at the University of Houston in 1982 when their collaboration arose in serendipity. They were working independently on similar projects when the idea struck. In a gleeful moment of why not, each stuck his hand in his respective bucket of paint — one green, the other pink — shook on the new identity, and slapped their paint-smothered hands on a piece of paper. The piece, which they titled *The art guys agree on painting*, served as the birth certificate for the Art Guys Ink.[1]

Although they have pursued private interests and individual works, the objects and situations they create as collaborators stand uniquely apart. Their work is aligned with the ephemera of Fluxus and Dada irreverence and irony. They glue things together into sculptures that are as pure as theoretical architecture and simultaneously as whimsical as a child's prank. Medicine capsules, bottles emptied of beer, and No. 2 pencils, are some of the unorthodox buildings blocks of their tangible creations. Other works are part body art, part performance, and fleeting by definition. On one occasion they grew goatees and sideburns, shaved them off and preserved them, keeping their shapes intact, like some latter day surrealist reliquary. Borrowing the vocabulary of Yves Klein, the Art Guise create incendiary drawings with matches arranged on a wall, sometimes on 200-pound rag paper, that burn briefly and intensely to leave a mere sooty trace of ephemeral action.

They came to Texas from different routes. Massing, born in Buffalo in 1959, moved when his father took a job in Houston. After one year at the Glassell School of Art, he transferred to the University of Houston. Galbreth, born in Philadelphia in 1956, had just graduated from the Memphis School of Art in Memphis, Tennessee, and was considering graduate school. He looked to the traditional institutions in the East Coast, but a friendship with sculptor James Surls, struck a few years earlier, persuaded him to try Houston. Surls, a dynamic teacher and leading figure in Texas' contemporary art scene, was head of the sculpture department at the UH at the time.

As with most collaborators, Massing, the light-hearted one, and Galbreth, the theoretician, cannot — or will not — identify who does what. In their anecdotal recounting, they complete each others' sentences. As in their fiery drawings, what matters is the memorable moment.

1. Galbreth and Massing spell their collaborative name in a variety of ways to change its meaning or merely its alphabetical place. The pronunciation remains the same.

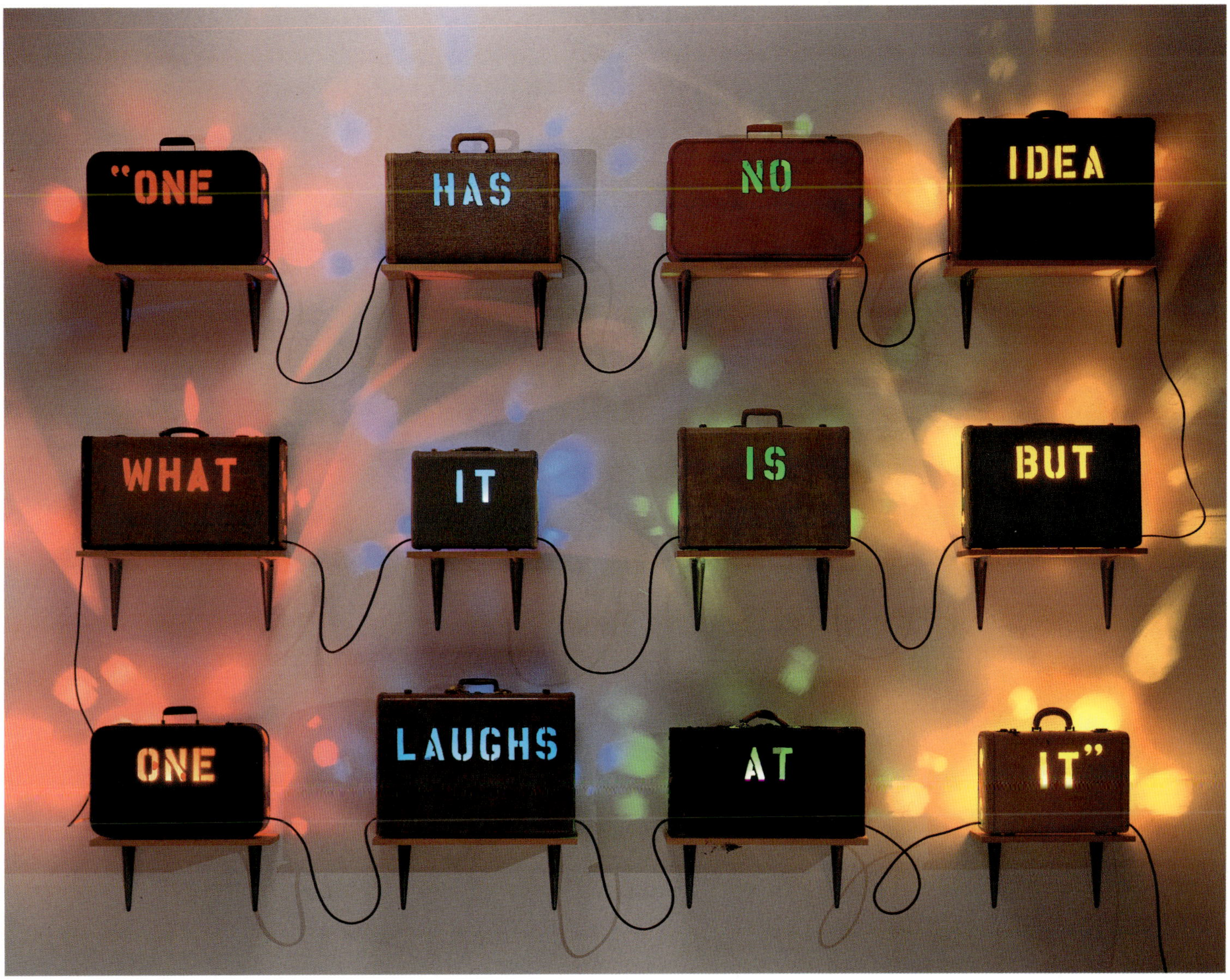


The Aaart Guys
**"The Definition of Metaphysics by Flaubert" or "The Boss Piece"**
Suitcases, lightbulbs, wire, variable size.
Courtesy of the artists

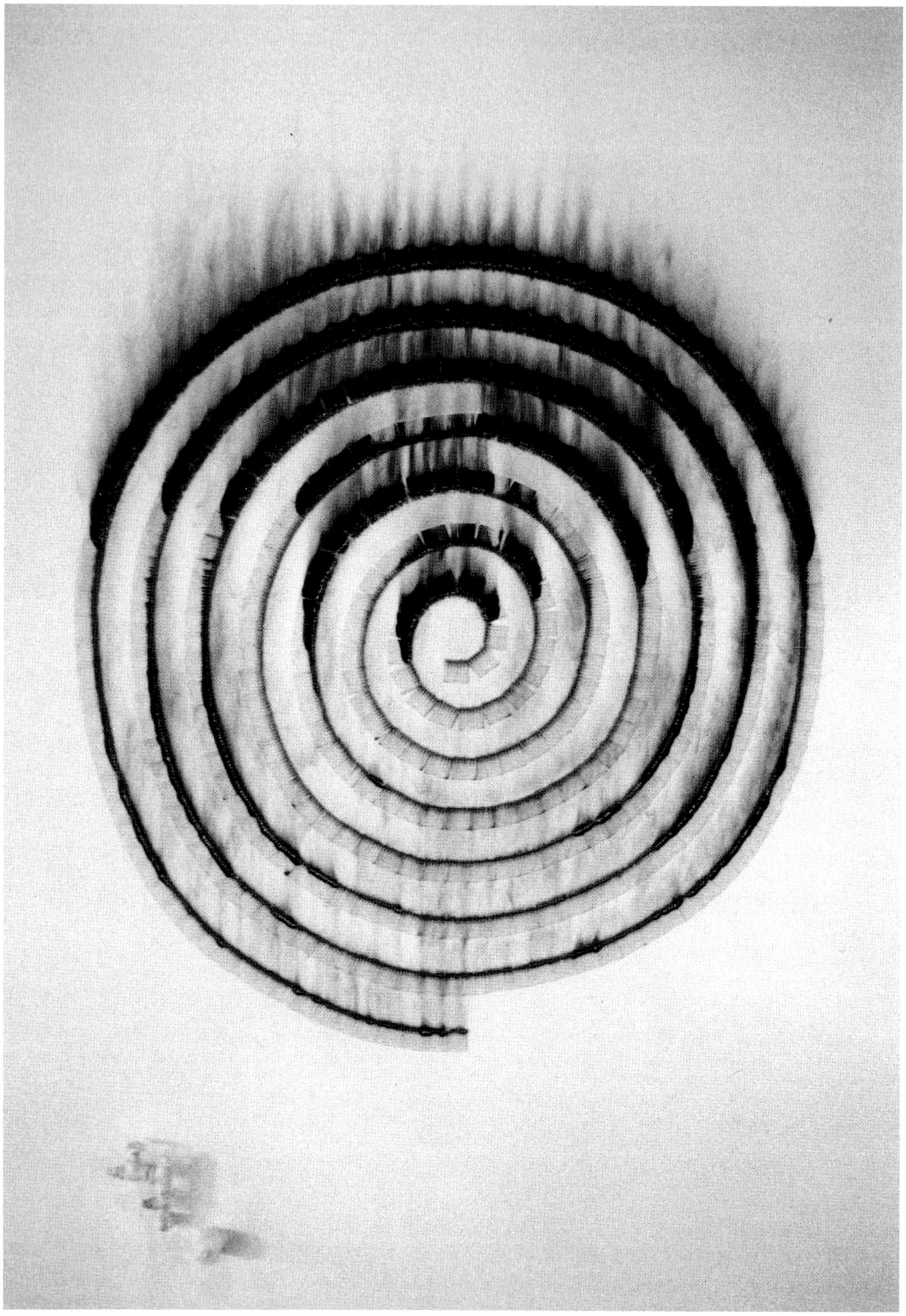

The Aaart Guys
**Match Installation #4**
1990, Matches (ephemeral drawing), 5' diameter.
Courtesy of the artists

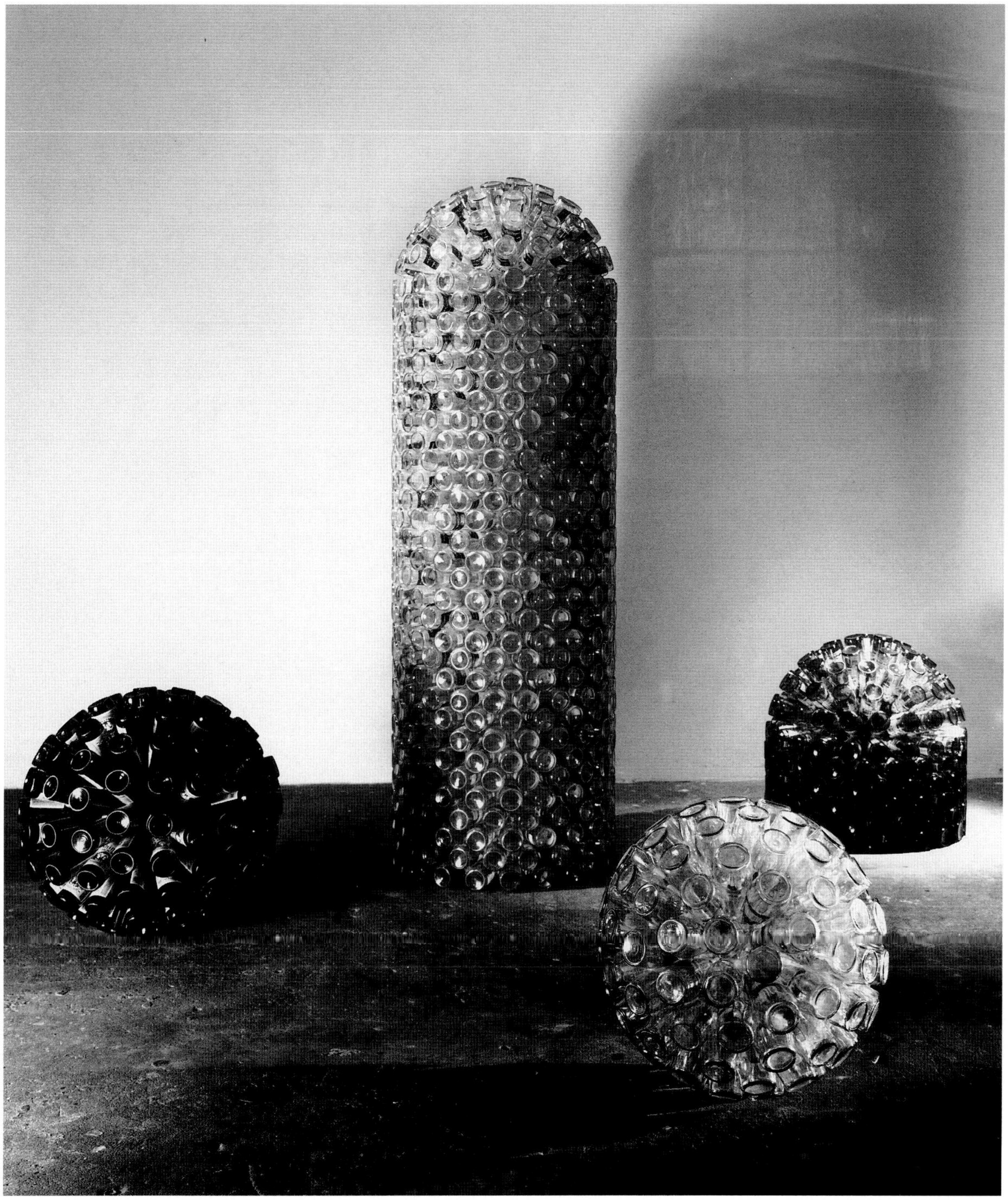

The Aaart Guys
**Bottle Pieces**
Glass beer bottles, silicone, Front right: "Clearly Canadian Ball", 27" sphere; Back left: "Shiner Bock Ball", 26" diameter; Center: "Corona Tower", 86" high, 27" base; Right: "Rolling Rock Nub", 29" high, 24" base. Courtesy of the artists

# John Alexander

When it comes to digging deep into the mystique of the Texas landscape to retrieve its passionate, contradictory components, John Alexander stands out. Even after more than a decade in New York City, his East Texas roots inform his exuberant paintings. His lush palette and energized brushwork fill them with snarls and gnashing teeth costumed as gorgeous foliage when the subject is a landscape, or in the opulence of material wealth when he turns to urban topics.

Alexander got his masters degree from Southern Methodist University in Dallas but had, he says, always wanted to live in Houston. In 1972, he joined the faculty of the University of Houston just as the art department was expanding its scope and faculty and the zeitgeist of the university was about to explode with new energy. His enthusiasm in the painting department matched James Surls' in sculpture's, and when James Harithas revolutionized the Contemporary Arts Museum, the synergy propelled Houston and its artists into the limelight. After a few years, though, Alexander got restless and felt he had done all he could for his career in Texas. Like others before him, he moved to New York.

"No one made money [here], so I didn't expect to. But I was 35 years old and I looked very consciously at what had happened to the really great artists who had stayed, to their careers, and I thought if I stay, it will happen to me, too. There was no reason for them to make art except their own drive."

His earliest paintings were "little ol' lady landscapes", as he describes them. By the late seventies, following a brief period of exploring abstraction and pure gesture, his compositions emerged with a ferocious surface that the eighties would call neo-expressionism. The rich paint described real and allegorical creatures, seething with danger that like the swamps of his boyhood, were irresistible. In the work of the 1990s, the resolution of his figures, creatures and context is lyrical and lush, but the lurking menace is never far beneath.

"I find myself in the beautiful Hamptons or the loft in SoHo, and in the middle of the night all the demons, all the smells of the roots and the leaves, the noises and images of the Texas woods and swamps, come back. The big difference between the North East and Texas landscapes is there's no danger here. We had alligators."

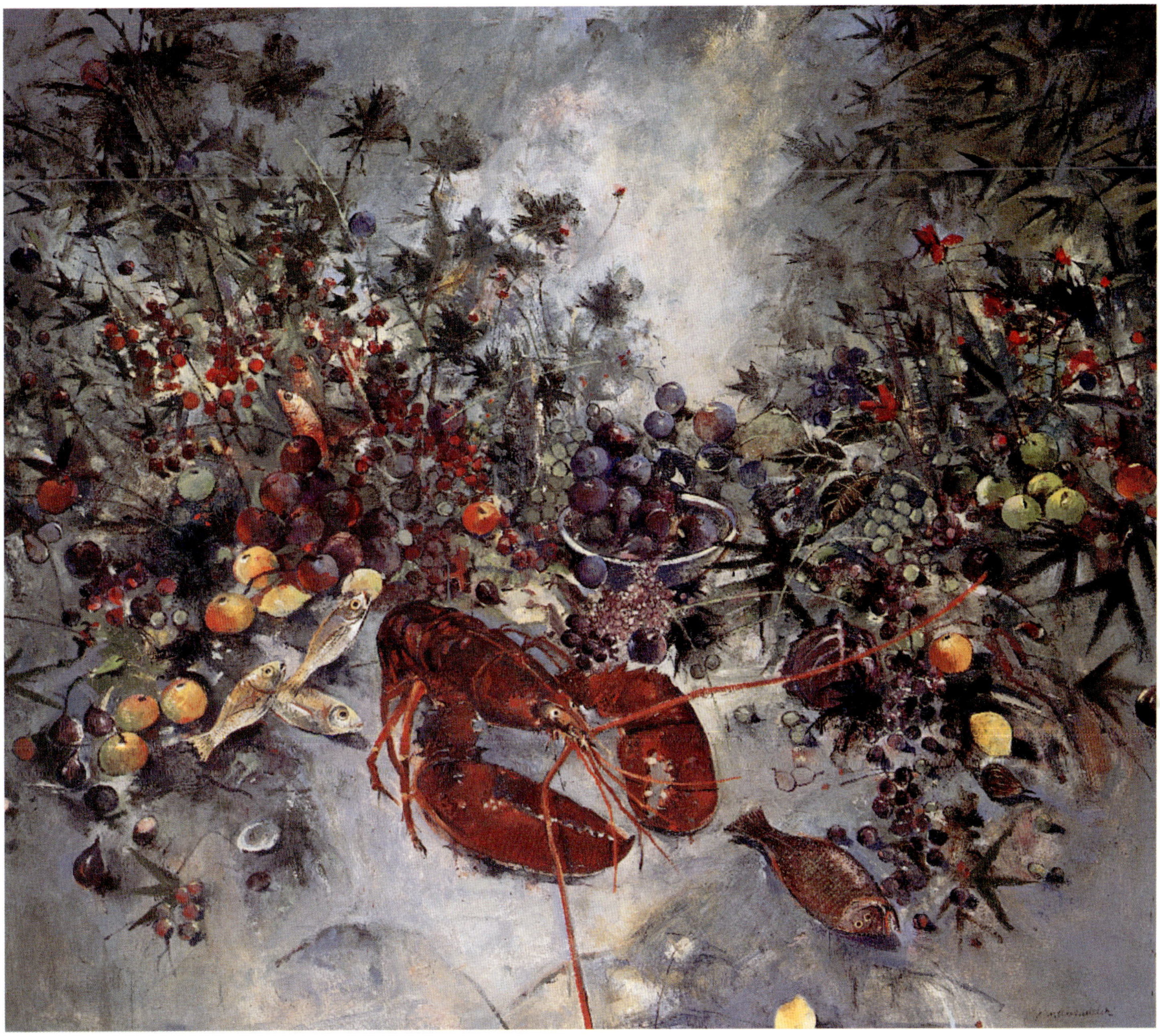

John Alexander
**Red Lobster with Blue Balls**
1993, Oil on canvas, 77" x 86". Courtesy of
Marlborough Gallery, New York

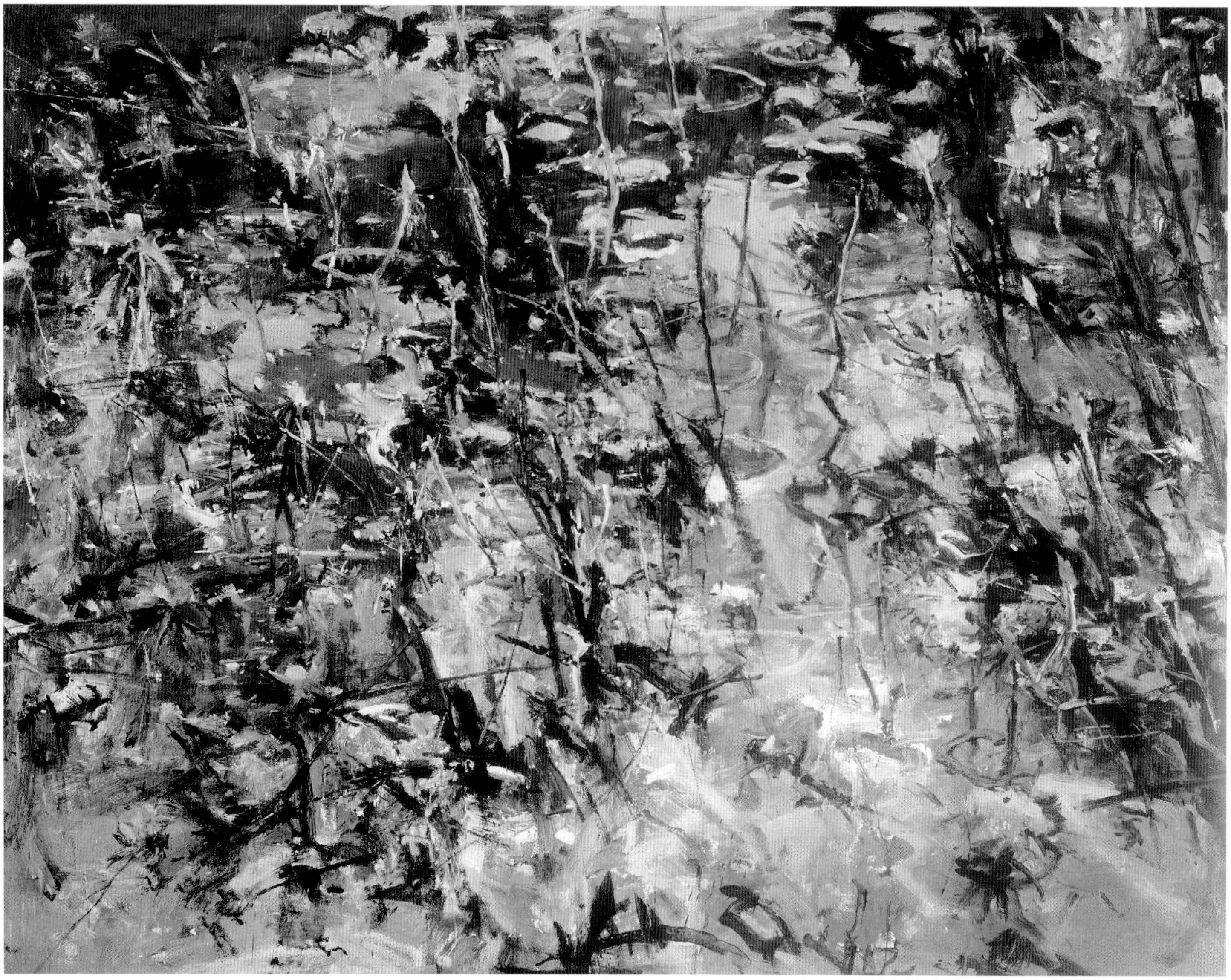

John Alexander
**Spring Frenzy**
1990, Oil on canvas, 76" x 96". Courtesy of Marlborough Gallery, New York

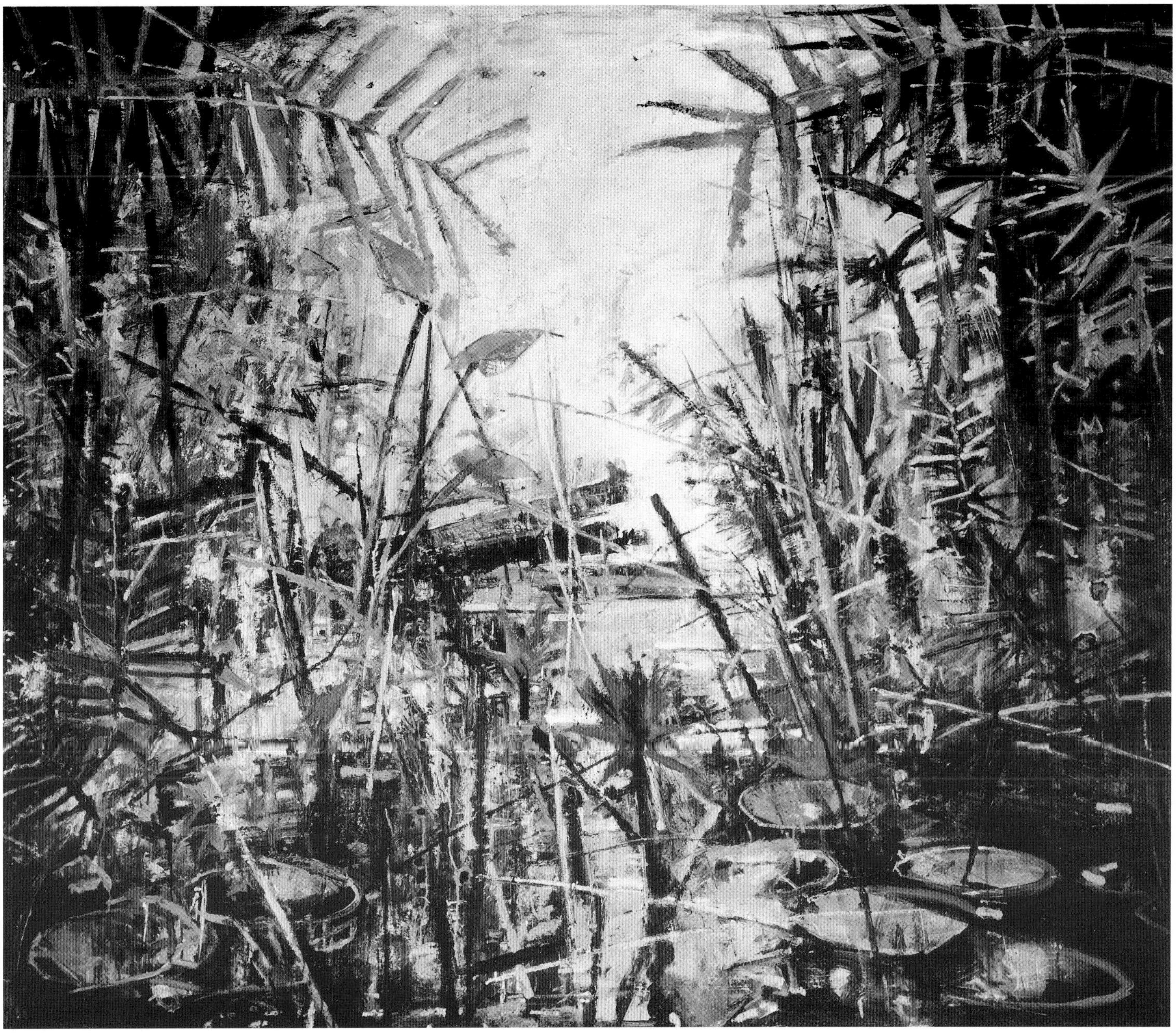

John Alexander
**Chauncey's Garden**
1989, Oil on canvas, 77" x 83". Private collection.
Courtesy of Marlborough Gallery, New York

# Terry **Allen**

In the long history of assemblage in this state, Terry Allen has added a new twist. He was a little boy in Lubbock and he wanted to be an artist, a writer, or a musician. He grew up to be all three, fusing sculpture, painting and drawing with theater, song and music.

"I don't think there's any difference in what you use. You say whatever it is that you're dealing with the best way that you can. Sometimes it's with music, sometimes words, and sometimes it's a picture or an object. I've never cared, never had priority for which one was better or more important. I've just never thought about making art about art. It's always been about being alive."

His father was a wrestling promoter and in the 1950s, a dance hall operator who booked bands into town. His mother had the dubious distinction of being the first woman to be expelled from Southern Methodist University for playing jazz piano in night clubs. His biggest influences, Allen says, were the musicians he heard, especially Hank Williams. Visually, there was nothing to dream on in flat, featureless Lubbock — except the horizon, Allen says, "which you always want to get on the other side of."

Getting to that other side is what Allen's life and work is about. In the cycles of work he has created for the better part of twenty years, he addresses the issues of personal identity and the multiple borders of our lives: physical, existential, emotional. Living on the border with Mexico, the complexity of Amerasians in Viet Nam, his personal make up as good ol' Texas boy who doesn't live in the state that defines him, enter his multifaceted constructions in narrative and metaphorical ways. A sense of irony and a sharp wit inform the plaintive stories of his country songs and define his richly layered assemblages where elements of popular culture rush headlong into lyrical passages whether melodic or painterly.

He married his childhood sweetheart, actress Jo Harvey, and left the Texas Panhandle in the late 1960s for California to attend the Chouinard Art Institute in Los Angeles. He hasn't lived in Texas since, and most recently, settled in Santa Fe, New Mexico.

But, Allen says, Texas is always home. "Everywhere else I've ever lived has just been a mailing address."

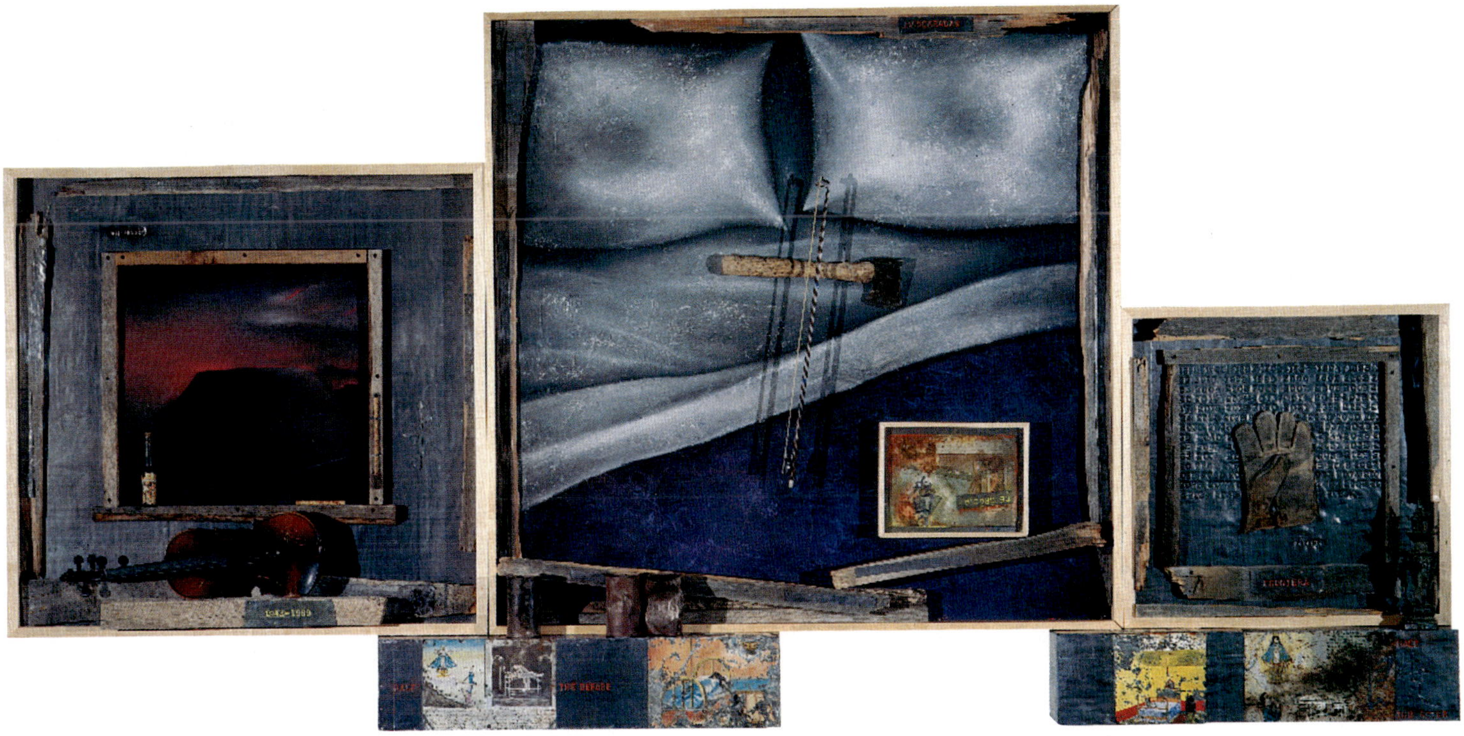

Terry Allen

**Mascaradas en Busca de Gracia**

1989, Mixed media, $55\frac{7}{8}$"h x 111"w x $5\frac{3}{4}$"d.
Collection of Dallas Museum of Art, Dallas, Museum League Purchase Fund. Courtesy of Moody Gallery, Houston

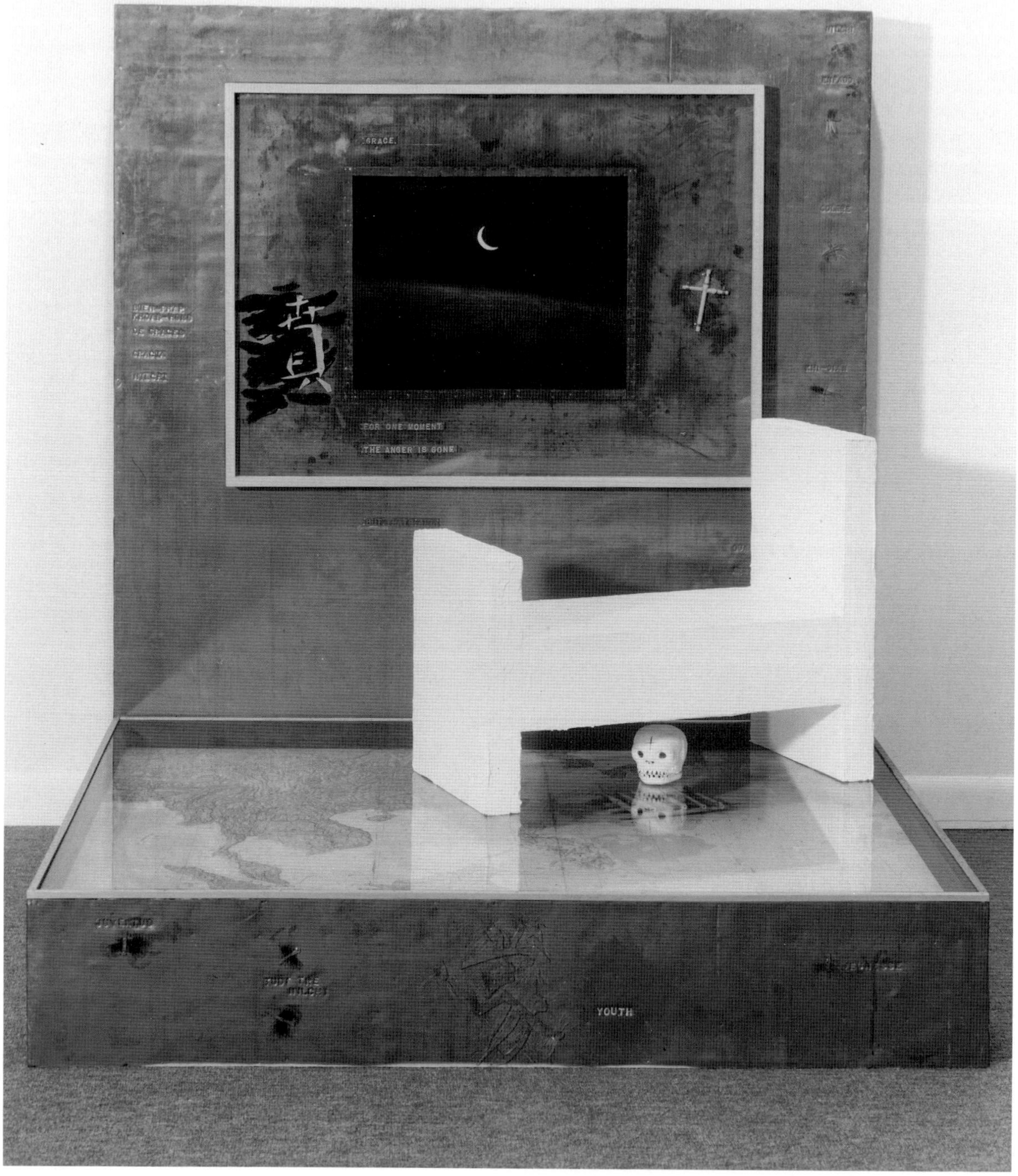


Terry Allen
**Grace**
1985, Mixed installation, 48"h x 41"w x 39¼".
Collection of Sheila and Wally Weisman, Beverly Hills.
Courtesy of Moody Gallery, Houston

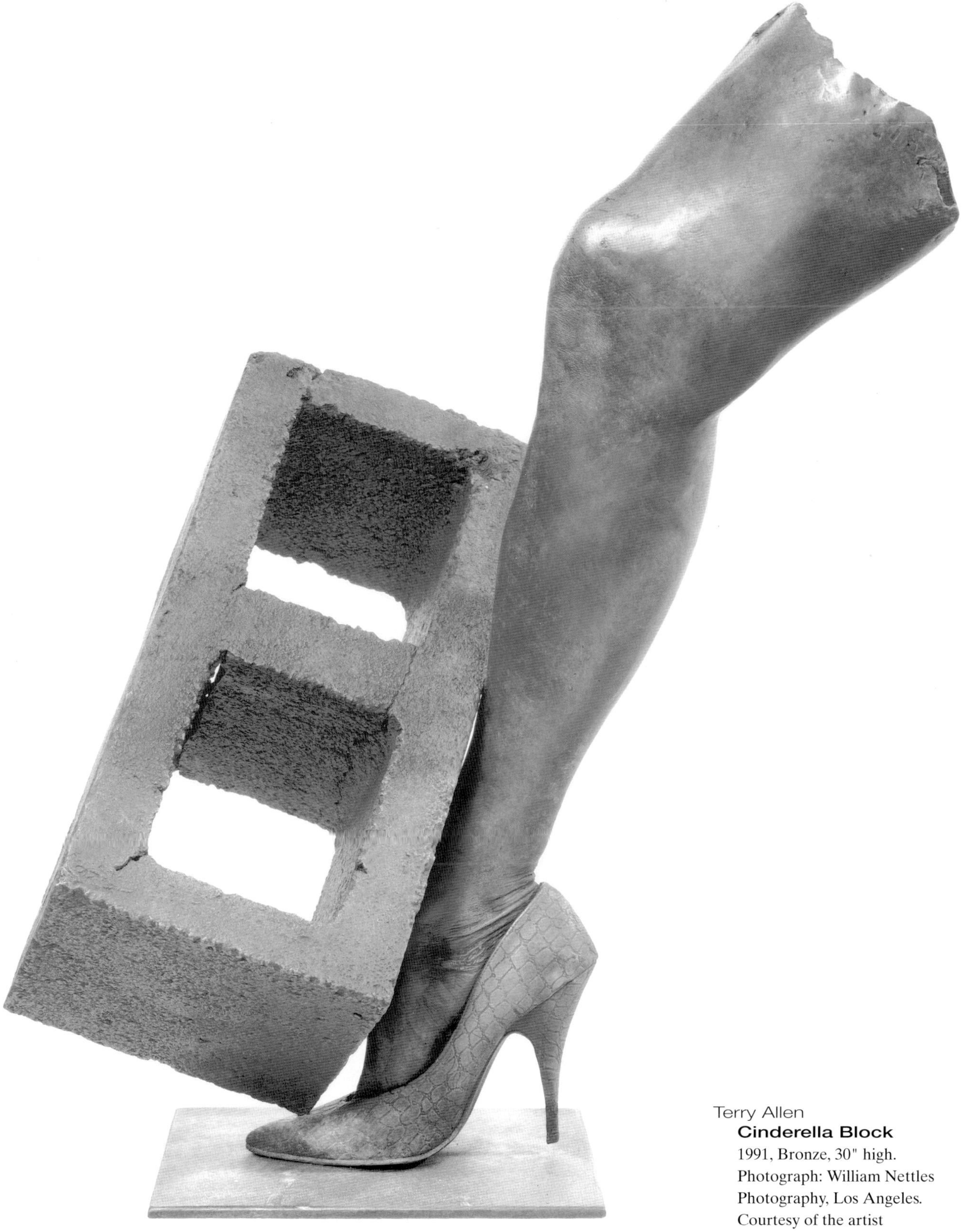

Terry Allen
**Cinderella Block**
1991, Bronze, 30" high.
Photograph: William Nettles
Photography, Los Angeles.
Courtesy of the artist

# Helen **Altman**

Helen Altman, born in Alabama in 1958, borrows Marcel Duchamp's irreverence for craft and penchant for the ridiculous parading as the meaningful to create her sculpture. She takes kitsch objects from the 1950s and reconfigures their essential falsehood into allusive assemblages that are both humorous and somehow sad. Her earliest works were quirky, miniature versions of the funky dioramas common in natural science museums until recently. By scaling them to the size of a cup and saucer, she emphasized the absurdity of the environments from which they derived: Those painted landscapes and dry vegetation intended to create illusion of life for the stuffed specimens served only to underscore the deadness of the creatures they housed.

Altman began using standard household appliances in 1988, finding their familiarity attractive and comforting. By simulating their function, adding a resin arc of water in the drinking fountain or flames impersonated by electric lightbulbs to a gas range, for instance, she transformed the useless contraptions into vehicles for emotional responses. Poignancy and nostalgia are involved, but as with the dioramas, the felicitous interpretation is revealed for the sham that it is.

Since 1990, the Fort Worth artist has been working almost exclusively with fake fire logs, achieving a clarity of purpose and deeper resonances than ever before. Altman arranges the cylindrical forms into freestanding or wall-dependent sculptures. Though disguised as abstract symbols such as an X, or piled to resemble a campfire or a clumsy snowman, she illumines them for maximum effulgence with electric bulbs and adds small electric fans that create a lifelike crackling sound to assume the aura of reality. The contradictory information conveyed in the manipulation alludes to other opposites, heat and cold, for instance. There is no warmth to be had from these illusory flames. But their appearance is persuasive, and if fire can be a source of life affirming warmth, it is also a destructive force.

There's something else informing the fire log pieces. As with the mass-produced appliances of her earlier works, they are an industrial product created by non-artist concerns. Altman pushes that fact further by sending rough drawings of her designs to the manufacturers who do the actual assembling.

"It's always a surprise when I open the package from the factory. Their craft is great, but it is not anything like what I would do. I'm interested in how they interpret the point of the piece. I relinquish control and can then ask why mine might be better."

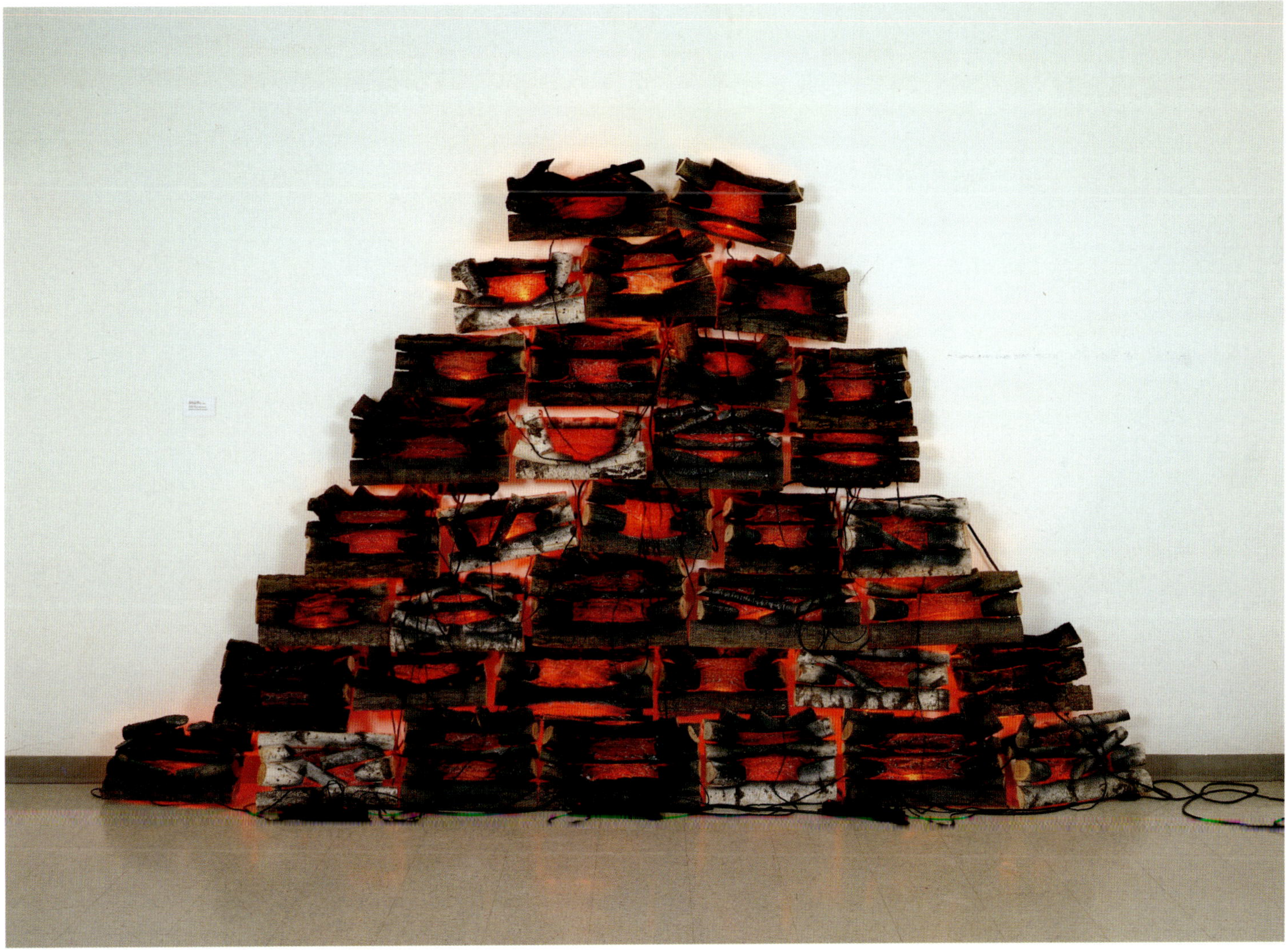

Helen Altman

**Signal**

1992, Electric fire logs, wire, other,
108"h x 162"w x 18"d.
Collection: The Barrett Collection, Dallas.
Courtesy of the artist

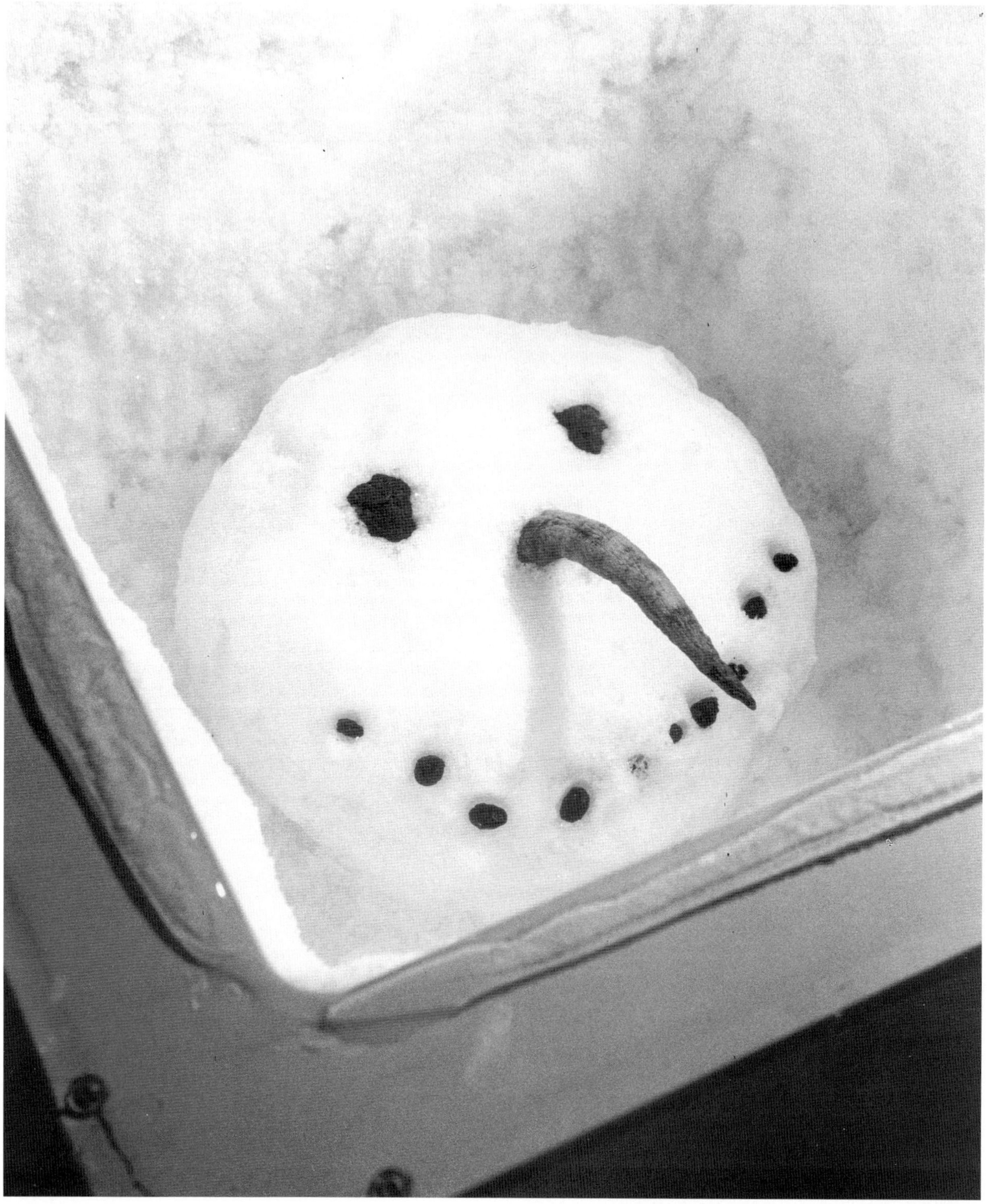

Helen Altman
**Snowhead**
(detail), 1992, Mixed media: electric freezer, ice, carrot, 38"h x 22" x 22". Courtesy of the artist

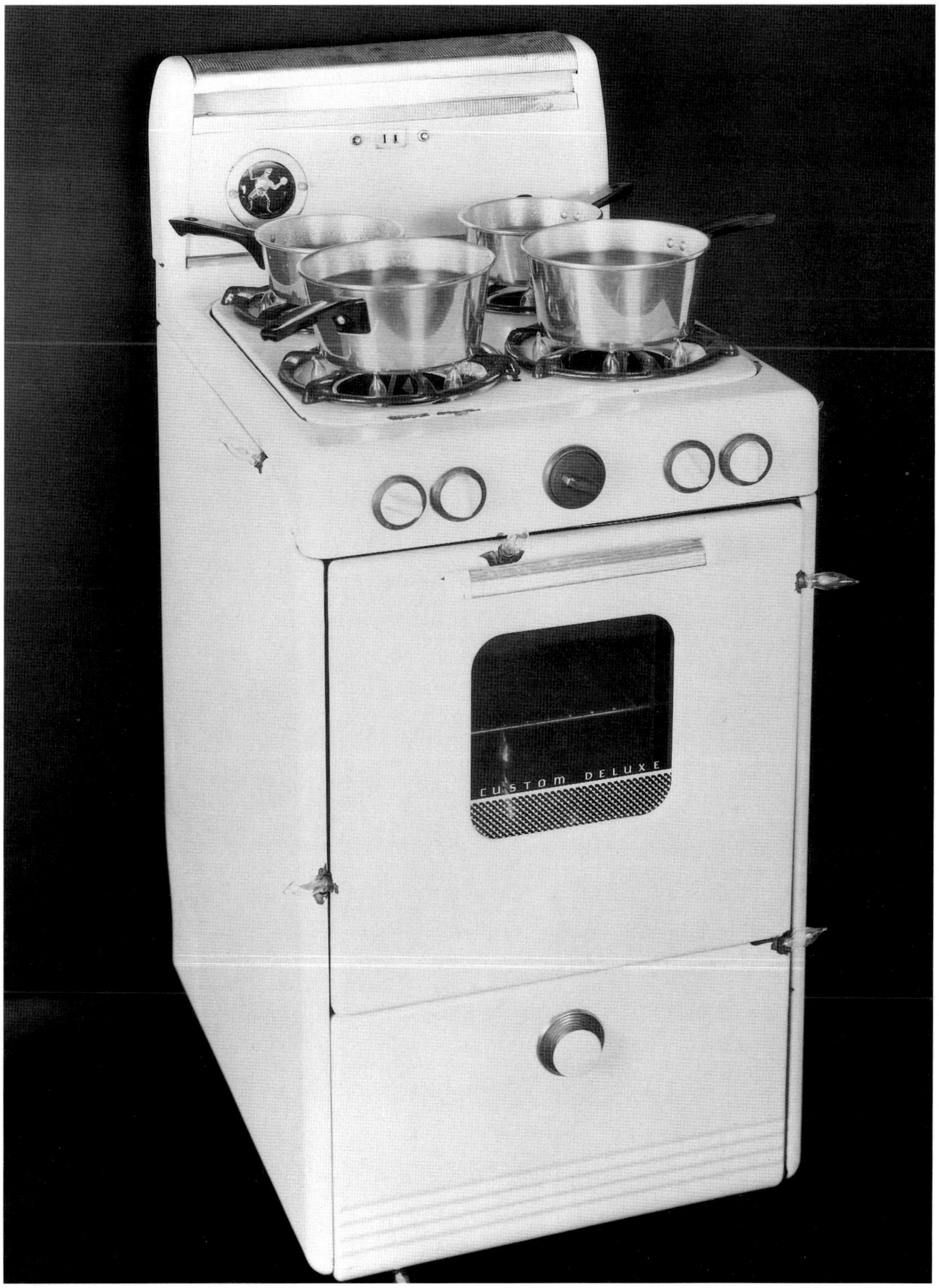


Helen Altman

**Custom Deluxe**

1990, Mixed media: stove, flicker flame bulbs, air pump, etc, 46"h x 24"w x 28½". Collection: The Barrett Collection, Dallas. Courtesy of the artist

# Jesse
# Amado

Jesse Amado originally chose to major in English, but ten years after graduating, returned to the University of Texas in San Antonio to pursue a degree in fine arts. He focused on ceramics then, and in 1990 was awarded his masters degree in painting. The decision to switch from the art of words to the visual language came not at a moment of epiphany, he says, but rather as the inevitable end to a gradual seduction.

Amado, born in San Antonio in 1951, is a second generation Mexican-American. Although the Chicano movement was flourishing across Texas when he was growing up, unlike older artists like painters Mel Casas, who had been his teacher, and César Martínez, Amado did not feel he belonged. His concerns were not artistic or social politics, but rather the conceptual problems of art in a post-modern world. He was not interested, he said, in art as propaganda. "I wanted to offer more to the viewer: If they didn't agree with the politics, there wouldn't be much left."

His work of the 1980s consisted mainly of installations and a variety of painting and sculptural assemblages in which he explored issues of American culture and appropriation. He exhibited widely, primarily in the group and juried shows that are the traditional venues for emerging artists. The elegant, self-contained felt and steel works of this decade, however, represent a breakthrough. The works of Joseph Beuys, which Amado had admired in reproduction for years and finally seen in a 1990 exhibition at the Menil Collection in Houston, were the inspiration. A prestigious grant to the Fabric Workshop in Philadelphia was the turning point.

"I think it's apparent I am very much influenced by minimalism, but I want to think of ways of overcoming it. I want to soften it, but keep its skeletal form. I want to make minimalism more personal, more subjective and ambiguous."

In the rolled cones and cylinders of felt with large brass zippers, Amado presents a potentially sexual image. Yet the clarity of the forms and the industrial nature of the materials precludes a merely prurient interpretation. He folds or wraps the felt components of diminishing sizes into each other and leaves their shiny closures agape. The ambiguity is provocative. They are neither hard nor soft, open or closed; they are both womb and a phallus, and recall a wound simultaneously suggesting a healing scar.

"They really are more about what is not there than what is. The simplicity of the form does not equal a simple experience. I try to make the pieces as essential as I possibly can. They are open-ended and ambiguous so the viewer may find in them what he brings to them."

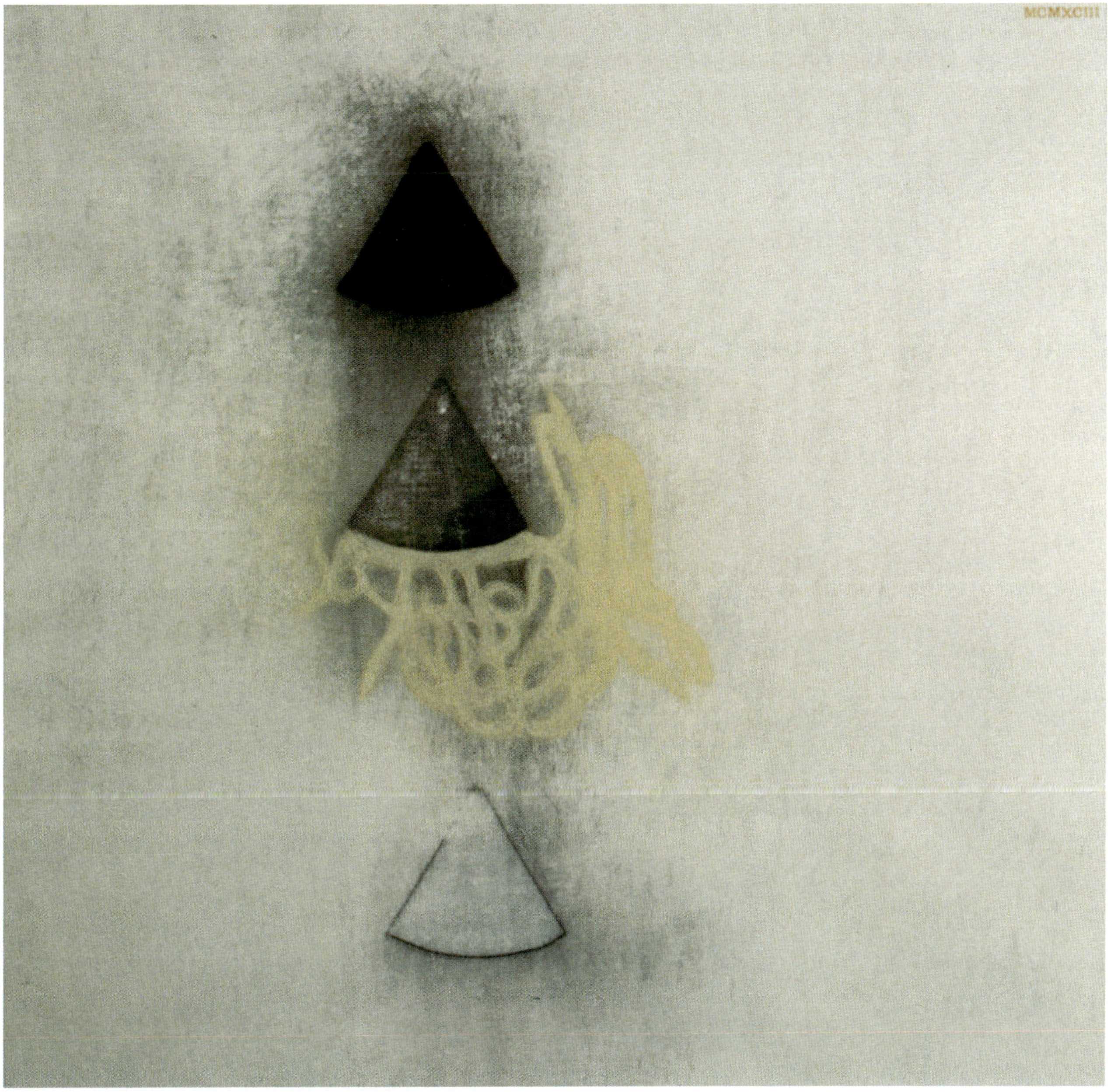


Jesse Amado

**Four (MCMXCIII)**

1993, Mixed media: charcoal, graphite, tire black on paper, 30" x 30". Collection: Jim McElgunn, Houston. Courtesy of Davis/McClain Gallery, Houston

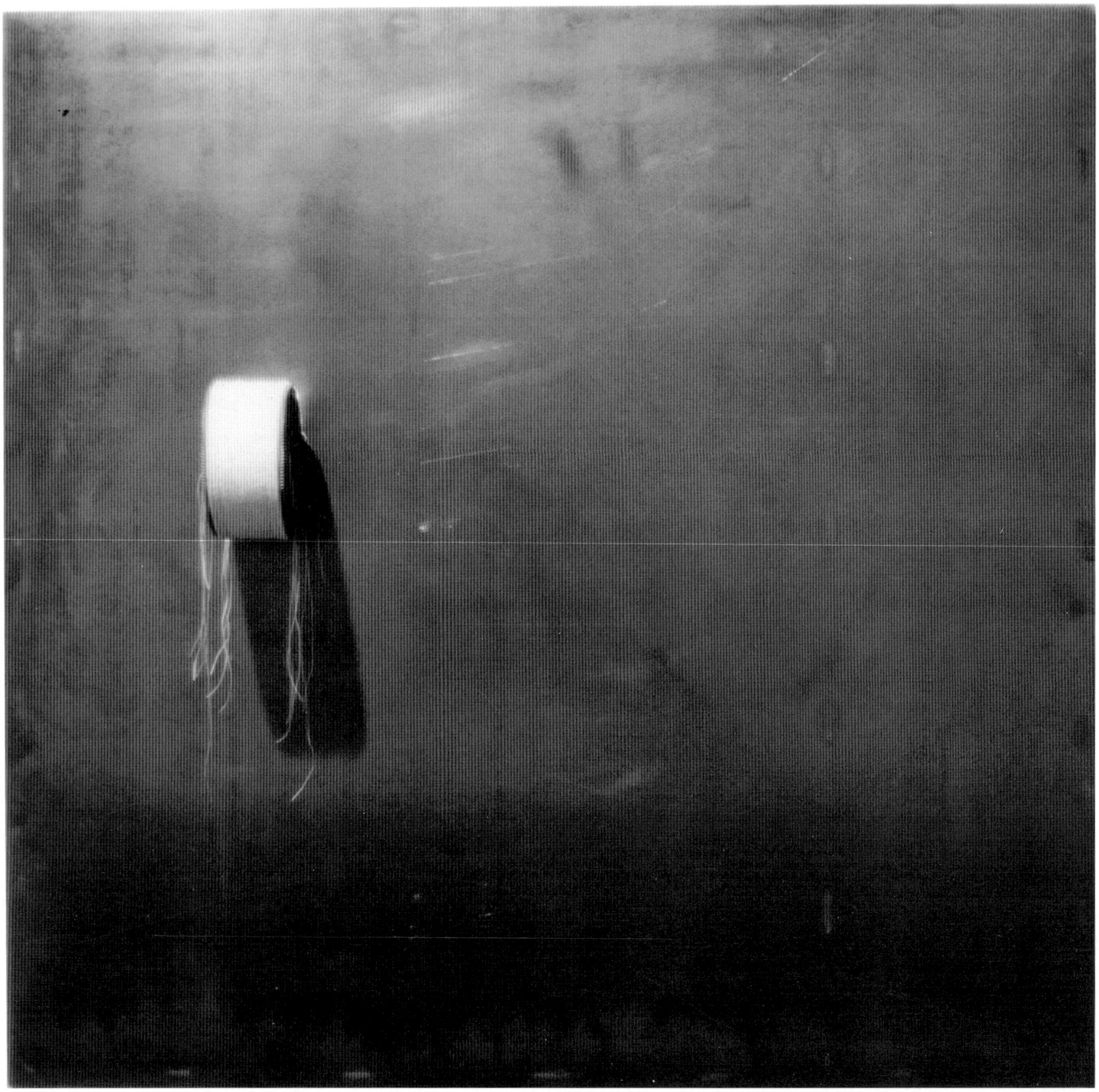

Jesse Amado
**Untitled (Felt IX)**
1993, Felt, brass, metal, 36" x 36". Courtesy of Davis/McClain Gallery, Houston

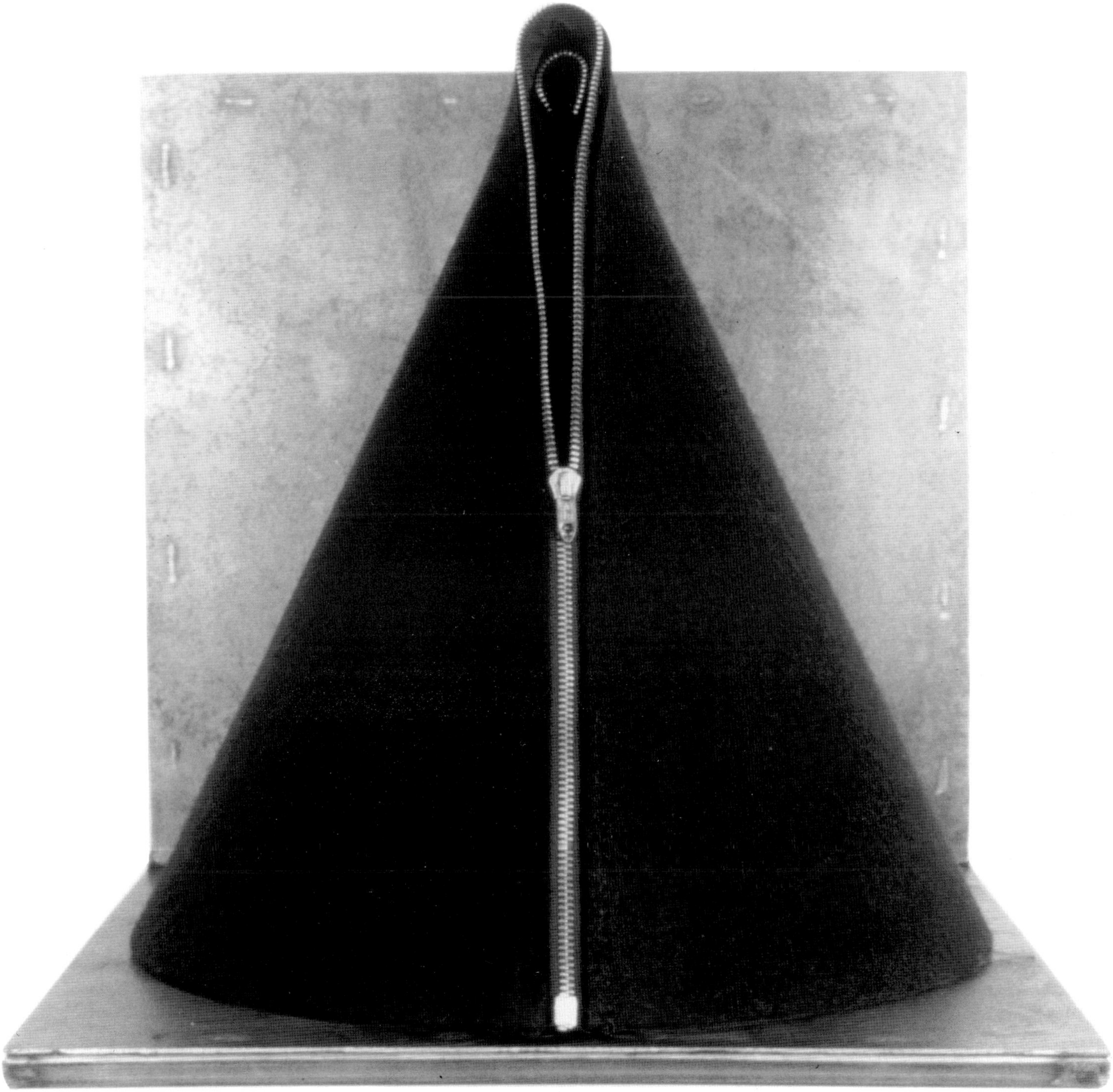

Jesse Amado

**Untitled (Felt VI)**

1993, Felt, brass zippers, metal shelf,
16" x 16" x 16". Courtesy of Davis/McClain Gallery,
Houston

# John
# **Biggers**

John Biggers moved to Houston from his native North Carolina at age 25 to establish the art department at Texas Southern University. The year was 1949, the school was known as Texas State University for Negroes, and segregation of blacks and whites was enforced. But Biggers, the grandson of a slave of mixed African and Cherokee Indian bloods, had a great dream.

"I intentionally did not go to the East or the West Coast. I felt that what I had to say and what I was involved with was in the South. I came here not only to teach, but I felt I wanted to get involved in attempting to express the lifestyle and spiritual aspirations of black people."[1]

Today, the search by black Americans for their African ancestry is celebrated and encouraged at many levels and at all ages. But when Biggers first arrived in Texas, acculturation into the white world was the goal. His dreams of visiting Africa were derided by colleagues at the university. Members of his department at TSU, he recalls, "wanted to visit Paris, London and Rome." Nonetheless, with a grant from UNESCO in 1957, he lived in West Africa for six months and four years later published his book, *Ananse, The Web of Life in Africa* (University of Texas Press, 1962). The book, art historian Alvia J. Wardlaw writes, "was a substantial and sensitive addition to that body of literature which addresses the African-American's perception of his African heritage. The *Ananse* drawings represented a critical point in the development of the artist and he was to return to them repeatedly for future inspiration."[2]

Texas had originally appealed to him as well because of its proximity to Mexico. Biggers identified the country with the "Big Three" of Mexico's muralist movement of the 1920s and 1930s — Diego Rivera, Jose Clemente Orozco and David Alfaro Siqueiros. He understood the artistic and didactic challenge and possibilities of the "painted Bibles", as Orozco described the monumental paintings. Biggers developed a powerful personal style and a curriculum for his students that addressed both.

Motifs of Southern black culture, including quilts, washboards, and the puzzle-like regularity of shotgun houses all in a row, provided the structure against which he depicts the life of the black community in the United States. Graceful archetypal figures — mother, sister, daughter, and symbolic creatures from West African creation myths — move across the surface in counterpoint to the geometric backgrounds. With transparent glazes of acrylic paint and a fine descriptive brush, Biggers achieves luminous surfaces of both narrative and formal richness.

"The role of art is to express the triumph of the human spirit over the mundane and material. It is also to express the universal myths and archetypes of the universal family of man."[3]

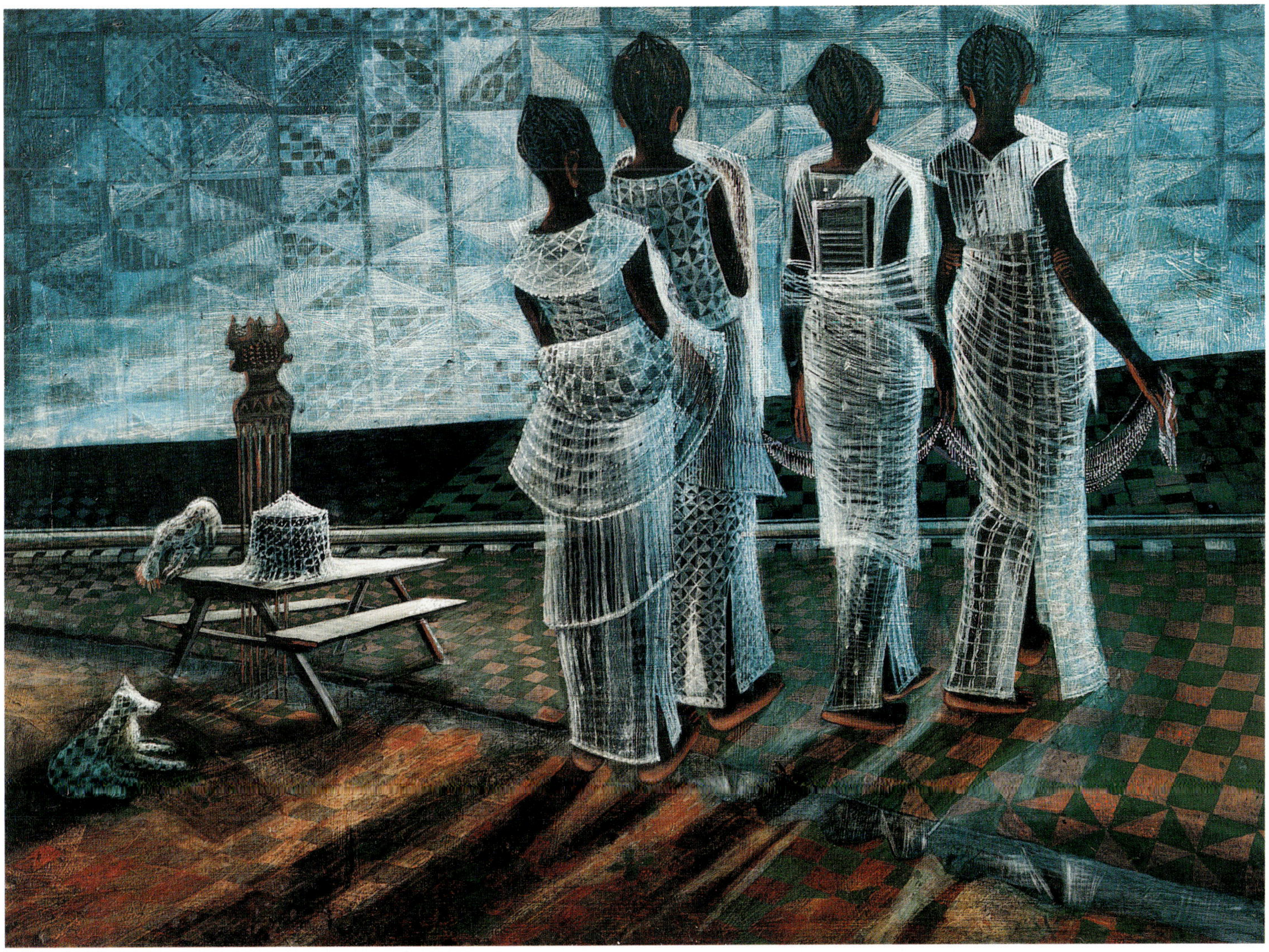

John Biggers
**Four Sisters**
1986, Acrylic on canvas, 36" x 48". Collection: Hampton University Museum, Virginia. Courtesy of the artist

In the summer of 1991, Biggers returned to Hampton University in Virginia, his alma mater, for a commission consisting of two murals, each 20 feet high, 10 feet wide, on opposite ends of the new library. A major retrospective of his work is being prepared by the Museum of Fine Arts, Houston, scheduled to open the spring of 1995.

1. Cited in "The mural of the story", by Patricia C. Johnson, *The Houston Chronicle*, Zest Magazine, Sunday, May 29, 1983, p. 16
2. Alvia Wardlaw, cited in *Black Art/Ancestral Legacy*, Dallas Museum of Art, 1989
3. Cited in Kalil, Susie, and Rose, Barbara, *Fresh Paint: The Houston School*, Museum of Fine Arts, Houston, 1985, p. 15

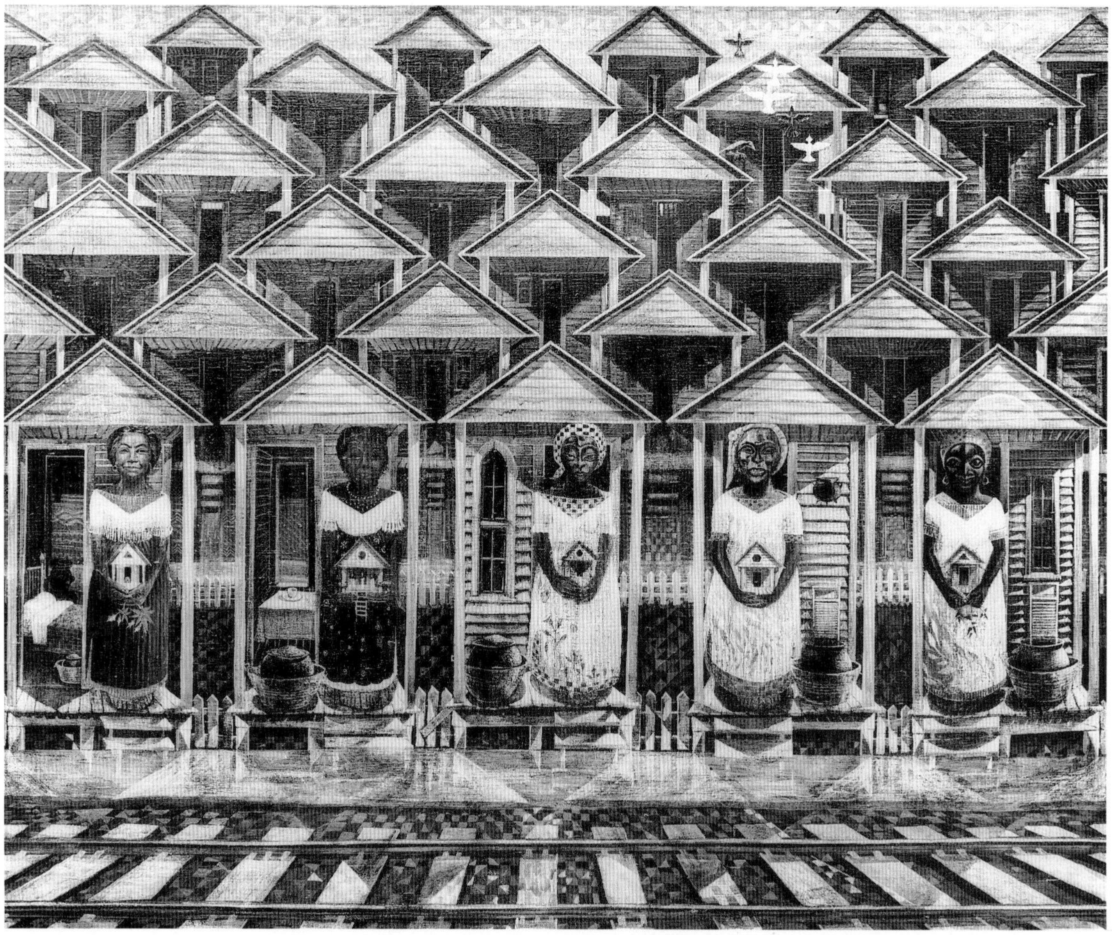

John Biggers
**Third Ward Shotgun**
1987, Acrylic on canvas, 40" x 56". Photograph: Earlie Hudnall, Houston. Collection: Andrew Moran, Houston. Courtesy of the artist

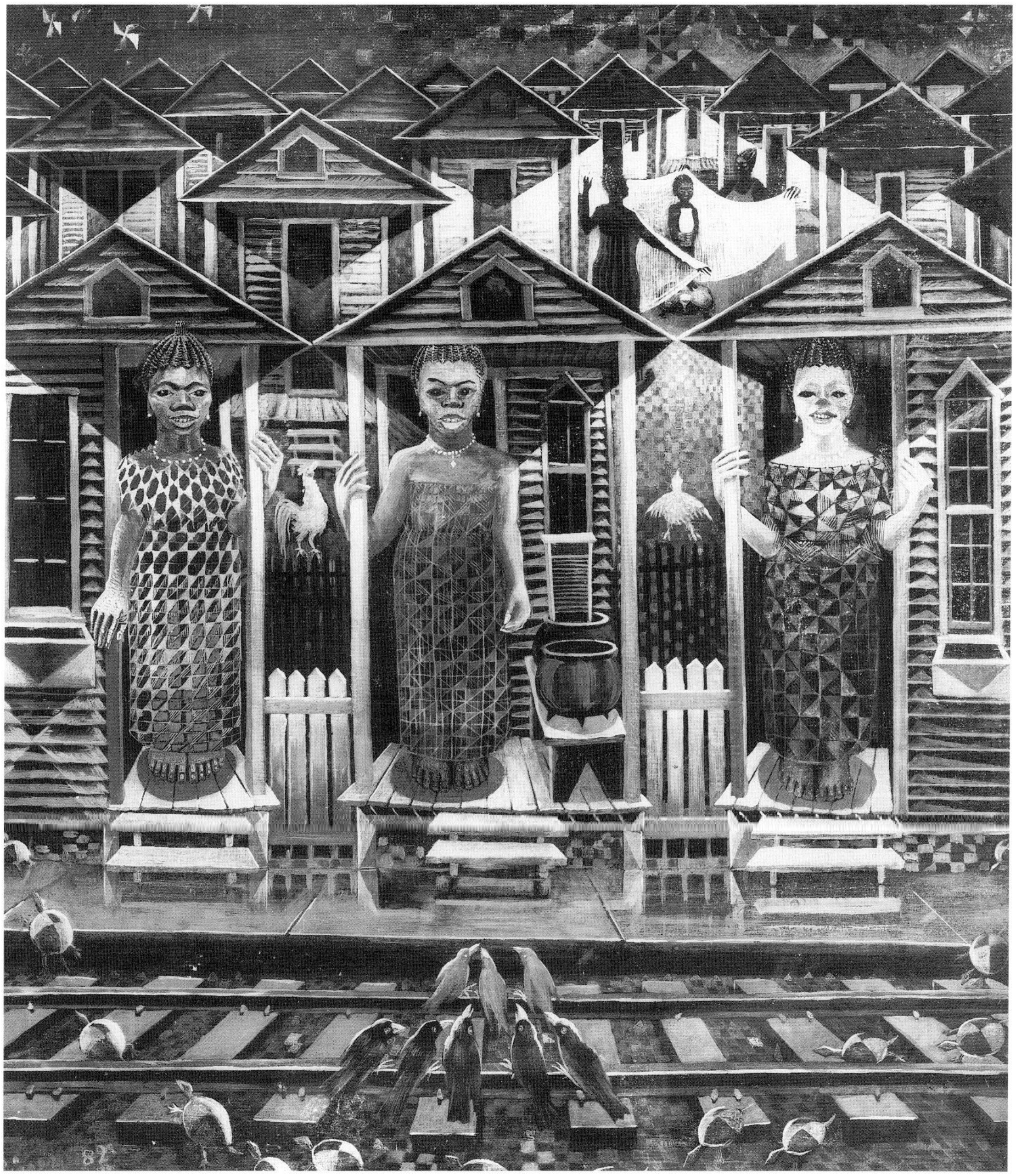


John Biggers
**Shotguns, Fourth Ward**
1986, Acrylic on canvas, 41¾" x 32". Collection: Hampton University Museum, Virginia. Courtesy of the artist

# Julie
# Bozzi

Julie Bozzi is meticulous in researching her subjects and precise in their rendering. She explores the traditional genres of Western art with the keen eye of the scientist and the sympathy of an anthropologist.

Born in Fresno, California, in 1943, Bozzi worked for eight years between receiving her bachelor's degree and returning for her master's at the University of California at Davis in 1979. There was a "short detour" into ceramics before she determined the classical areas of painting were what interested her. Landscape, still lifes and portraiture, she says, "are the historical areas of painting and there is a certain resonance when you deal with subject matter which is so heavily loaded."

Bozzi is best known for her landscapes, their long, narrow format a signature quality like her delicate palette. She approaches this genre traditionally, making sketches outdoors to be rendered in full later in her studio. Photographs have always been important references, too, but more so since moving to Fort Worth in 1980, where the climate isn't always cooperative. Her format is intimate rather than heroic, and the scenes seemingly featureless mundane lengths of highways or walls, rather than visibly beautiful or dramatic. But because Bozzi also prefers to work in series, painting the exact same site several times, she reveals hidden meanings or relationships, and the subtleties of nature.

Still lifes have not been a major part of her oeuvre, but in 1991, Bozzi finished an extraordinary assemblage of diminutive sculptures seven years in the making titled *American Food*. It consists of thousands of individual and exact facsimiles of breakfast cereals, ethnic dishes, candies and pastries in a sweeping array Bozzi painstakingly recreated in wood, clay and paint. It is an exhaustive and stunningly beautiful cultural document of America's diet, organized, analyzed and identified as methodically as a Victorian collection of pinned butterflies or a malacologist's obsession.

"The food I wished to describe was non-domestic and idiomatic on a national rather than a regional scale: the food of restaurants, supermarkets and advertising … I had to rely on unorthodox research materials such as menus, magazines, trade periodicals and observation. Cumulatively, this project is about food as product, subject to stylization, mutation, and obsolescence. The result is a still life representing a passing moment in the transitory language of American food."[1]

1. Cited in *American Food*, Museum of Contemporary Art, San Diego, California, 1992

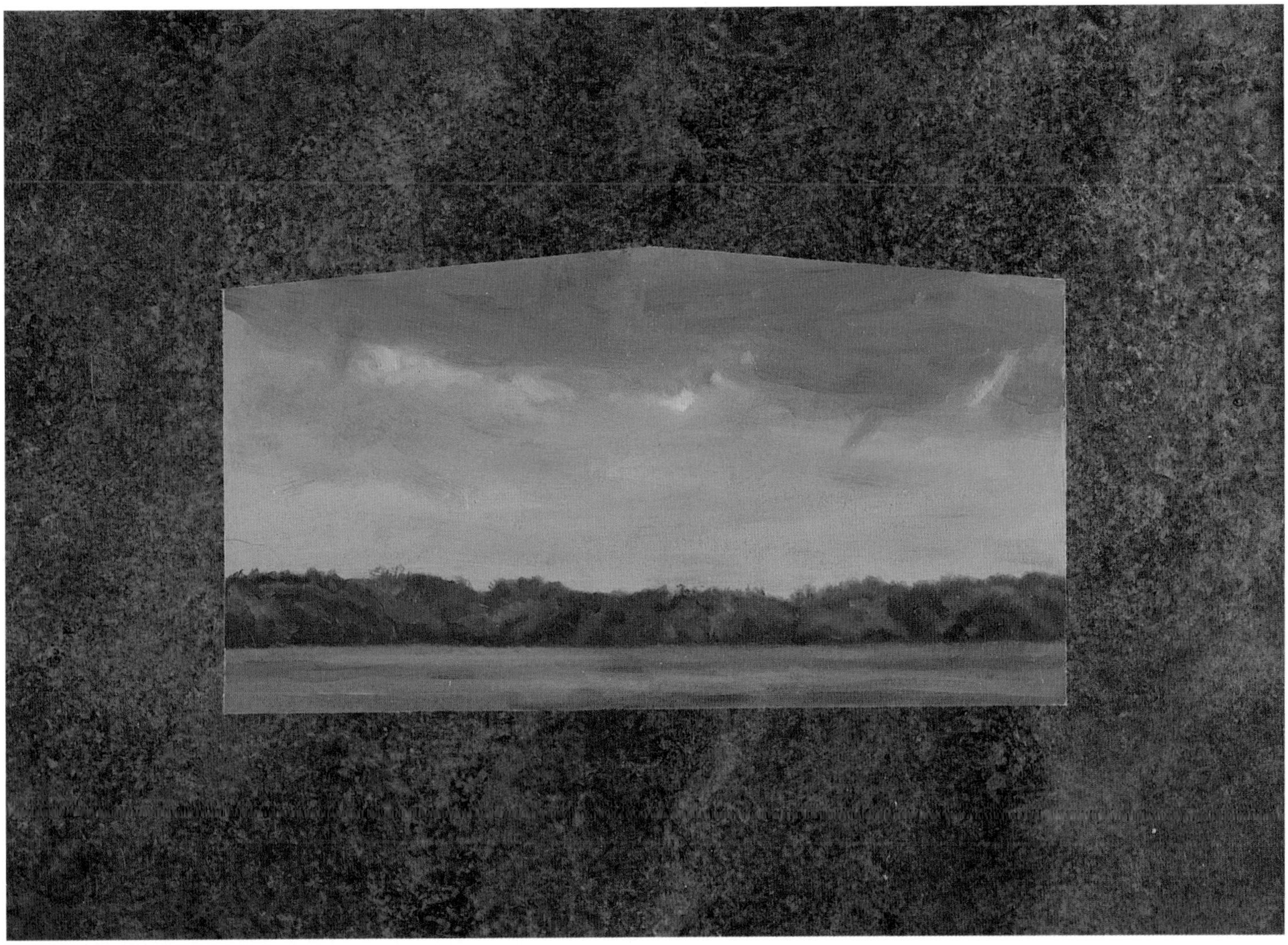

Julie Bozzi
**Untitled (Landscape)**
1989, Oil on paper, 10¼" x 14⅛". Courtesy of Texas Gallery, Houston

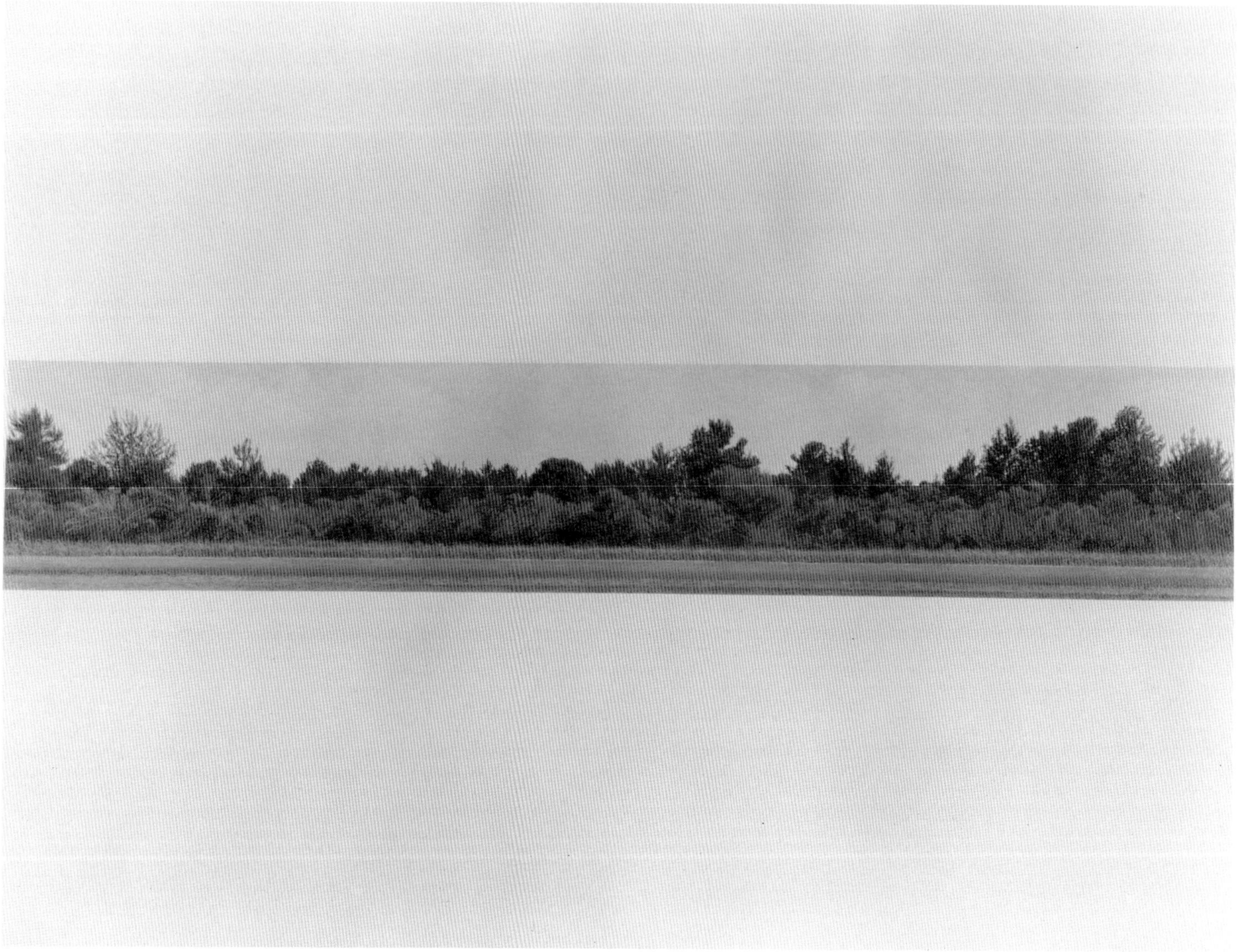

Julie Bozzi

**Edge of the Piney Woods**

1987–88, Oil on paper, 22" x 30" (paper size).
Collection: Modern Art Museum of Fort Worth,
Museum purchase, The Benjamin J. Tillar Memorial
Trust. Courtesy of Texas Gallery, Houston

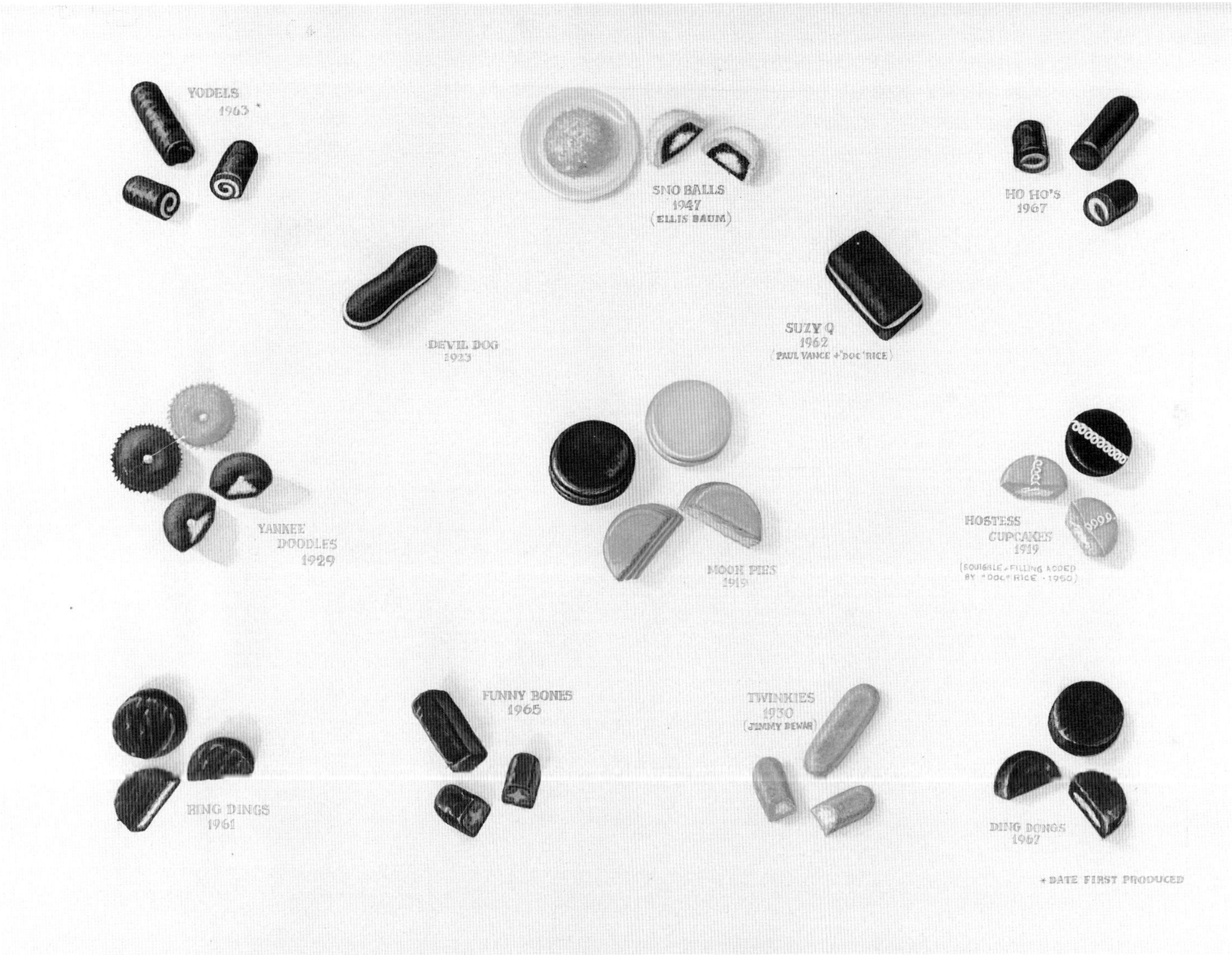


Julie Bozzi

**Classic Snack Cakes (from American Food)**

1991, Gouache on paper, 17" x 22".
Collection of the artist. Courtesy of the artist

# Karin **Broker**

Karin Broker pursued a rigorous and traditional education in printmaking, but frustration and professional ambition compelled her to push her knowledge to extremes. "I realized a long time ago printmaking was going to be limiting to me size wise, but also career wise. Printmaking has always been just kicked around, especially by painters."

Born in Pennsylvania in 1950, she received her bachelor's degree at the University of Iowa in 1972, and her master's from the University of Wisconsin eight years later. In the interim, she spent six months working with Stanley William Hayter, the innovative master printer, at his renowned Atelier 17 in Paris. The experience was unpleasant but crucial.

"Hayter was 73 and a dirty old man. He always had his hands all over the students. And the shop was a primitive situation. There was no room and no light. But he was a dramatic, dynamic guy. Everything he said stuck. His ideas about movement, about popping out images, really apply. I have used them from that moment on."

Her subjects are autobiographical. Love found and love lost are constants, frequently complicated by a feminist edge that rebels against the woman's need for the man. Broker imbues the work with the power of conviction. In her lexicon of the human condition, loneliness is the flip side of anger. Life-size figures emerge from backgrounds of complex tonality and implied movement, scratched, rubbed, and redrawn to give them volume.

Since coming to Houston to teach printmaking at Rice University in 1980, she has pursued two main expressive avenues. Combining the essential techniques of printmaking with others from the fields of commercial engraving, she makes marks with conte crayon, sandblasters and by attaching fluorescent lights onto her flat surfaces. At first, the grounds were plastic laminates on sculptured shapes simulating domestic furniture; most recently, her surfaces are sheet steel. These latter, wall-dependent works occupy real space and demand physical confrontation. She calls them "drawings", but they actually bridge the distance between two and three dimensions.

In 1989, Broker began making hermetic, fetish-like objects that are as intimate and discrete as her steel drawings are heroic in demeanor. Assembled from recycled metal and embellished with nails, *milagros* (small votive images from Mexico, usually made of silver or brass) and mementos from her past, they would seem to totter on sentimentality, were they not so evidently a form of exorcism.

"I make boxes when I'm feeling bad about something, when I feel impotent. In the boxes I can incorporate all those feelings of frustration. They are about being a woman."

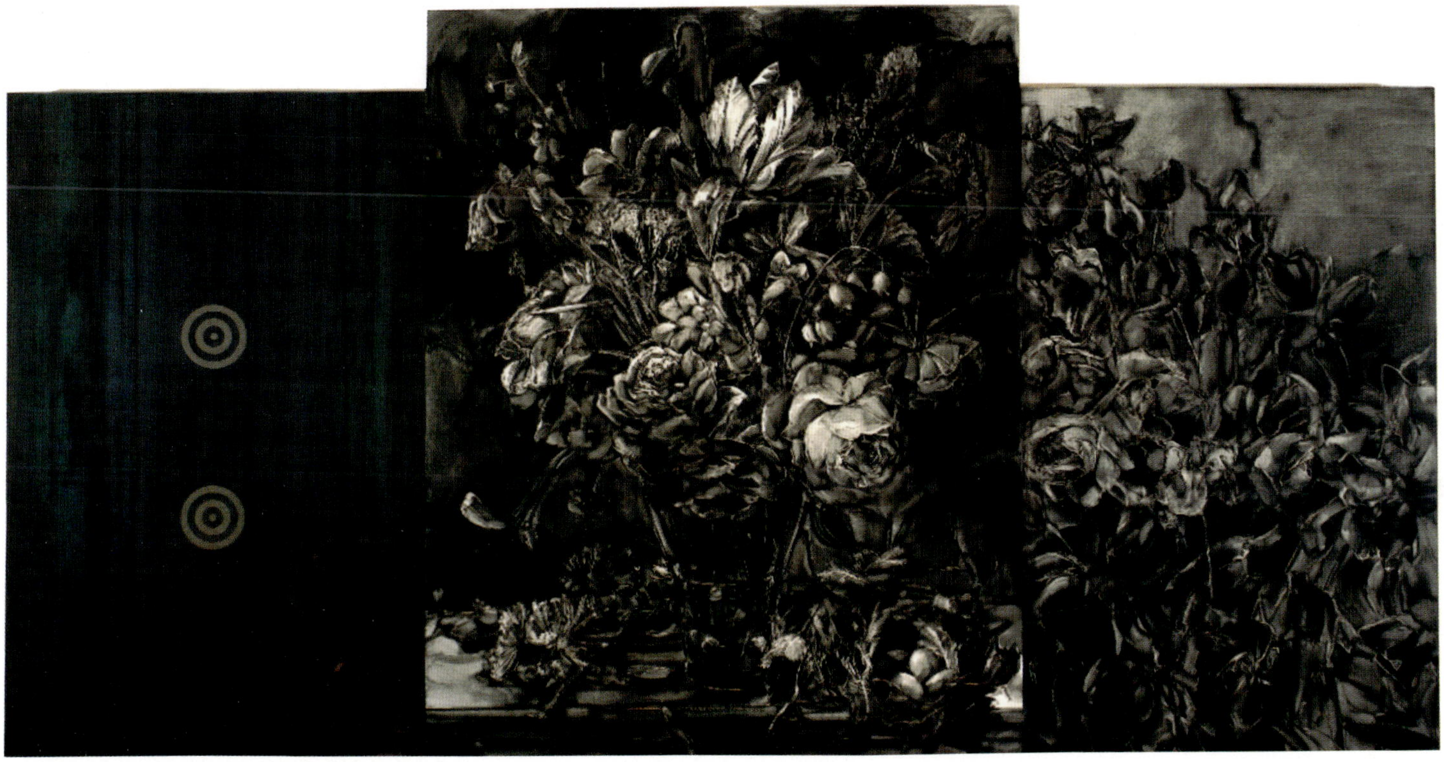

Karin Broker
**Big Girl Lie #1 (S.C.B.)**
1992, Conte on formica and steel, 108" x 205½".
Courtesy of McMurtrey Gallery, Houston

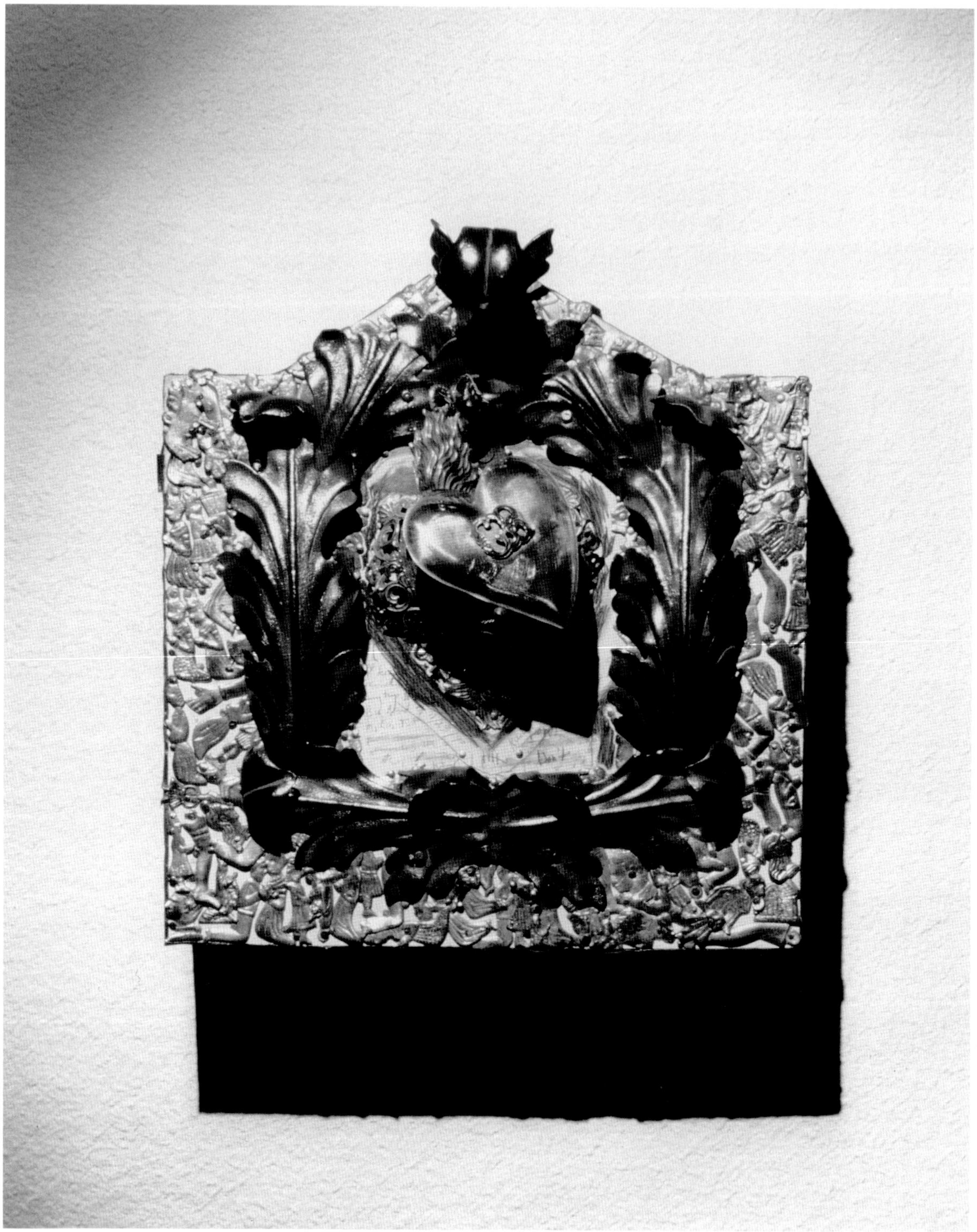

Karin Broker
**Rusted Heart #3**
1990, Mixed media including metal *milagros*,
$9\frac{1}{2}$"h x $8\frac{1}{2}$"w x $5\frac{1}{4}$". Courtesy of McMurtrey Gallery, Houston

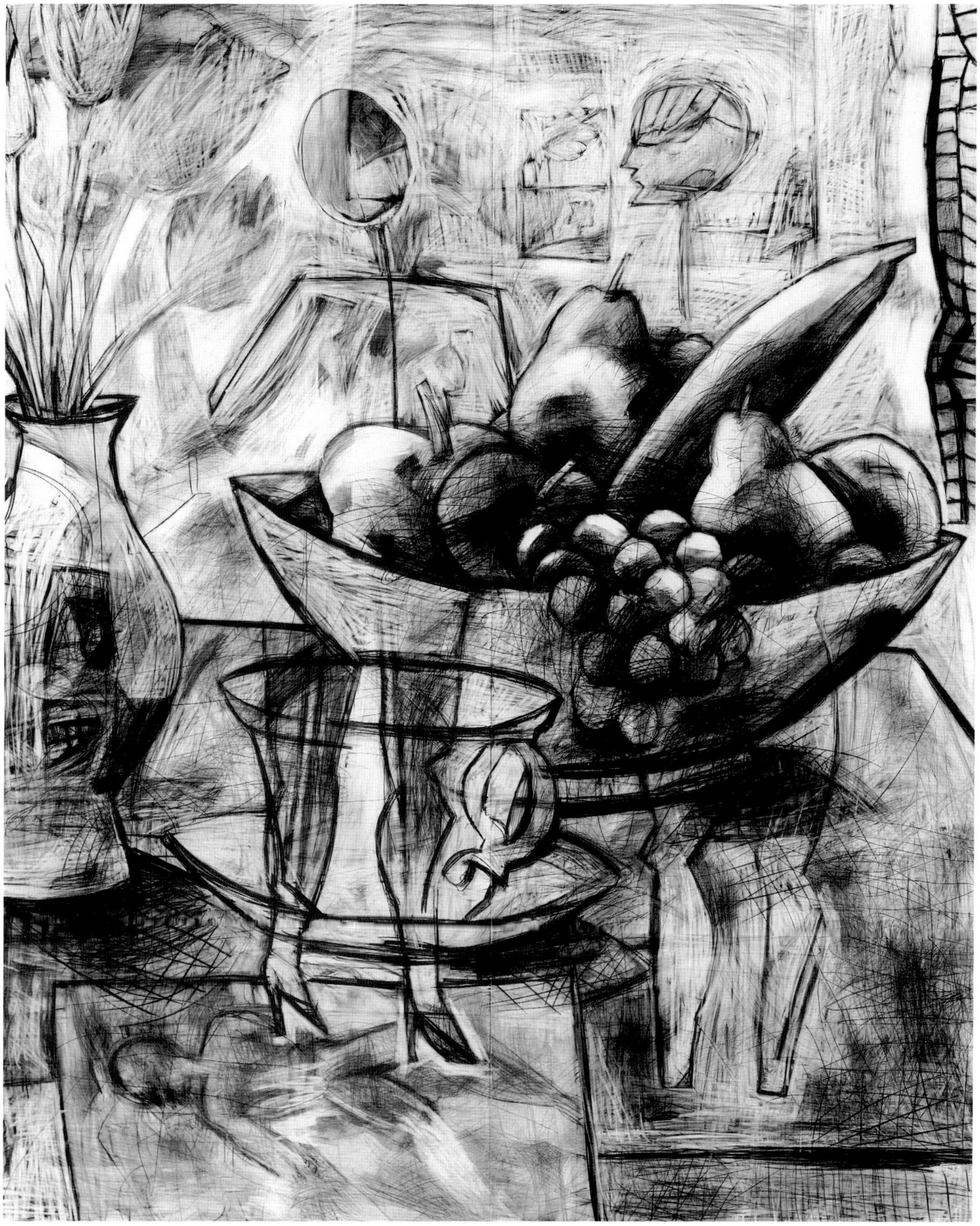

Karin Broker
**Stilled Life**
1988, Conte and pencil and formica, 108½" x 87½" x 3". Collection: Mia Jones. Courtesy of McMurtrey Gallery, Houston

# Keith
# **Carter**

Photographer Keith Carter knows his part of the world intimately. His camera, an extension of his compassionate eye, records the lives which unfold against the rural background around Beaumont — the farmland, swamps and piney woods of deep East Texas where he grew up. The images, warm, richly toned black and white silver gelatin prints, are up close and personal, but never intrusive.

Carter, born in Wisconsin in 1948, began taking pictures as a teenager. His mother was widowed when he was five and she earned the family living photographing children. But he was 22, with a degree in business administration and an idea about being a picture framer, before he considered the camera a means to make a living or think of it as an expressive tool. A friend in Beaumont, sculptor David Carnegie, had been lending him books on art through the years and taking critical interest in Carter's youthful photographs. Now he gave Carter a book on Henri Cartier-Bresson. "I had been making photographs out of ignorance," he said. "Cartier-Bresson's 'decisive moment' was a new vocabulary for me." In photography, light is the the verb that articulates the image; in Carter's images, the space the subject inhabits assumes the narrative lead.

"I'm rooted in the tradition of documentary photography, but I feel my work is more visionary. I've chosen to live here and work here, because my interest has to do with rural people and rural communities — the superstition, religion, everything that is a life, and how it fits together. I deal with questions I cannot answer."

Carter works in series, defining them first with a title that is both allusive in meaning and specific in content. *From Uncertain to Blue*, the first of three portfolios he's published in book form (Texas Monthly Press, 1988), consisted of images of 100 small crossroad communities in Texas with alluring names. His most recent series, *On Higher Ground*, looks at life in the extreme poverty of the Mississippi delta, and is scheduled for publication the winter of 1994. A statement he made in the text of the evocatively titled *The Blue Man* (Rice University Press, 1990) encapsulates who this sensitive photographer is and why his images are so enormously appealing.

"There are an extraordinary number of people who have these great lives of the spirit. They work hard to make their lives interesting. [My images] are about imagination in the boondocks."

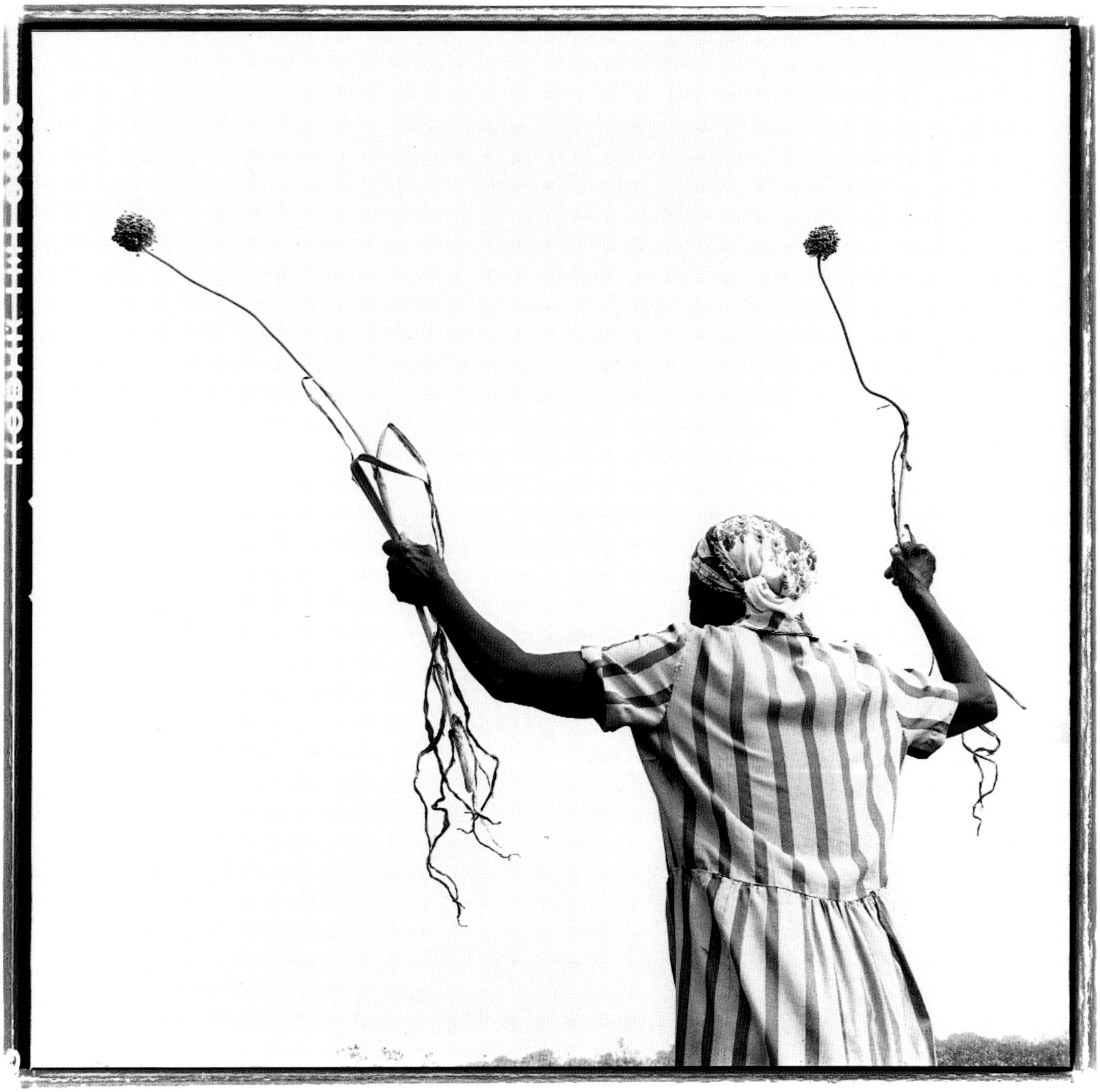

Keith Carter
**Garlic**
1991, Gelatin silver, 15" x 15". Courtesy of the artist

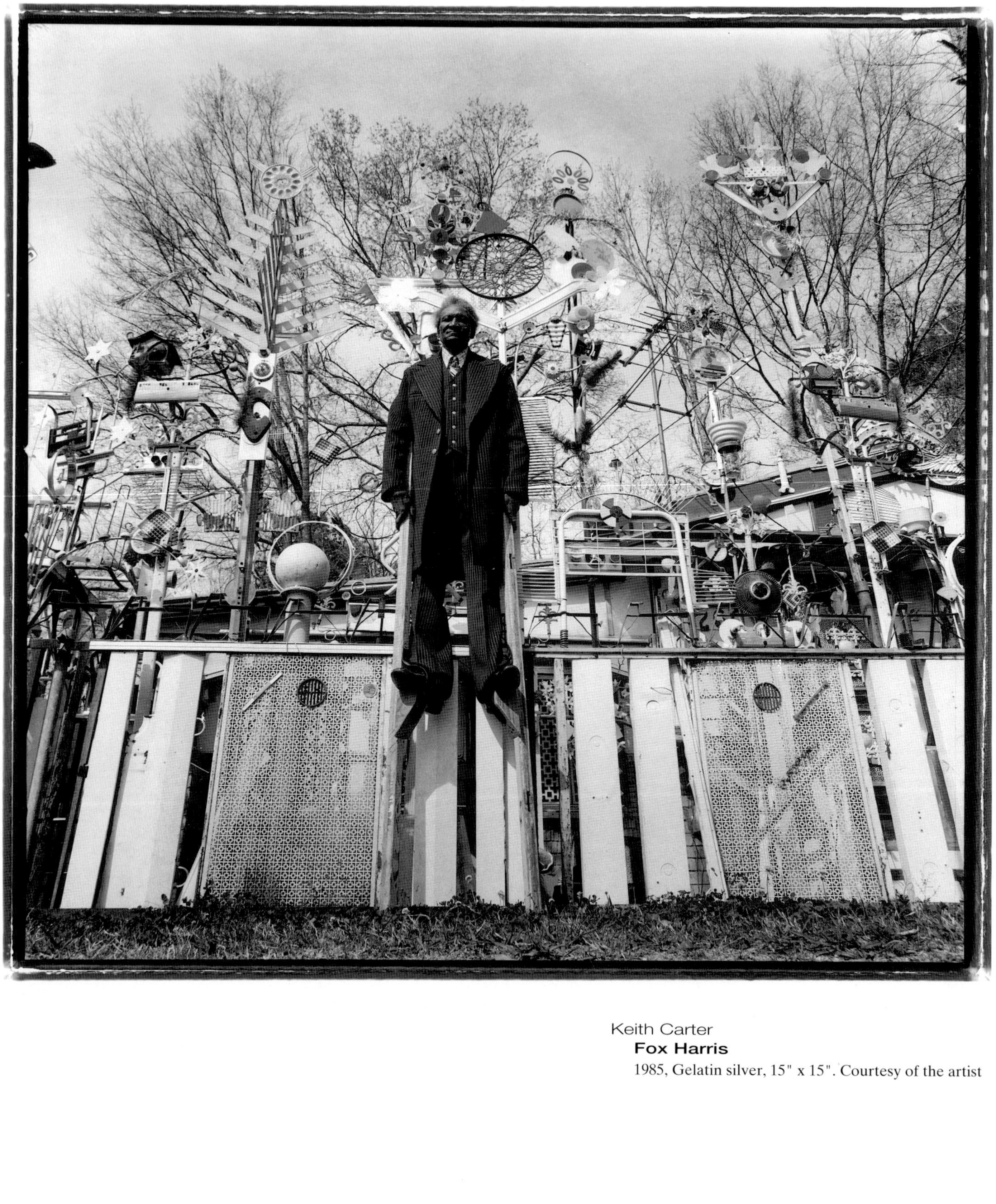

Keith Carter

**Fox Harris**

1985, Gelatin silver, 15" x 15". Courtesy of the artist

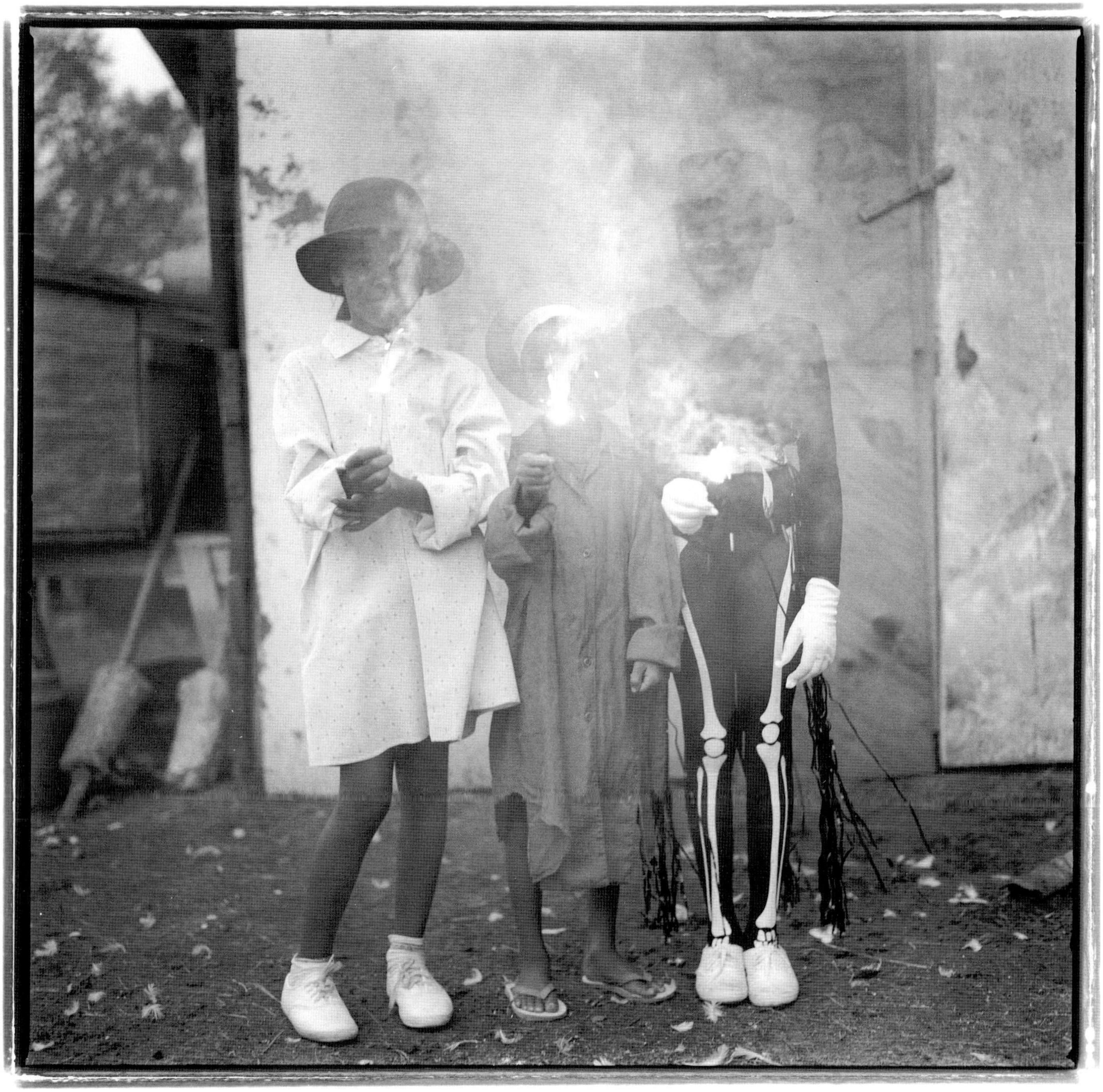

Keith Carter
**Chicken Feathers**
1992–93, Gelatin silver, 15" x 15". Courtesy of the artist

# Mel
# Chin

With a mind-boggling array of materials drawn from nature and industry, Mel Chin compresses the universe into poetic objects and environments loaded with meaning. The humanities are his sources and the natural sciences inform his concerns. His meticulous research combined with a unique sensibility for manipulating substances result in precise metaphors where nothing is gratuitous. "I feel an obligation to the facts," Chin states.[1]

Chin, a first generation Chinese-American, was born in Houston in 1951. His formal education was at George Peabody College for Teachers (Nashville, Tennessee) where he studied ceramics. The pliable, humble clay was an auspicious material, fraught with historical and cultural references. It led him to explore other transformative and expressive media, even as his curiosity took him to myriad sources of image and content. He selects his materials for their inherent symbolism or practical applications, and often designs and constructs the tools he needs to make what he's envisioned.

The apparent simplicity of his concise forms belie their multi-disciplinary and intellectual genesis. One sculptural example from 1988 helps illustrate. *The Opera of Silence* addresses the long-standing conflict between China and Tibet. It is a large-scale replica of ceremonial drums used in Chinese operas. Chin fashioned the beating surface from hog skins stitched into the stylized eagle that is the emblem of the Central Intelligence Agency. It is stretched over a concave funnel, the shape of a satellite dish, which he coated with white theatrical make-up, symbolic of deceit. The drum balances precariously, like an animal trap, on a human figure carved from an animal thigh bone.

Increasing demands for information and access to human resources compelled his move to New York City in the mid-1980s. His most recent projects are environmental, formally and in terms of topicality. They range from *Revival Field*, an experimental garden of plants known as hyperaccumulators that are capable of leaching toxins from contaminated soil, to *The State of Heaven*, which addresses world ecology.[2] To realize his concepts, Chin works with experts, an extension of his uncompromising quest for knowledge and precision. Dr. Rufus Cheney of the U.S. Department of Agriculture, for instance, was instrumental in the implementation of *Revival Field*. For the *State of Heaven*, Chin has called upon intellects and craftsmen, from computer experts to Kurdish weavers, to realize an art work that is, indeed, global.

1. Cited in "True to form", by Patricia C. Johnson, *The Houston Chronicle*, Zest Magazine, April 16, 1989, p. 15
2. *Soil and Earth*, a partial installation of this multi-media work in progress, was presented at the Fabric Workshop and Swarthmore College, Philadelphia, October 1–November 30, 1992

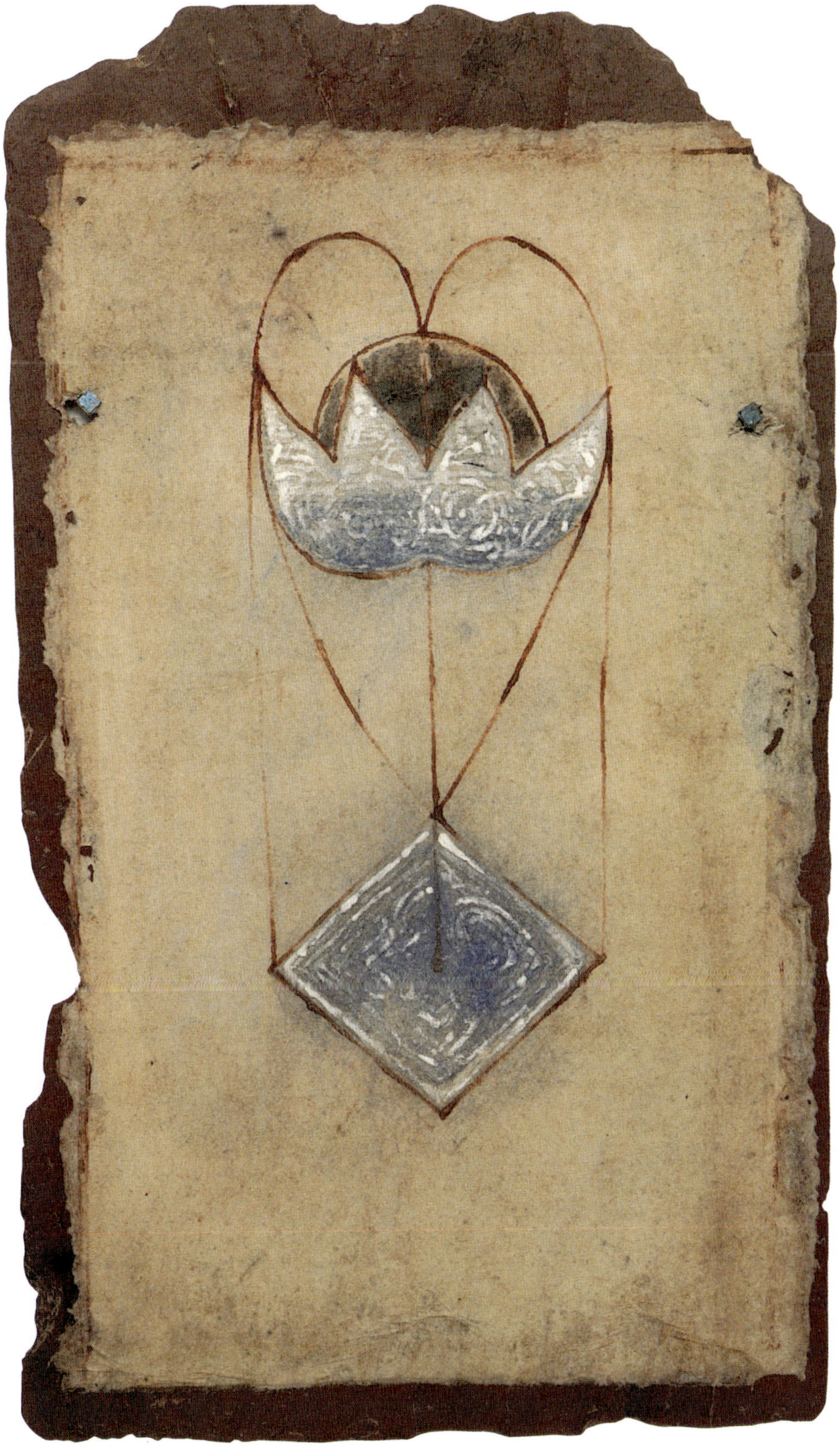

Mel Chin
**Degrees of Paradise,**
**"Tantric" Dream Diagram**
(detail) 1991, Pigment on paper on slate, 13½" x 7½". Courtesy of the artist

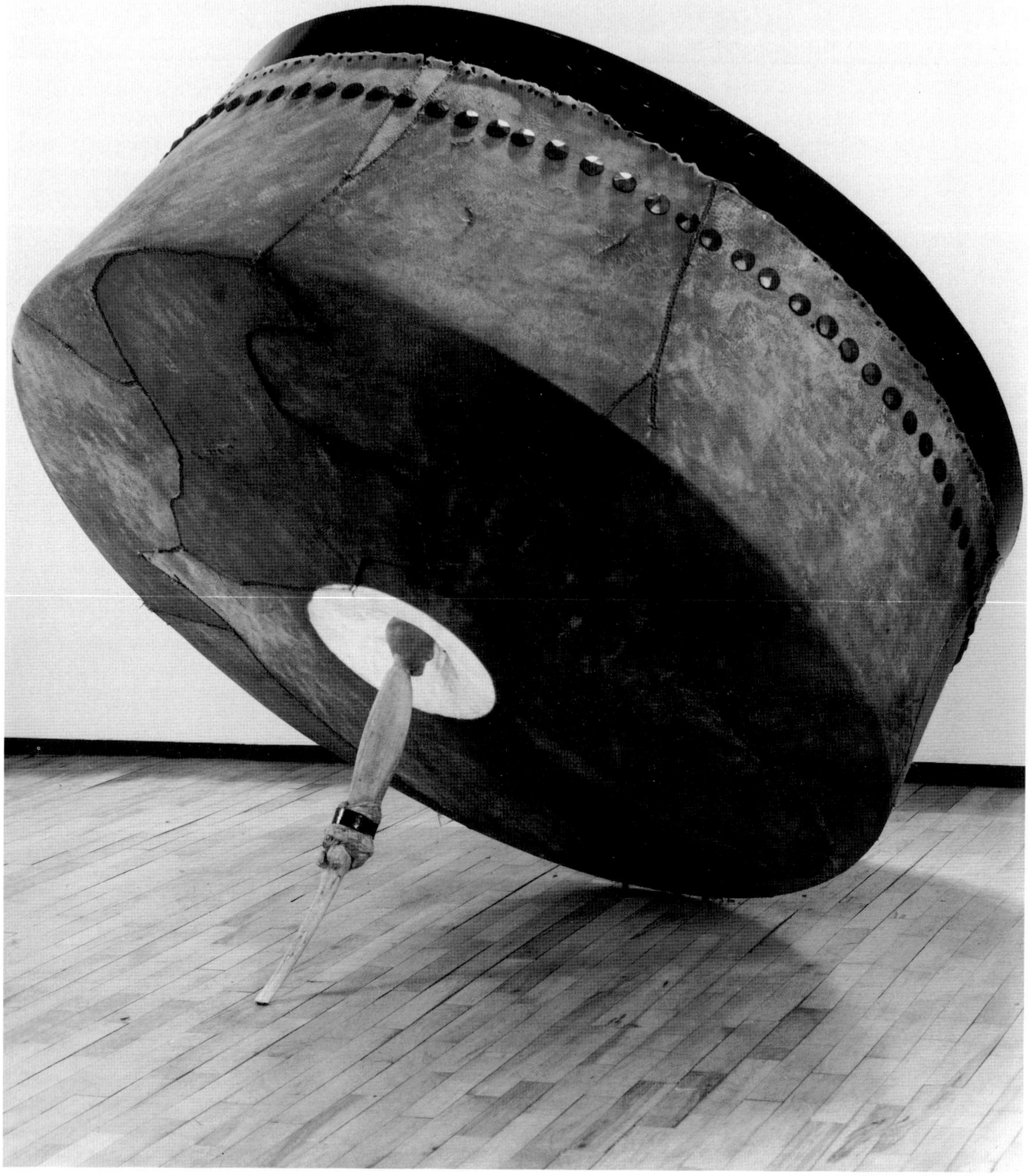

Mel Chin
**The Opera of Silence**
1988, Mixed media: hog hides, wood, steel, white face, etc, 60"h x 70" x 67". Collection: Walker Art Center, Minneapolis, T.B. Walker Acquisition Fund, 1990. Courtesy of Walker Art Center, Minneapolis

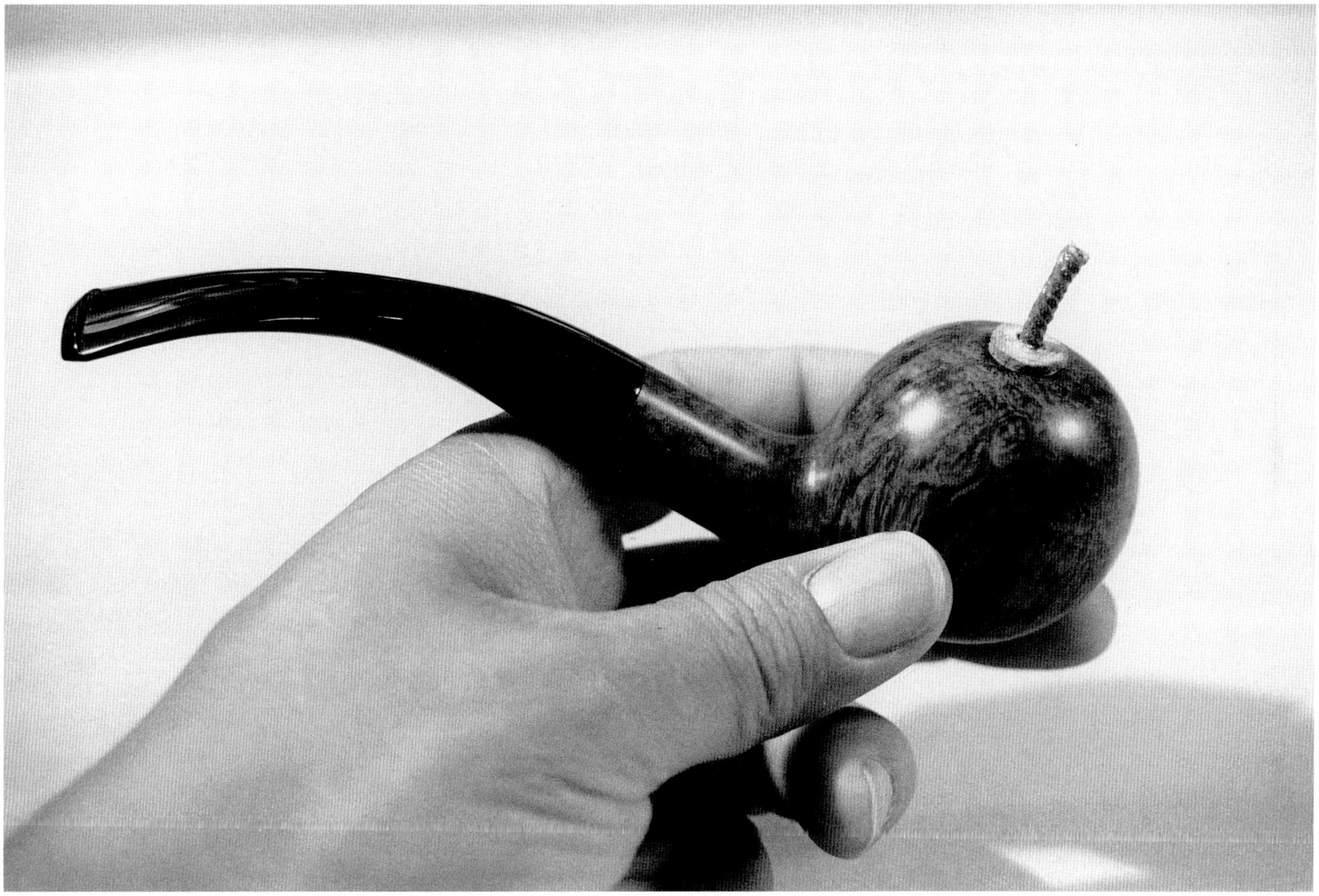

Mel Chin
**Elementary Object (Prototype)**
1993, Mixed media: approx. 8" long. Courtesy of the artist

# James **Drake**

James Drake doesn't think of himself as an artist "of the border". El Paso is home, not a political statement. His mother and her sister moved there in the late 1950s and started an import business that continues to support the family. Drake has taken a hand in the business since he was a teenager, speaking Spanish and absorbing cultural nuances through daily contact with the Mexican craftsmen whose work is the company's lifeline.

But living in El Paso affects his art profoundly. "The Pass", on the Rio Grande on the U.S.-Mexican border, is different historically, socially and economically from any other Texas city. The precarious existence on the Rio Grande informs the content of Drake's work as much as classical draftsmanship describes his style. He deals with the human condition through powerful, expressive charcoal drawings and steel sculptures directly in the semi-narrative work of the eighties. *The Raft of the Medusa* (1988), a pivotal piece in his career, drew analogies between the infamous incident of 19th century France that inspired Theodore Gericault's masterwork of that title, and the present condition of Third World refugees in the United States. In the nineties, Drake has taken a more symbolic approach, presenting issues such as drug trafficking and its attendant violence, through elegant metaphors such as the gun benches, menacing and horribly seductive at once.

Born in Lubbock in 1946, Drake, like his friend Terry Allen, thinks the featureless, flat landscape of his childhood had everything to do with his becoming a visual artist for it forced the imagination to search within. And like many Texans of his generation, going to art school meant leaving the state. Drake chose the Center College of Design in Los Angeles, receiving his BFA in 1969 and his masters the following year. But what was really happening, he says, was outside the school, especially at Walter Hopps' Ferus Gallery and exhibits like Edward Kienholz's at the Los Angeles County Museum of Art.

"My work is a necessity for me, and if it is honest, people will pick up on that. Nobody gives a damn about my life, but if somehow I can [touch] theirs, and they can relate to something I've done, then, I think, something has been accomplished. If I had stayed in Lubbock, I don't know what I would have been doing, but obviously it wouldn't have been anything about Mexico and Central America and El Paso, or how it relates to me and the United States and Texas."

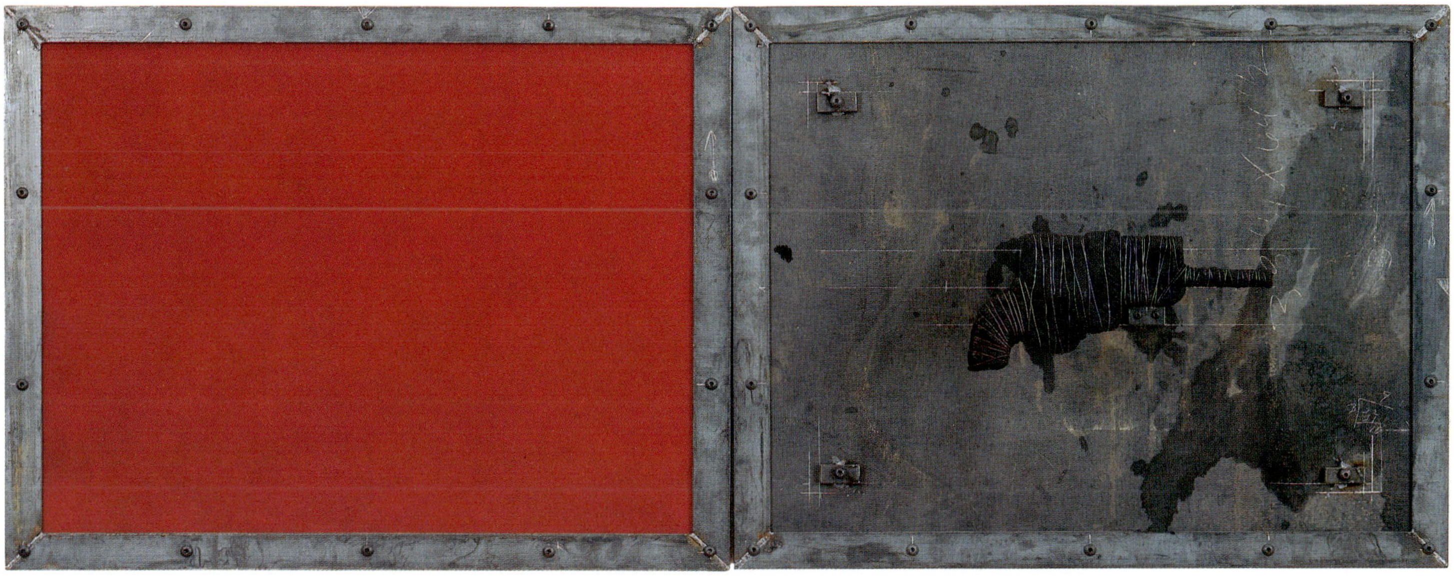

James Drake
**Untitled (Wrapped Gun)**
1989, Mixed media: steel, paper, pastel, fabric, tar, 30"h x 76"w x 10"d. Photograph: Rick Gardner, Houston. Courtesy of Texas Gallery, Houston

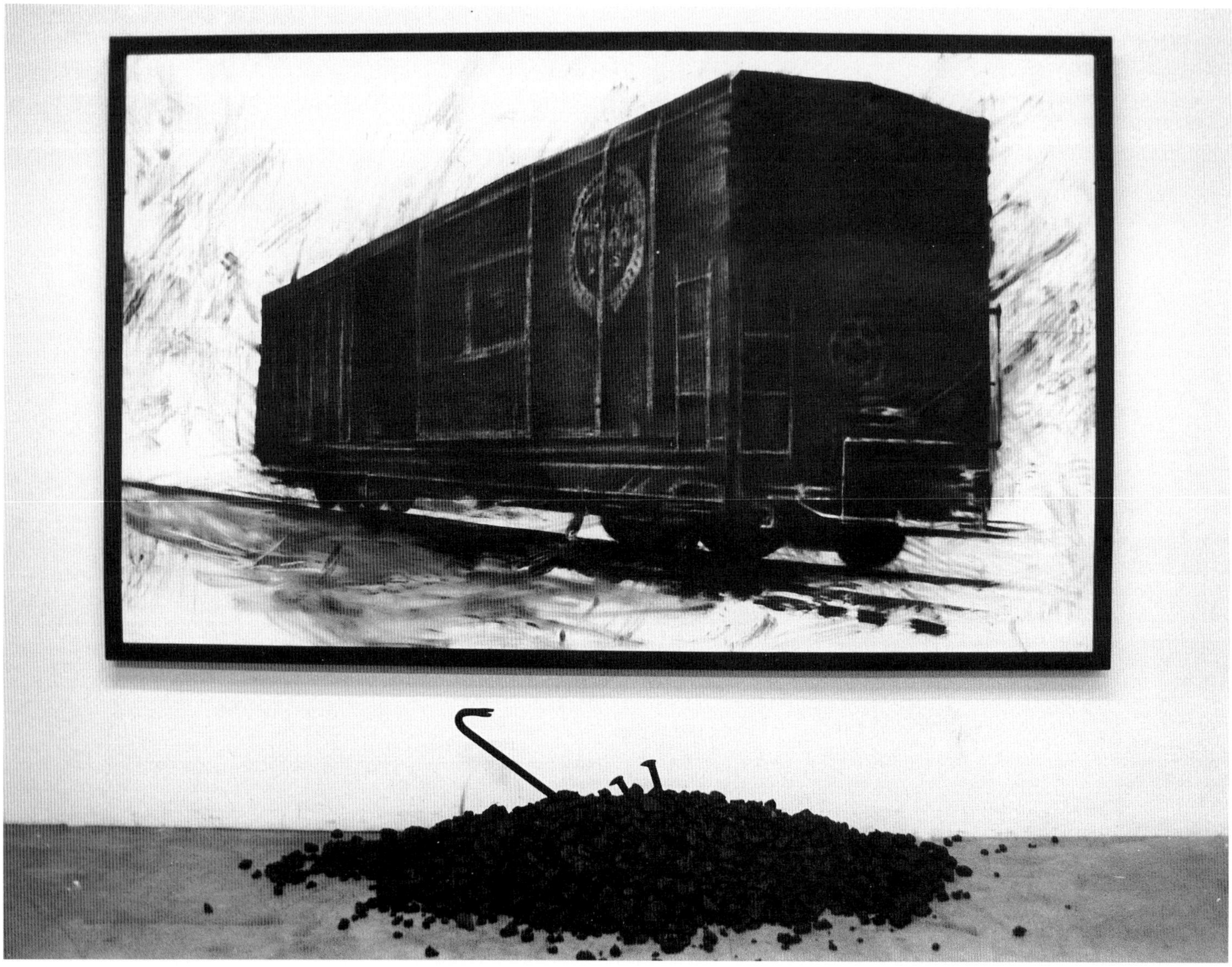

James Drake
**Juarez / El Paso (Boxcar)**
1986–89, Charcoal on paper mounted in steel frame and coal, railroad spikes, crowbar, 87"h x 110"w x 30"d. Collection: The Museum of Fine Arts, Houston, Museum purchase with funds provided by an anonymous donor in memory of Hugo V. Neuhaus, Jr. Courtesy of the artist

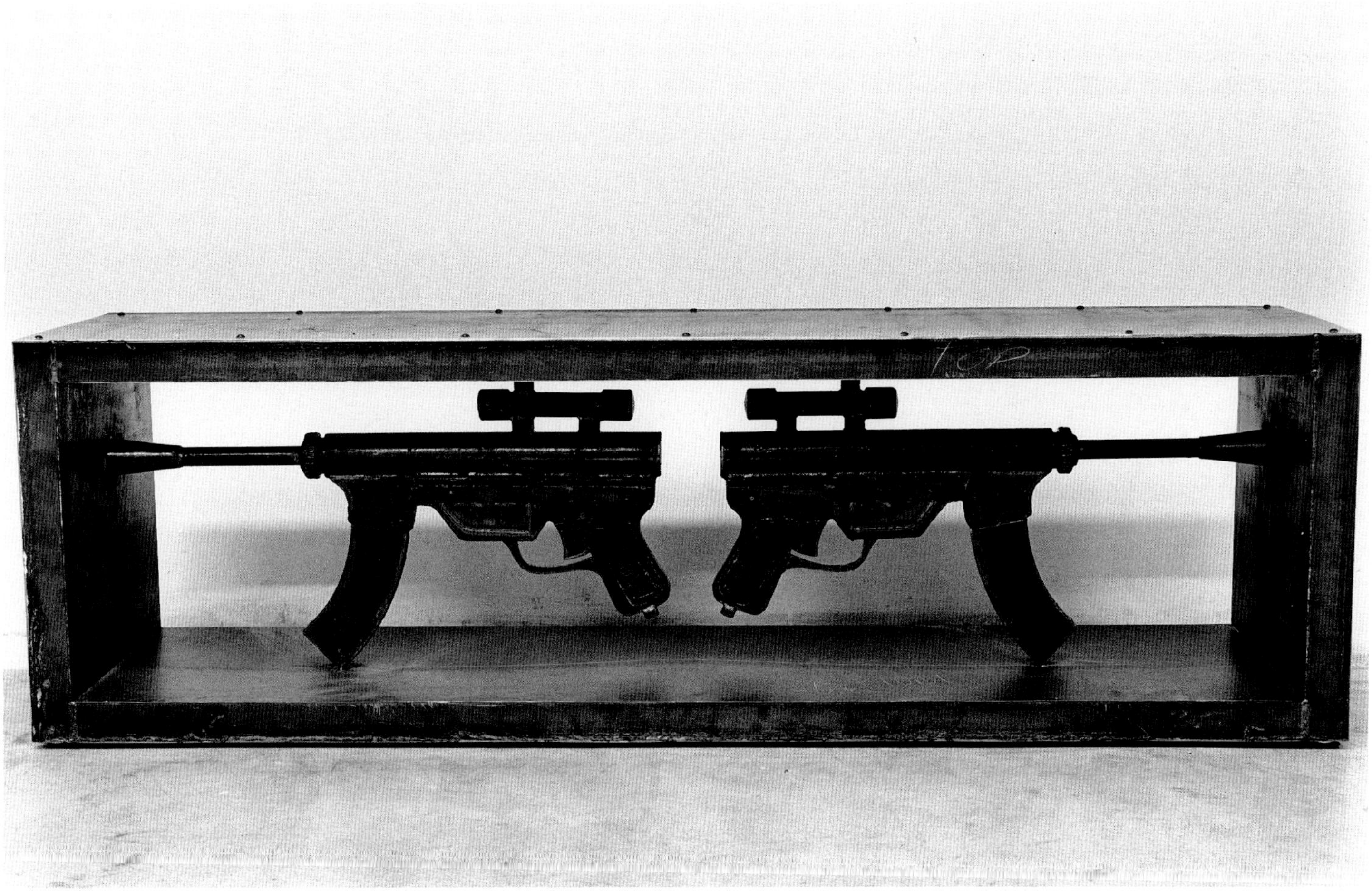

James Drake
**Gun Bench**
1989, Steel, 20"h x 60"w x 18"d. Courtesy of the artist

# Sharon
# **Engelstein**

Sharon Engelstein has been making things from the time she was a child. She doesn't recall usual activities like painting, but rather tinkering with things, pulling them apart and rebuilding them. Born in Canada in 1965, she received her bachelor's degree in fine arts and journalism from the University of Florida and a master's in sculpture from The Claremont Graduate School in California before moving to Houston in 1989 as a fellow in the Core Program of the Glassell School of Art.

Engelstein acknowledges Eva Hesse and Louise Bourgeois as her most important, nameable influences. She feels she's at the stage, though, where she must bury her artistic mothers, to pursue other components of her aesthetic. They are less concrete, and have to do with the way she sees the physical and mental landscapes, the conflict between nature and technology and how the perception of each affects the other.

She juxtaposes biomorphic shapes against mechanical elements, seeking a resolution to the inherent contradiction. Her bulbous forms are swollen and organic with strongly sexual overtones. Cast in resins or plaster, sometimes they suggest internal organs, other times they are explicitly male or female. She attaches prosthetic eyes and industrial clamps to the sensual objects keeping the artificial union obvious. In more recent work, however, her intentions are the persuasive integration of contradictory elements. A temporal installation piece she created for the Contemporary Arts Museum in Houston in early 1993 seems to have been the turning point. The untitled piece consisted of ten small plaster breasts seamlessly embedded in the wall. Set at eye level and equidistant from each other, the small protuberances created a simple, appealing pattern. At a deeper level, they suggested a process of transformation, as if the support wall were actually a living, breathing thing — or vice versa, the body of which the breasts were evidence was disappearing, like some ghost, into the wall itself.

"I think that piece successfully communicates where the body meets the person-made object, where our fleshy selves connect with cold, hard fabricated objects. The subtlety of the piece and its disturbing aspect draws you in. But it also has a humorous aspect that appeals to me."

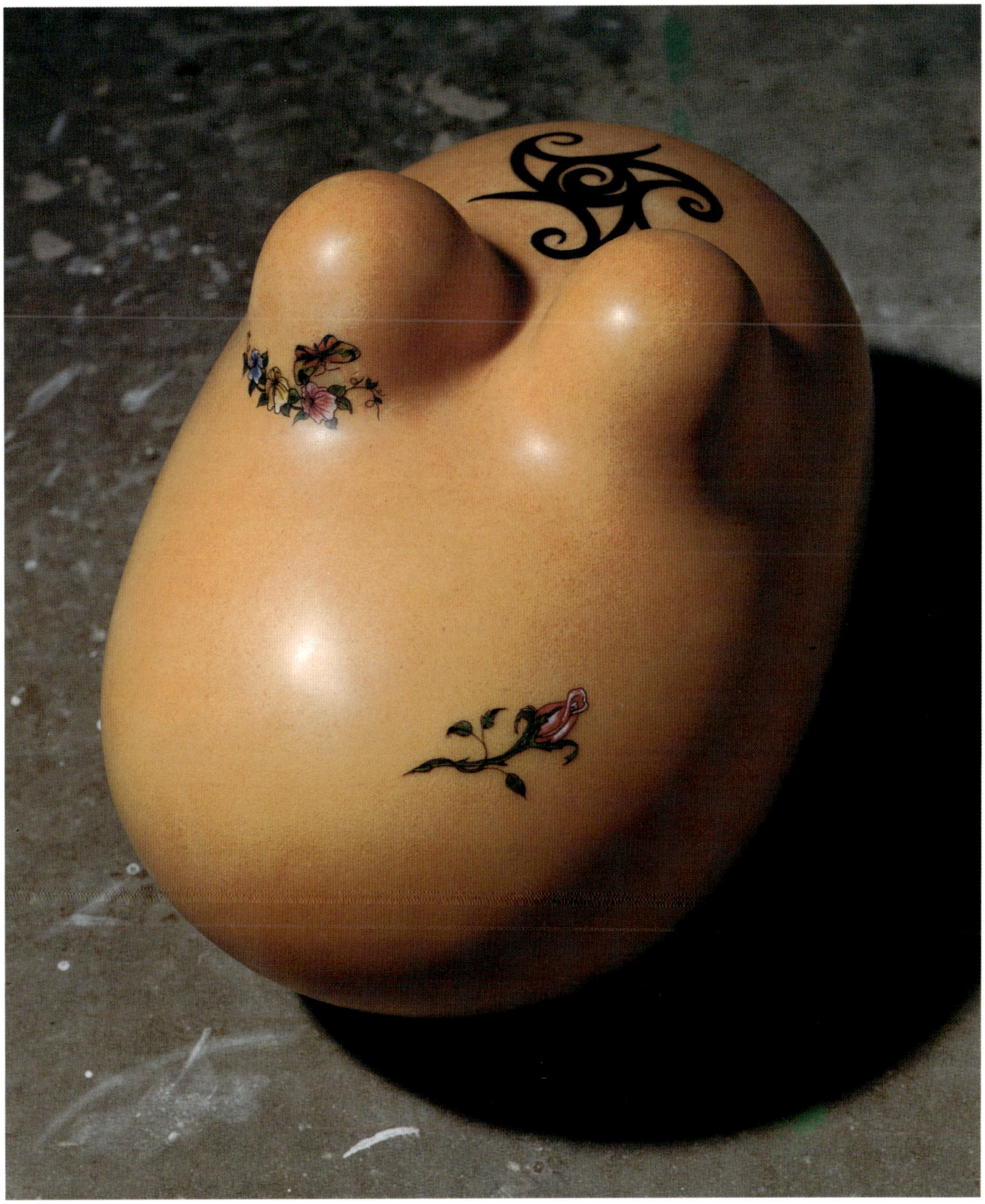

Sharon Engelstein
**Untitled I**
1993, Polyfoam and fiberglass, painted tatoos (tatoos by Angela Collins), 22"h x 18"w x 32"d. Photograph: Aaron Parazette. Courtesy of the artist

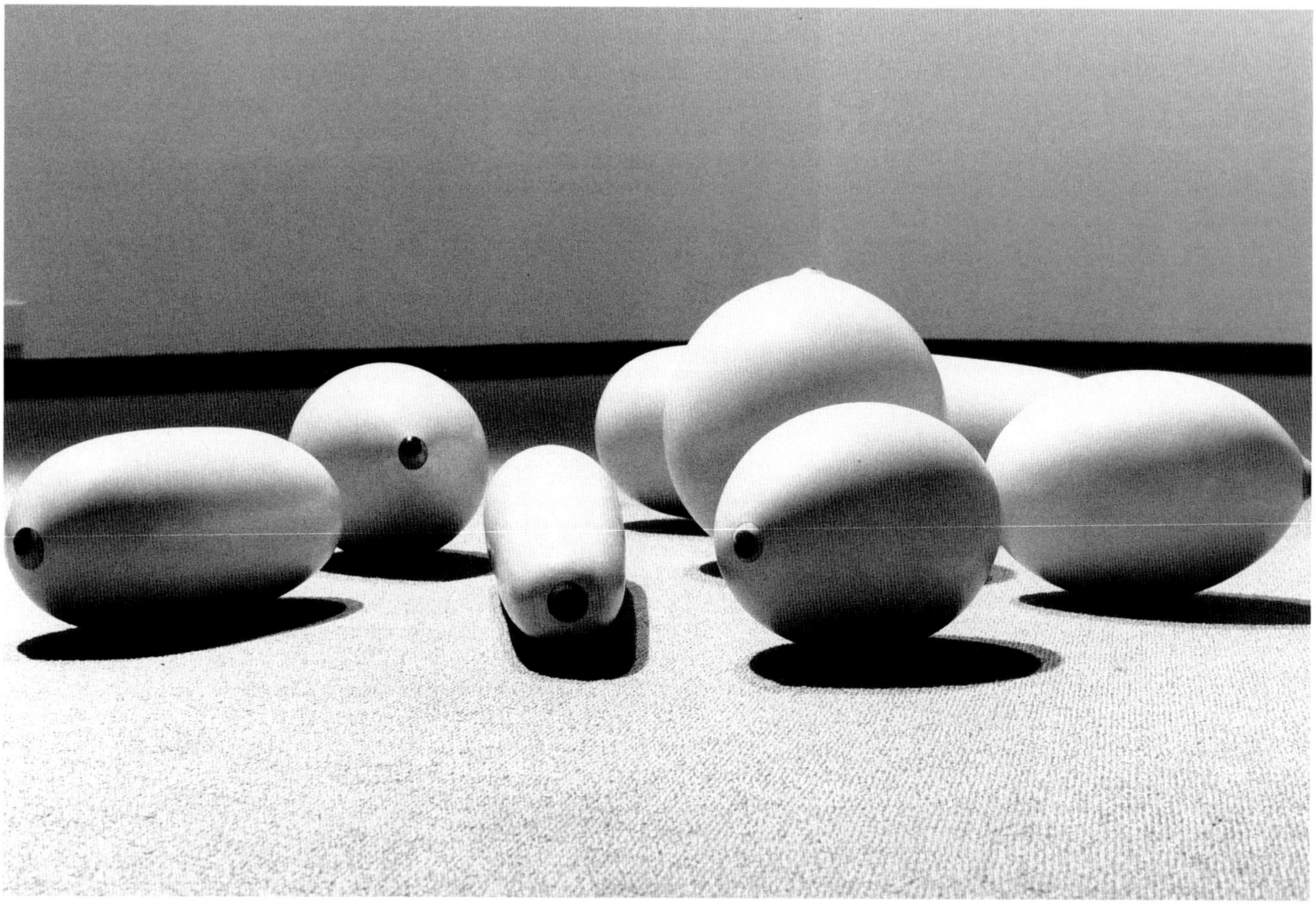

Sharon Engelstein
**Untitled (eight components)**
1993, Mixed media and prosthetic eyes.
Photograph: Aaron Parazette. Collection: Karen and Stephen Sussman, Houston. Courtesy of the artist

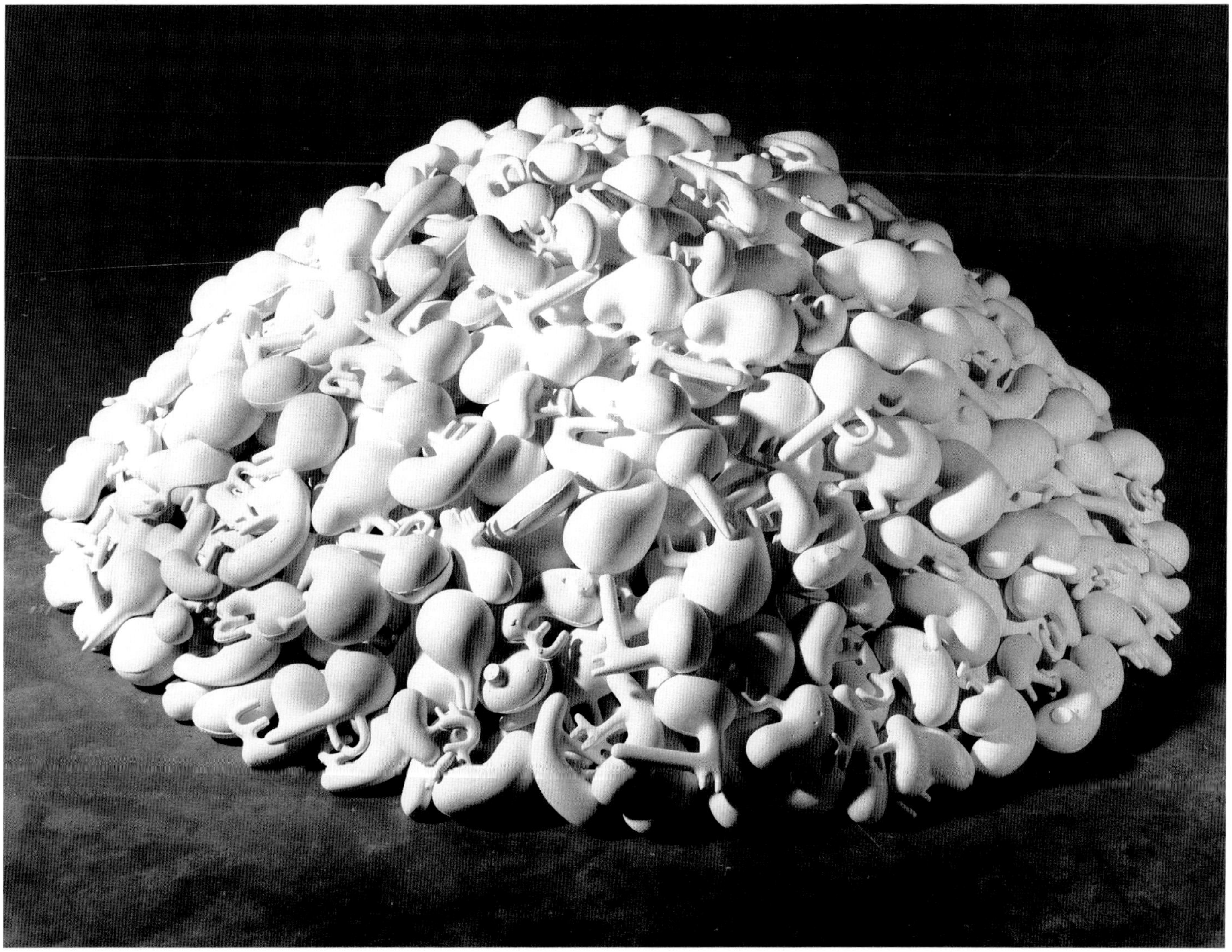

Sharon Engelstein

**Ten Forms Multiplied**

1991, 1000 cast plaster pieces, 72" diameter (variable).

Courtesy of the artist

# Vernon **Fisher**

Looking at Vernon Fisher's work is like seeing rain in the landscape. The distance at which one's eye focuses determines whether one perceives raindrops or the trees behind the soaking scrim. The renowned artist meshes word narratives with object-paintings. His terse short stories, three to three dozen sentences long, may be anecdotal and autobiographical; they are apocryphal and metaphorical. The words themselves become taut linear elements on his multi-layered surfaces where photographic images, actual objects, and painted shapes demand simultaneous attention.

Born in Fort Worth in 1943, Fisher received his B.A. degree in English literature and, finding some time on his hands, enrolled in some art courses and "just got hooked". He pursued his M.F.A. from the University of Illinois in Champaign-Urbana in 1969 and through most of the 1970s concentrated on painting what he describes as "mindlessly beautiful pictures of the abstract sublime". But the purely formalist emphasis appeared to him as a closed system. The word pictures John Baldessari and Ed Ruscha were making in California in the 1970s (and Jasper Johns, Robert Rauschenberg and Roy Lichtenstein before them) presented an alternative. It was as if permission had been granted to finally break the mold of traditional landscape and figure, and explore the inner mind instead. Fisher developed a bridge between the written and pictorial image with his unique voice. Inclusion in three major exhibitions of contemporary American art in 1981 — The Whitney Biennial, the "Directions" exhibit at Corcoran Gallery of Art and "Emerging Americans" at the Museum of Modern Art — was a prestigious external validation.

Sometimes, his allusive compositions are self-contained objects. More often, Fisher constructs wall and room installations where his interest in nature, language, culture and the unconscious is manifest, and where his concerns over a trivialized existence are expressed in masterful analogies. The immediacy of his art belies the wry and rigorous intellect which conceives it. He proposes relationships that at first seem absurd, not unlike Magritte's denial that his image of a pipe was not a pipe, but which are observations about nature and culture — reality and illusion — and the distance between them.

"From your side the mountains are an illusion, but from my side they are a technique … behind every story there are machinations that can put things together in any number of ways."[1]

1. Vernon Fisher, 1988. Cited in the brochure *Moonrise, Hernandez, N.M.*, 1951, Center for Creative Photography, October 1992

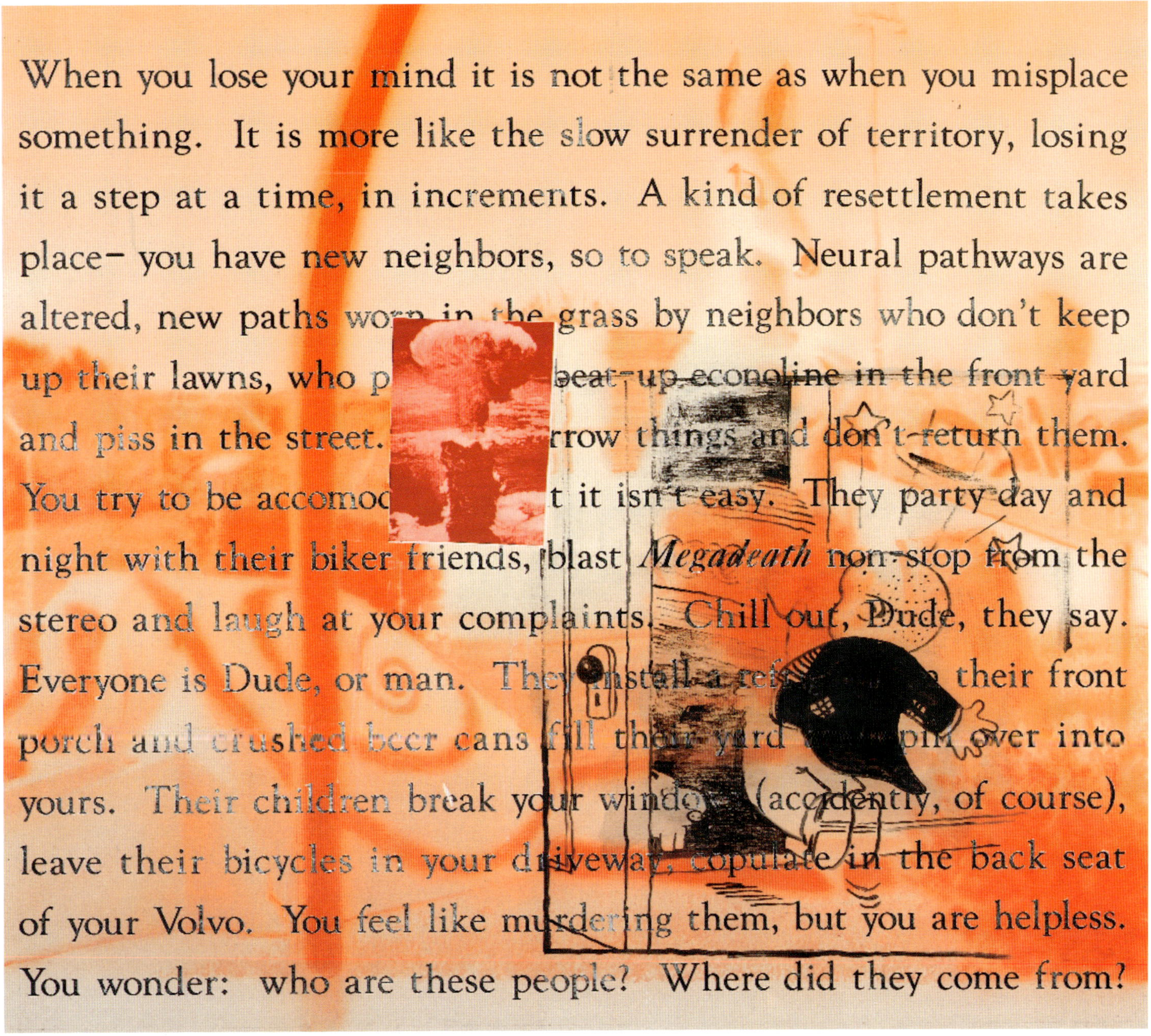


Vernon Fisher

**When You Lose Your Mind**

1991, Oil and acrylic on canvas, 57½" x 63½". Collection of Michael A. Caddell and Tracey Conwell, Houston. Courtesy of the artist

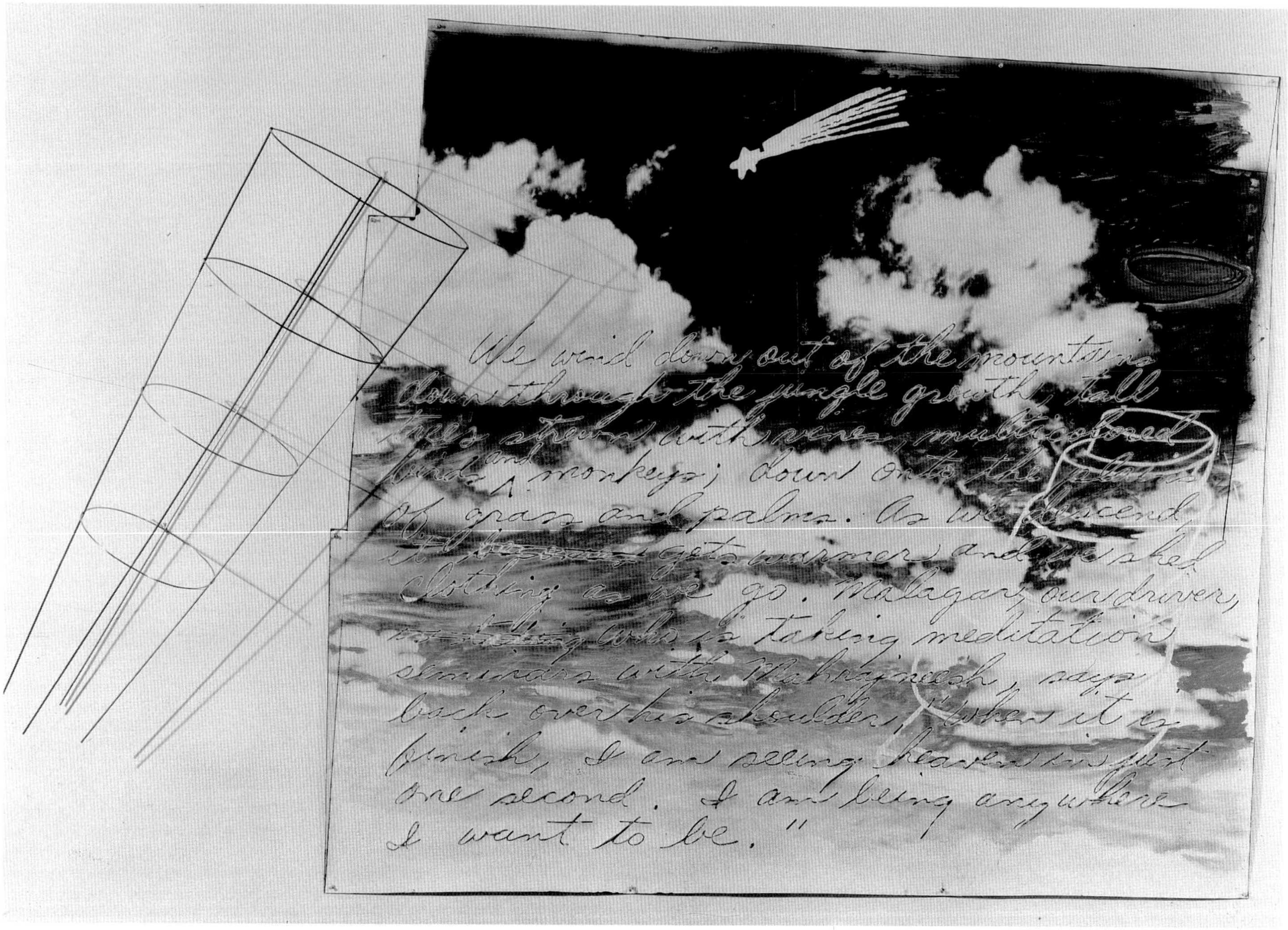

Vernon Fisher

**White Cloud / Black Sky**

1984, Mixed media, 76½" x 108". Collection of the Walker Art Center, Minneapolis, Walker Special Purchase Fund, 1987. Courtesy of the artist and Hiram Butler Gallery, Houston

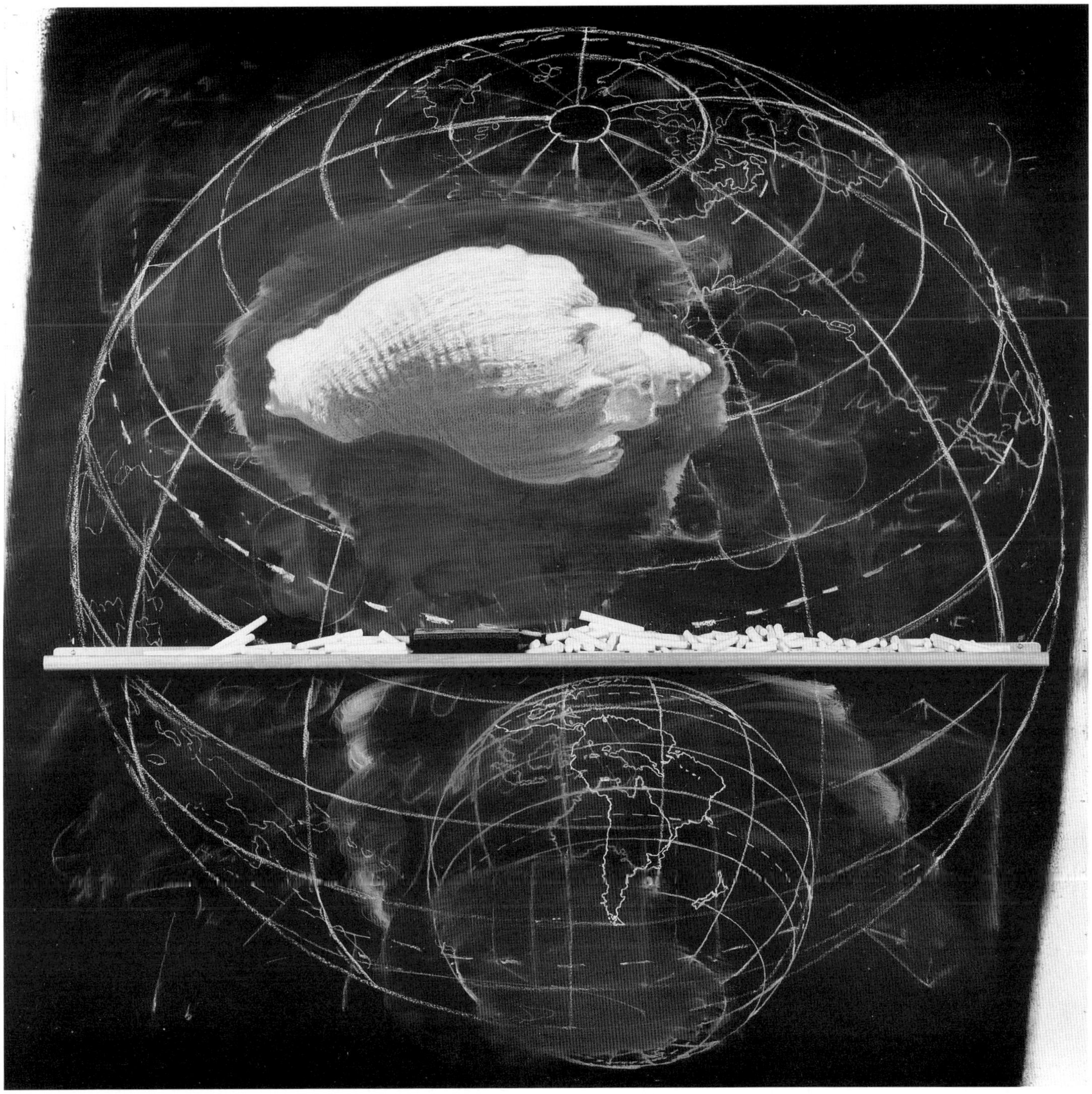

Vernon Fisher

**Below the Equator**

Mixed media: oil on blackboard, slating on wood, chalk tray, chalk, eraser, 54"h x 54"w x 6½"d. Courtesy of the artist and Modernism Gallery, San Francisco

# Roy **Fridge**

Roy Fridge, along with Jim Love and David McManaway, occupies a special niche in the history of contemporary art in Texas. They were part of its definition in the 1960s in Dallas, and subsequently in Houston. All are assemblagists, working in the intuitive mode which defines so much of Texas art with its surrealist strains and wit.

In 1963, Fridge ran away to the beach. He was 36 years old and successful in the fledgling television advertising industry in Dallas. He had a degree in film from Baylor University in Waco, and a background in journalism and graphics. He was making films, including one of Claes Oldenburg's happening at Dallas Center for Contemporary Art, in 1962, and building avant-garde theater sets, but he wasn't satisfied. On the isolated beaches of Port Arkansas on the Gulf of Mexico, he found a place where he could play at being a hermit and pursue his interests in Jungian psychology.

"It wasn't that I went to the beach to make art. I went to the beach to find a life, and in finding that life, discovered making art was part of it. I've never been able to appreciate art as a historical concept, so I can't make art that is about art. I can only make art that is about Roy Fridge."

For many years he called himself a whittler rather than a sculptor. It was not false modesty, but a genuine sense of who he was. He directed his intellectual pursuits to the areas of psychology and native magic — shamanism — discerning a relationship between the two areas which connect intimately to his own self. Introspective by nature, the beach appealed to him, too, as a metaphor. Boats of all kinds — from seaworthy lone-man sailing boats to metaphorical ships capable of crossing the River Styx — are a major motif in his work.

The boxes with movable parts he "whittled" and the totems he constructed from both found and made objects early on, gave way in the late 1970s to more formal, controlled works that are also more intensely personal. Fridge began to document the transformations in his own life through photographic self-portraits, and became more rigorous in his journals. Keeping a journal, he explains, was a self-imposed discipline from his days in Dallas, that gradually became documents of his dreams — the source of his surrealist forms — and a record of his interior life.

*The Hermit Shrine*, in the collection of the Menil Collection in Houston, in many ways exemplifies what Fridge does and conceptualizes. In this freestanding cabinet from 1977 he presents himself as an antlered being, a shaman. Built from bones, the skeletal figure wears one of the artist's shirts, and stands between two open shelving sections in which he's placed the carefully annotated journals. An archive of a life lived.

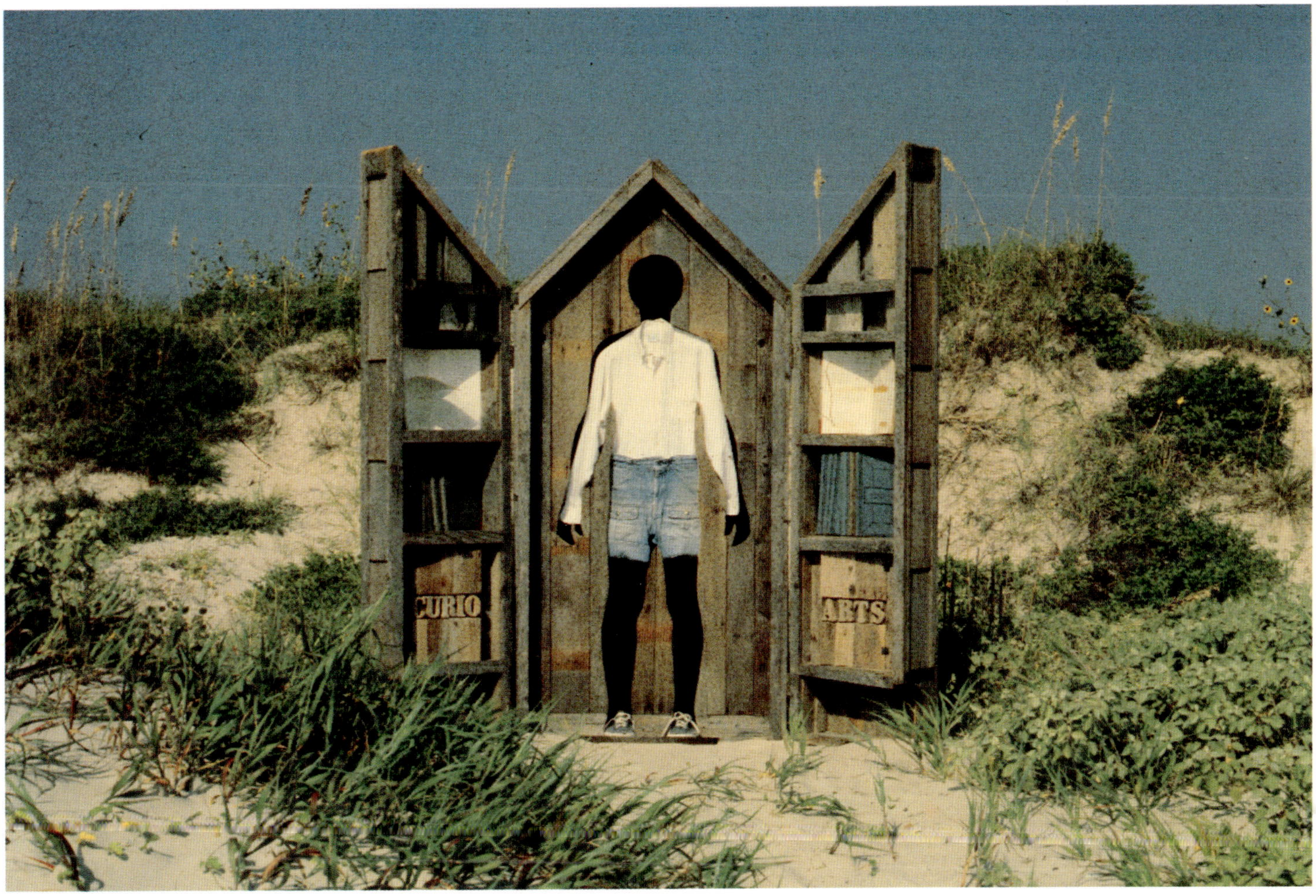


Roy Fridge
**The Hermit Shrine**
1977–present, Mixed media: wood, bones, cloth, paper, 83"h x 62" (closed) x 35"d. Collection: The Menil Collection, Houston. Courtesy of Moody Gallery, Houston

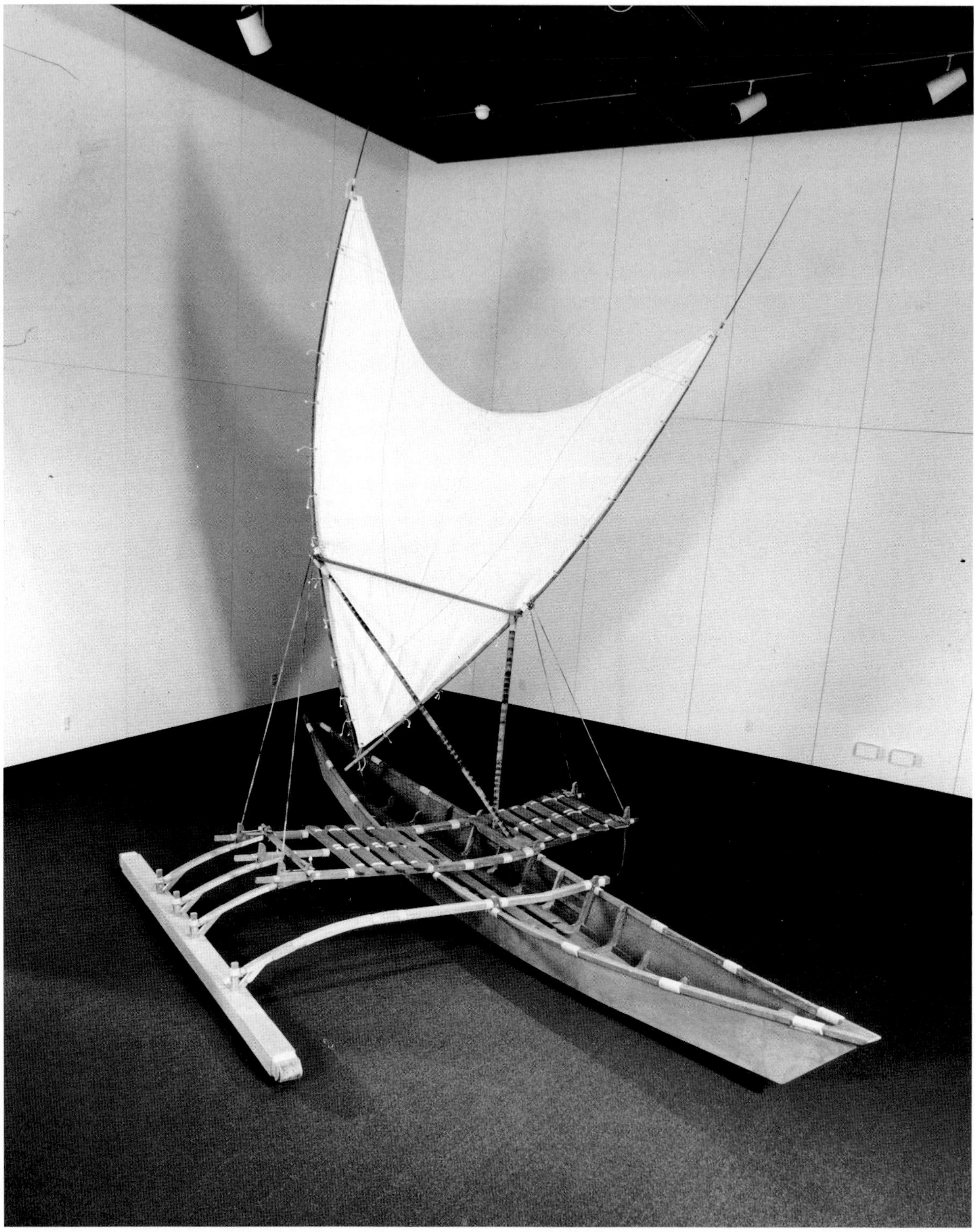

Roy Fridge

**Flying Proa: Souvenir of a Voyage**

1979, Mixed media: mahogany, rope, canvas, bamboo, 180"h x 216" x 96". Collection: San Antonio Museum of Art. Courtesy of Moody Gallery, Houston

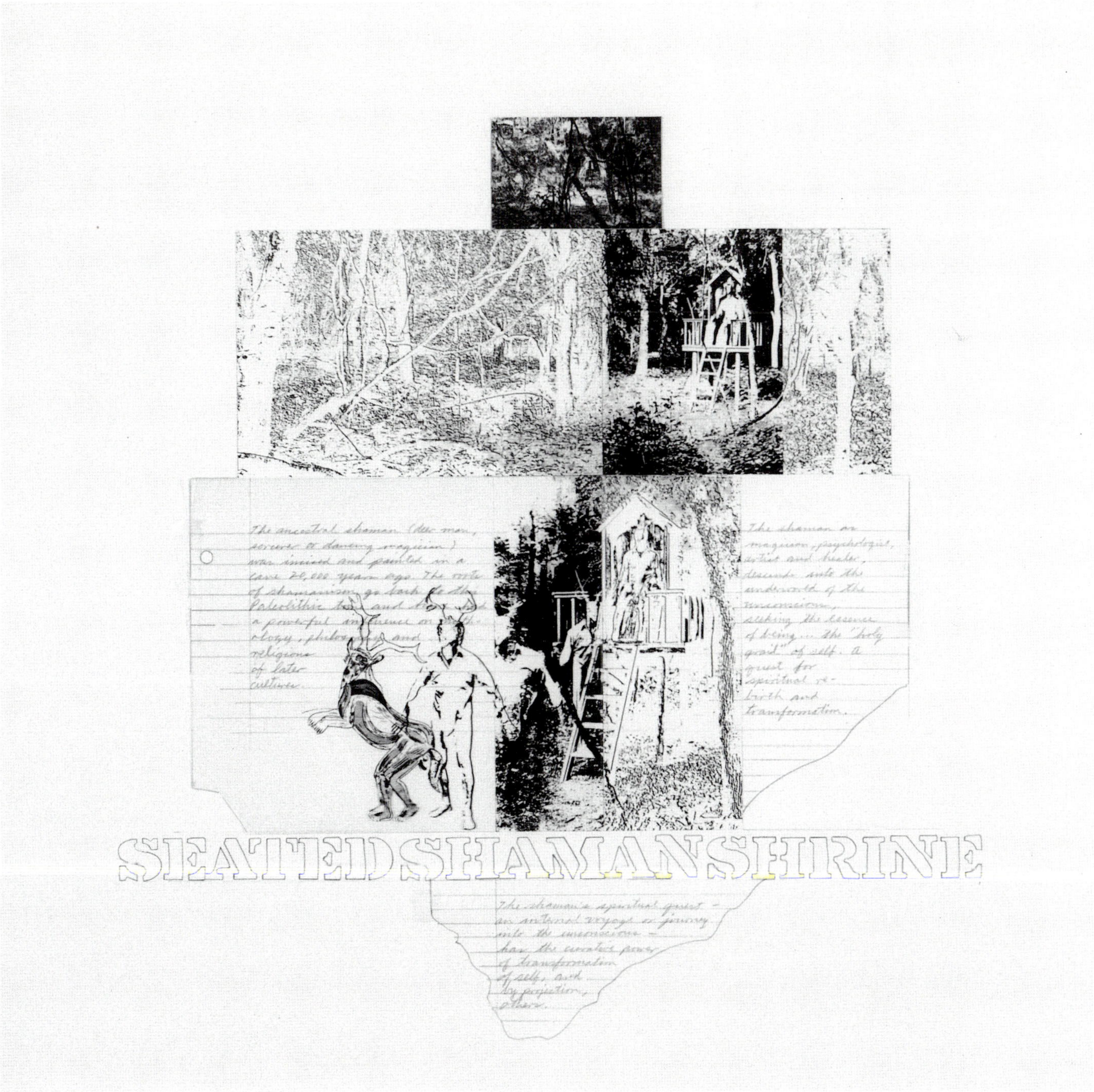


Roy Fridge

**Seated Shaman Shrine**

1982, Collage: graphite, watercolor, photograph,
20" x 20". Photograph: Frank Golden, Houston.
Collection: Betty Moody and Bill Steffy, Houston.
Courtesy of Moody Gallery, Houston

# Joseph
# **Glasco**

Joseph Glasco was the young kid at the 1950s gatherings in the legendary Cedar Bar in Manhattan's Lower East Side neighborhood. He was 25 years old and would drink in more of the conversation than beer at the table where the revolutionary American artists later knows as the Abstract Expressionists would gather to talk and drink away the night .

Glasco, born in Oklahoma and raised in East Texas, traveled with his father to wherever the Army sent him. His education, though not formal, was global. In New York City of the 1950s, global was as rare as the money in the artists' pockets. Glasco supported himself with odd jobs and painted at night. He was working with figures then, abstracted into voluptuous surrealist forms reminiscent of Cycladic idols with a dash of Jean Dubuffet. In 1952 he was invited by the Museum of Modern Art's legendary curator Dorothy Miller to lend a work for her "Fifteen Americans" exhibition. It was an auspicious beginning for Glasco's long career.

For the next two decades, the romantic artist traveled widely — from Manhattan to Taos, to Texas where his family had settled, to Morocco, Greece and New York once again, forging profound and lasting friendships everywhere. Finally, in the early 1970s, Glasco "fell in love with Galveston", and the genteel Southern thinker found his home.

In the relative isolation of this island city, Glasco has produced canvas collages made from pieces he's cut or torn from other paintings he's made. The dynamics of color couples with harmonious patterns. Dots and stripes of paint in shades from jewel to black and white, zig and zag across the surface, suggesting glass puzzles, always in equilibrium and ending at a point of rest that energizes and satisfies the eye.When he showed in New York in 1979 after an absence of nearly 10 years, Hilton Kramer wrote, that "if this is what an absence from the New York scene can do for a mature and thoughtful artist, it might be something worth thinking about as a regular program".[1]

The most recent work assumes a freer hand. Bold gestures appear to blow across the surfaces. The collage elements are changing as well. Glasco has added newspapers and rags to his usual assortment of pre-painted and cut canvas or paper components. The textures add a literal other layer to the lyricism of the freeform compositions. The eye penetrates easily, but the richness within engages and holds it there, gently at first, insistently long after one has gone on to other things.

1. Cited in *Joseph Glasco, 1948–1986*, Contemporary Arts Museum, 1986. p.17

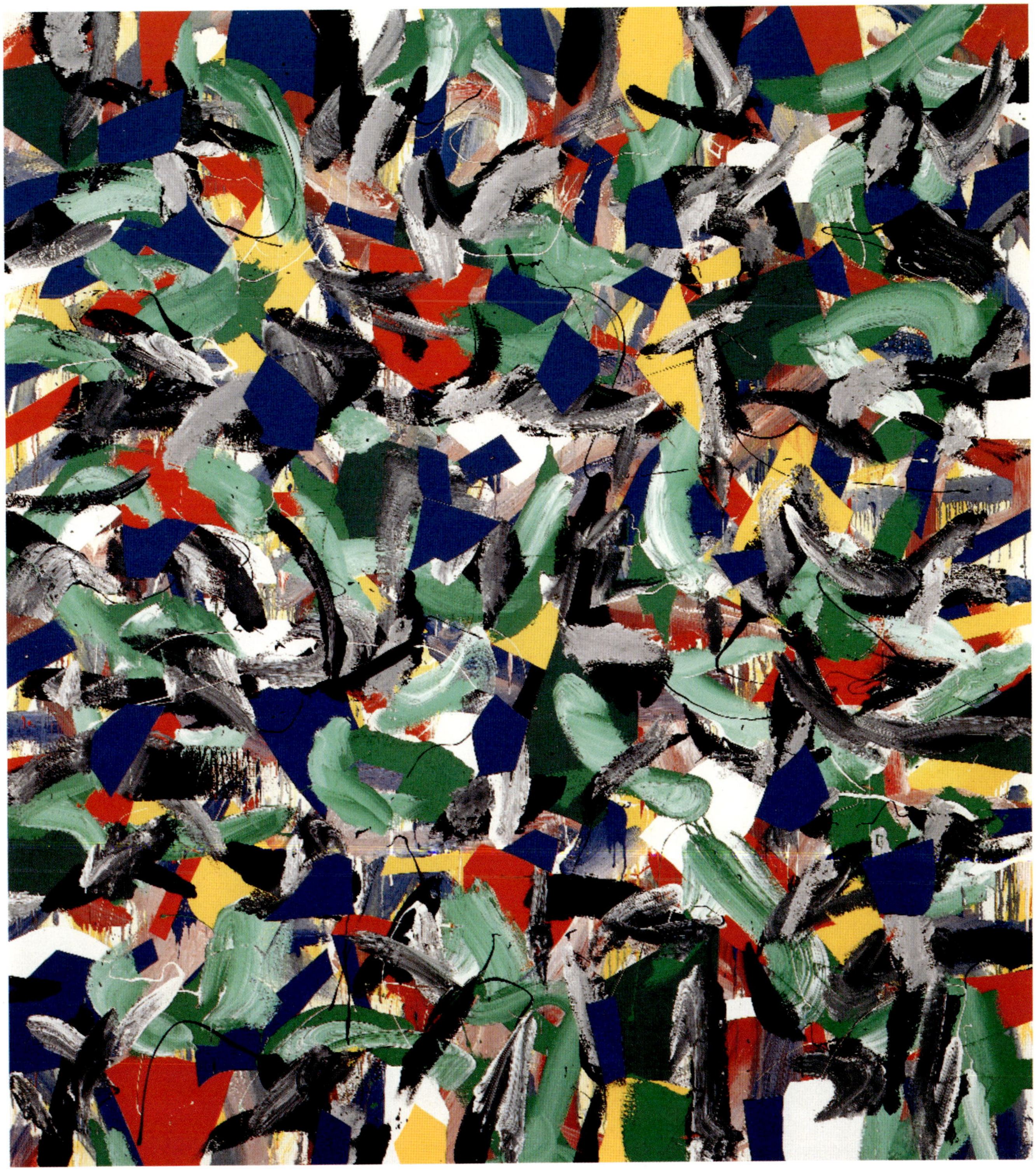

Joseph Glasco
**Untitled No. 5**
1989, Mixed on canvas, 96" x 84". Collection: Leslie Waddington, London. Courtesy of the artist

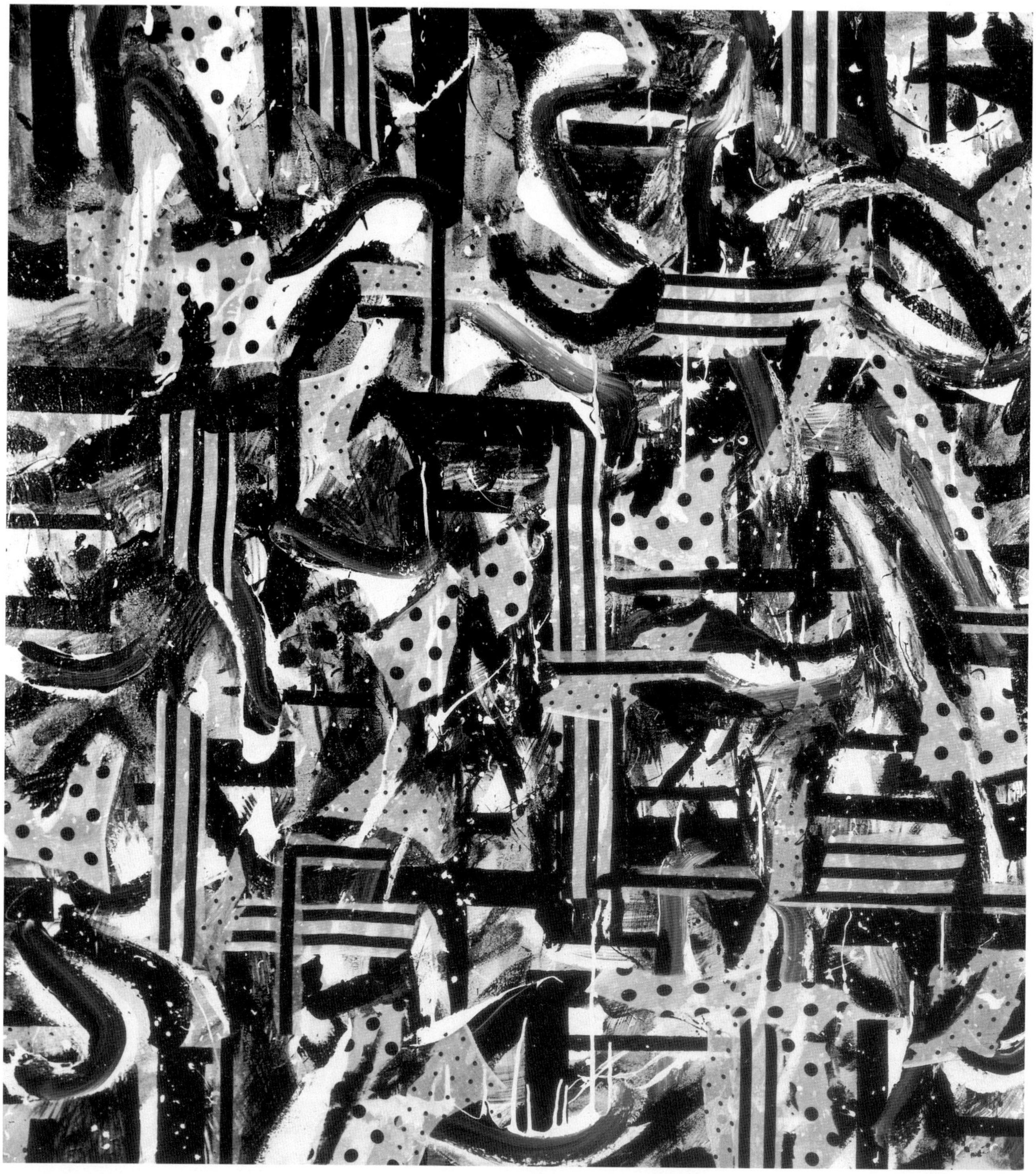

Joseph Glasco
**Untitled**
1993, Acrylic and fabric collage on canvas,
96" x 84". Courtesy of the artist

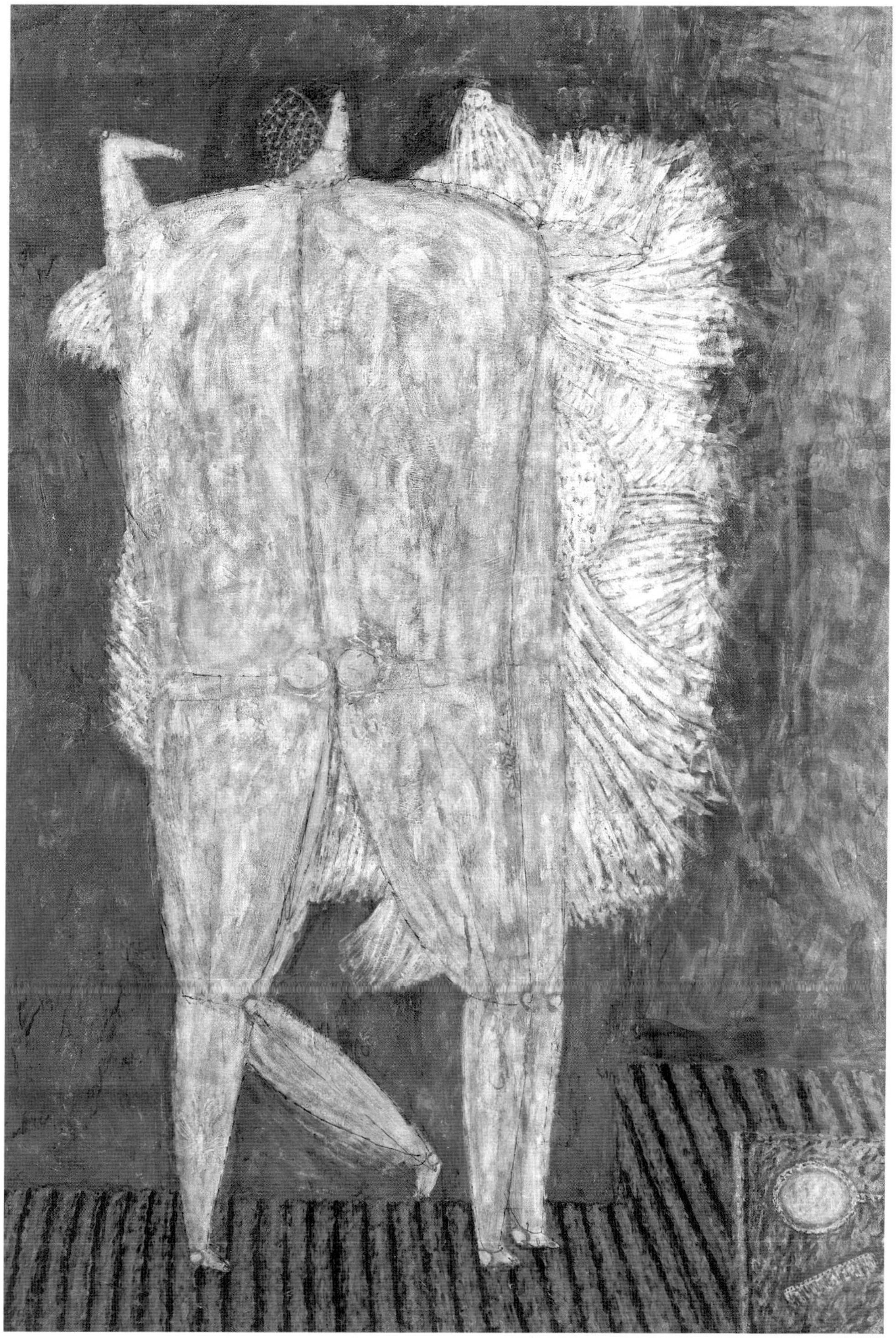

Joseph Glasco
**Leda**
1956, Oil on canvas, 59⅛" x 39⅛". Photograph: Geoffrey Clements. Private collection. Courtesy of the Contemporary Arts Museum, Houston

# Virgil
# Grotfeldt

When Virgil Grotfeldt graduated from the University of Eastern Illinois in the 1971, he truly believed he was on his way to fulfilling his childhood dream. From the day he started earning his living at age 13, he wanted to be an art professor. His natural draftsmanship, he says ruefully, would "let the fair-haired boy succeed and escape from poverty". But even with the master's degree, earned in 1974, teaching opportunities were scarce, as were exhibitions. Growing increasingly disillusioned, he had to rethink his goals.

He eventually made his way to Houston in 1977 with his wife and child, lured by an item he chanced upon in an art magazine proclaiming the city as the next art center. Grotfeldt painted in the isolation of an abandoned church for four years, fighting weariness and bitterness, and avoiding any kind of "art scene."

"I saw everything as a giant illusion. Illusion of success. Illusion of communication. We (the artists) weren't doing much, just neat things people would stick up on their walls and accumulate through a lifetime. I had learned to make marks all along, but they were meaningless for the most part. I knew there had to be more, I just didn't know what it was."

The breakthrough came and he realized what had eluded him all those years: It wasn't a conscious effort, he says, but his attitude changed. Overcoming his own facility, the liquid paintings with their powerful suggestions of spiritual transformation began to emerge. For the first time he felt he was doing something genuine. He moved to a cooperative studio where his visibility was greatly increased and exhibition opportunities multiplied. His first major solo exhibition was in a gallery in The Netherlands in 1987. The same year, he visited Mexico for the first time, and it was a revelation.

"I found another world there, outside what I'd been taught, or I had understood, that was very important. The attitudes and the spirituality I sensed made a huge impact. That's when my work took a turn for the better."

Using bronze powder on canvas wet with acrylic medium, Grotfeldt allows gravity and accident to define the essentials. In the pools and streaks of liquid powder, he discerns forms that interest him and coaxes them into higher resolution, sometimes as a flower, often as shamanistic silhouettes. Mostly, they are spirit beings, translucent shadows that metamorphose from the gilded veils, and in the past two years, into bronze sculptures.

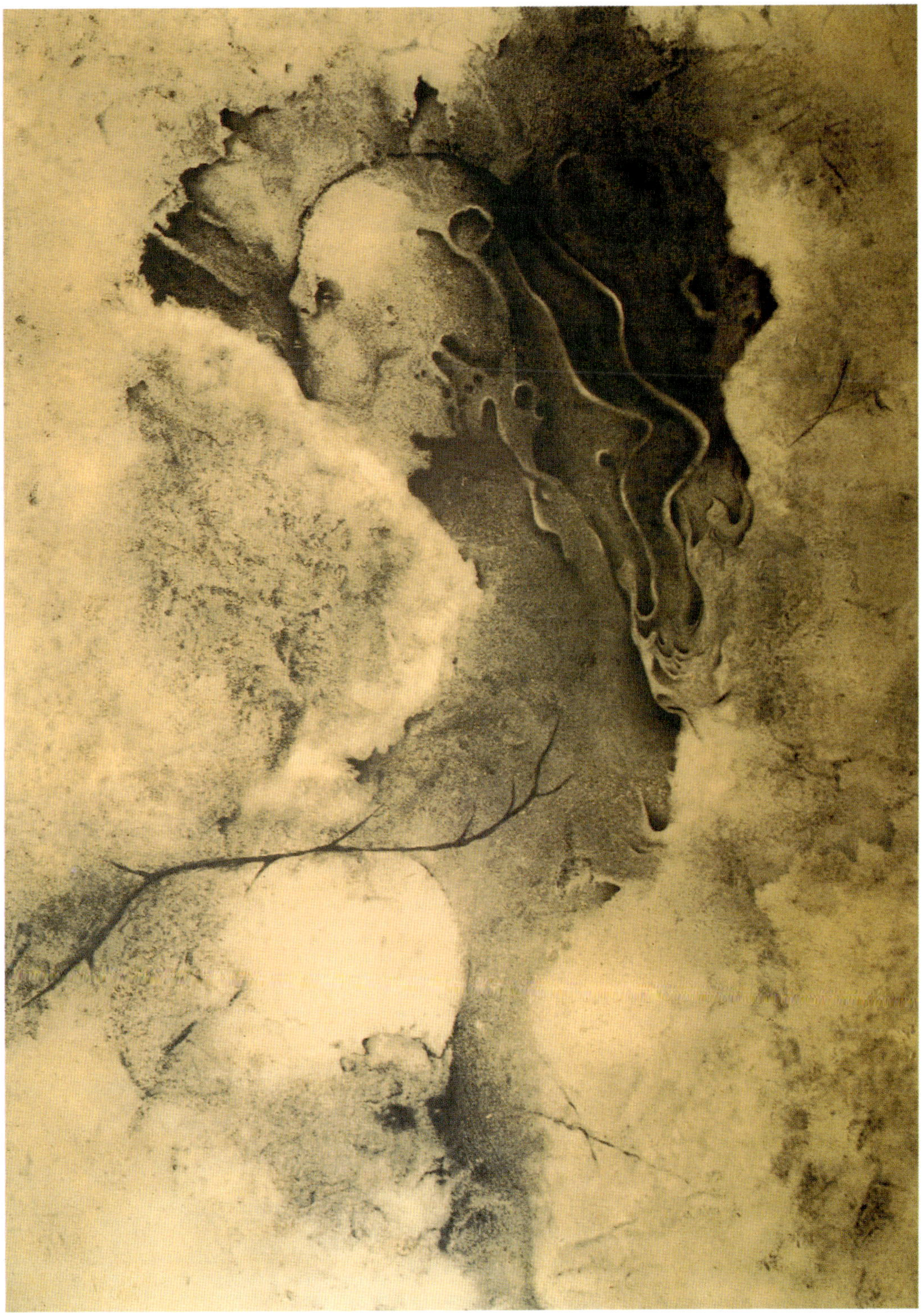

Virgil Grotfeldt
**Crevice**
1992, Acrylic and bronze power on canvas, 93" x 65".
Courtesy of the artist

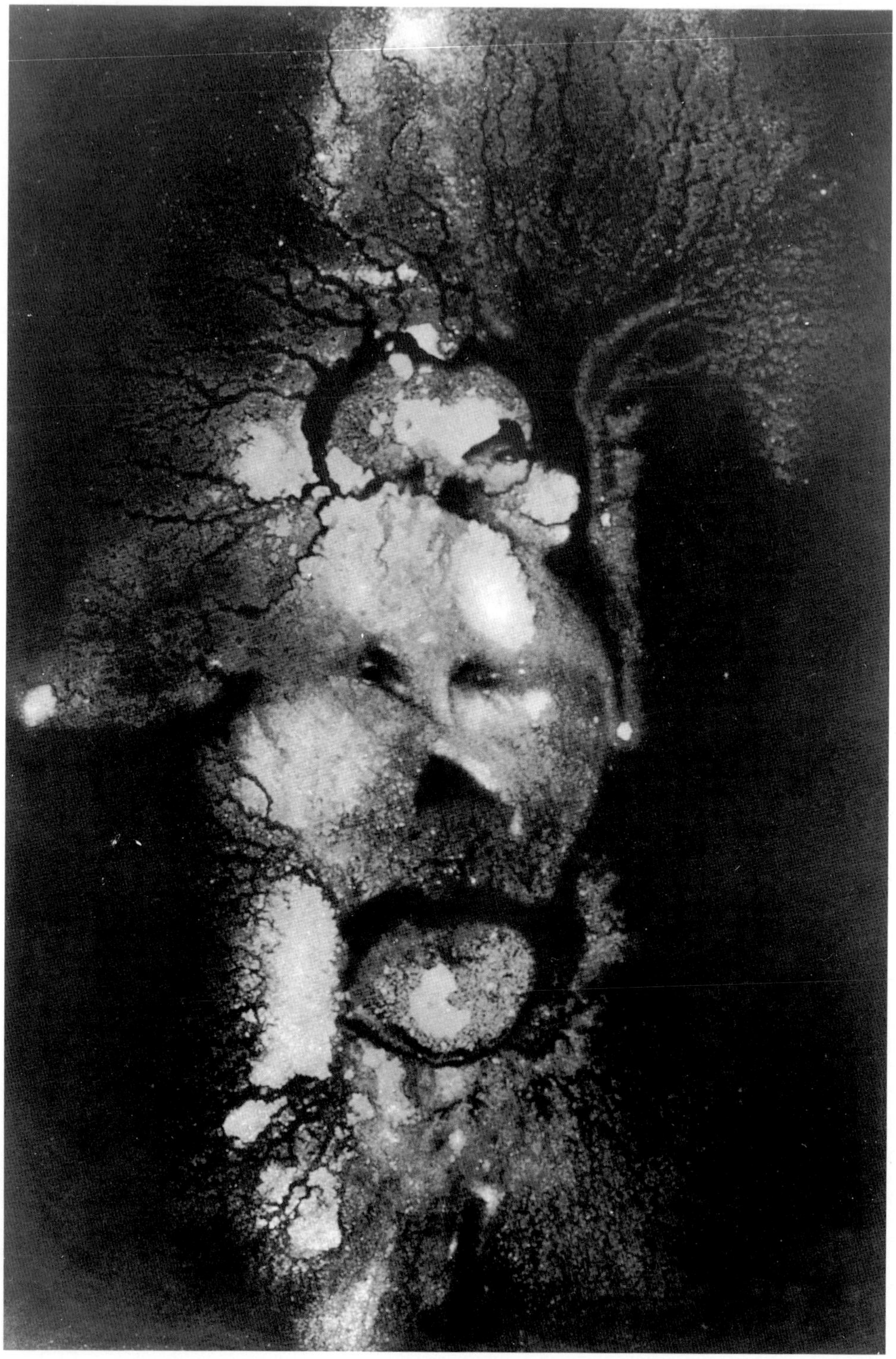

Virgil Grotfeldt
**Headdress**
1993, Acrylic and bronze powder on canvas, 66" x 44".
Photograph: Jeffrey Nixon. Courtesy of the artist

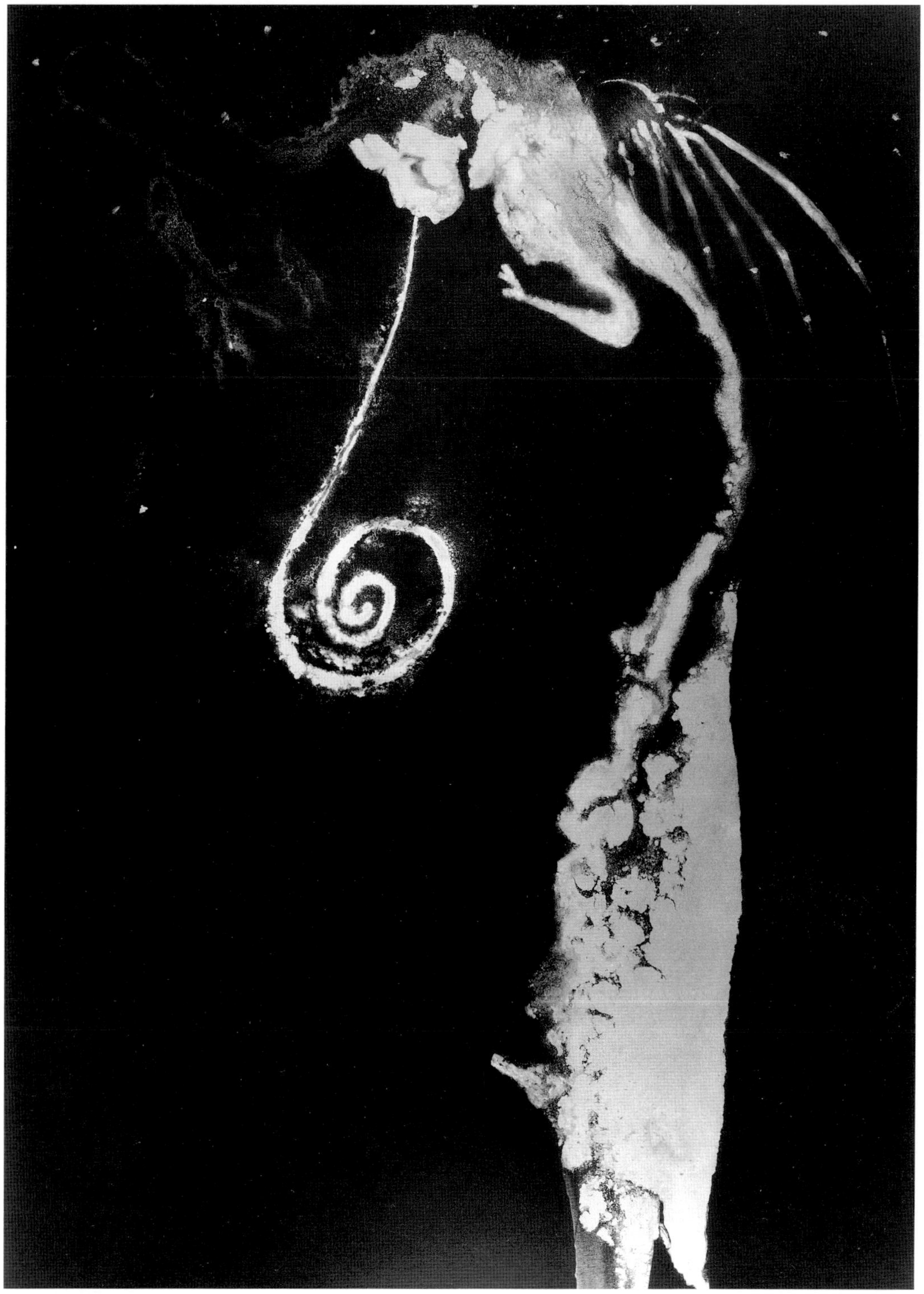

Virgil Grotfeldt
**Night Nymph**
1993, Acrylic and bronze powder on canvas,
93¼" x 65". Photograph: Jeffrey Nixon. Courtesy of
the artist

# Joe
# **Guy**

Joe Guy's drawings have the power to suggest color where there is none and elicit complex spiritual yearning with the simplest of forms. The artist works exclusively with graphite on paper stretched taut like a canvas, frequently hinged and shaped like Renaissance altars. With the delicate calibration of his black and white abstractions, he entreats the viewer to discover fresh paths to intellectual meditation.

Born in 1943 in upstate New York, Guy moved to Fort Worth at age 33 and "snaked" his way, as he phrases it, through various art schools. He did not set out to be an artist, he says, but to discover a means to externalize that which he found unsayable.

"The deepest part of myself has always wanted to make these things that are a kind of negation, a clearing where these realities are allowed to present themselves. Ever since I can remember I've wanted to find a way to express, to convey a certain feeling I had, a certain attitude. I make these things because they have something to do with my life. They have to do with temperamental attitude."

Guy's studies in Eastern religion and Christian mysticism led him to explore his craft. He taught himself the technique of Japanese folding screens by the very modern method of a videotape on the ancient craft.[1] And he dedicated years to formulating a bridge between contemporary American art, specifically the abstract modernism of Ad Reinhardt and Mark Rothko, and the ancient tradition of *byobu* (folding screens).

His technique is central to the works. Grounded in the gestalt of minimalism, Guy builds a lattice support of wood slats over which he laminates sheets of mulberry or block printers' paper. As he works with graphite and wax on this tight matrix, building translucent layers gradually, burnishing some areas with a stone or a cloth and re-drawing others to deepen the darkness, the wood support reveals itself as a grid pattern to become the visual element as well as being the physical definition of the piece.

Yet the serenity of his limpid chiaroscuro arises from a need deeper than aesthetic conviction.

"Many of my pieces are titled *Waiting. Listening*. If you listen to the work you don't get caught up in trying to see something, even though it's primarily a visual experience. The deepest part of myself has always wanted to make a clearing where these realities that are inexpressible are allowed to present themselves."

1. Produced by the Freer Gallery of Art, Smithsonian Institution, Washington D.C.

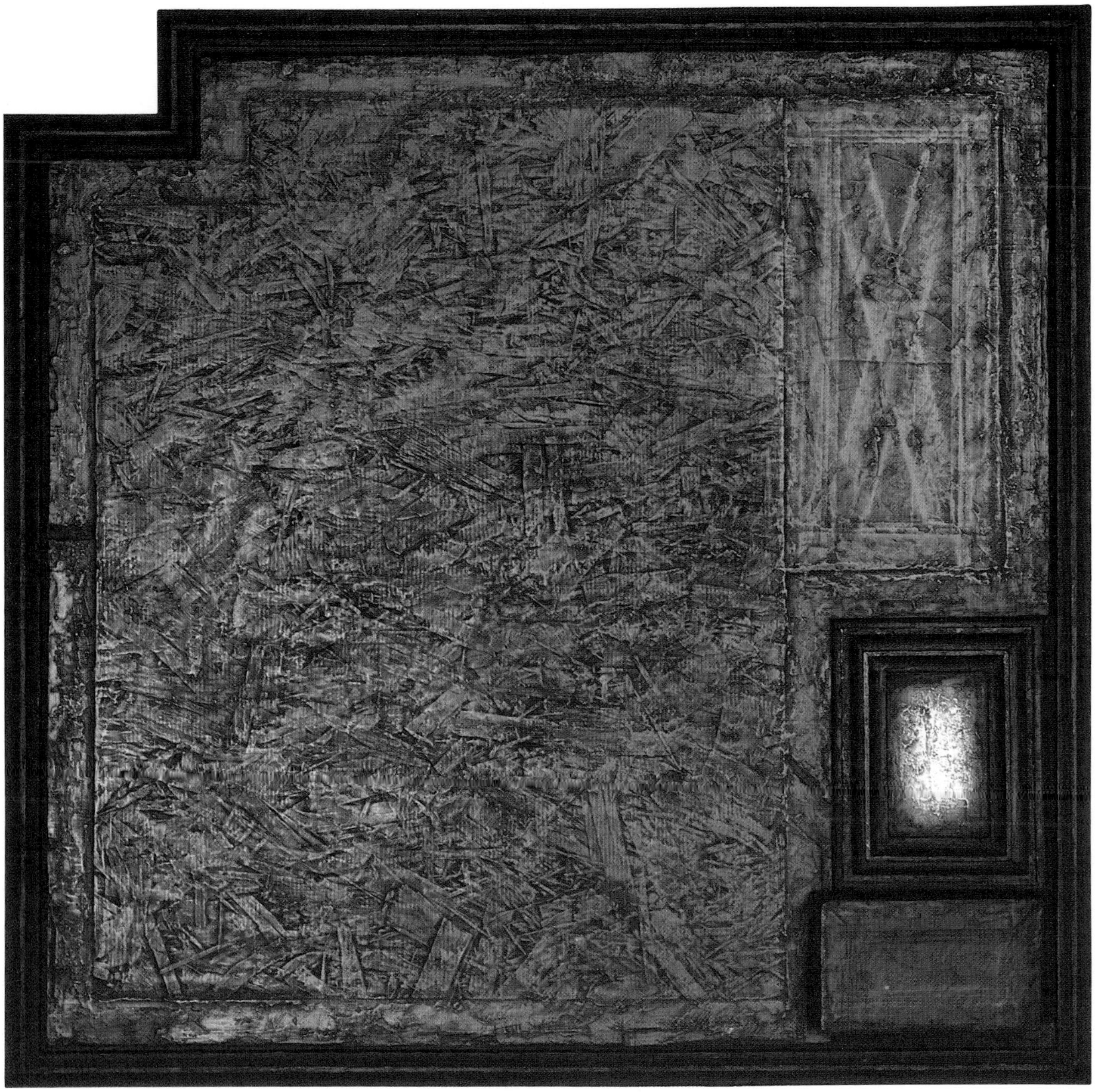

Joe Guy
**Forgetting**
1991, Mixed media: graphite, paper, etc,
34¾"h x 34¾"w x 4½"d. Collection: Adams-Middleton Gallery, Dallas. Courtesy of the artist

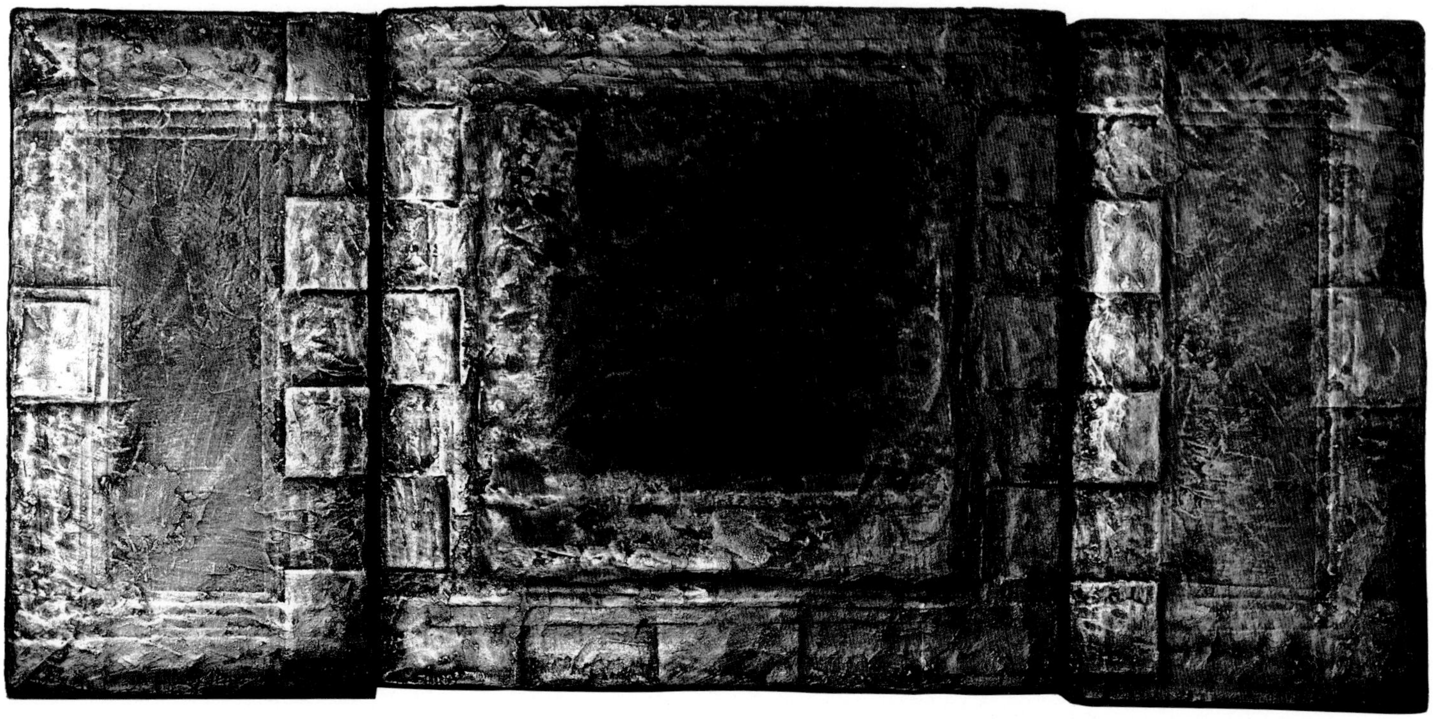

Joe Guy
**Homage: In a Darkless Time**
1986–87, Mixed media: graphite, paper, etc,
$10\frac{1}{4}$"h x $20\frac{1}{2}$"w x $1\frac{5}{8}$"d. Collection: Victoria Gaumier.
Courtesy of the artist

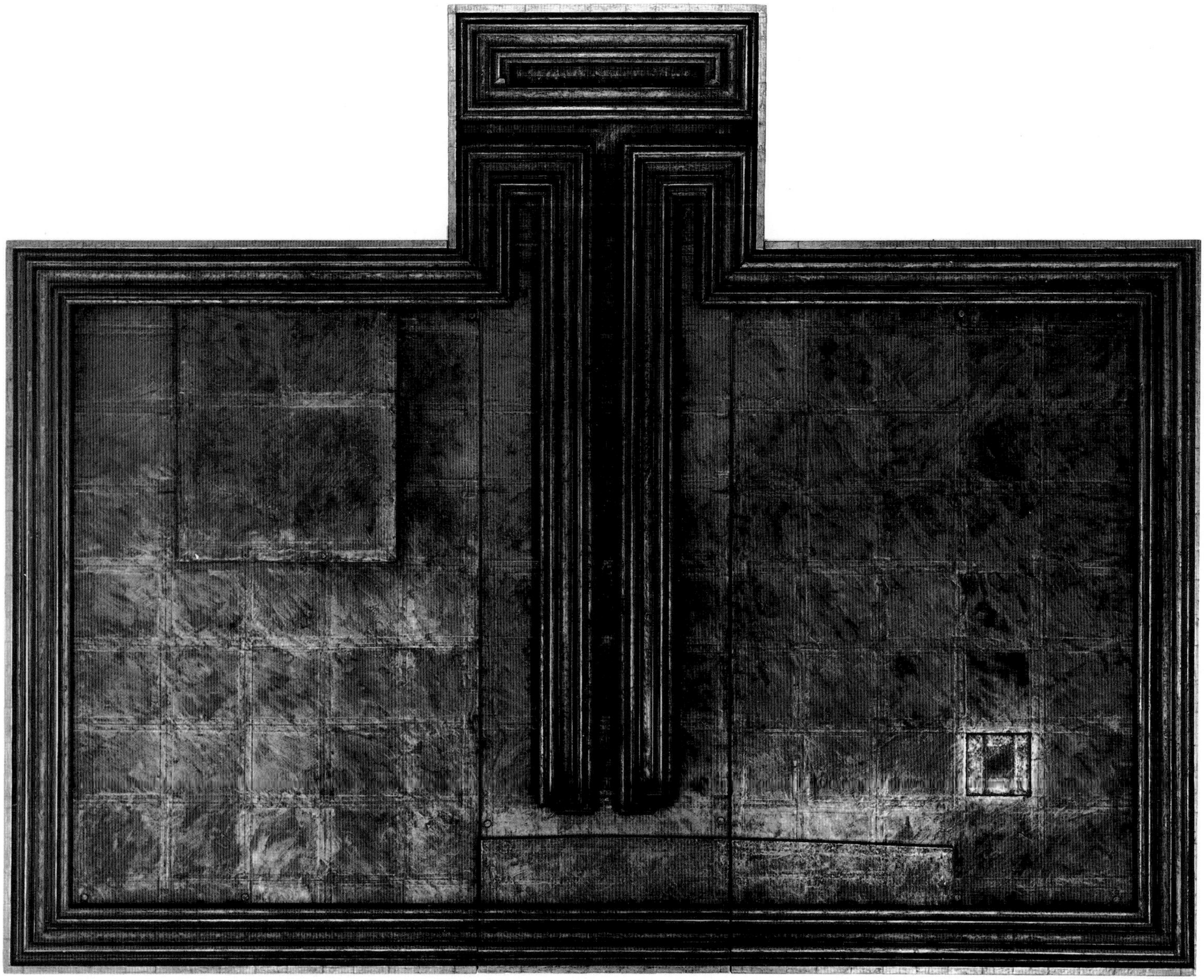

Joe Guy
**Descent**
(destroyed) 1987–88, Mixed media: graphite, paper, etc, 88½"h x 109"w x 5"d inches. Courtesy of the artist

# Joseph **Havel**

Joe Havel has always been very catholic about his media. As a student, he explored painting, drawing and ceramics with verve, and since moving to Houston as associate director of the Glassell School of Art in 1991, he has concentrated on lyrical assemblages.

He had several options when he graduated from the University of Pennsylvania in 1979. Offers to teach had come from schools in Pennsylvania and Illinois, which would have allowed him to stay close to art centers of the East Coast. But Austin College in Sherman, Texas, near Dallas, needed to replace Vernon Fisher, who had resigned. In spite of misgivings, Havel also sensed adventure and a certain romance associated with Texas remembered from a childhood trip across the state.

"It was a good situation for me to come into, though I was very isolated in the beginning. Dallas was difficult to integrate into and it was very strange after all the attention I'd had (in the East). I went into a work crisis. But it was good for me. It gave me time to think about what I wanted to teach, and what I wanted to do with my art. I reworked things that interested me about paintings I had done, about various cultures. I accumulated a lot of information."

Far from attempting a narrative or even a system of thought, Havel suggests arrested moments in time, an instant within which past and future are clearly discernible. In sculptures from the mid-1980s, the basic components were domestic artifacts like chairs, window sashes and doors which carried their own history. He sliced, laminated, glued and otherwise reconstituted them into arching or columnar stabiles. His more recent sculptures include a mix that ranges from the exotic, like Japanese paper lanterns, to the mundane broom stick and lamp shade. He combines them in supremely fluid presences that seem to be in suspended animation. In the past two years, he has cast some of the assemblages in bronze, giving them the finality and classicism inherent to the medium. If in the process a certain spontaneity is lost, that sense of permanence transforms the objects yet again.

"People think my work is different now, but actually it's just a kind of accumulation of investigations. I like my pieces to be loaded with association, information, and history."

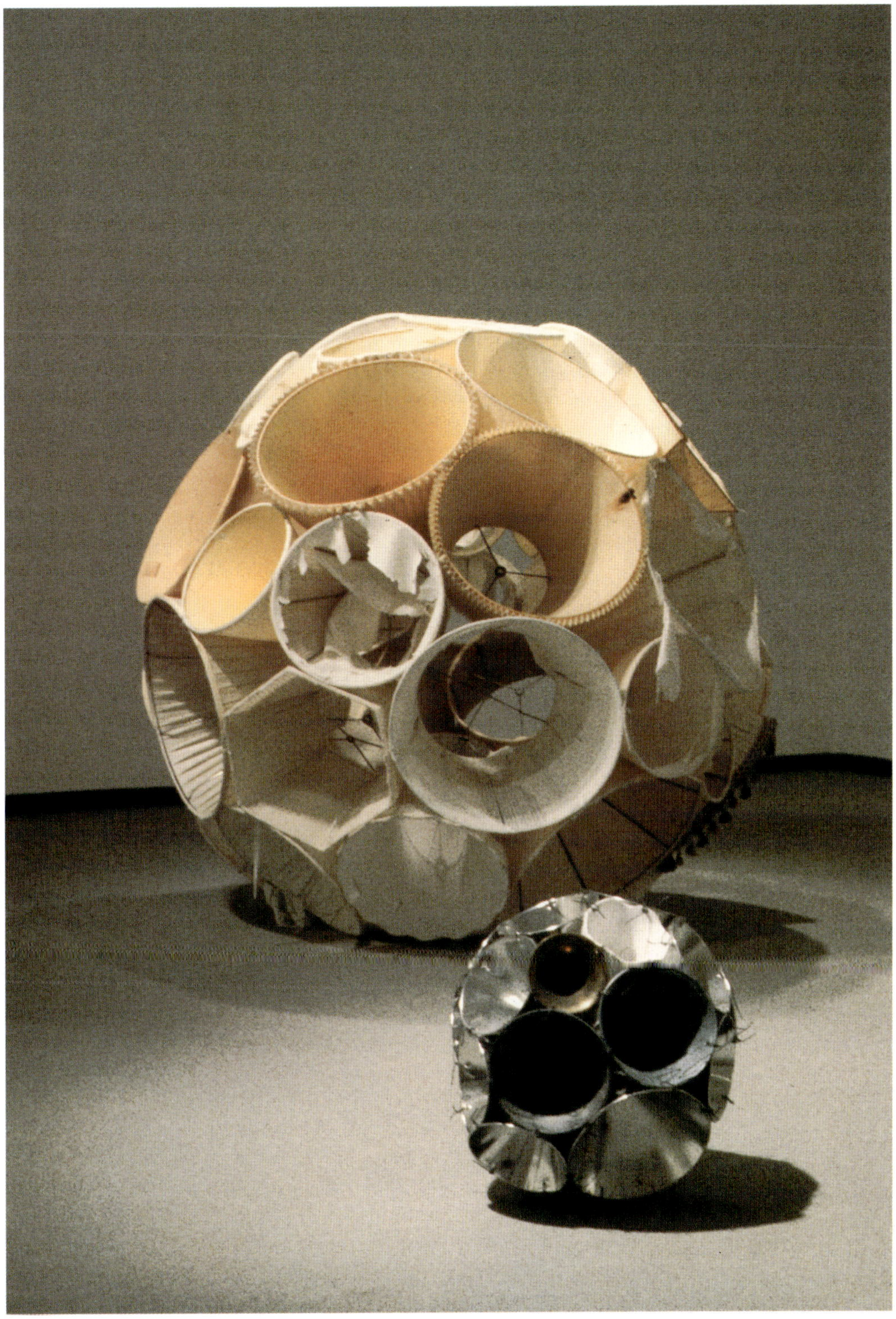

Joseph Havel
**Germ of Gossip, Spore of Silence**
1993, Mixed media: fabric, metal, thread, plastic,
72"h x 156"w x 72" (variable). Courtesy of the artist

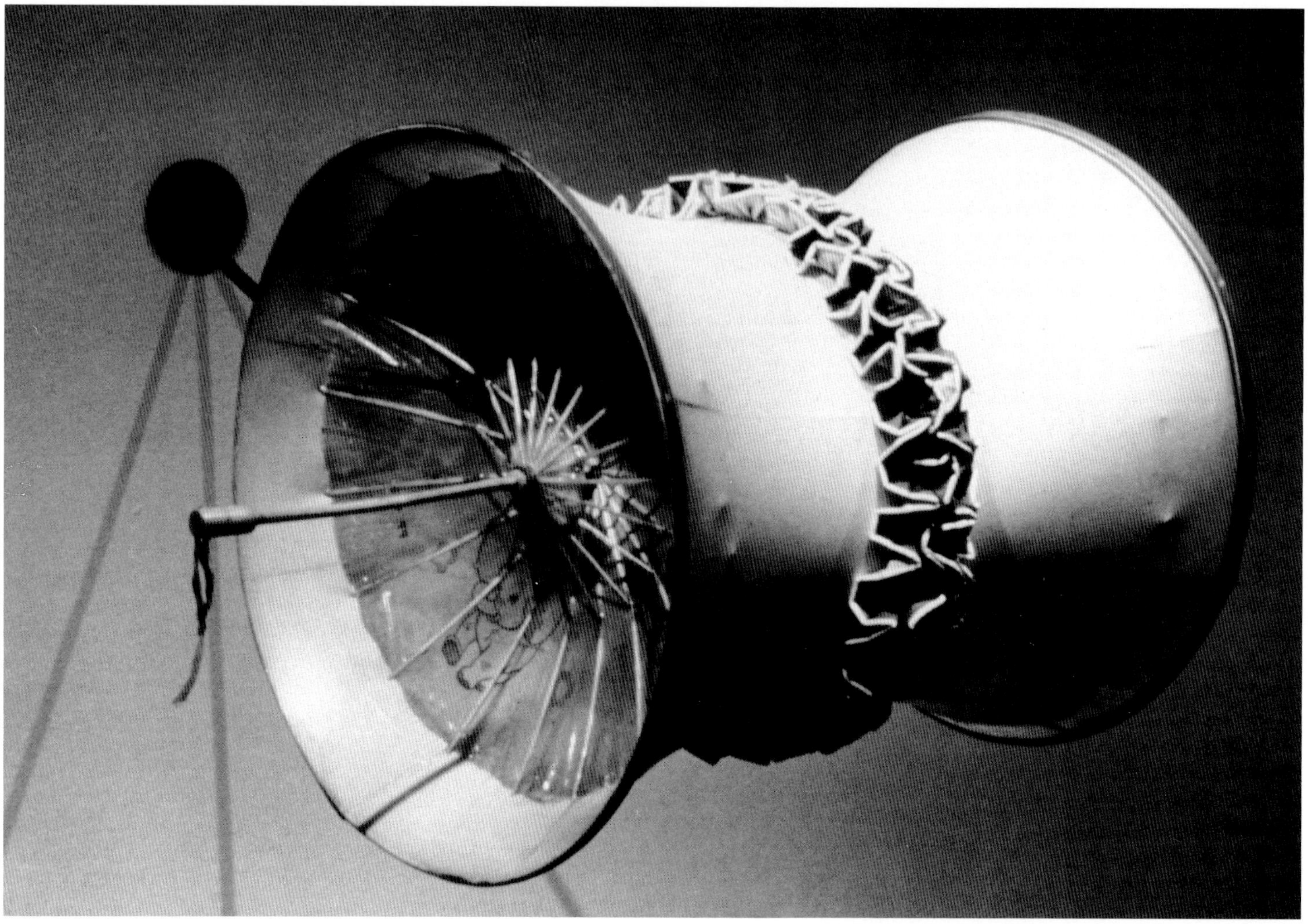

Joseph Havel
**Virus**
1992, Mixed media: fabric (lampshade), paper (parasol), bamboo, $19\frac{1}{4}$"h x 28"w x 41"d. Courtesy of the artist

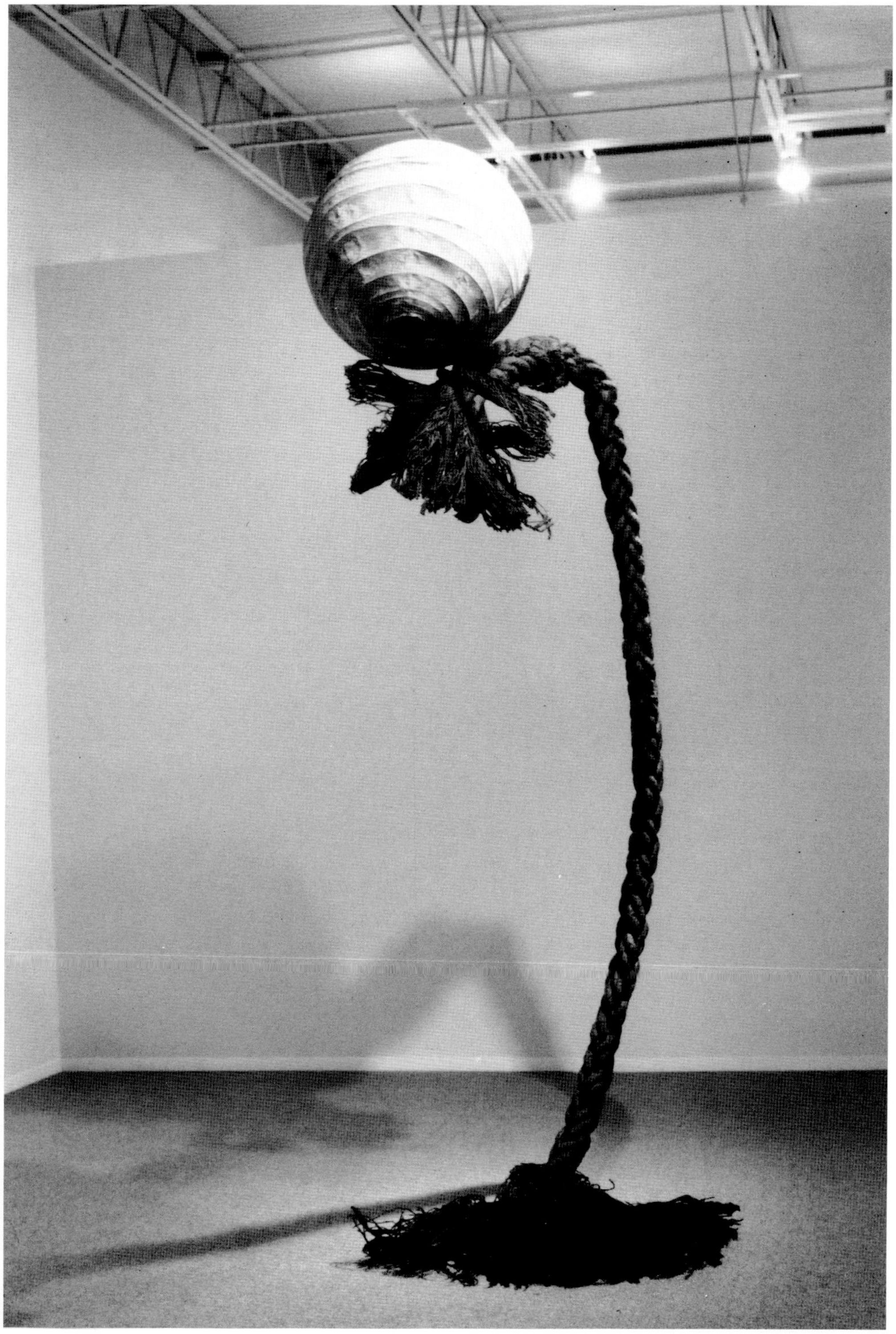

Joseph Havel
**Untitled**
1992, Bronze, 115"h x 49" x 49". Courtesy of the artist

# Rachel **Hecker**

Rachel Hecker recycles images from the commercial arena and renders them in the reductivist stylization of billboards. Snapshots of movie stars gleaned from magazines, cartoon characters, and icons of American products become hybrid symbols of a consumer society. She keeps her palette in the dull grayed tones of industrial printing, depersonalizing it further by applying it with an airbrush. "I want to push it as far as I can in that direction and still have them seen as paintings," she says.

She moved to Houston from her native Rhode Island in 1982 as assistant to Alan Hacklin, her former professor and newly appointed director of the Glassell School of Art. Born in 1958, Hecker graduated Summa Cum Laude in sculpture from Moore College in Philadelphia, but chose to pursue painting for her master's degree from the Rhode Island School of Design. It was a political decision, she says, "because it was the eighties and everybody was talking about the rebirth of painting, but everyone was really cynical about it. It also felt very male. I couldn't think of any women who were making paintings that I liked."

Her large acrylic paintings, like her diminutive gouache drawings, are easy to read at a casual glance. They are much richer, though, seriously funny and somehow moving when contemplated for longer periods of time. Unlike her contemporaries for whom appropriation is a way of expediting image-making, for Hecker it is an intriguing form of making images that are already public even more so. In the process, she exposes their commercial and sexual specificity.

Unlike the consumer-driven images she has adopted as her format, her composites derive from her activist stance: Empowerment of women, civil and health issues, the abuse of power for economic gain, are the provocative themes she embeds just beneath the slick surfaces of her acrylic paints — subliminal messages, if you will. Hecker sets up paradigms in her paintings against which the viewer judges him or herself.

"I think historically, art has been political. I'm not interested in making paintings that are about single issues, and when you're not focused that way, the message tends to get diffused. But true activism doesn't have to beat you over the head with an agenda."

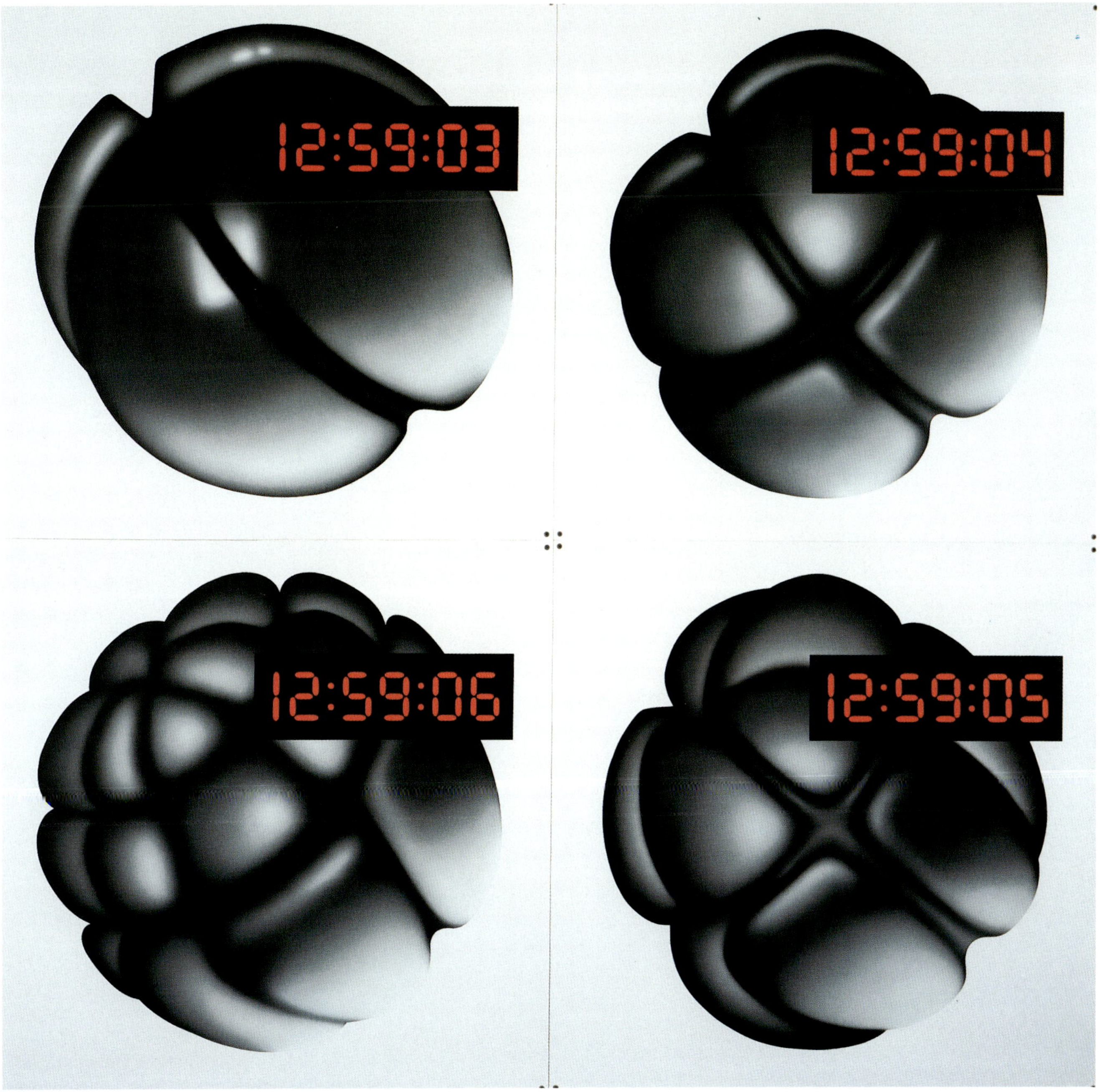


Rachel Hecker
**Cell Division (Plain View)**
1991, Acrylic on mahogany, 96" x 96". Courtesy of the artist

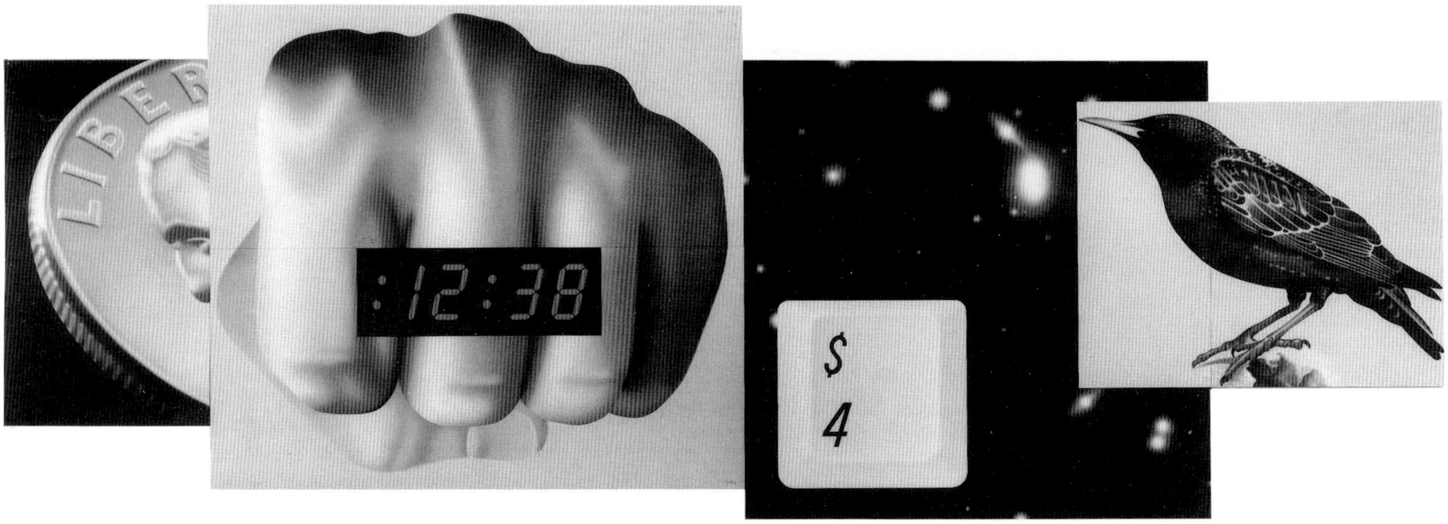


Rachel Hecker

**Tailgate**

1991, Acrylic on wood, 108" x 258". Photograph: Art Industrial, Houston. Collection: The University of Houston. Courtesy of the artist

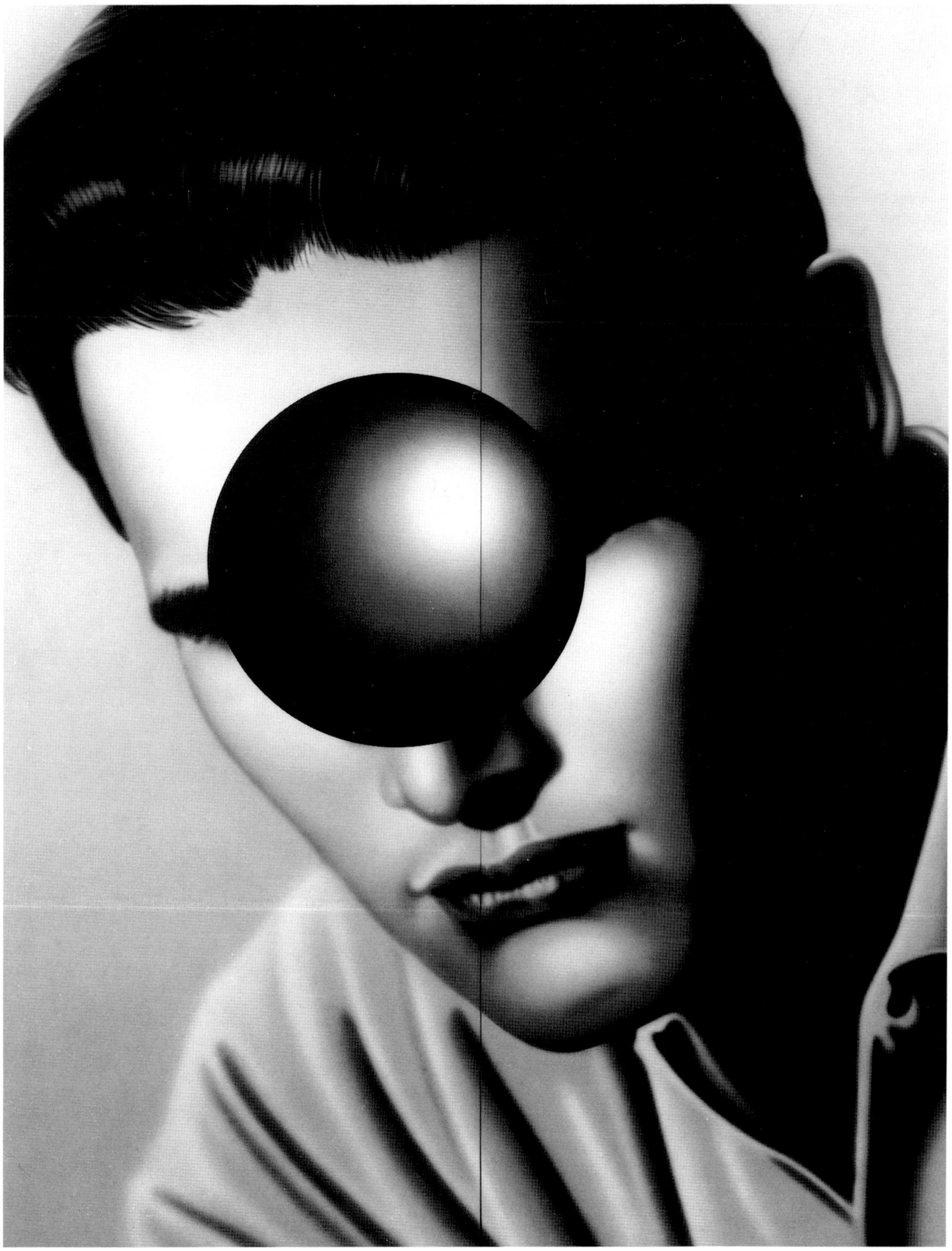

Rachel Hecker

**Bowling Trophy**

1992, Acrylic on wood, 80" x 60". Photograph: Art Industrial, Houston. Courtesy of the artist

# Ron **Hoover**

Ron Hoover works slowly and exhibits infrequently, but he has earned the respect of colleagues and collectors. Born in Liberty, Texas in 1944, Hoover received a bachelor's degree from the University of Houston in 1975. He left for the University of Oklahoma in Norman to pursue a masters degree just as UH was about to explode with the energy of sculptor James Surls and painter John Alexander. He returned two years later as the city was becoming the focus of art world attention.

His paintings consist of many layers of shimmering oil paint, applied with delicacy and meticulous precision. The technique belies a rage against a political system which he condemns for ignoring the weakest citizens while worshipping power and fostering greed. He shapes generic portraits of social types, but sometimes with the exaggerated specificity of an editorial cartoon. His symbols, including things like flags, skulls and evil grins, are readily understood, but the subtle richness of his surfaces and what they contain reward only the patient eye.

His abstracted figures appear surreptitiously, like shadows or ghosts materializing in fog. Their presence is insidious among the veils of pale color, echoing the subterfuge they represent. The looming figure of a soldier rises from a mound that startlingly reveals itself as the dead of battle in this vast field of camouflage greens. The politician or the patriot are almost invisible against the stippled paint describing flags and fireworks; only his broad grin filled with contrasting, sharp little teeth gives him away.

The power of an image, any image, though, resides as much in what it is as how it is rendered. Hoover is first and foremost a painter. Inspired by "all the big time artists", he names Willem de Kooning and Francis Bacon specifically. Hoover has nonetheless chosen to work in a way that resembles the revolutionaries of 19th century Paris rather than the Americans of the 1950s. His process is time consuming. He begins with a silhouette shape cut from newspapers which he uses as a guide to the composition. Once the principal form is anchored on the surface, he applies diminutive brush strokes, working from light to dark or vice versa, in a pointillist technique that allows him to maintain clarity and luminosity of tone — and critically, that allows him to make his blunt point with enormous subtlety.

"I feel that all artists have something to give others. My painting deals with the human figure — an interest and concern about the human condition. My works refer to the environment and what man has done to it and himself. I view painting as a form of communication — and I do like painting for painting's sake."[1]

1. Cited in *Fresh Paint: The Houston School*, p. 134

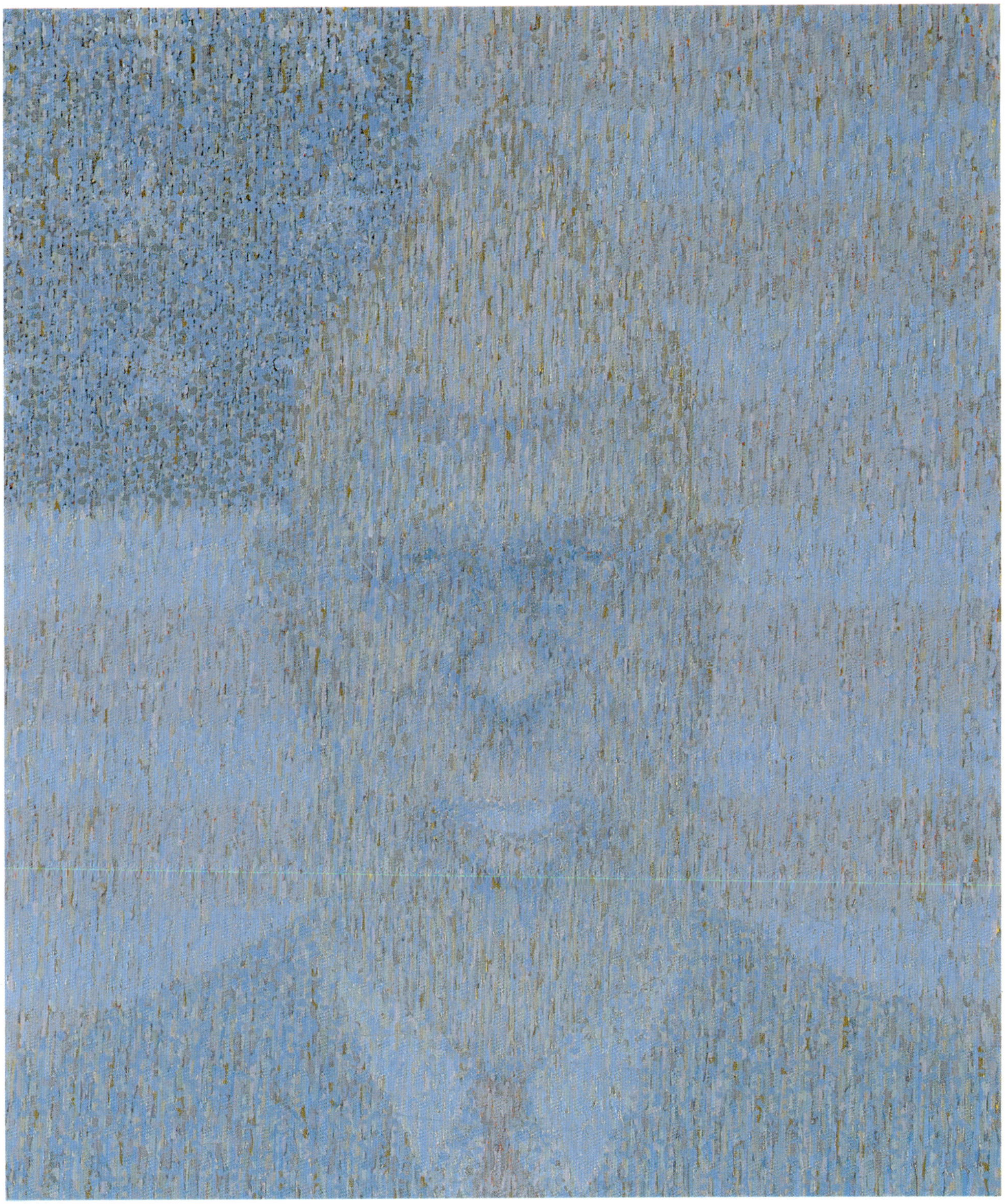

Ron Hoover

**Elected Reactionary**

1990, Oil on canvas, 24" x 20". Private collection.

Courtesy of the artist

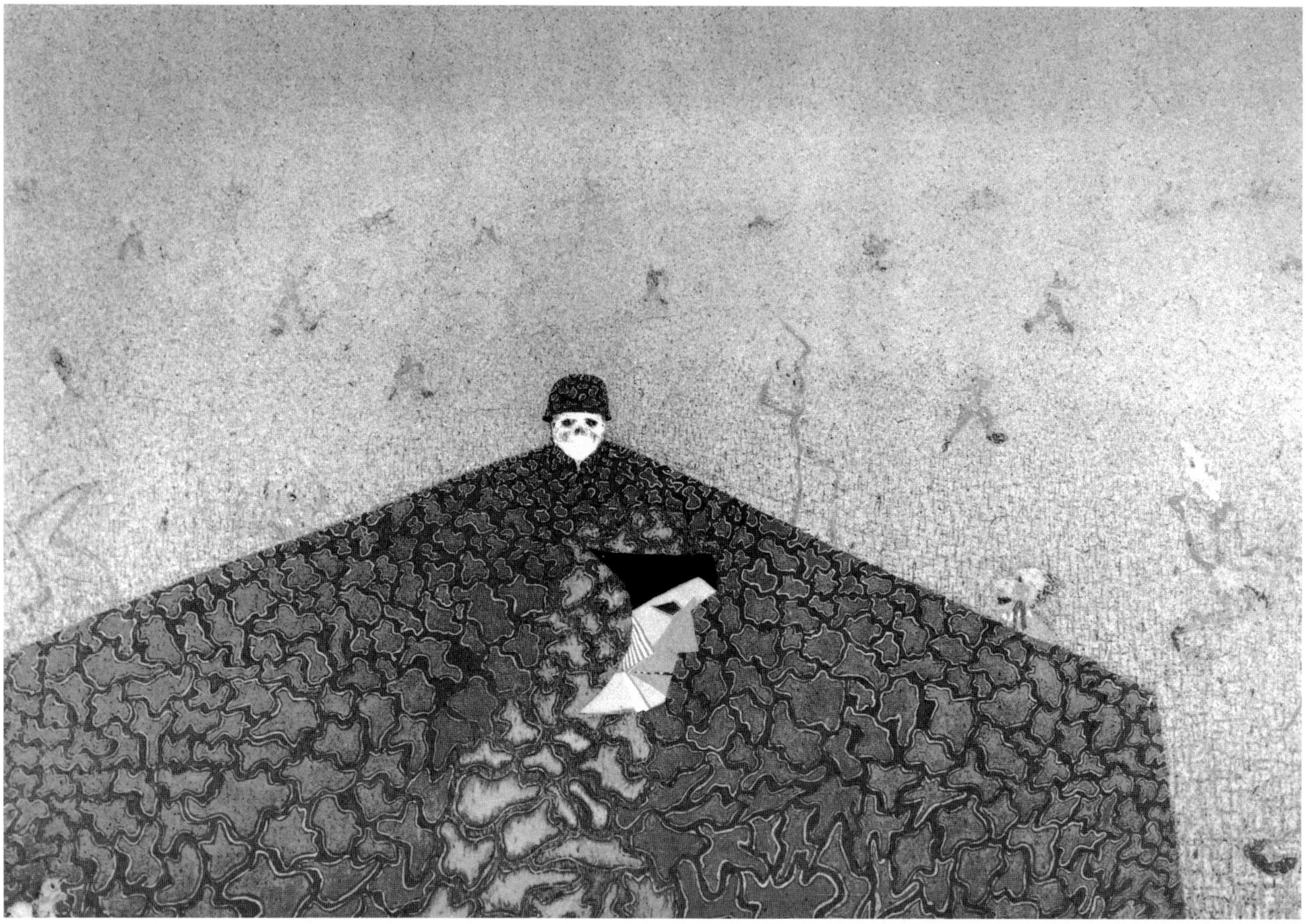

Ron Hoover
**Your Tax Money**
1983, Oil on canvas, 48" x 68". Collection: Estate of William A. Graham, Houston. Courtesy of the artist

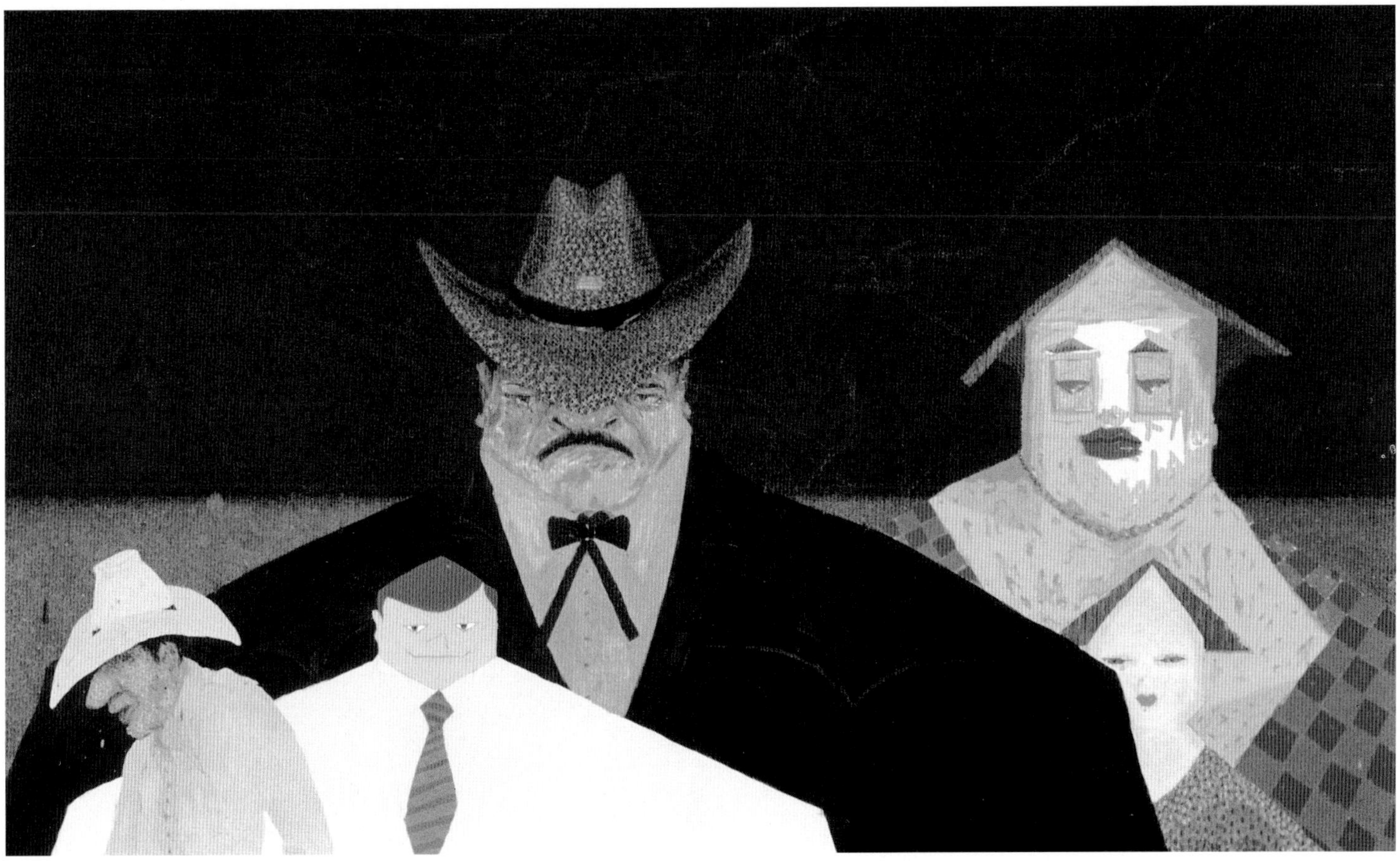

Ron Hoover
**Beef Production in America**
1985, Oil on canvas, 50" x 84". Collection of the artist. Courtesy of the artist

# Perry **House**

Over the years, Perry House has simplified his paintings to a few, primarily neutral colors, and a handful of objects he calls his "cast of characters." The characters are unremarkable things in themselves — a brooch, stairs removed from any structure, a ship of sails. And yet, isolated against the painterly grounds that at first appear flat, they become highly evocative objects. House describes their forms in complex scrollwork reminiscent of the wrought iron typical of Southern architecture. They snare the eye with the illusions of volume, but never quite free themselves of the ground.

His process of distillation has been long and often unrewarding. House began exploring the domestic objects of his current repertory in the early 1980s. The palette then tended toward the acid and frequently garish. In the skewered, multiple perspectives he employed, beds and armoires, chairs and lamps, collided in cramped spaces like the jumbles of junk stores. As he began to dissect the shapes, detaching elements and abstracting form to reveal intrinsic geometry, the space became shallower. Ovals, loops and triangles pushed at the surface, competing for primacy in a chaotic, dynamic dance. Paradoxically, as the description of forms turned ever more simple, the relationship between figure and ground, color and form, gained in complexity. Everything appeared to be on the surface yet some things were "in front" of others.

Born in Orange, Texas in 1943, House, like many of his colleagues, went to California to pursue his master's in fine arts.

"There was no program anywhere in Texas. I chose California instead of the East Coast because it was much less formal. Also, I was fascinated with customized cars and the California car aesthetic was really appealing. I've always acknowledged Von Dutch (a legendary practitioner of car painting especially renowned for pin striping) as my biggest influence."

In the 1990s, his isolated, melancholy objects float against layered veils of color. House developed a technique to make the characteristic opacity of acrylic paint seem as transparent as oil glazes. The milky and monotonal surface of first viewing reveals itself to be in fact the result of many colors, and the chromatic subtlety seductively romantic.

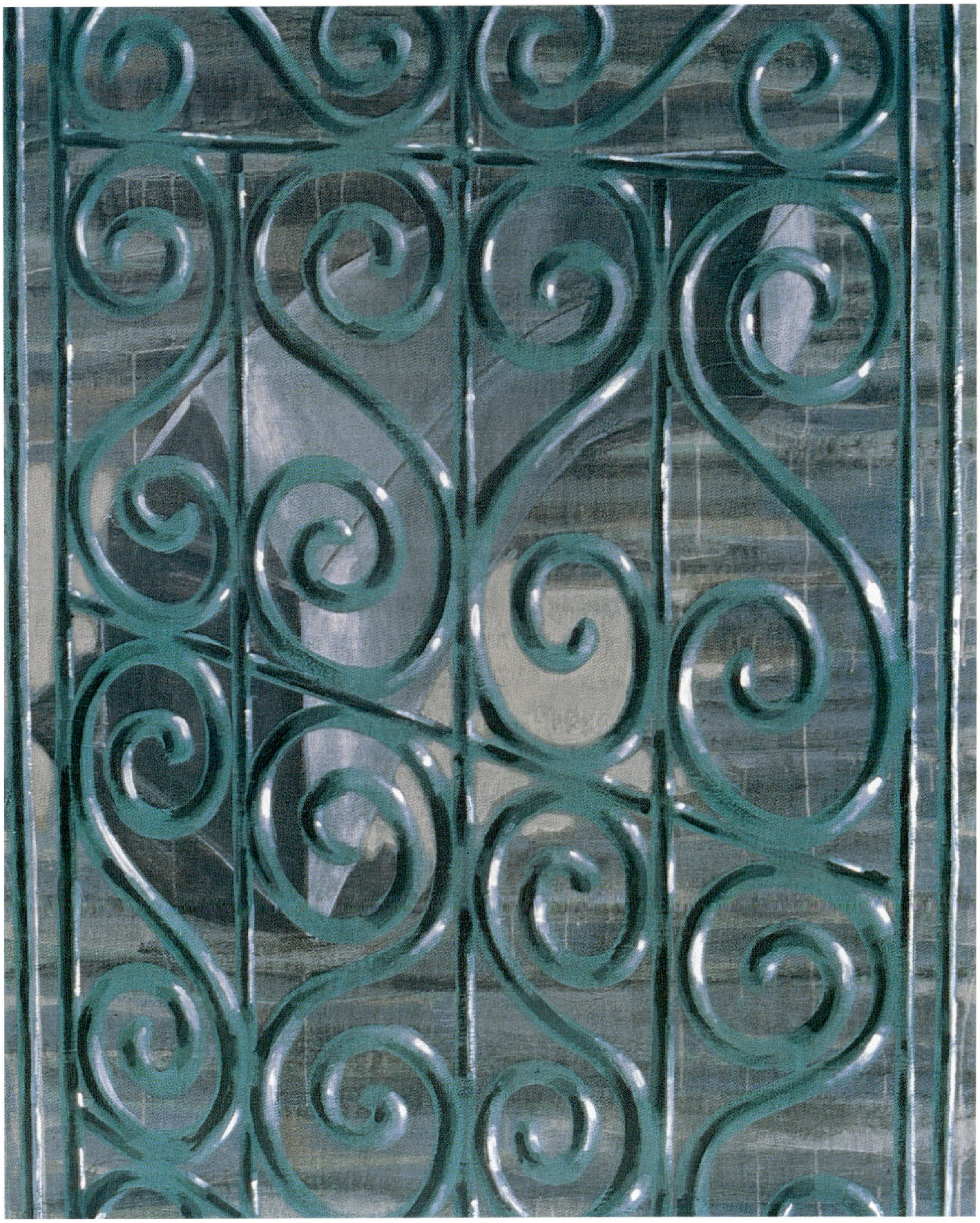

Perry House

**The Gate, The House**

1993, Acrylic on canvas, 60" x 48". Courtesy of Davis/McClain Gallery, Houston

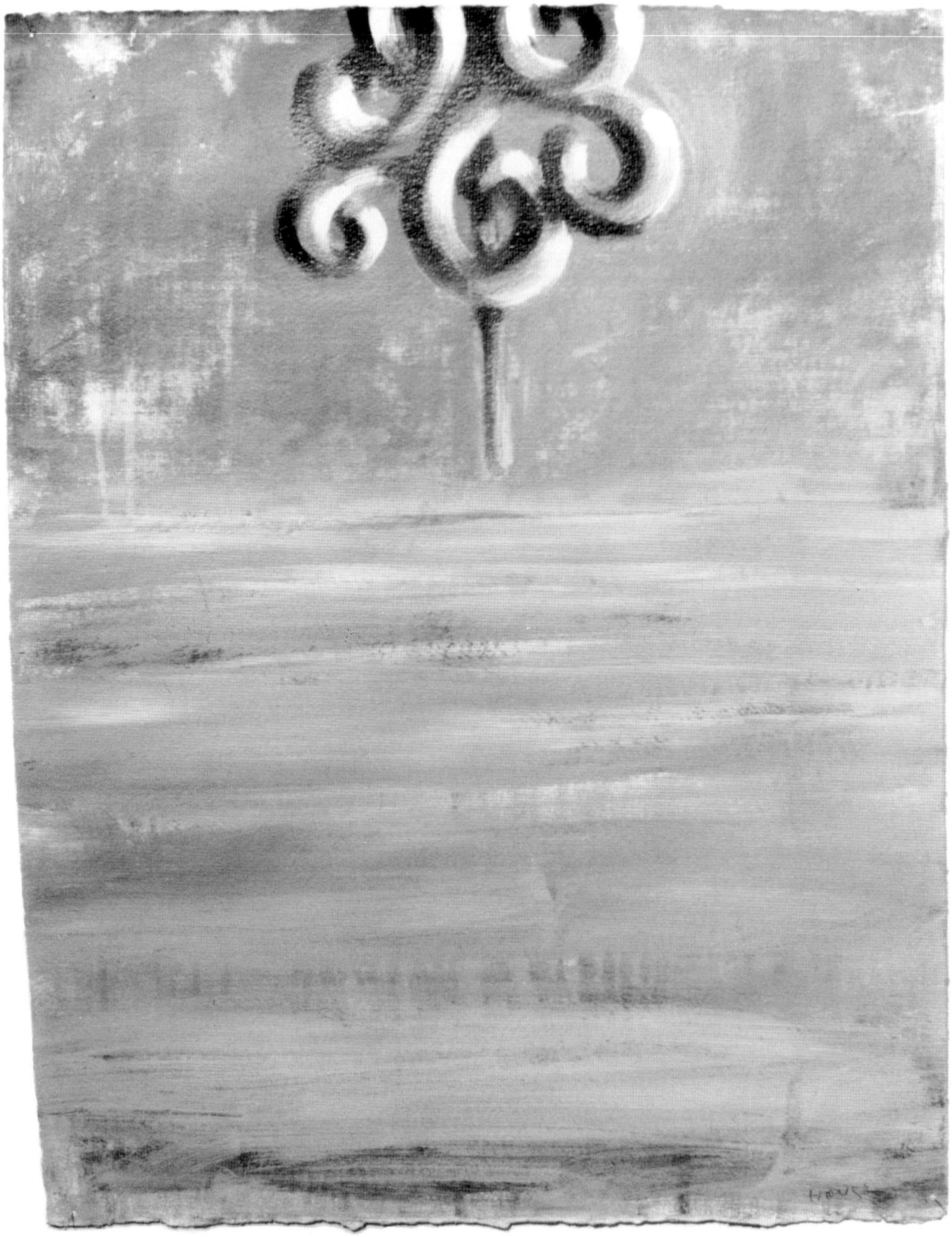



Perry House
**S.F. #3**
1991, Acrylic on paper, 30" x 22½". Courtesy of Davis/McClain Gallery, Houston

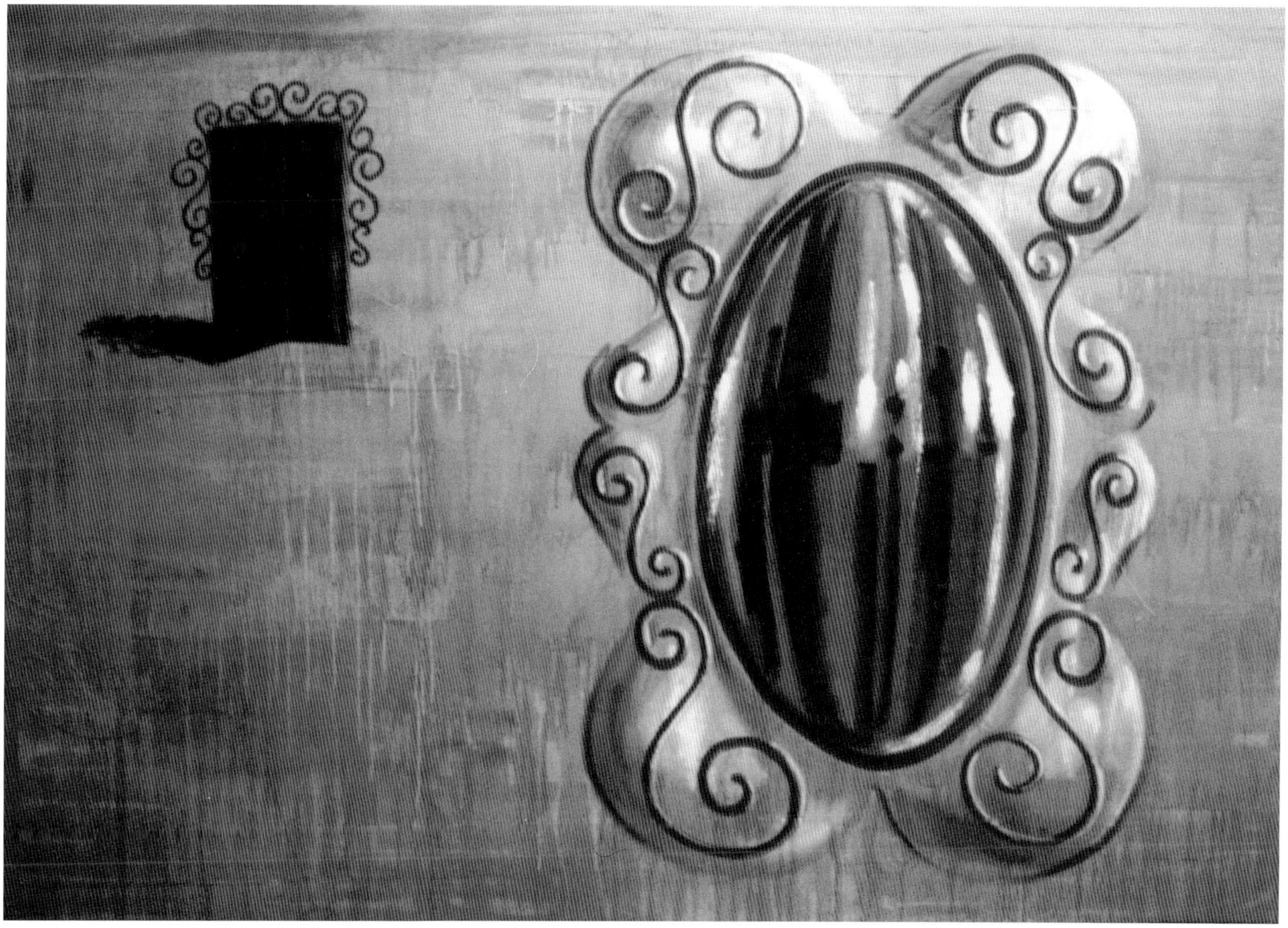

Perry House
**The Mirror, The Brooch**
1993, Acrylic on canvas, 60" x 84". Courtesy of Davis/McClain Gallery, Houston

# Luis
# **Jimenez Jr**

Luis Jimenez's vision encompasses the mix of cultures manifest on both sides of the Rio Grande. On the one hand, European classicism defines the forms and proportions of his figures, heroic in scale and emblematic in meaning. On the other, he chooses the materials of popular culture, like fiberglass, and the lurid palette of outdoor advertising.

Born in El Paso in 1940, he grew up working in his father's sign shop where he was groomed to take over the business. But visits to his grandparents in Mexico City introduced him to the heroic murals of 20th century Mexico whose imagery he understood and the scale of which impressed him. In spite of strife, and the eventual rift with his father, he graduated from the University of Texas in Austin in 1964 with a degree in art and just shy of a second degree in architecture, and promptly left for New York. In the heyday of Pop Art, Jimenez's ironic depictions of both American and Mexican clichés quickly rose to prominence. But the conflict between his family's expectations and his desire to make art, were painful. He felt he somehow had to justify his choice.

"I finally made some peace with myself by feeling I could work in art and through art, I could help affect change in the larger society by affecting the way people think."

Far from being didactic, however, Jimenez is interested in public art that is accessible, and that simultaneously revitalizes — and realigns — Western myths. He investigates the myths from a historical perspective. In the monumental *Vaquero* for example, he presents the cowboy not as the John Wayne of popular America, but in the more historically honest demeanor as the Mexican ranch hand who populated Texas and was the original cowboy.

The sheer visual impact of his forms and their colors tend to disguise the craft and deep art-historical references Jimenez masters. To envision the *Vaquero* cast in bronze or carved in marble, is to see equestrian statues in Europe's (and Mexico's) plazas. In his sculpture *Howl*, the clichéd coyote of the Southwest is reinfused with meaning as a creature of the land, and a symbol whose artistic ancestor is the She-wolf of Romulus and Remus.

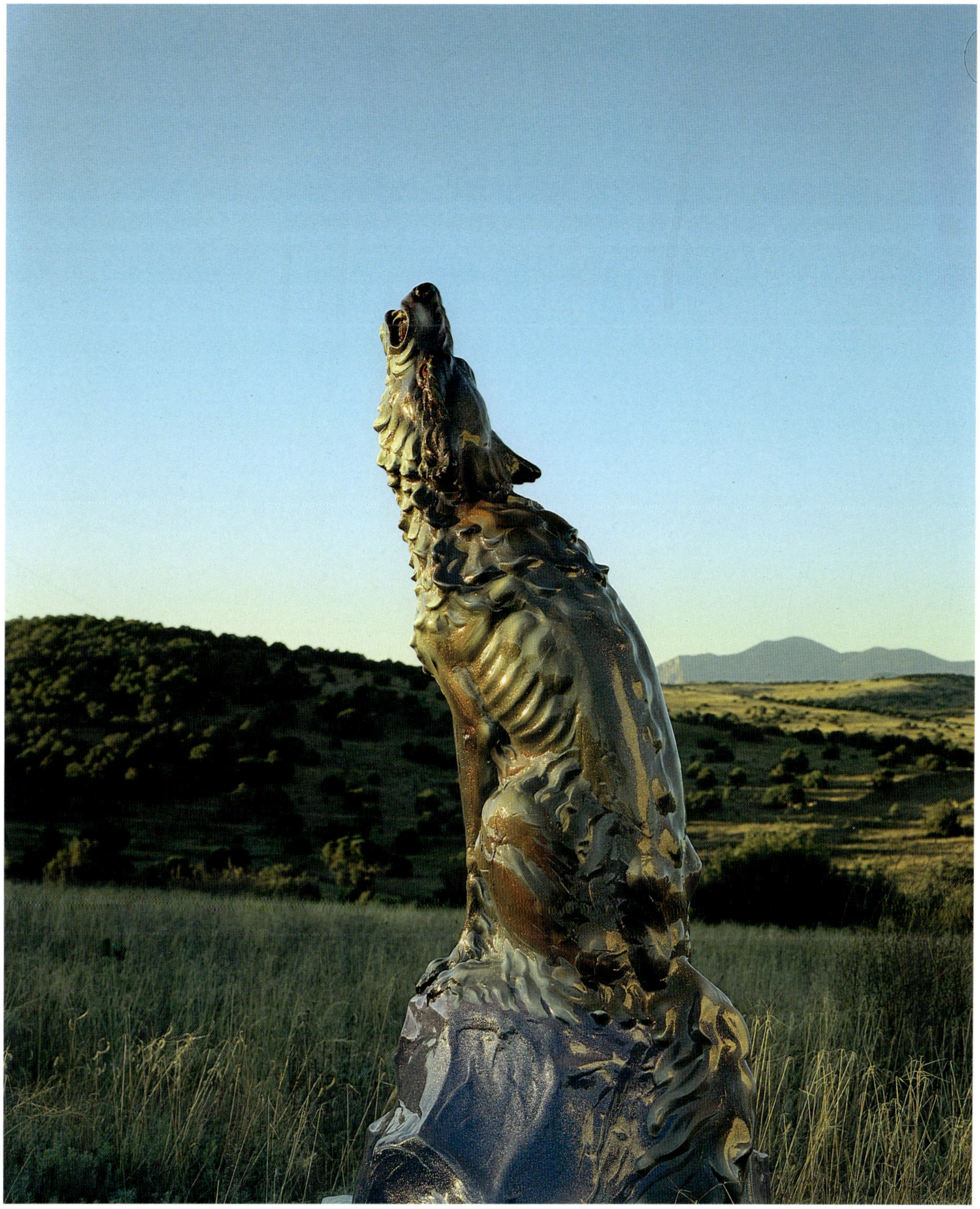

Luis Jimenez Jr
**Howl**
1986, Fiberglass, 62"h x 29" x 29".
Photograph: Bruce Berman. Collection of the artist.
Courtesy of the artist

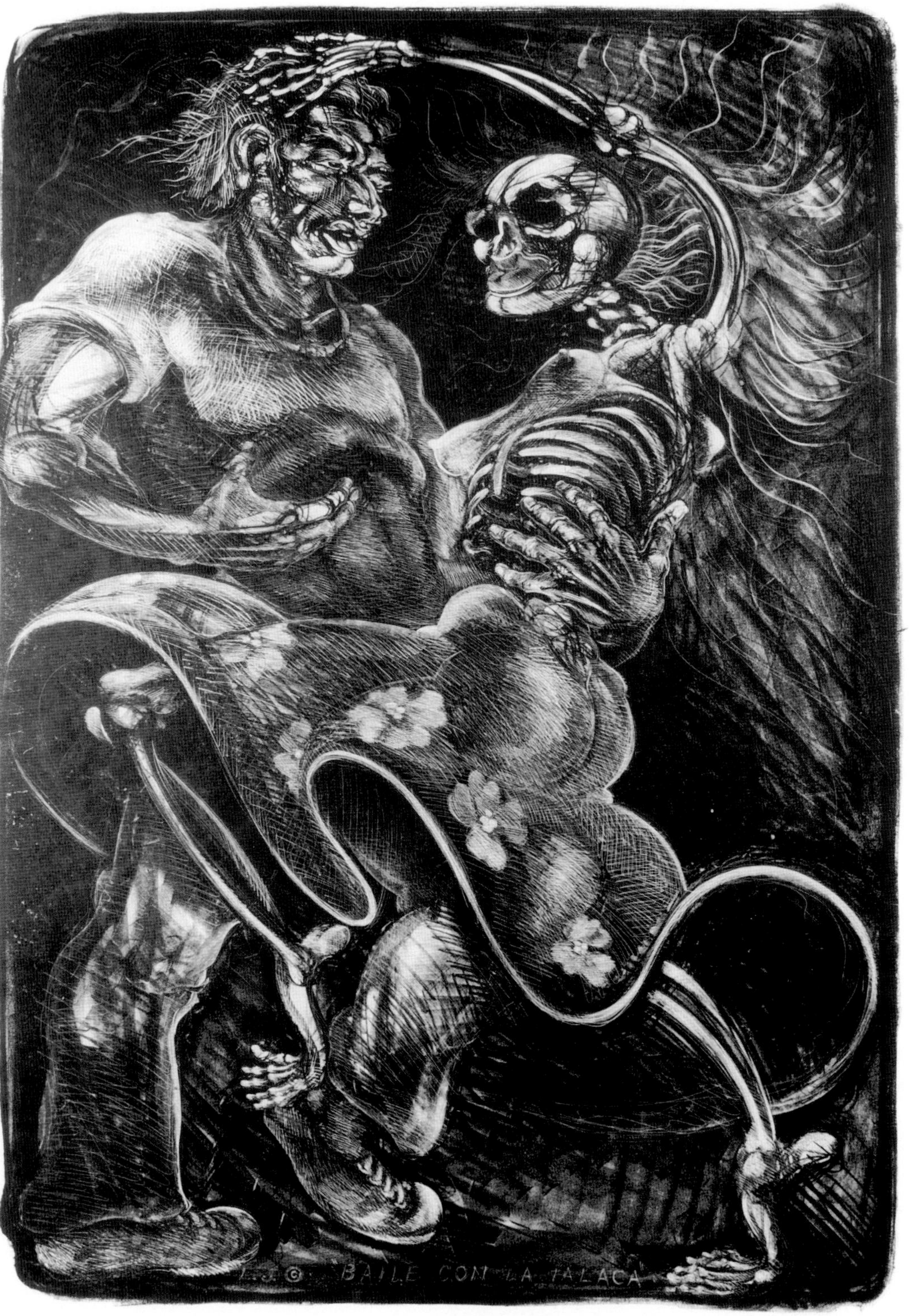


Luis Jimenez Jr
**Baile Con La Talaca (Dance with Death)**
1983, Lithograph, Edition 100, 39" x 26¾". Courtesy of the artist and Moody Gallery, Houston

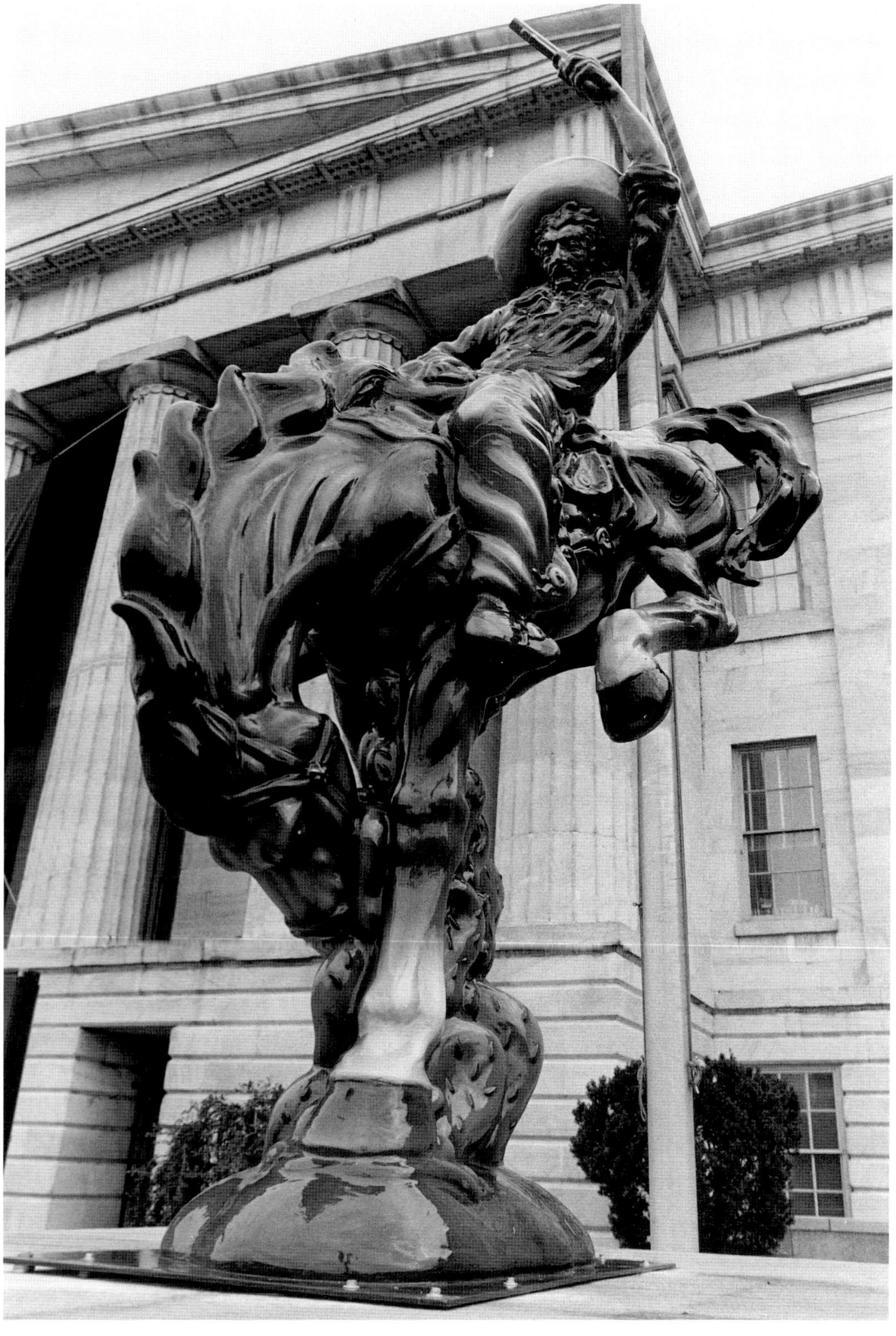

Luis Jimenez Jr
**Vaquero**
1980, edition of 5, Fiberglass, 16½'h. Photograph: courtesy of the artist and the National Gallery of Art, Washington D.C.

# Lucas **Johnson**

Lucas Johnson always knew he was going to be an artist, he just took some detours on the way. The first time he saw a painting, Thomas Gainsborough's *Blue Boy*, his twelve-year-old mind just knew it was magic. But the Connecticut Yankee, born in Hartford in 1940 and raised in southern California, enrolled in marine biology at the University of California in Los Angeles, not art. He left after his junior year to go where his curiosity led him. From a cattle ranch in Wyoming, to the streets of New Orleans where he taught himself to draw and studied Ralph Mayer's *Artists' Handbook*, to a cold-water walk-up in lower Manhattan, it eventually led him to Mexico City in the early 1960s.

The timing was auspicious. A new generation of artists was flourishing, taking the best of traditional humanism and making it fresh. Jose Luis Cuevas and Francisco Toledo, among others, were revitalizing the figure in paintings and drawings mixed with the surrealist soul of Mexico. Surrealist Leonora Carrington, living in the capital city since the mid 1940s, became a good friend. Johnson felt he was home, and stayed ten years.

"I got off the plane and everything felt good — the food, the street life — everything, though I didn't speak a word of the language. The first time I ordered in the restaurant I thought I was asking for enchiladas but got a fruit salad instead. But it was very comfortable. I got the first studio in my life in a three-story building I shared with four other artists with whom I showed sometimes. My work was figurative and I was just another painter. After a while I wasn't a *gringo* anymore."

Johnson sifted Mexico's myths and cultural traditions in ink drawings and paintings, perfecting his craft and developing a style which some critics at the time identified as magic realism, named, like European Surrealism, after a literary movement. His images, however, have never been descriptive, but symbolic. His subjects then as now are the little — or even major — miracles and tragedies which occur daily but which go mostly unperceived, or unrecognized. The theme of death and resurrection is the leitmotif, witnessed by people or by nature itself, willingly or not. It is manifest in ink drawings of lyrical lines and rich, modulated black washes, and in a luminous palette of Renaissance clarity.

Since moving to Houston in 1973, Johnson's work has become increasingly abstract and introspective without losing its figurative grounding. Alternating between drawing and painting, he is using the landscape to express the eternal conflict between soul and body, magic and realism, only hinting at the human presence which defines it.

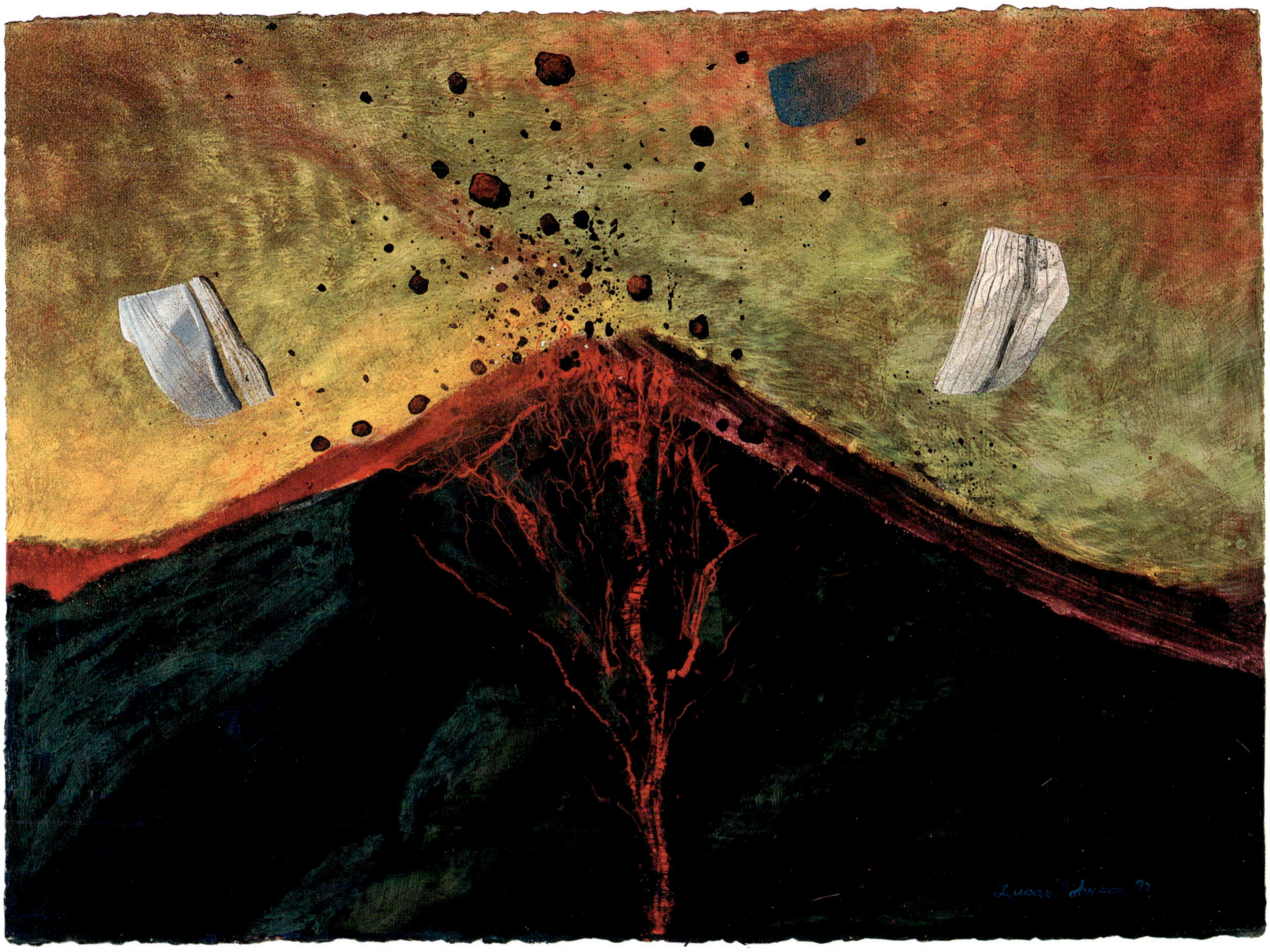

Lucas Johnson

**Untitled (Volcano Series)**

1993, Acrylic on paper, 22½" x 30". Courtesy of Moody Gallery, Houston

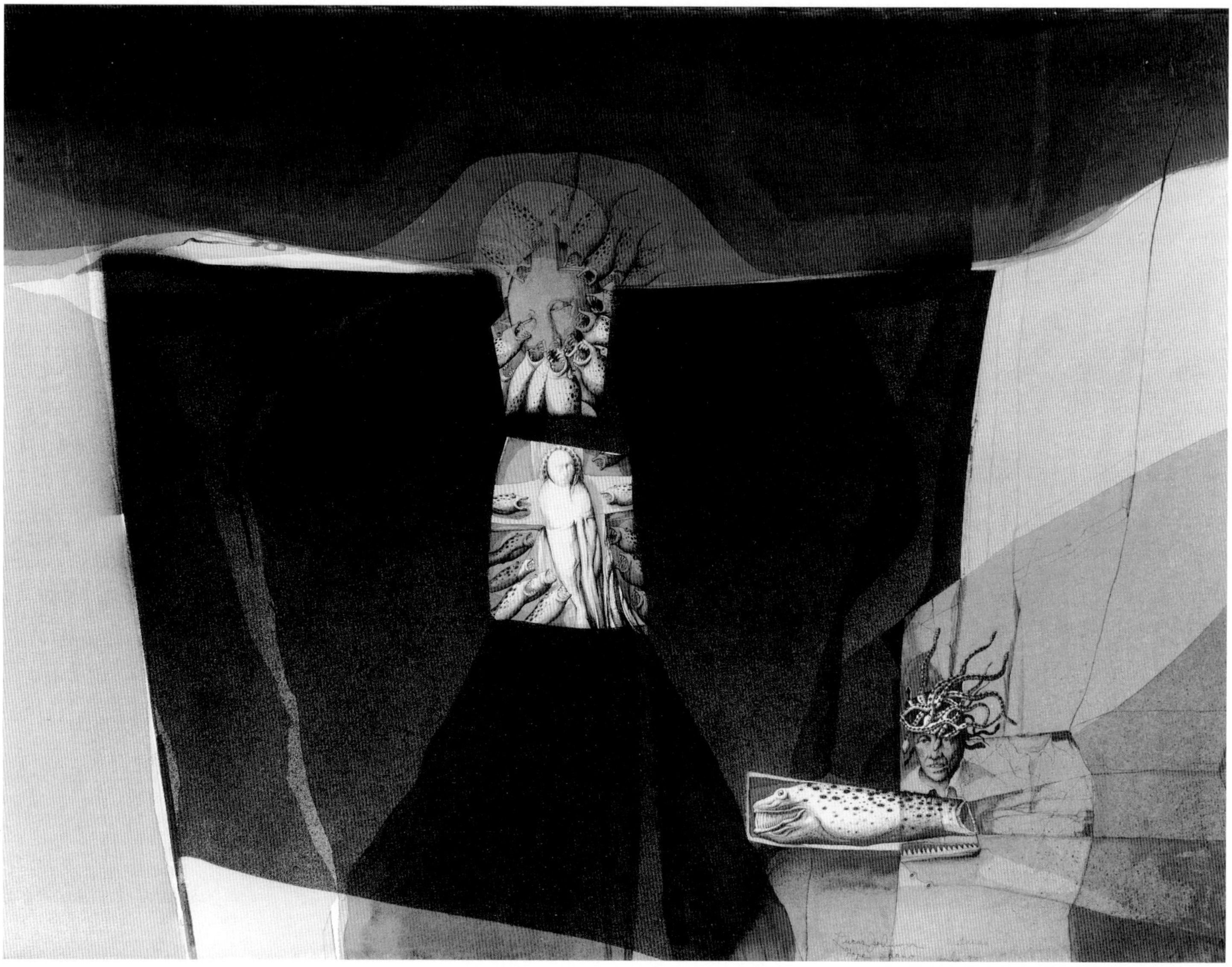

Lucas Johnson
**Witness (Drawings from the Underworld)**
1993, Ink and enamel on paper, 22½" x 30". Collection: Edward and Nancy Reddin Kienholz, Hope, Idaho. Courtesy of Moody Gallery, Houston

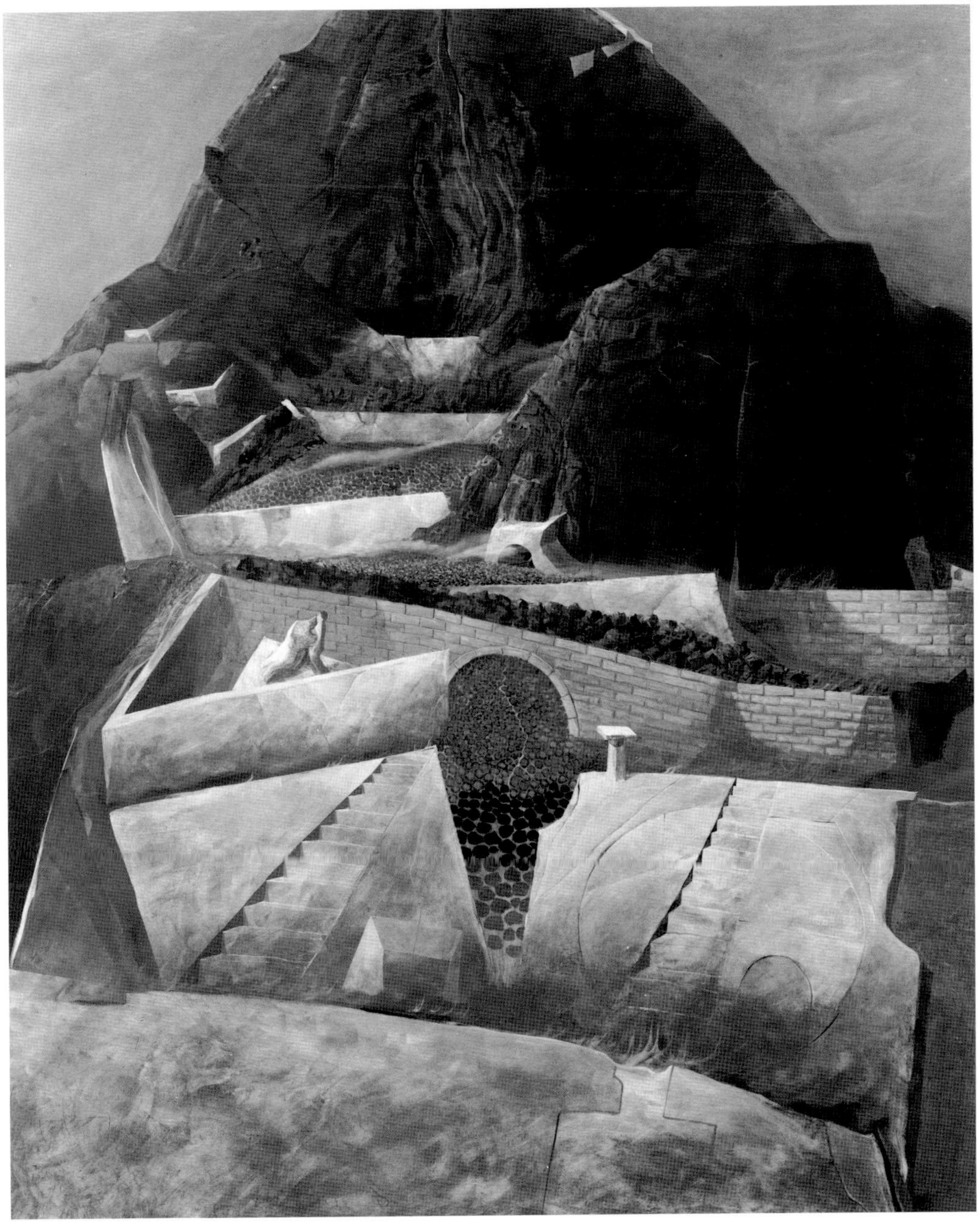

Lucas Johnson
**Volcano Series, No. 3**
1991, Acrylic on canvas, 60" x 48". Collection: The Museum of Fine Arts, Houston, Museum purchase with funds provided by Crowley, Marks and Douglas in memory of Diana Faz.
Courtesy of The Museum of Fine Arts, Houston

# Donald **Judd**

Donald Judd was internationally renowned when he chose to make Texas his home base in 1971. He was lured by the myth of the West, the dreams dreamed by a child in Missouri reading Frank Dobie stories, but what the adult artist wanted was nothing less than to build a perfect museum where his immaculate minimalist sculpture could be displayed in perpetuity.

Born in Missouri in 1928, Judd traveled a fairly traditional art school route that included the Arts Students League in New York City. Following his discharge from the army, though, he pursued a degree in philosophy from Columbia University. Upon graduation, Judd turned to painting. The expressive abstraction of the 1950s still had a strong hold on the market and the institutions, but Pop art was beginning to steal lightning with its cynical, humorous appropriations of commercial design. Judd could relate to neither. He abandoned painting gradually, at first adding three-dimensional components to his painting surfaces and eventually removing the flat surface altogether in favor of the pure geometry that would become known as minimalism.

The minimalist aesthetics defined in the 1960s had changed the appearance of contemporary art. More importantly, the austere elegance of minimalism's gestalt had also changed what collector's could acquire and what a general audience could look at. With a firm reputation in the major centers of the world, Judd made the decision to create a place where this intellectual art could exist in a pure context.

He found the remote *despoblado* — the uninhabited place — of West Texas, an austerely beautiful landscape where high plains desert and the tallest mountains in the state meet under almost a painful clarity of light. The abandoned Fort D.A. Russell in Marfa, 200 miles southeast of El Paso, had served as an army base for U.S. troops during World War II. Between 1976 when he began his visionary museum, and 1987, when the Chinati Foundation opened to the public, Judd transformed the dilapidated barracks, artillery sheds and indoor arena of the fort into immaculate exhibition spaces illumined exclusively by natural light. In redesigning the fort's existing buildings, Judd conceived of the whole — the buildings, the art they would house, and the grounds — as a sculpture in itself.

"The art and architecture of the past that we know is that which remains. The best is that which remains where it was painted, placed or built."[1]

Since his death in February 1994, Judd's legacy as artist and architect, and the Chinati Foundation he created, are more inseparable than ever.

1. Donald Judd, Statement for the Chinati Foundation, in *Donald Judd Architecktur*, 1989, p. 67

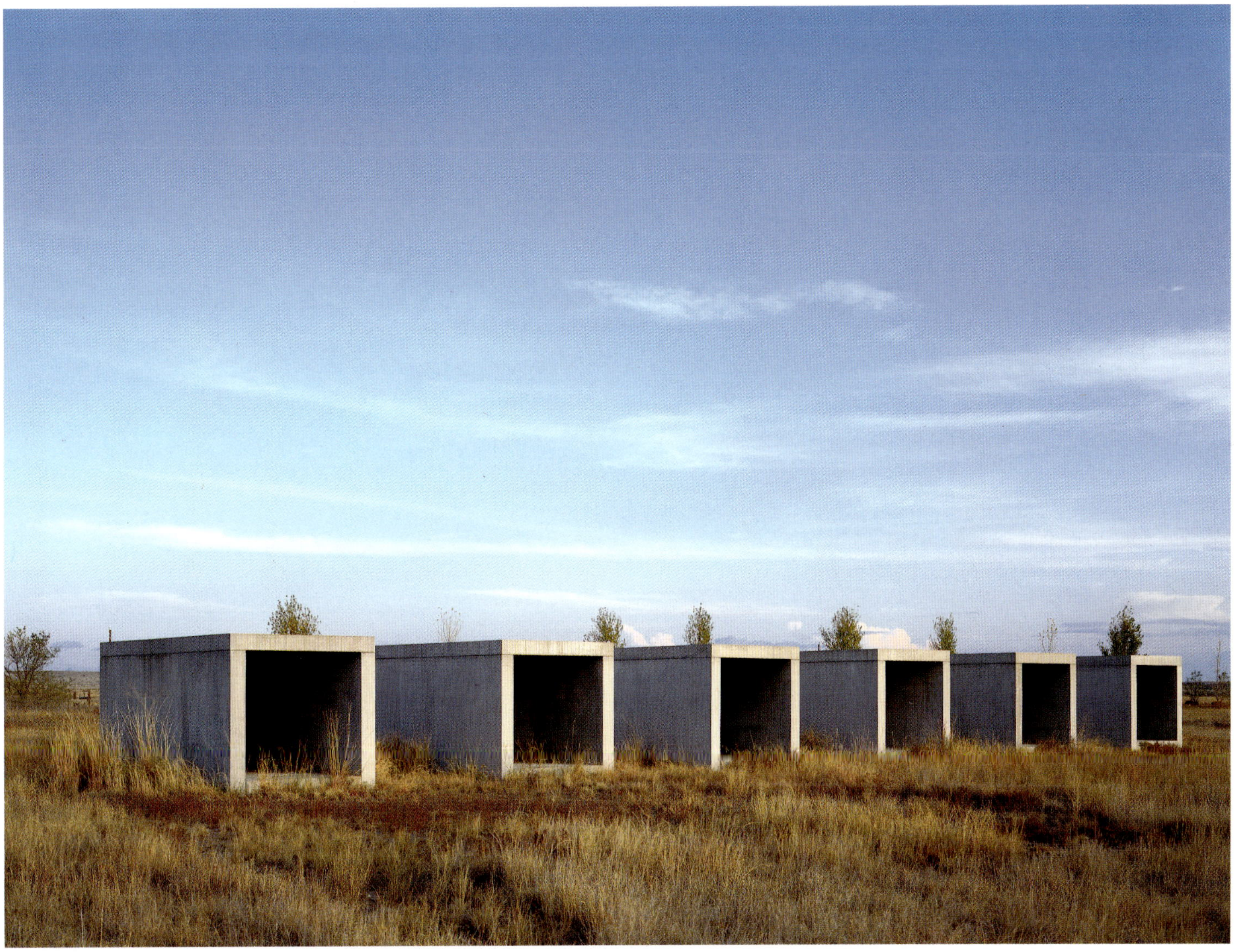

Donald Judd

**One of "Fifteen Concrete Works"**

1980–84, Cast concrete, six units, each unit: 98 7/16" x 98 7/16" x 196 7/8". Photograph: Todd Eberle. Collection: Chinati Foundation, Marfa. Courtesy of the artist

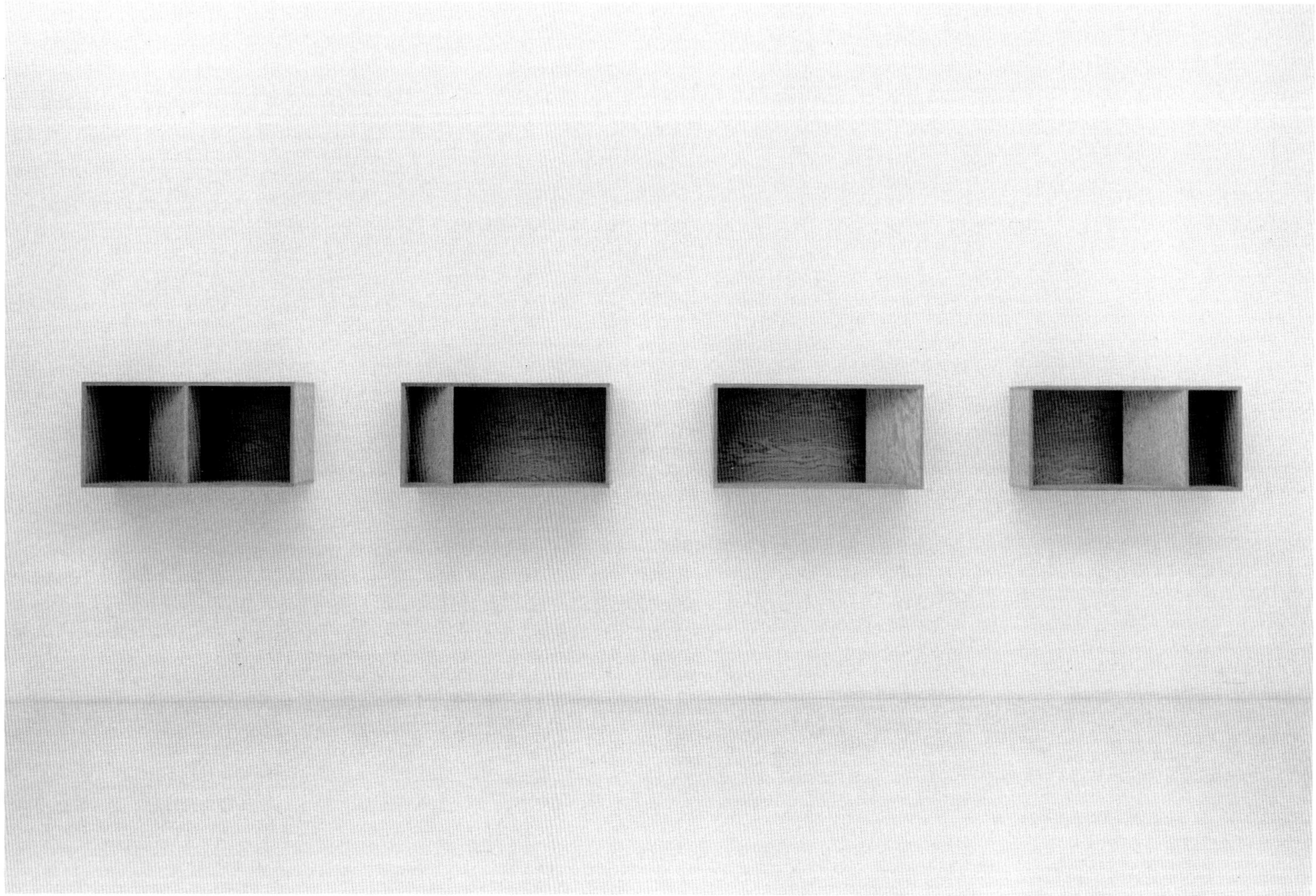

Donald Clarence Judd
**Untitled**
1991, Plywood, four units, each unit: 19⅝" x 39⅜" x 19⅝".
Photograph: Bill Jacobson. Courtesy of Pace Gallery, New York

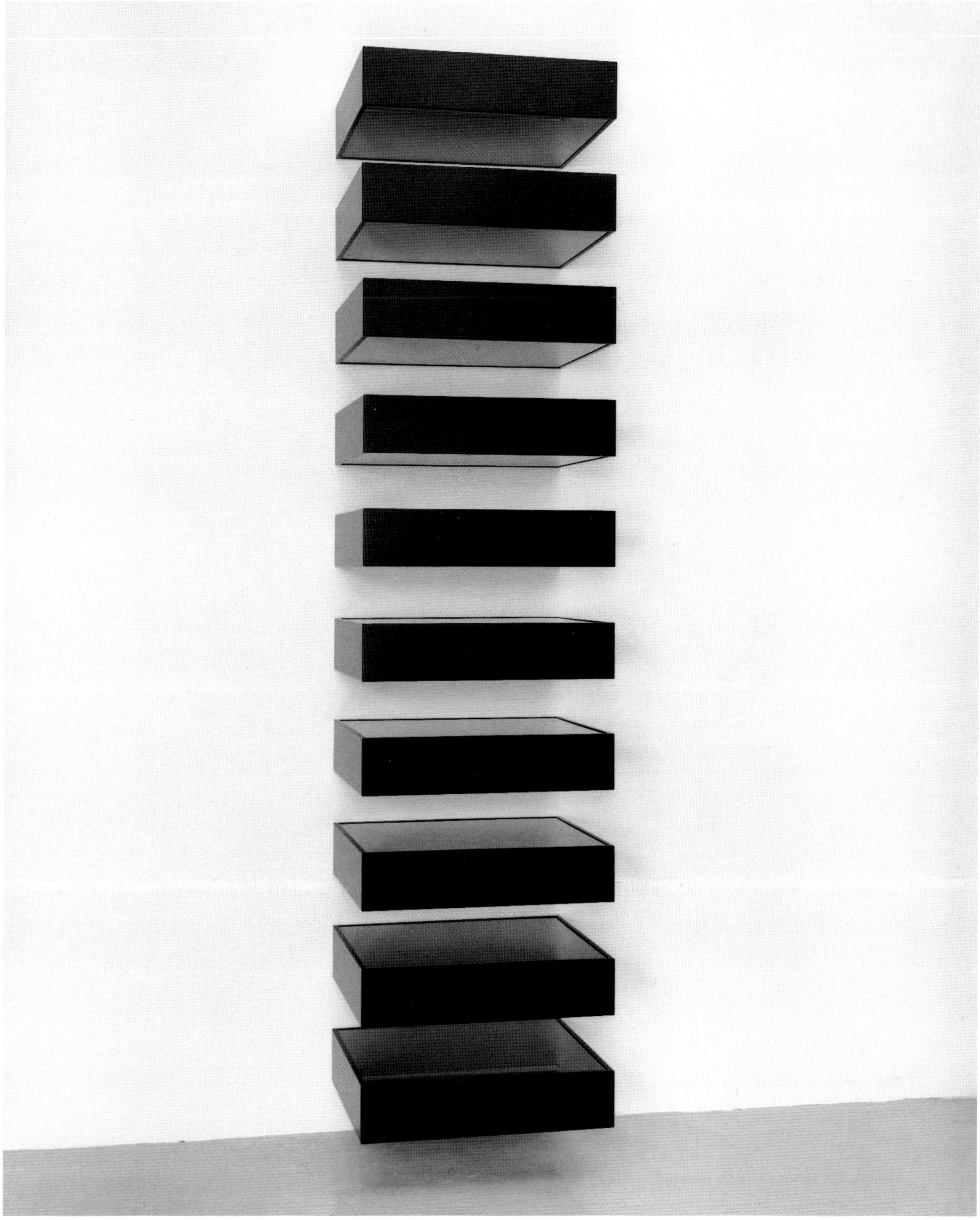

Donald Clarence Judd
**Untitled**
1990, Black anodized aluminium, bronze plexiglass, ten units, each unit: 6⅛" x 27" x 24". Photograph: Bill Jacobson. Courtesy of Pace Gallery, New York

# Paul
# **Kittelson**

Paul Kittelson's playful figures are human and animal and come in a wide range of scale and materials. From a life size chipmunk he modeled from the clay of Buffalo Bayou in Houston in 1984, to the 10-foot tall headless body builders of black rubber skin, he coaxes his forms and allows them to exist on their own terms.

"I think art exists not in the object but in the dialogue between people and the object. That's why it doesn't matter if the sculpture is permanent. The memory stays, like dance."

He does work with permanent materials sometimes, including concrete. Among the memorable works he's molded with it, is the parade of cars, one-quarter scale, he embedded in the banks of the bayou. He also shaped the Seven Dwarfs of fairy tale, and the biblical Seven Sins, from this material, perhaps alluding to their enduring moral lessons without relinquishing any of his personal wit.

Most recently, he has explored traditional plaster, albeit in characteristic untraditional ways. For his 1993 exhibition at the Art Museum of Southeast Texas in Beaumont, Kittelson used the chicken wire he normally uses purely as armature, as both the structure and form. He shaped the pliable web by wrapping it around willing friends, including his wife, sculptor Carter Ernst. He then coated the resulting silhouette by flinging brightly colored plaster and allowing it to cling to the wire like lichen on a stone. The results are surprisingly painterly.

Kittelson, born in Minnesota in 1959, received his bachelor's degree from the University of California at Santa Barbara and transferred to the University of Houston in 1982. California, he said, was too much about style "in clothes, in what you eat, even in what art looks like." At UH, he found quite the opposite. The energy of the Lawndale Annex, a warehouse off campus where senior and graduate students had their studios, was at a high point and the sense of freedom exhilarating.

Kittelson firmly believes in art that is public, and just as firmly, that it exist in a public place for an audience that may or may not know anything about art. His strong convictions have led to multiple projects in the civic as well as artistic arenas. Working in collaboration with other sculptors, especially Carter Ernst, the artist designed and built a playground featuring plaster dinosaur bones for a public elementary school, and conceived an art park on city land where artists can exhibit their work.

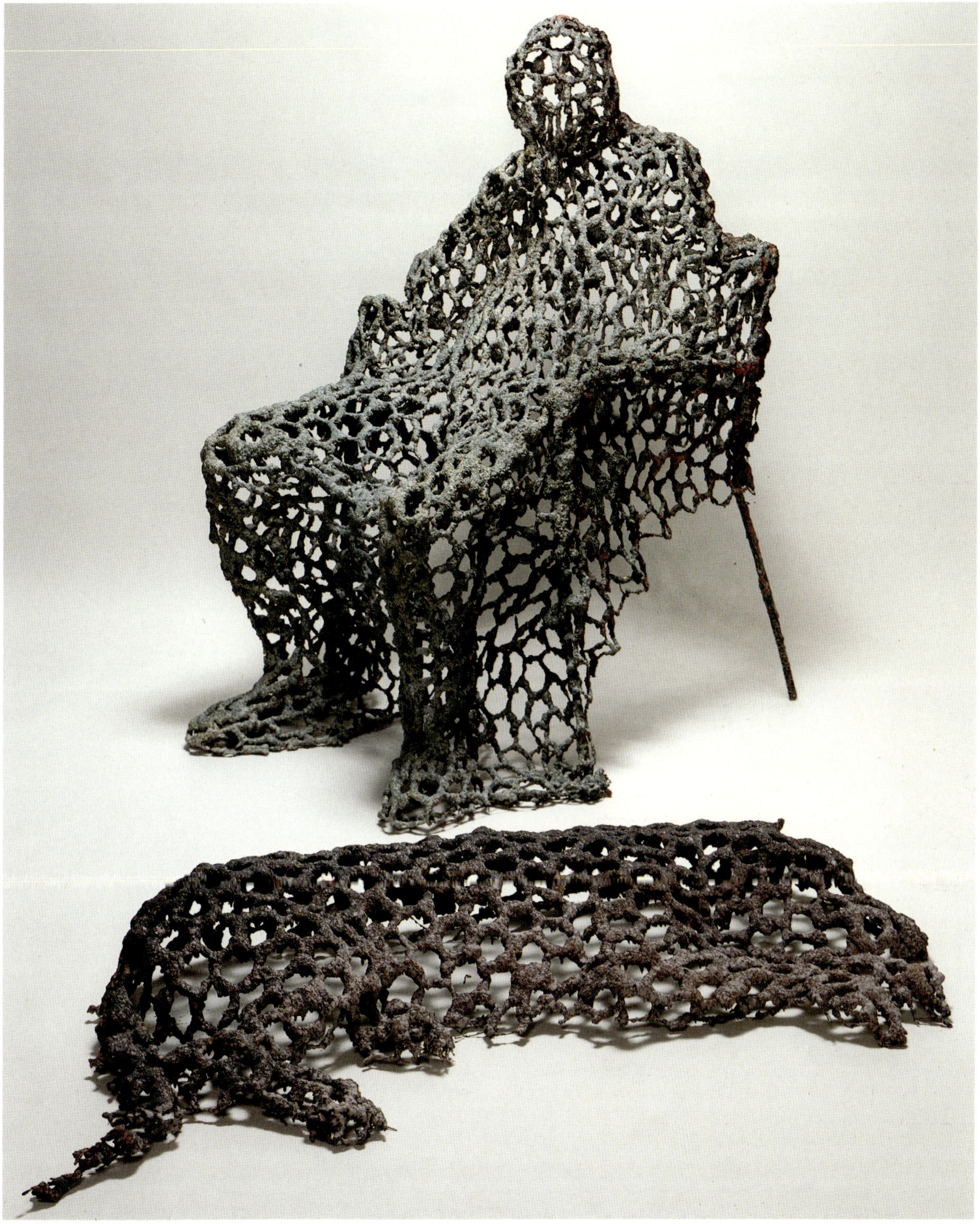

Paul Kittelson
**Noah and Earl**
1993, Hydrocal on chicken wire, 42"h x 36"w x 16"d.
Photograph: Clem Webb. Courtesy of the artist

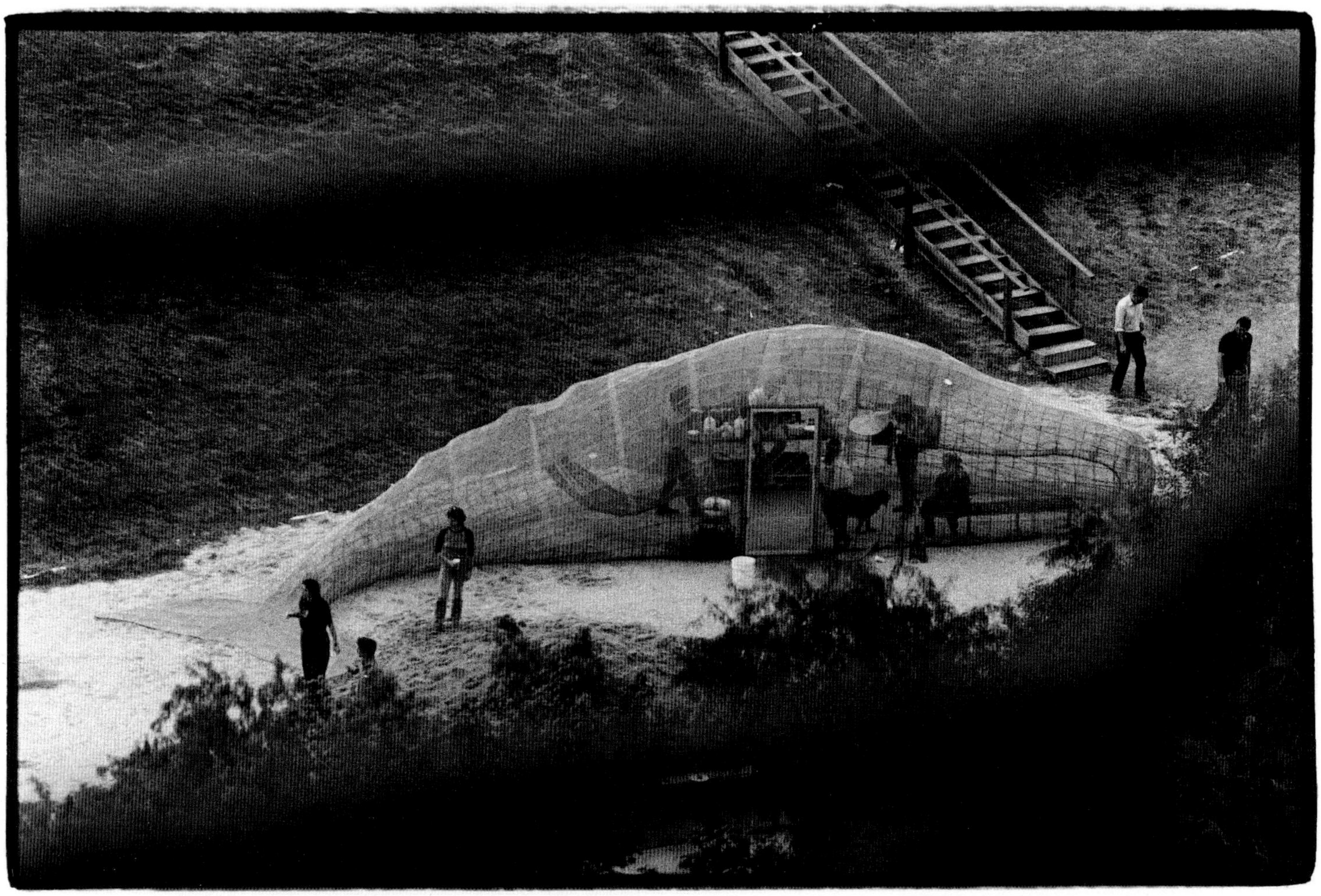

Paul Kittelson with Olin Calk

**Whale**

(Installation) 1987, Steel and window screen, 144"h x 45'l x 108"w. Collection of the artist and Carter Ernst. Courtesy of the artist

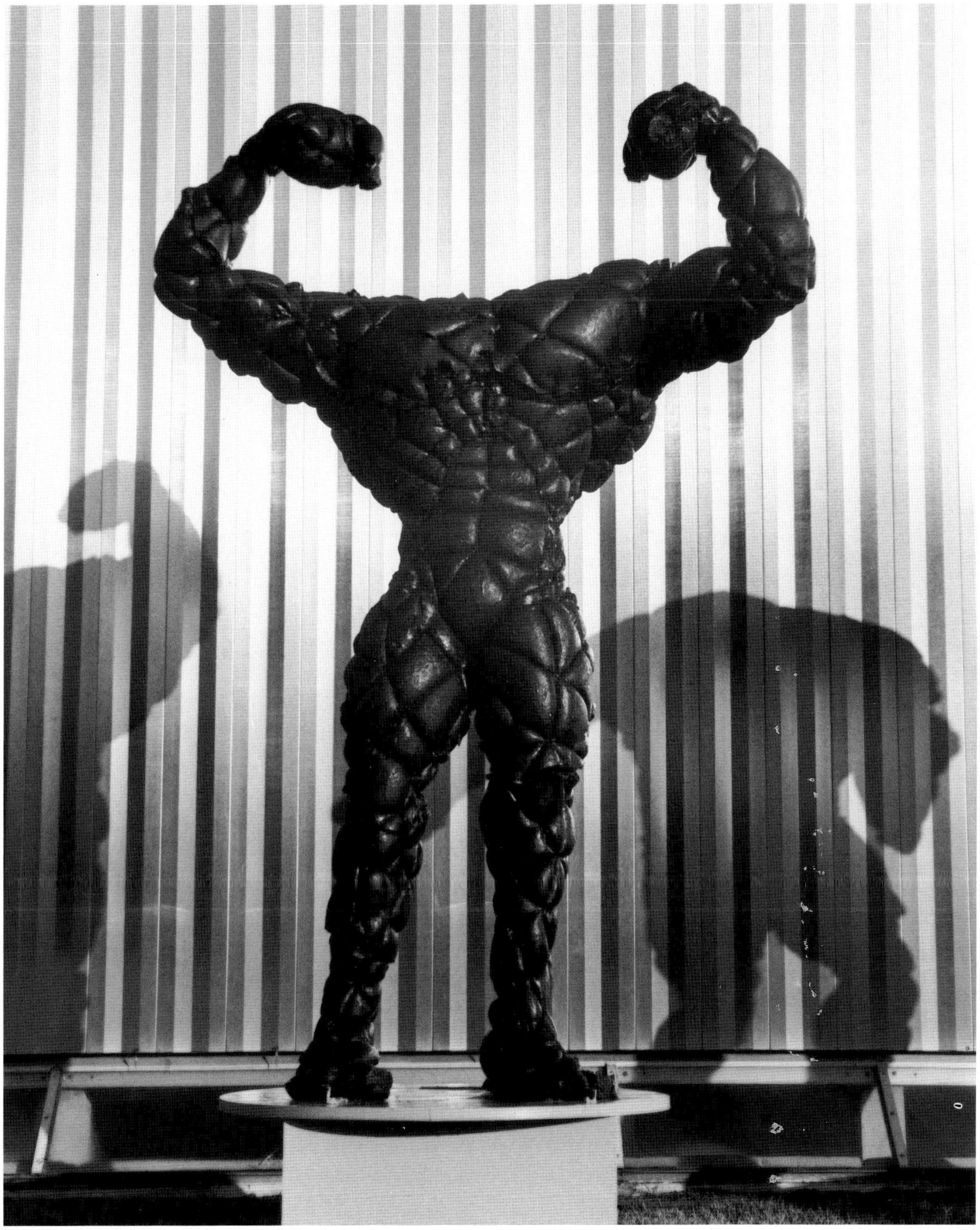

Paul Kittelson
**Mindless Competition**
1988, Steel, foam rubber, latex, 144"h x 60" x 60".
Courtesy of the artist

# Sharon **Kopriva**

Sharon Kopriva received her master's degree from the University of Houston in 1981 after a hiatus of nearly ten years. She concentrated on painting, landscapes primarily, working evenings that followed full days of teaching in public school. A visit to the ancient ruins of the Inca in Peru, however, opened her eyes to the possibilities of sculpture. Mummies ensconced in niches carved from the rock face near Cuzco left an indelible mark on her mind's eye. The dry and brittle remnants of human life from centuries ago, Kopriva says, "were beautiful. They weren't frightening. But they make you think about your own mortality."

In her studio in Houston, the memory of those desiccated figures began to insinuate themselves into her paintings. The fragility and texture she remembered appeared as timid reliefs made from clay and glued or sewn to her canvas. They asserted themselves gradually, becoming increasingly complex as she began to attach actual bones and cloth, their clotted mass and greater weight demanding stronger supports. By 1986, her mummy-like figures were as fully sculptural as they were powerful reminders of life's mysterious but inevitable destiny.

"Death is confronted as a question of the phenomenology and transcendence of the spirit. Kopriva treats death as a primordial condition that takes place under the sign of the known and the unknown."[1]

She taught herself the mechanics of building in three dimensions. Her painting background had not prepared her for it, but assemblage was quite natural. Using hardware like tomato cages and lumber, Kopriva built the armatures for the fragile figures she composes with gauze, glue, paint and bones.

As the physical demands of her heavily textured figures, singly and in groups, increased, so did their religious specificity. Her Catholic upbringing led her to literally objectify the remembered rituals and those who performed them. Bishops and nuns become vessels through which Kopriva continues to probe the duality of life and death, the transformation of matter into spirit, and her private investigations of belief.

"My work often depicts the contradictions between formal religion and nature. It is not intended to be a negative statement about death, but an exploration of it as a form of change or transformation."[2]

1. Bloom, Suzanne, and Hill, Ed. "Review: Sharon Kopriva", *Art Forum*, May 1989
2. *Fresh Paint*, p. 144

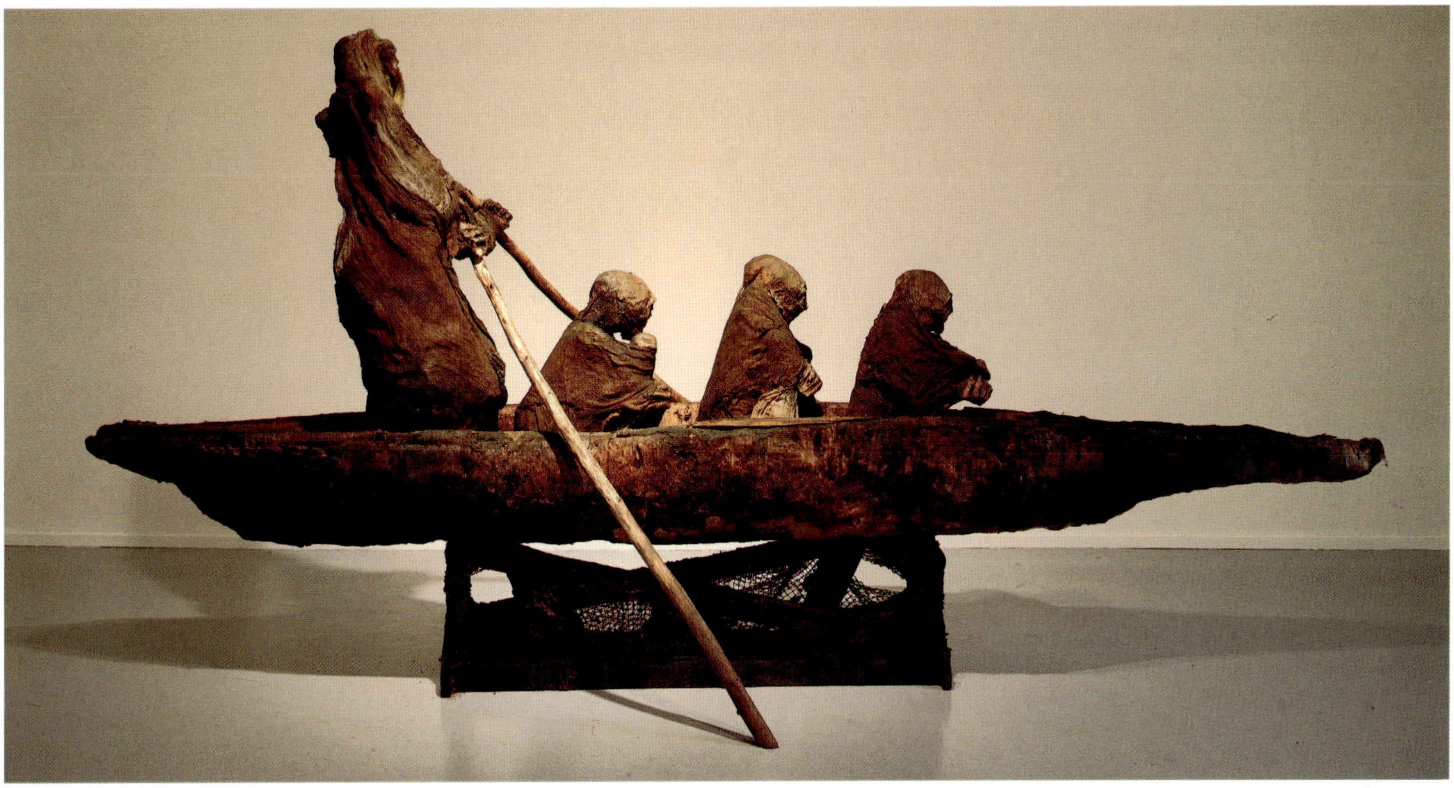

Sharon Kopriva

**Rite of Passage**

1991, Mixed media: papier-mâché, bone, wood, cloth, 60"h x 132"l x 72". Collection: Edward and Nancy Reddin Kienholz, Hope, Idaho. Courtesy of the artist

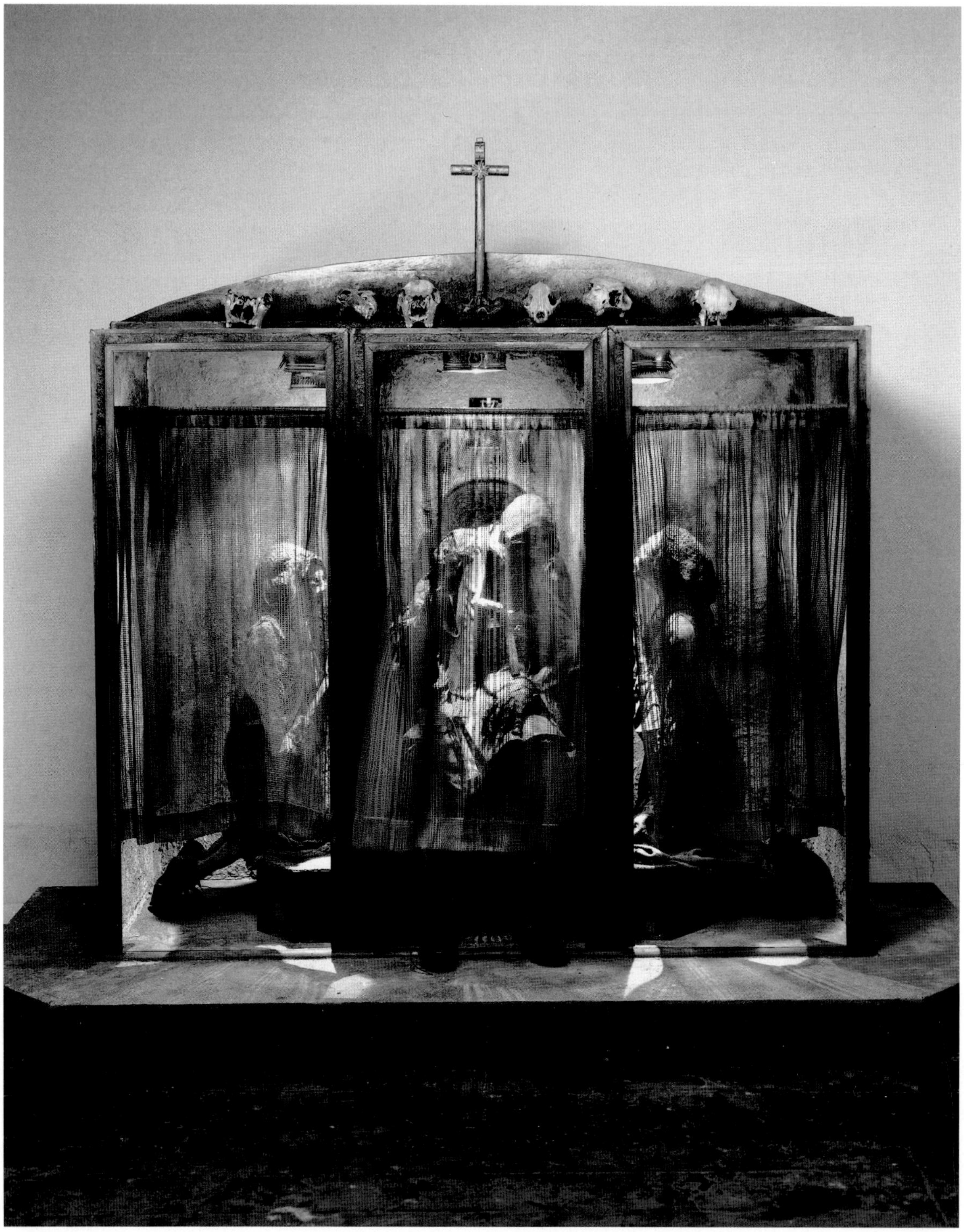

Sharon Kopriva
**The Confessional**
1992, Mixed media: wood, papier-mâché, fiberglass, bone, 84"h x 96"w x 36"d. Collection: Edmund Pillsbury Collection, Fort Worth. Courtesy of the artist

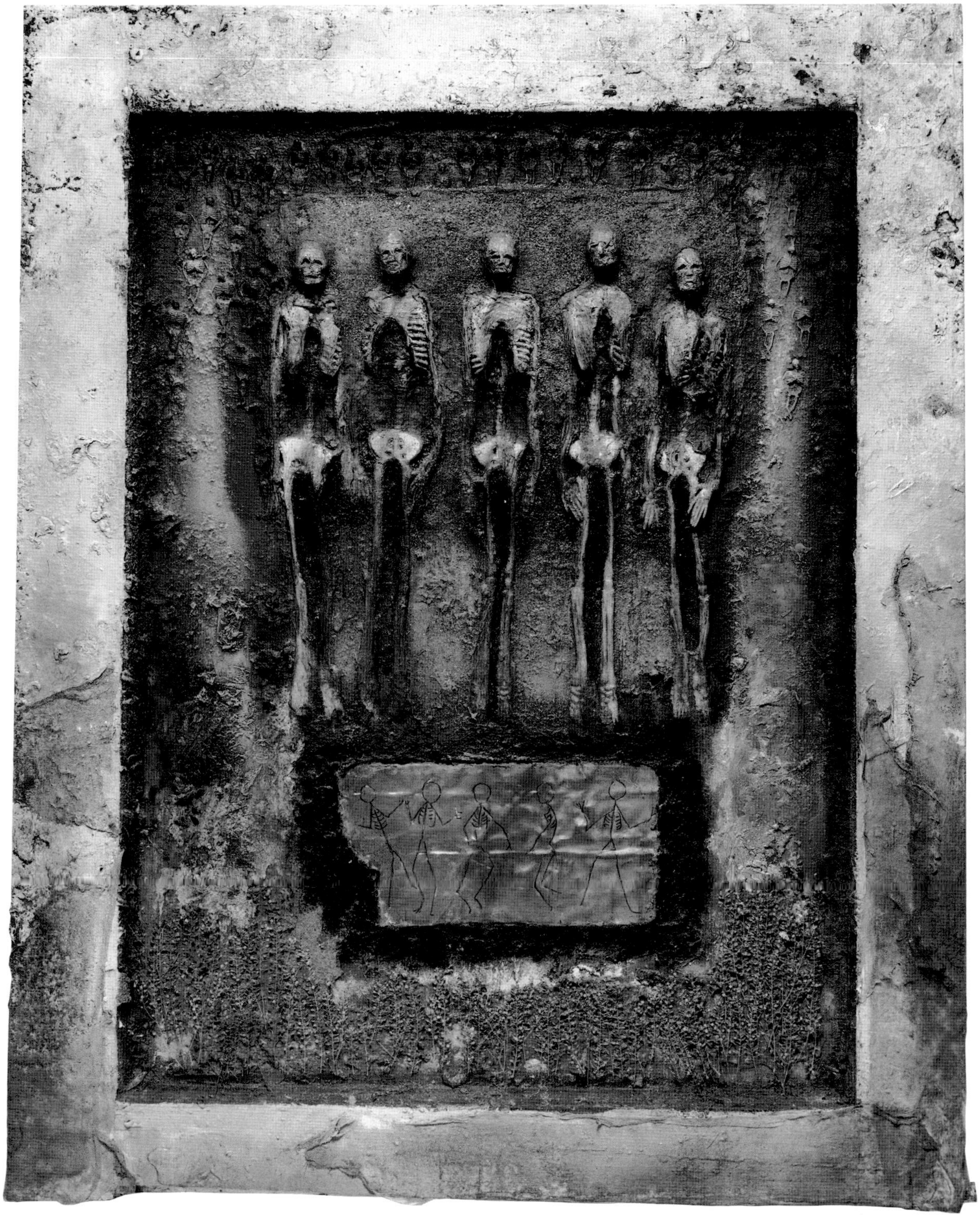

Sharon Kopriva
**Five that Jive**
1993, Mixed media, wall relief, 46"h x 36"w x 3"d.
Courtesy of the artist

# George **Krause**

For more than three decades now, photographer George Krause has focused his camera on classic subjects — people, places and things. But the sensuous, beautifully toned silver gelatin prints are quirky as often as iconic, and funny as frequently as mysterious. He remembers going to art school while his friends played football in the working class neighborhood of his native Philadelphia. He won scholarships to the Philadelphia College of Art and kept winning prizes in drawing and sculpture. He was 20 years old and serving in the U.S. Army when he picked up his first camera in 1957. The experience, he says, was "like being on fire"[1], but when he returned to college, it was to study everything else.

Nonetheless, Krause began the first of four major series he continues to explore. A retrospective in 1991 organized by the Museum of Fine Arts, Houston, pulled the work together for the first time.

"[Krause] relishes the drama embodied in changing appearances as well as using physical transformation as a metaphor for emotional or spiritual change. Most of Krause's images are too evocative to accept on literal terms alone. His work is perpetually relevant because his issues are basic and vital to the human condition."[2]

The untitled group of life on the streets portrays children and old people, men, women, rich and poor, going about their business in Philadelphia, in Barcelona, in Rome. *I Nudi* deals with the human body as an expressive language of its own. He poses lithesome female models and his own body in compositions ranging from a humorous alphabet to allegories and illusive transformations. The third group, titled *Qui Riposa*, consists of alluring pictures of gravestones and markers from the ancient cemeteries of Italy. The series, *Saints and Martyrs*, cuts a broad portrait of religious rituals and icons in the world's Catholic countries, especially in Spain and in Mexico, that are sometimes horrifying and other times awesomely moving.

In spite of the early lack of promise in the field, by the time Krause came to Houston in 1975 to help shape the department of photography for the University of Houston, he had an international reputation that included nearly every national and international prize in the medium. His presence in Texas was critical. The department of photography was being formed at the museum, and students whose prior photography option had been within the journalism or advertising departments, discovered a master for a teacher in the fine arts.

1. Cited in "The Artist", by Patricia C. Johnson, *Houston Chronicle*, August 5, 1984
2. Tucker, Anne W., *George Krause*, Rice University Press, 1991, p. 17, 18

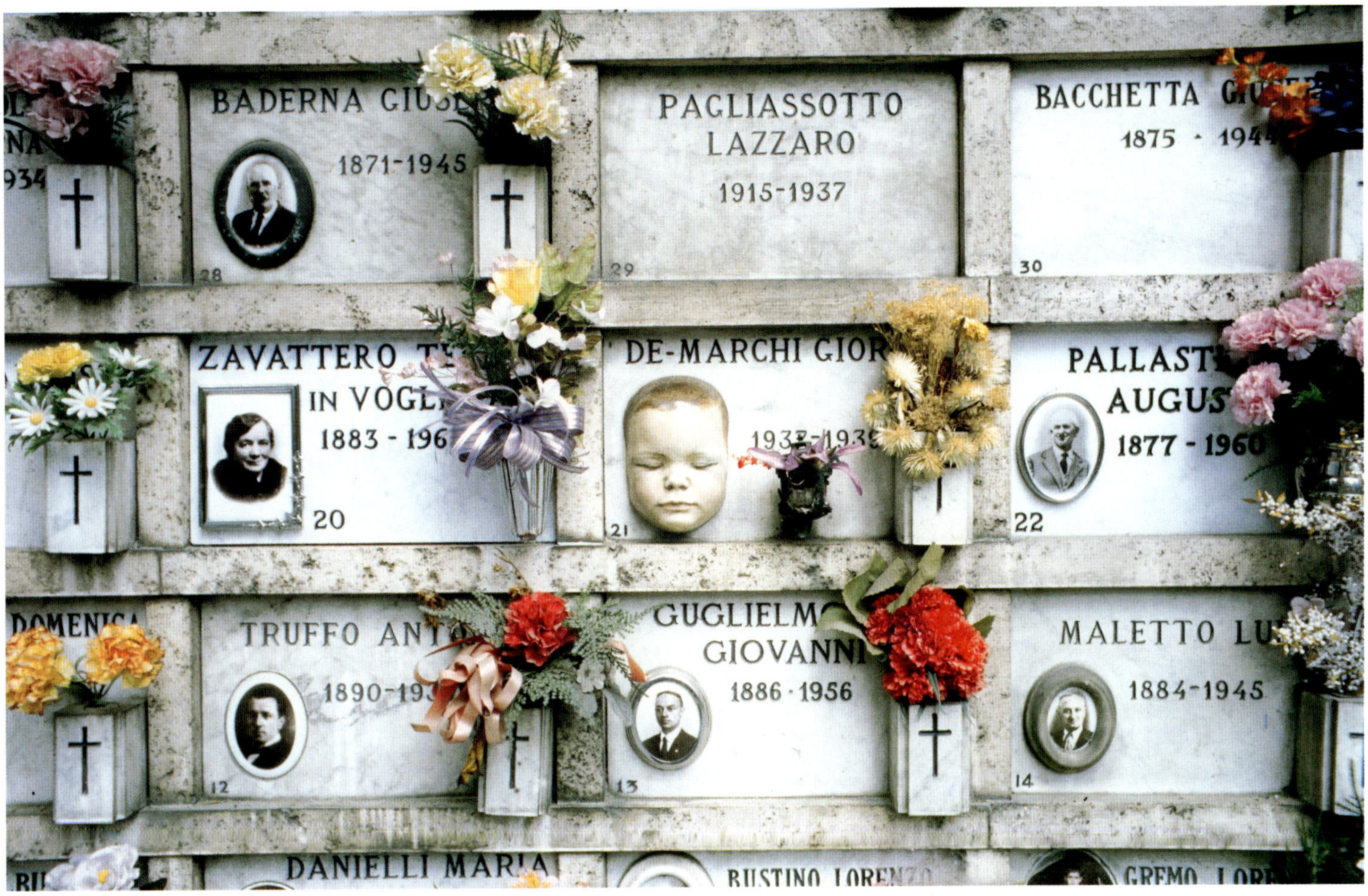


George Krause
**Untitled ("Infant Death Mask" from Qui Riposa series)**
1980, Cibachrome, 5" x 7". Courtesy of the artist

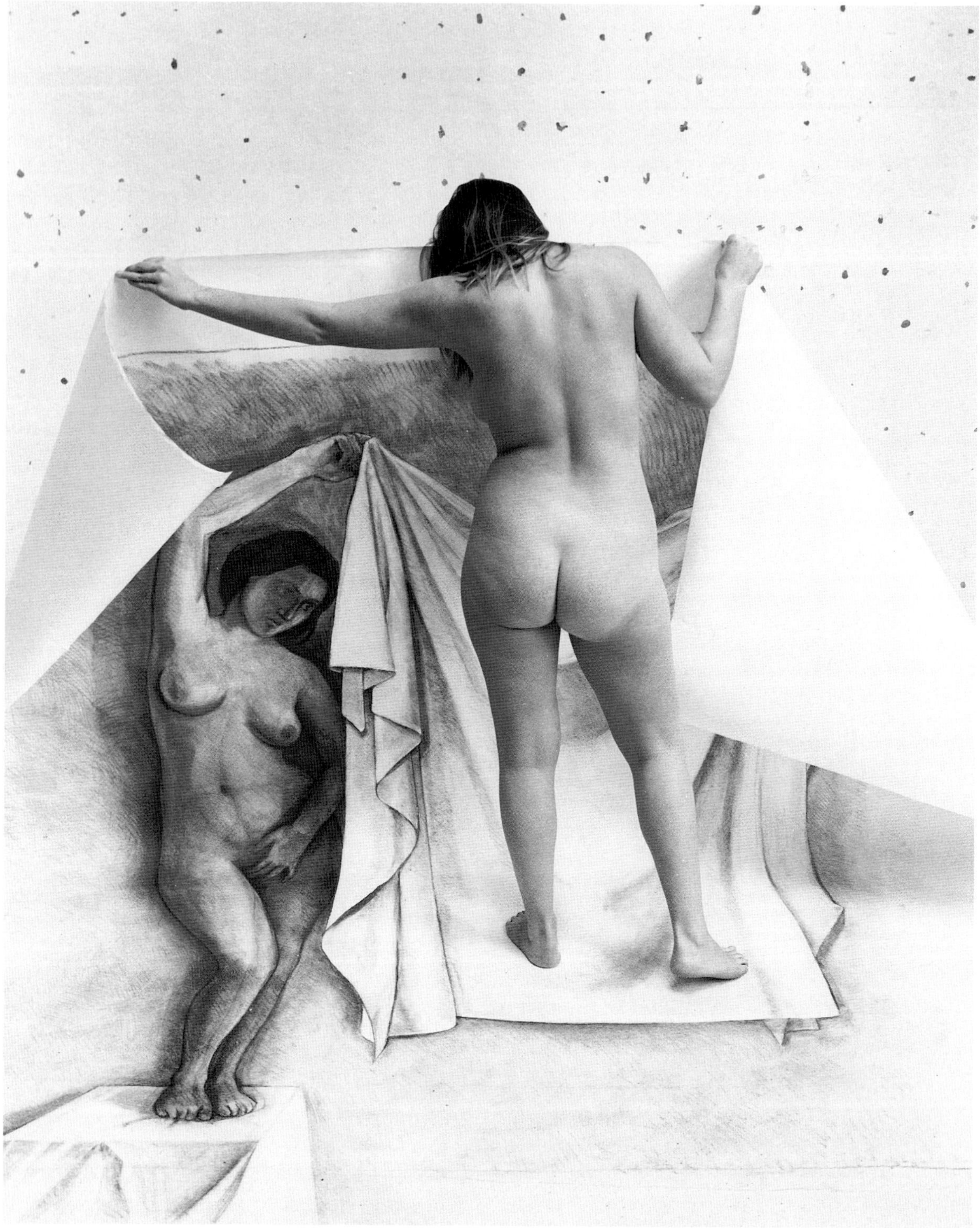

George Krause
**Drawing, Rome**
1980, Toned silver gelatin, 20" x 16". Courtesy of the artist

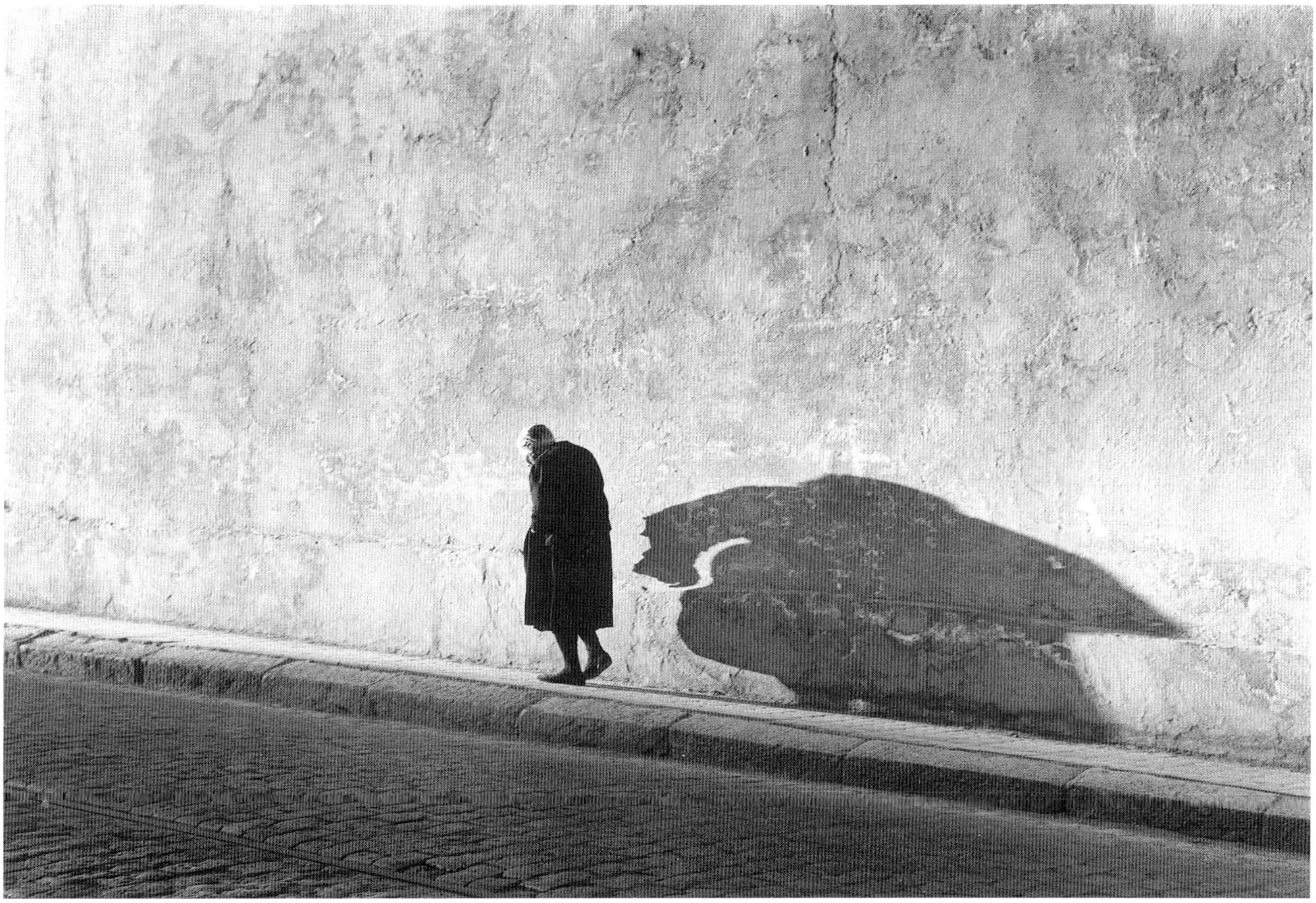

George Krause
**Shadow**
1964, Toned silver gelatin. Courtesy of the artist

# Jean
# **Lacy**

Jean Lacy, like John Biggers, came to Texas early in her career and helped change the ground rules for blacks in the community. Born in Washington D.C. in 1932, she was introduced at an early age to the writings of black philosophers and educators, including Alain Locke and W.E.B. DuBois. Her formal training is in art education, from Southern University in Baton Rouge, Louisiana. When she moved to Dallas in the early 1970s, Lacy pursued additional studies in museum education at Southern Methodist University. After the sophistication of the black communities she knew, moving to Texas was a culture shock.

"I worked in several urban churches in Los Angeles during the 1960s. My husband and I were very active in the civil rights movement, and of course, this was at the time of the Watts riots. Before that, I had been in Louisiana, and raised in Washington D.C. A lot of creative things happened at the SMU campus, but Dallas still wasn't like any place I had lived."

The urban experience lies at the heart of Lacy's fragile collages and small constructions. She combines history, humor and street smart observation in constructing the works. The delicacy and surface beauty of the paper works belie the multifaceted content of the African and African-American history and culture as experienced in urban tenements and on the streets. The comic aspects of the small constructions, too, disguise the subtle irony in reliquary or toy-like forms.

Although she has been creating the narrative compositions from the time she was in Los Angeles, it wasn't until 1988 that her artistic career took flight. She crossed two important thresholds that year. First, she resigned her positions in the Dallas Independent School District after nearly two decades of teaching high school and thirteen years as director of the district's African-American Cultural Heritage Center, to dedicate herself entirely to her art. Second, she was prominently featured in the traveling exhibition "Black Art: Ancestral Legacy". Organized by the Dallas Museum of Art, the exhibition explored art by black artists in the 20th century United States and the Caribbean, in a range of styles from folk to conceptual. For Lacy, it was the first significant exposure to a national and mainstream audience.

In 1993, she completed a commission for 53 windows, averaging 3 feet by 6 feet each, of faceted glass for the new St. Luke United Methodist Church in Dallas. Instead of designing the traditional religious compositions, she chose instead, to "deal with the Civil Rights movement, with the historical, cultural and biblical presence of black people."

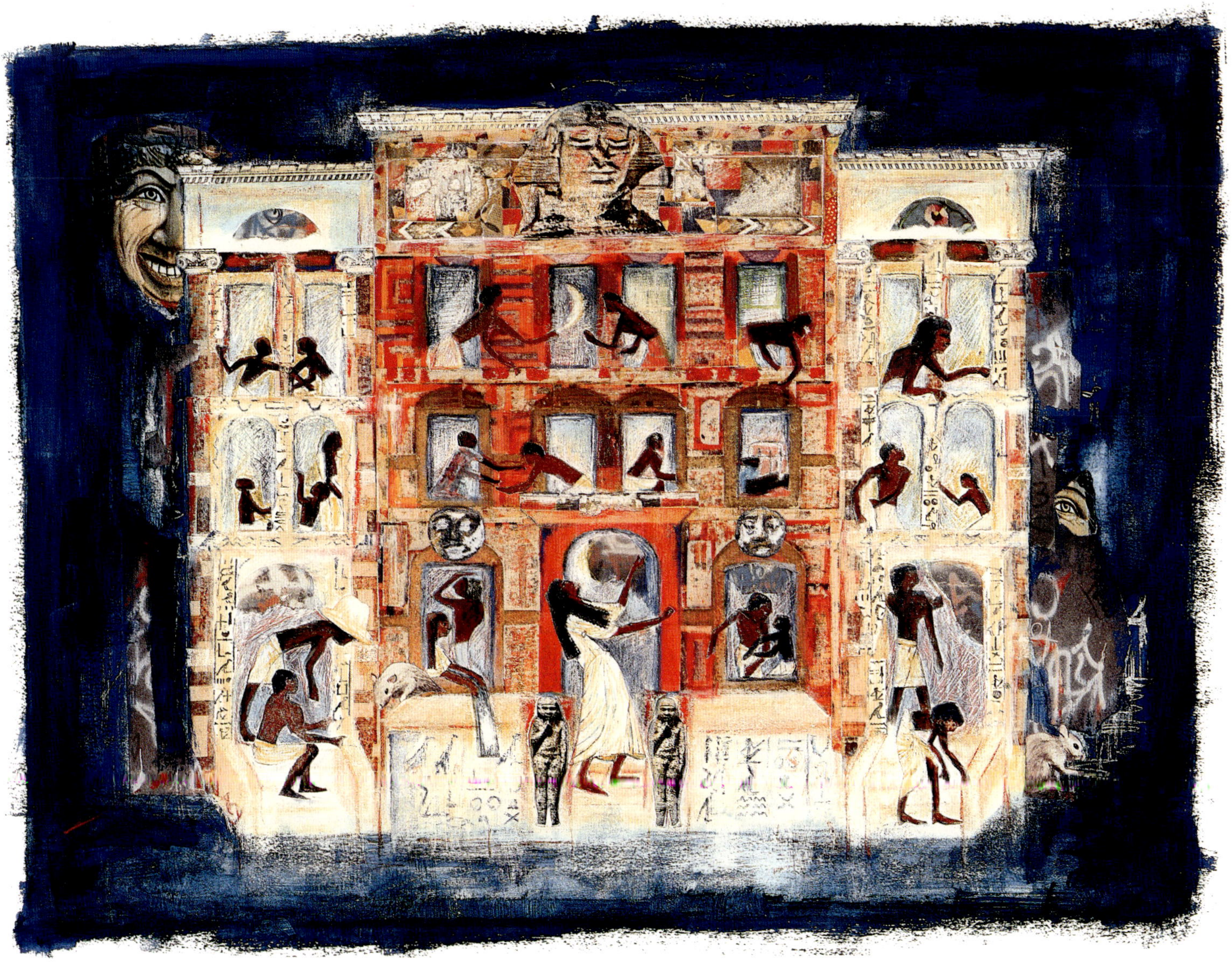

Jean Lacy

**Little Egypt Condo/New York City**

1987, Mixed media on museum board, 10½" x 13½".
Collection: Dallas Museum of Art, gift of Dallas
Links, Inc. Courtesy of the artist

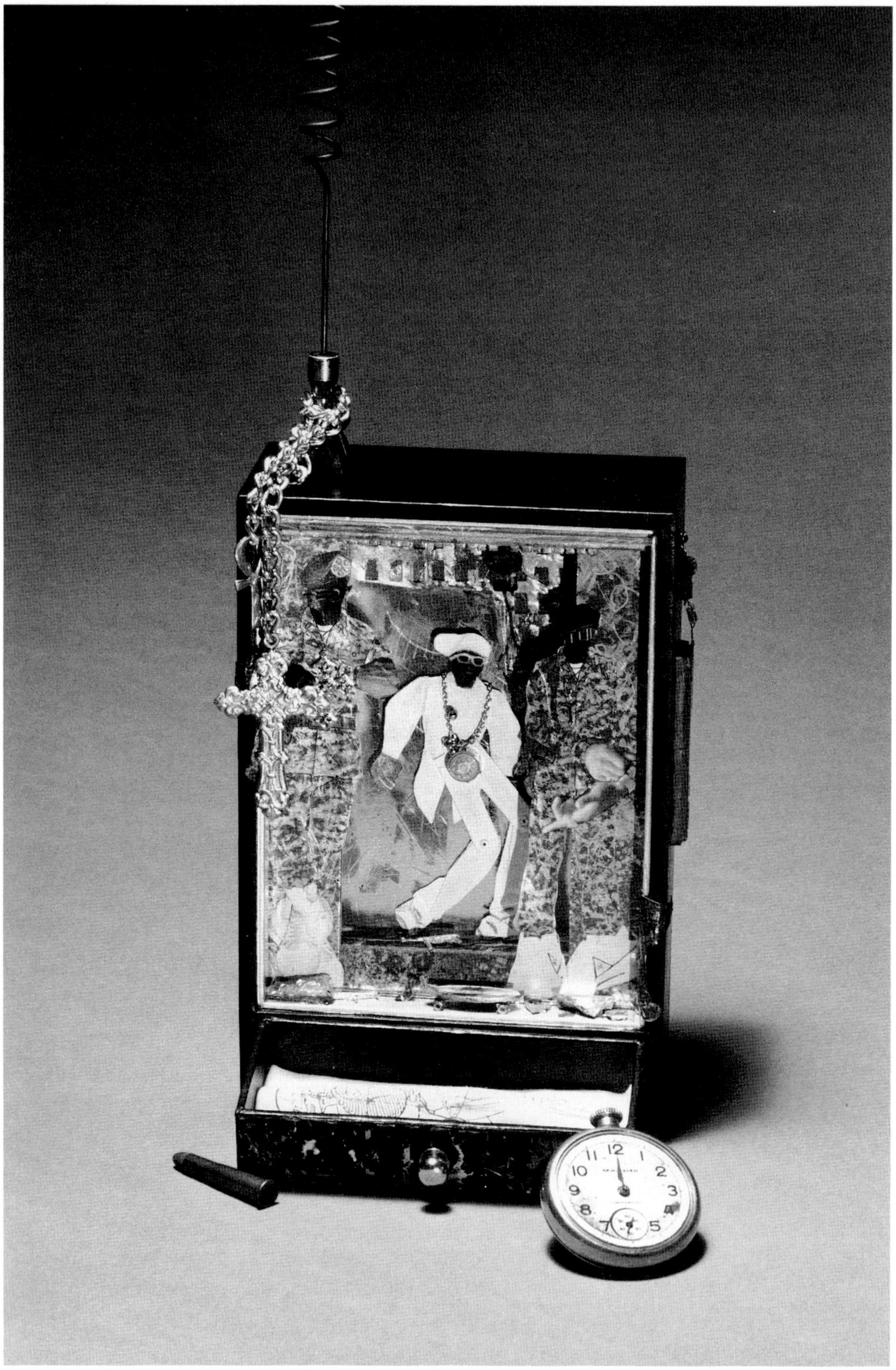

Jean Lacy

**Wake Up and Smell the Real Flavor**

1990, Mixed media: animated music box,
8¼"h x 5½"w x 2¾"d. Courtesy of the artist

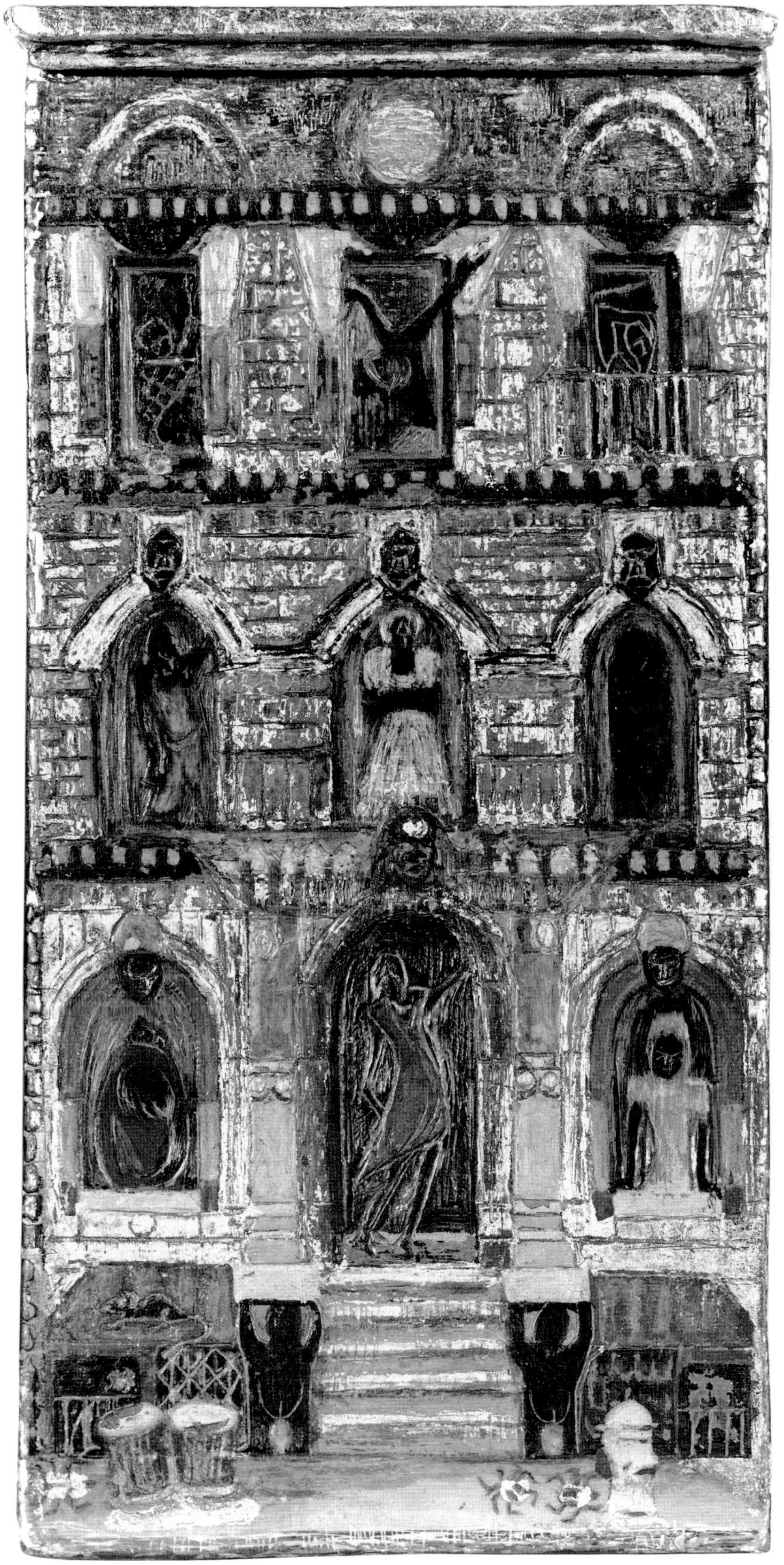

Jean Lacy
**Welcome to My Ghetto Land**
1986, Mixed media on wood panel, 6⅛"h x 3"w x ⅝"d. Photograph: Tom Jenkins. Collection: Dallas Museum of Art, Metropolitan Life Foundation Purchase Grant. Courtesy of the Dallas Museum of Art

# Jesse
# **Lott**

Jesse Lott discovered the entertainment and economic value of discarded paper as a kid growing up in one of Houston's low income neighborhoods. He made papier-mâché figures and sold them to neighbors and relatives for enough coins to pay for a movie or buy sweets. As a young man in his 20s, making these objects became the path of economic sustenance.

Lott constructs a diverse cast of characters intuitively. He twists rebar and various gauge wires including industrial cable and the copper strands of commercial electrical wire, into bristling life-size people and animals, and smaller, fetish-like forms adorned with shiny bits of glass, plastic and leather. When he works in assemblage, however, Lott retains the integrity of the cast-offs found in the city streets and dumpsters. In words that echo fellow sculptor/assemblagist Jim Love, Lott waits for the perfect part to "show up" to complete the envisioned shape.

"You always observe, otherwise you don't know anything. You learn to make decisions based on your observations [and] if the observation is good from the beginning, it's not necessary to modify the found material."

Born in Louisiana in 1943, Lott came to Houston with his father in the late 1950s, when the city was booming. The family moved again in the sixties, this time to Los Angeles. After two years in state and city colleges, Lott enrolled at the Otis Art Institute and played jazz late nights at Shelly Mann's Hole, (closed in 1970). But the late sixties were the time of great social and political unrest. There were riots in Los Angeles, and Lott was radicalized by the civil rights movement.

"I was swept up into it," he recalled in a 1989 interview, "till I wised up and stopped being a fool. To make positive changes, you don't set up yourself in opposition to the government. You make positive changes by changing people's lives. As artists, we have to try to solve some of the big problems."[1]

Making paper sculptures became a political act. Paper is free, Lott says, so anyone can use it as a tool of self-expression and as a means to economic sufficiency. He keeps an open-door policy at his studio in one of Houston's poorest neighborhoods that attracts area residents, especially children. They help him sort the raw material for assemblages, and learn through participation as much as by example. Lott begins with armatures made from cardboard cones, adding multiple layers of paper gradually, shaping archetypal figures ranging in size from less than 12 inches in height to ten feet. Their relative simplicity belies Lott's subversive intent. He calls his technique the *piñatero* method, a term derived from the Spanish *piñata* — the festive clay and paper toy children smash to get at the candies and fruits hidden inside. It's an apt metaphor.

1. Cited in "Jesse Lott and the art of transformation", by Patricia C. Johnson, *Houston Chronicle*, Zest Magazine, November 12, 1989, p. 14

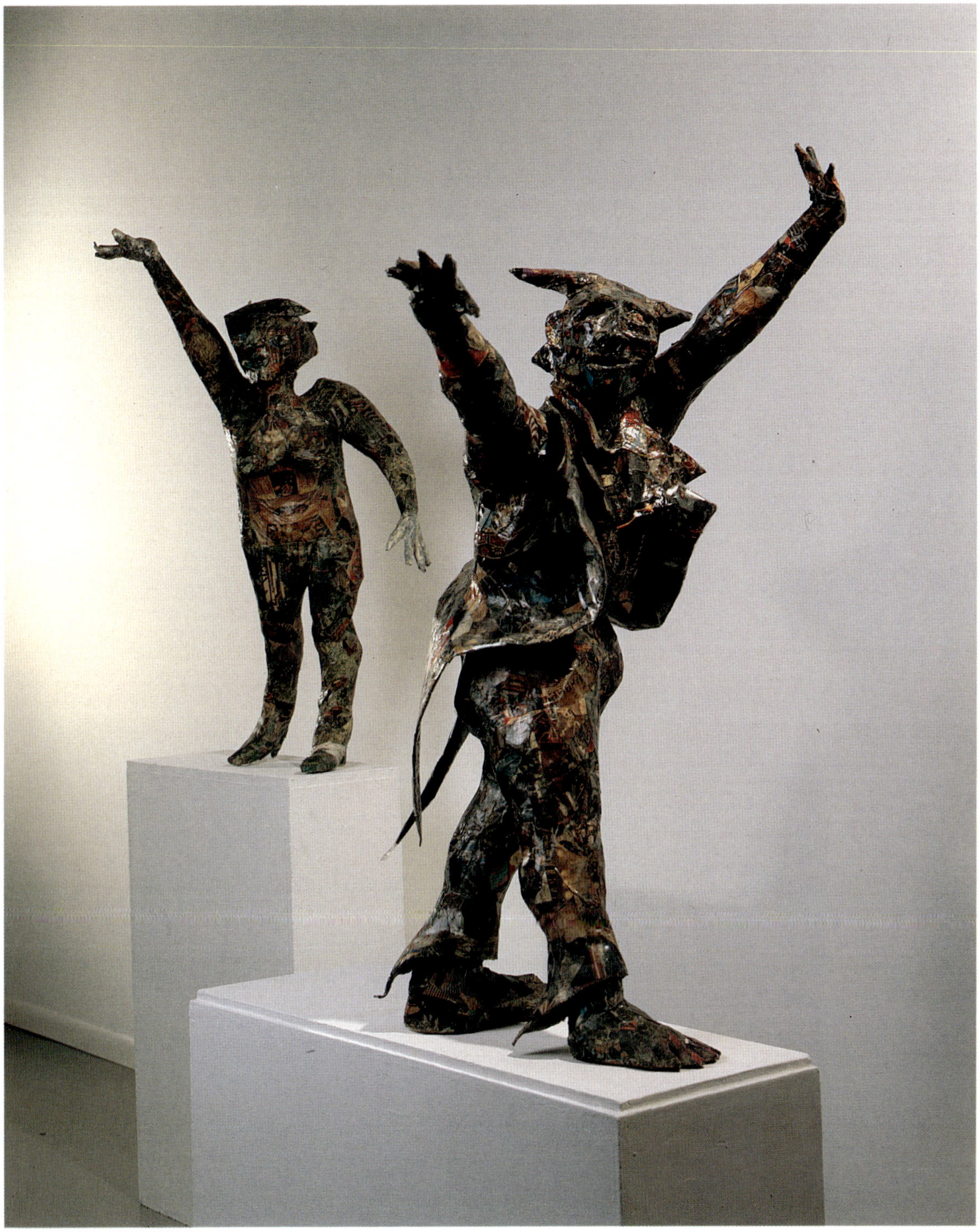

Jesse Lott

**Piñatero Figures**

1983–84, Papier-mâché, Front: 48"h. Collection: James Surls and Charmaine Locke, Splendora, Texas; Back: 36"h. Collection: Harriet Lott, Los Angeles. Photograph: Louie Psihoyos. Courtesy of the artist

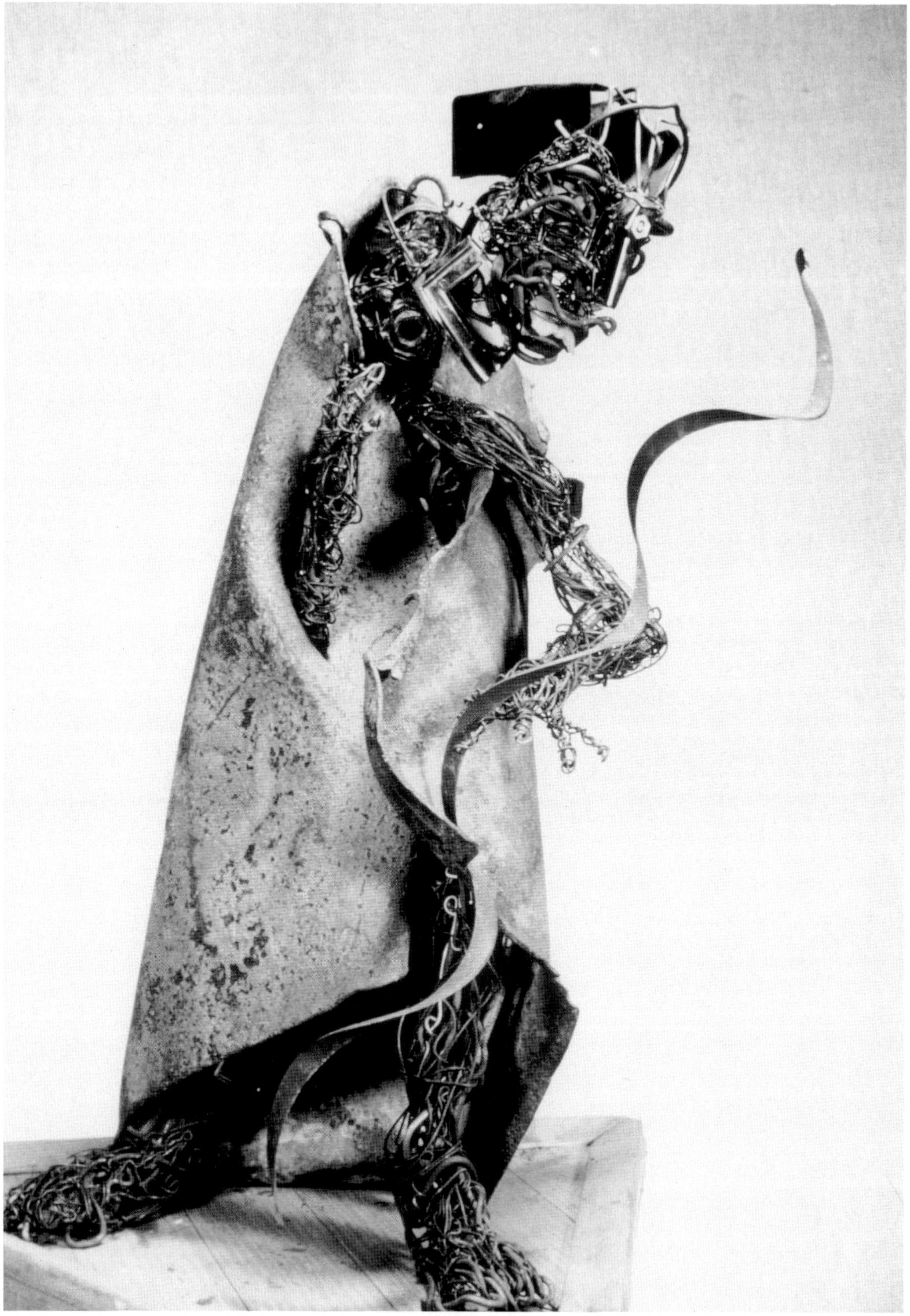

Jesse Lott
**Hierophant**
1983, Mixed metal, glass, 25"h. Collection: Robin and William Lodin, Houston. Courtesy of the artist

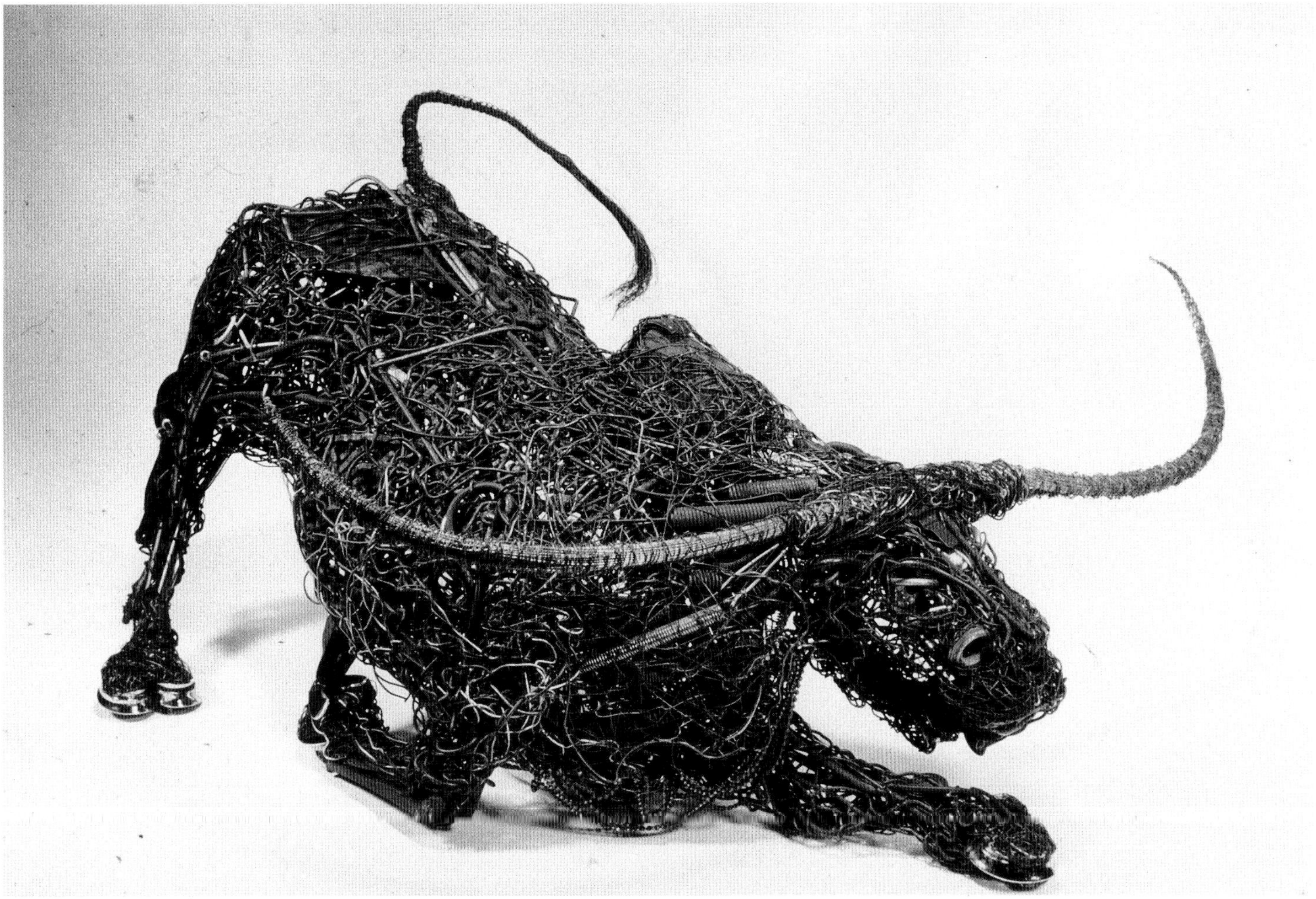

Jesse Lott
**Bull**
1976, Mixed metal and found objects,
32"h x 42"w x 42"d. Collection: Vivian Ayres,
Mt Vernon, New York. Courtesy of the artist

# Jim
# Love

Jim Love has always insisted he got into art "sideways". He was aiming for a degree (which he did get) in business administration at Baylor University in Waco, Texas, when his girlfriend, a theater major, and Roy Fridge, introduced him to the magic of make-believe. Love got involved with making sets for Paul Burke's little avant-garde theater in Dallas. A job as lighting director for the fledgling (established in 1947) Alley Theater brought him to Houston in 1953.

Jermayne MacAgy in the meantime had been hired by John and Dominique de Menil as the first professional director of the Contemporary Art Association in Houston, now the Contemporary Arts Museum. A call from her in 1956 asking Love to assist as preparator, changed the course of his life. He was 28 years old and claims to this day he doesn't know how she got his name.

However that happened, he was working with what he calls "fantastic stuff" — paintings and sculpture by the masters of modernism and surrealism that were MacAgy's and the de Menils' forte. He wanted to learn how to "do stuff", and taught himself to weld. His exceptional eye had led him to discover, too, the poetry hidden in the junk heaps of a rapidly growing city. A faucet looked like the head of a bird, and a hoe like that of a bear. Gears from the motor of an antiquated tractor were potential blossoms in a giant, metallic bouquet.

The hybrids gleaned from the junk heaps gave away to the clean intentionality of welded steel in the mid 1970s and most recently, to bronze. But the process of discovering the form, whether for a monumental public sculpture or one scaled to the human hand, is similar. The chaos through which he swims to reach the purity of what he envisions, and the philosophical difficulties of explaining life, disappear in his concise, immaculately crafted sculptures. Their peculiar beauty and economy of form distract one from the complexity of their genesis.

It pains him to verbalize, for every thought engenders its opposite and its corollary. In his sculpture, Love ably compresses them into inarguable wholeness.

"In my world, there's less planning than might be thought to have happened. You keep shuffling things and try to stay alert for whatever it is that might pop up. We want tomorrow to bring full pardons, good weather, timely magic, instant wisdom, and occasionally a white horse. I am one of those for whom the fact that it seldom does, never kills the hope."[1]

1. Cited in "Jim Love", by Patricia C. Johnson, *Houston Chronicle*, Zest Magazine, July 7, 1985, p. 16

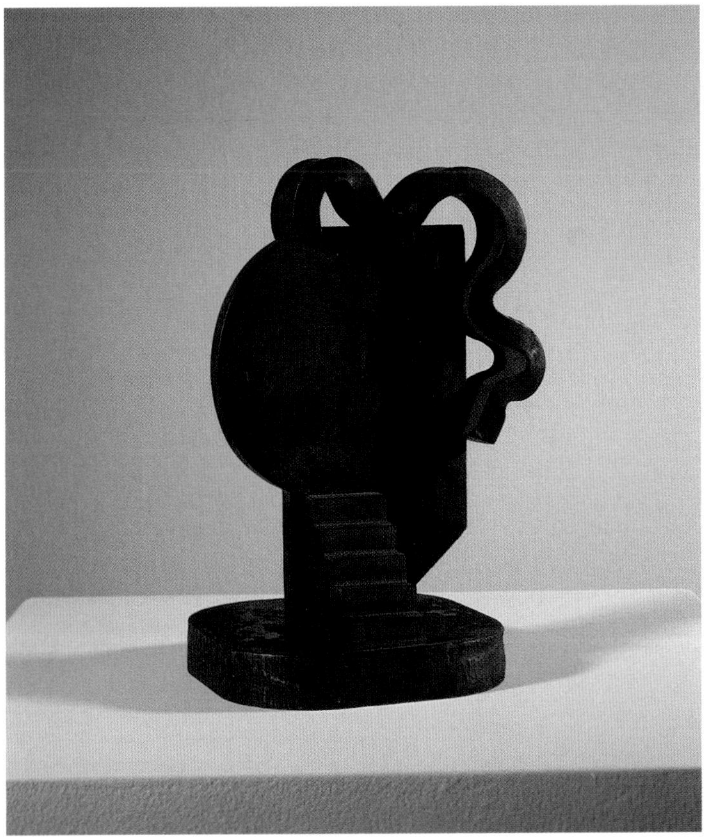

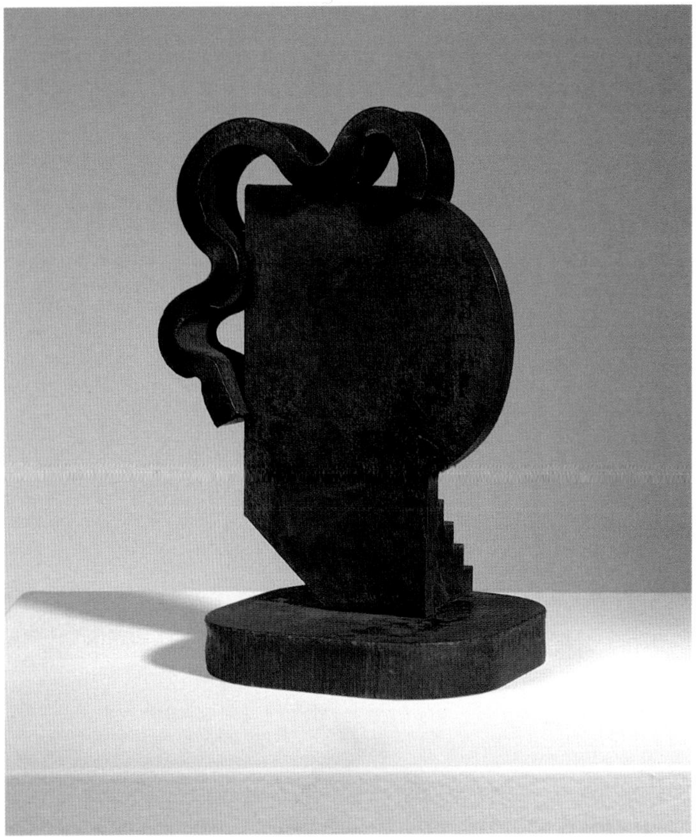

Jim Love
**"Portrait" two views**
1993, Steel, $10^{3}/_{8}$"h x $7^{1}/_{4}$"w x $5^{3}/_{4}$"d. Courtesy of Moody Gallery, Houston

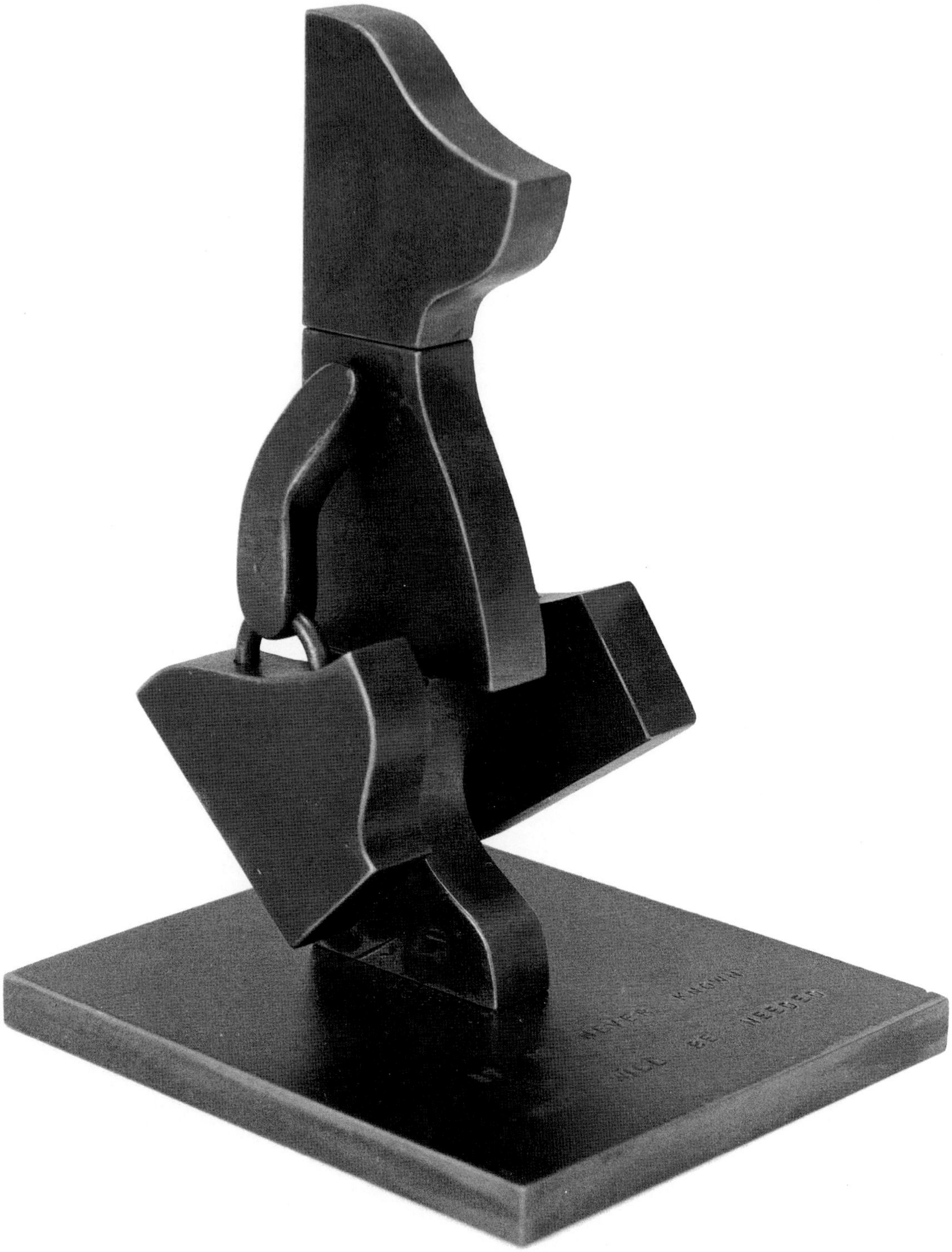

Jim Love

**It Is Never Known What Will Be Needed**

1984, Steel, $4\frac{3}{8}$"h x 4"w x $6\frac{3}{8}$"d. Photograph: Vincent Gargotta. Courtesy of Janie C. Lee Gallery, Houston

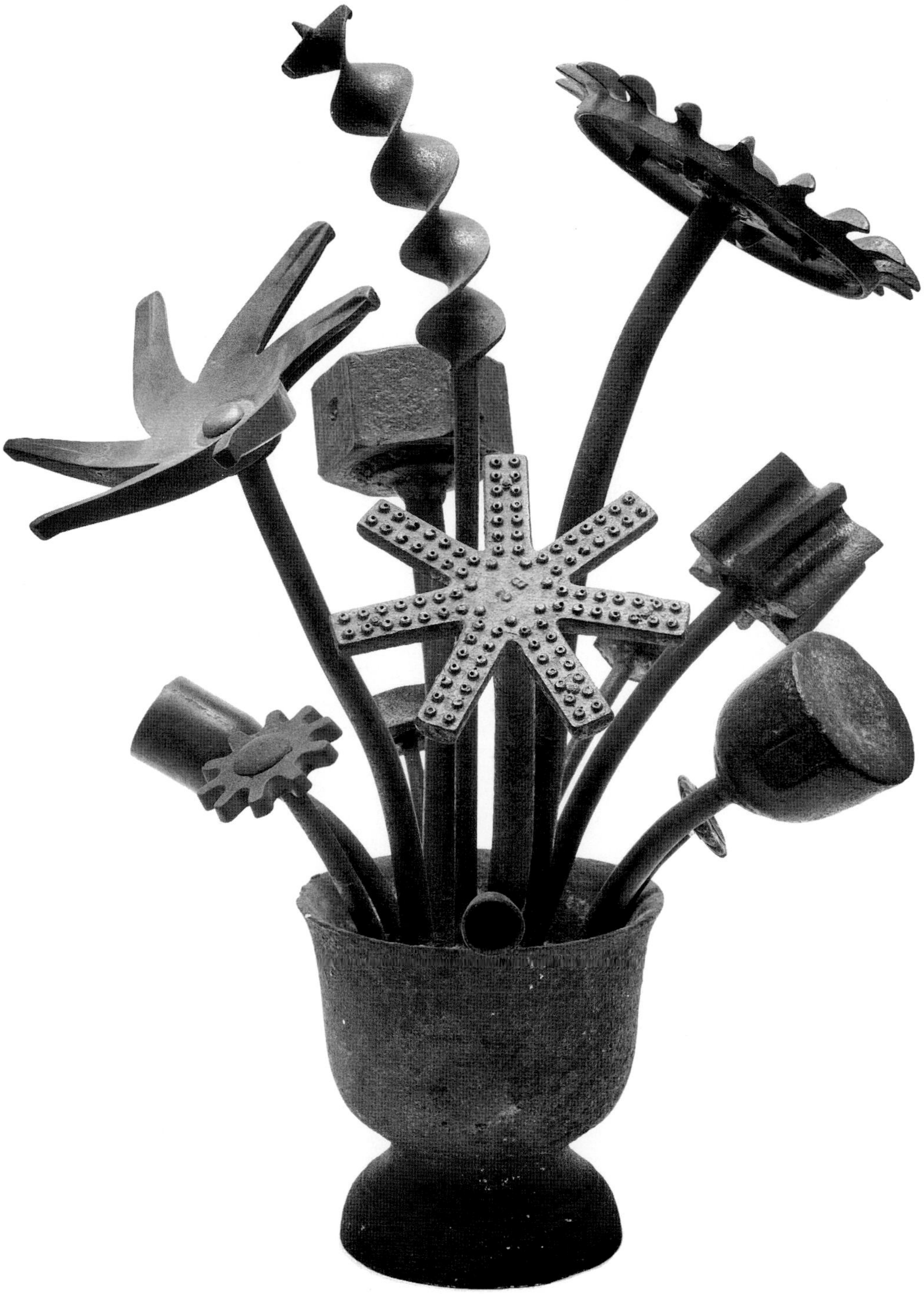

Jim Love
**Flowers**
1965, Steel and cast iron, 27⅝"h x 19" x 17½"d.
Photograph: Hickey-Roberston, Houston. Collection: The Menil Collection, Houston. Courtesy of The Menil Collection, Houston

# David **McManaway**

David McManaway has been constructing his magical *Jomo* boards for three decades. They are mostly two-dimensional assemblages of found objects with no story to tell or wisdom to impart, but ineffably mysterious and witty. His materials are of every conceivable type: Old brushes, stones, stuffed toys, tools, glass and colorful plastics, lengths of string, twigs — arranged on a flat support. His poetic eye and unerring sense of placement result in the absolute transformation of detritus into a oneness that appears predestined. *Jomos*, like the Surrealists' visual alliterations, belie the intellect that created them to anchor in the depths of the imagination.

"I assemble my stuff. But the objects, the materials and what have you, are just a three-dimensional aspect of pigment that can result in imagery. And it's not non-objective at all. I trust my intuition and my eye, what I call the third thing."

Born in Chicago in 1927, McManaway arrived in Dallas in the late 1950s via serendipity after finishing art school at the University of Arkansas. Within a year of his arrival, Douglas MacAgy assumed the directorship of the upstart Dallas Center for Contemporary Art, and exhibited McManaway's assemblages in several breakthrough exhibitions, including "The Art of Assemblage" (1961) and "The Art that Broke the Looking Glass" (1962). For McManaway, along with Roy Fridge and Jim Love, among others, the shows legitimized and in some way elevated, what they were doing.

He says he cannot define exactly what a *jomo* is. The origin of the word, however, is a scene from a 1942 movie titled *Juke Girl* in which a black man (actor Willie Best) stands on the corner holding a board with the words "Get a Jomo" printed on it, and small pouches hanging from its edge. Something about it, McManaway says, triggered in his mind a recognition of connectedness to something inexplicable. Jokey but completely serious, the power of the *jomo* tore McManaway from painting, his first passion, to absorb him totally.

"It was one of those momentous decisions that at the time you don't know is going to be that momentous. I went from one day to the next and said, 'I'm not going to do THAT anymore, pointing to the painting; I'm going to do THIS,' pointing to the 20 little constructions I had done. It was fear at the pit of my stomach. And I still want to paint all the time."

"A Jomo is something one made in all honesty that turns out to have more than its intended aspects," painter Bill Kommodore offered. "Jomos, discarded toys, etc., are usually humorous to the observer for reasons other than planned by the maker. Or morbid, or sexual, or everything. In other words, they are like other Art."[1]

1. Cited in *One i at a time*, by Douglas MacAgy, Meadows School of the Arts, Southern Methodist University, Dallas, Texas, 1971, p. 36

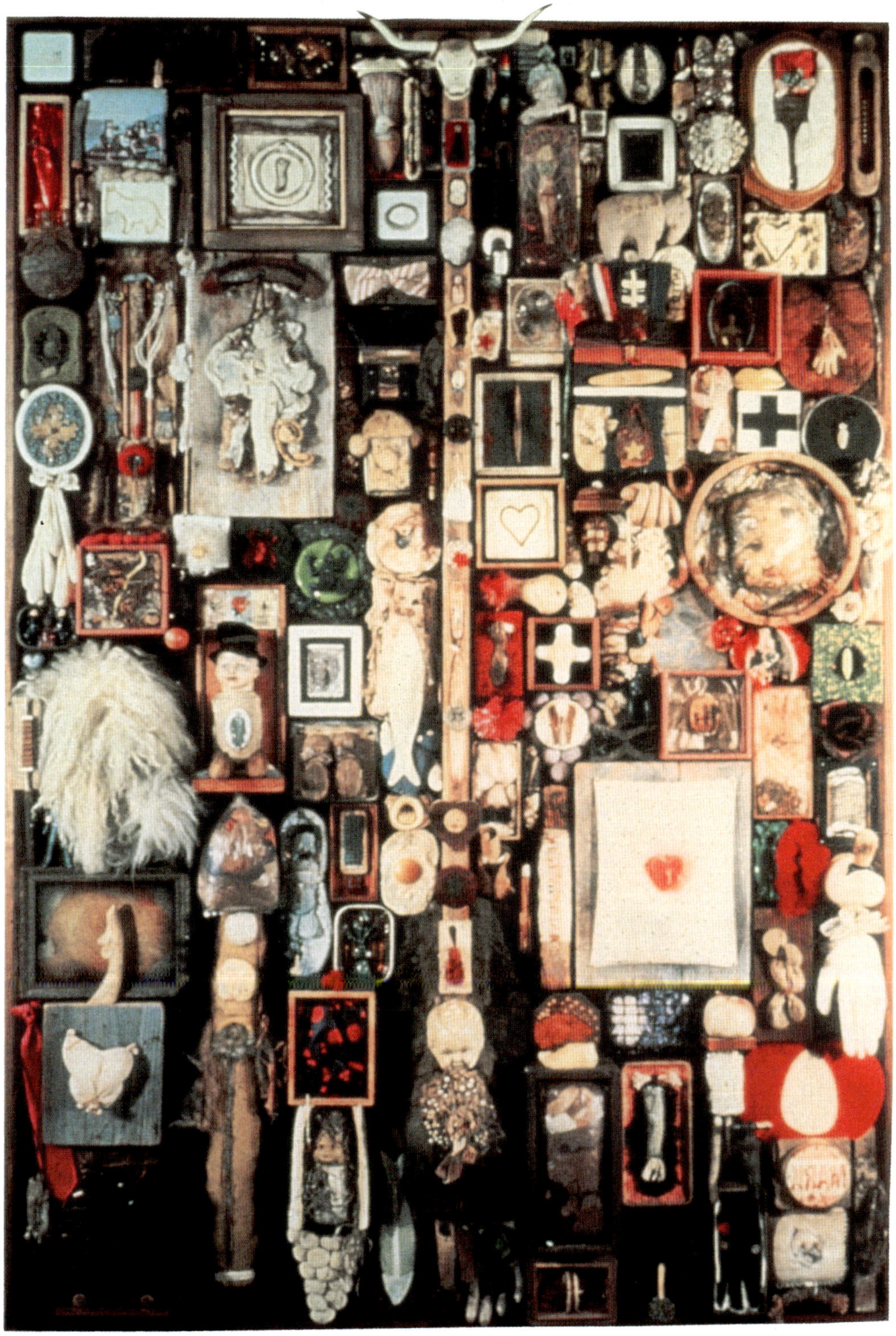

David McManaway
**Jomo Board #6**
1973–75, Mixed media, 73" x 49". Courtesy of Moody Gallery, Houston

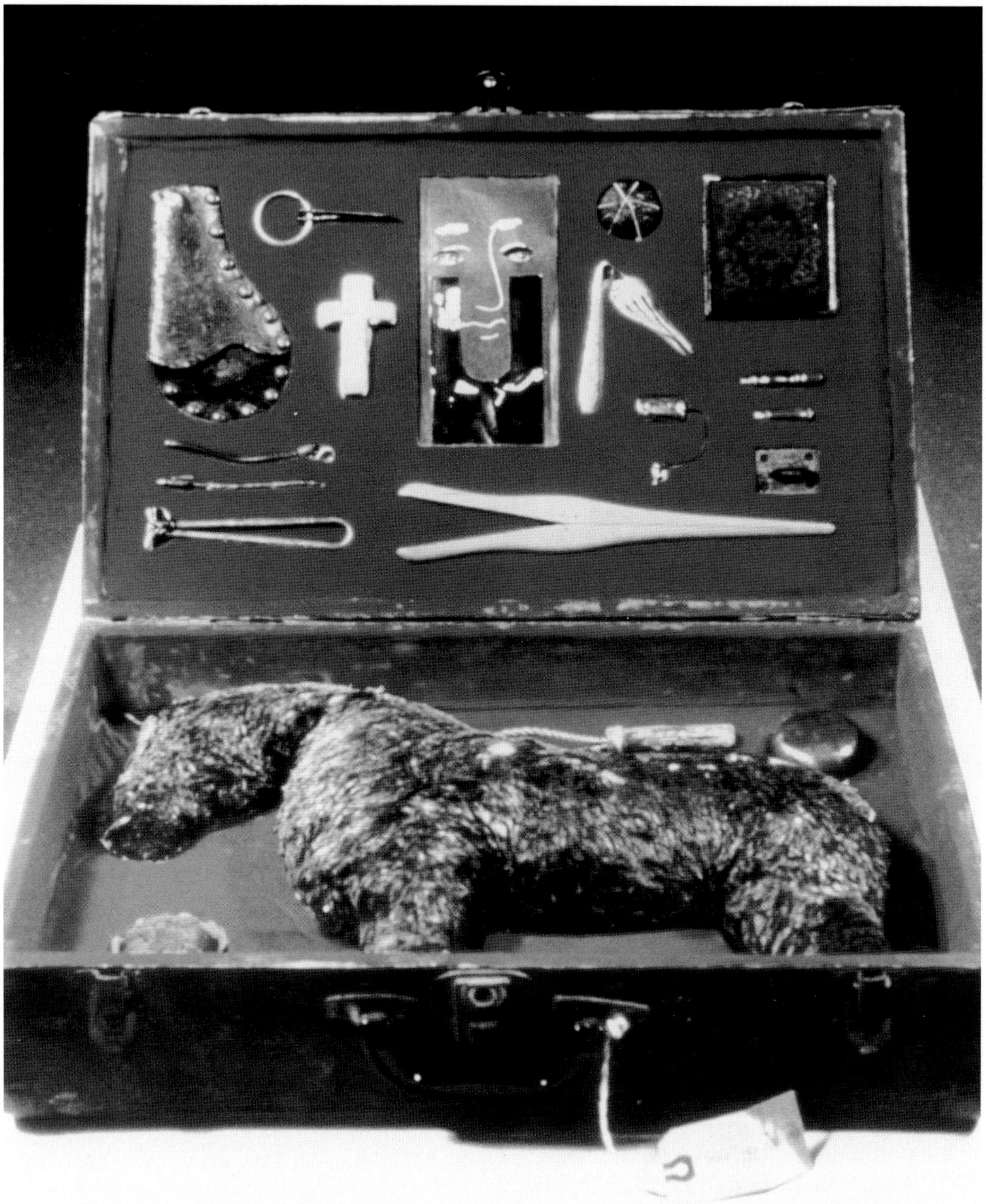

David McManaway
**Jomo Travelling Case**
1959, Mixed media, 6"h x 20"w x 12"d (closed).
Courtesy of Moody Gallery, Houston

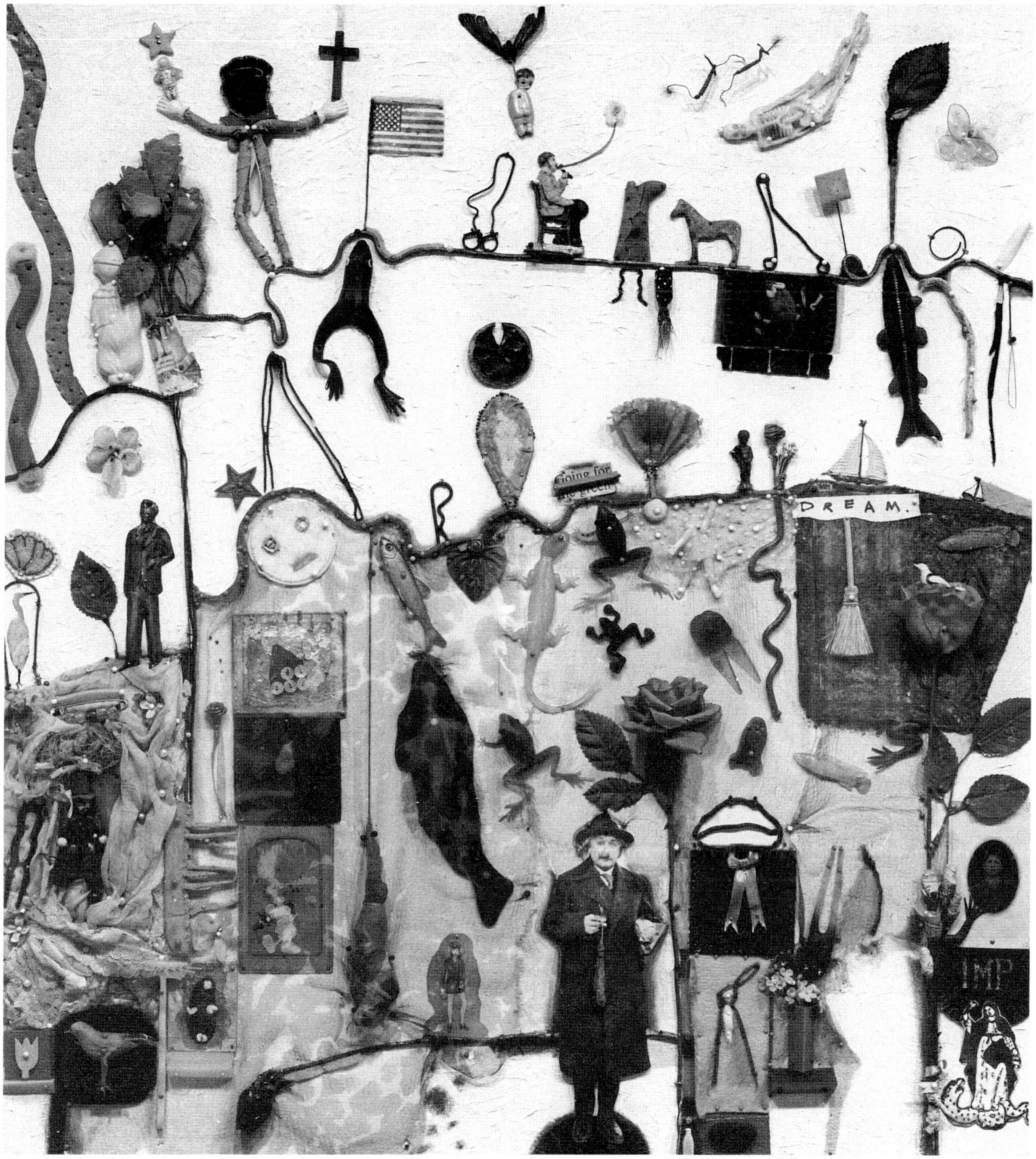


David McManaway
**Jomo Landscape**
1991, Mixed media, 38½" x 35". Photograph: Lynn Lennon. Collection: Mark Srere and Jayne Jenkins, Washington D.C. Courtesy of the artist

# Douglas **MacWithey**

Between 1988 and 1992, Douglas MacWithey worked almost exclusively on a series titled "The Noisome Corpse". It consists of 250 separate, delicate collages in which he combines fragments of nature and words, the fragments of language. The fragility of each is enhanced by a technique that defies permanence. He secures the multiple, segmented shapes with translucent tape on the paper surface, a process that both enhances and obscures their presence, and alludes to the concept of the work. "Decay is something not actively referred to," MacWithey says, "but it's the nature of nature. Everything changes. It's part of life."

Born in Ames, Iowa, in 1952, MacWithey moved to Dallas with his family at a young age. He always knew he wanted to be an artist. The example of the Dallas artists in the late 1960s known as the Oak Cliff group, showed him it was possible. At first, MacWithey channeled his creativity to theater, writing and directing performances in various venues around the city. In the mid-1980s, he made the leap to concentrate on making objects. Vernon Fisher's word-and-image compositions would present a powerful model.

In his collages, MacWithey typically centers on the page a leaf or a wildflower translucent with age whose inherent shape may recall other things, like a bird or a branch of coral. He surrounds it with letters, full words and occasional phrases gathered from many sources, including medieval manuscripts, arcane treatises, proverbs and his own writings. Sometimes they are typeface characters and other times, handwritten in pencil. They provide a rhythmic linear element which contrasts with the organic object, but rather than elucidate, they present an intriguing obstacle to "reading" specificity into the work.

In recent years, MacWithey has been exploring sculptural forms. Unlike the seemingly insubstantial collages, his assemblages, composed from plaster birds and metal tubs, have a sturdy materiality. The elements of water (contained in the tubs) and light (from light bulbs that are integral to the piece) simultaneously suggest impermanence. Taken together with the birds (air) and the metal tubs (earth/minerals), these elusive untitled pieces suggest the philosophical, alchemical and physical elements.

"I didn't set out on this course, but in retrospect, I see certain concerns at the basis: The concept of interior/exterior life and all its connotations — mind/body, body/soul — the supposed opposites, are a whole. If you take everything back, it leads you to primary cause."

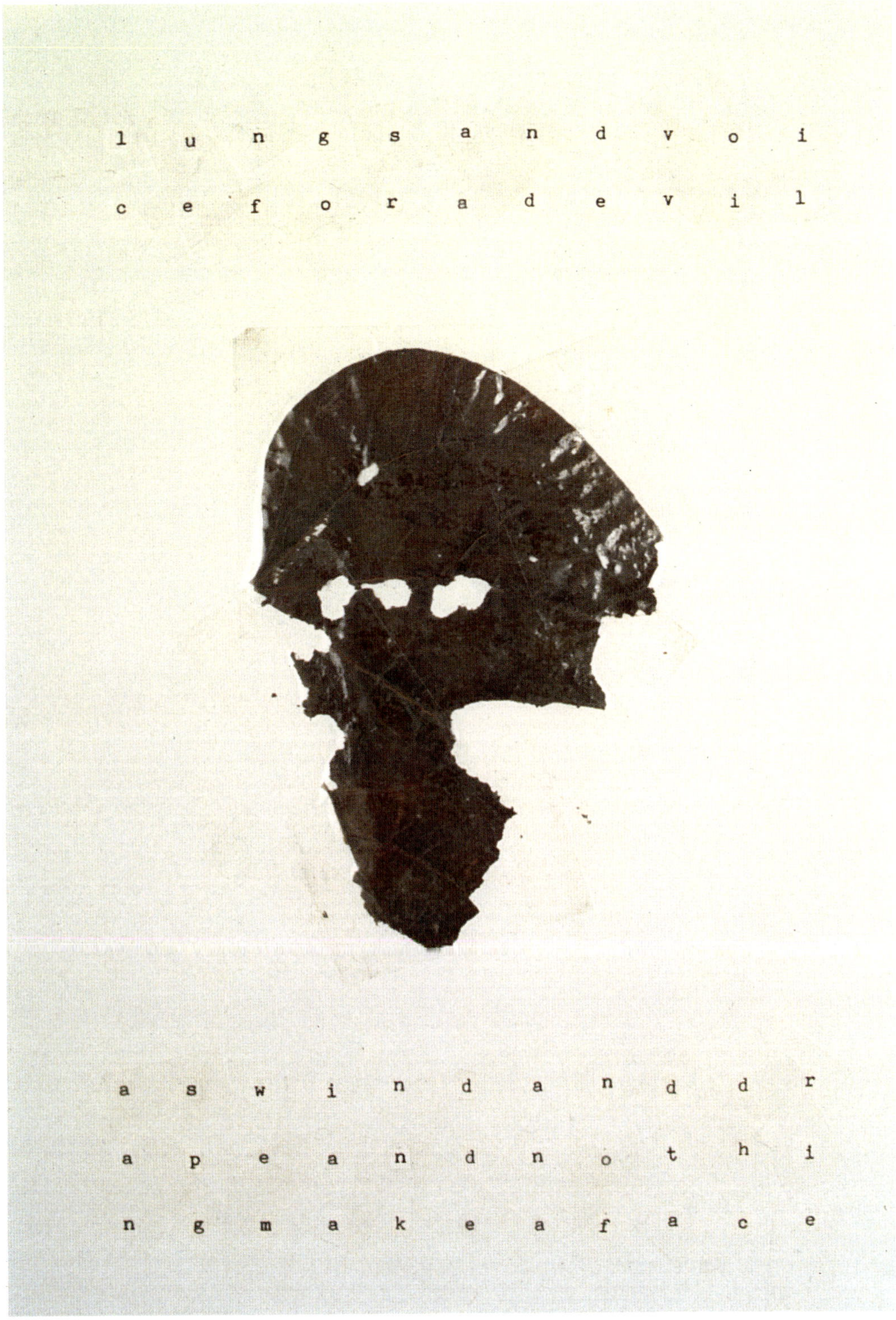


Douglas MacWithey
**The Noisome Corpse**
(Detail) 1991–93, Mixed media on paper, 20" x 12".
Courtesy of Barry Whistler Gallery, Dallas

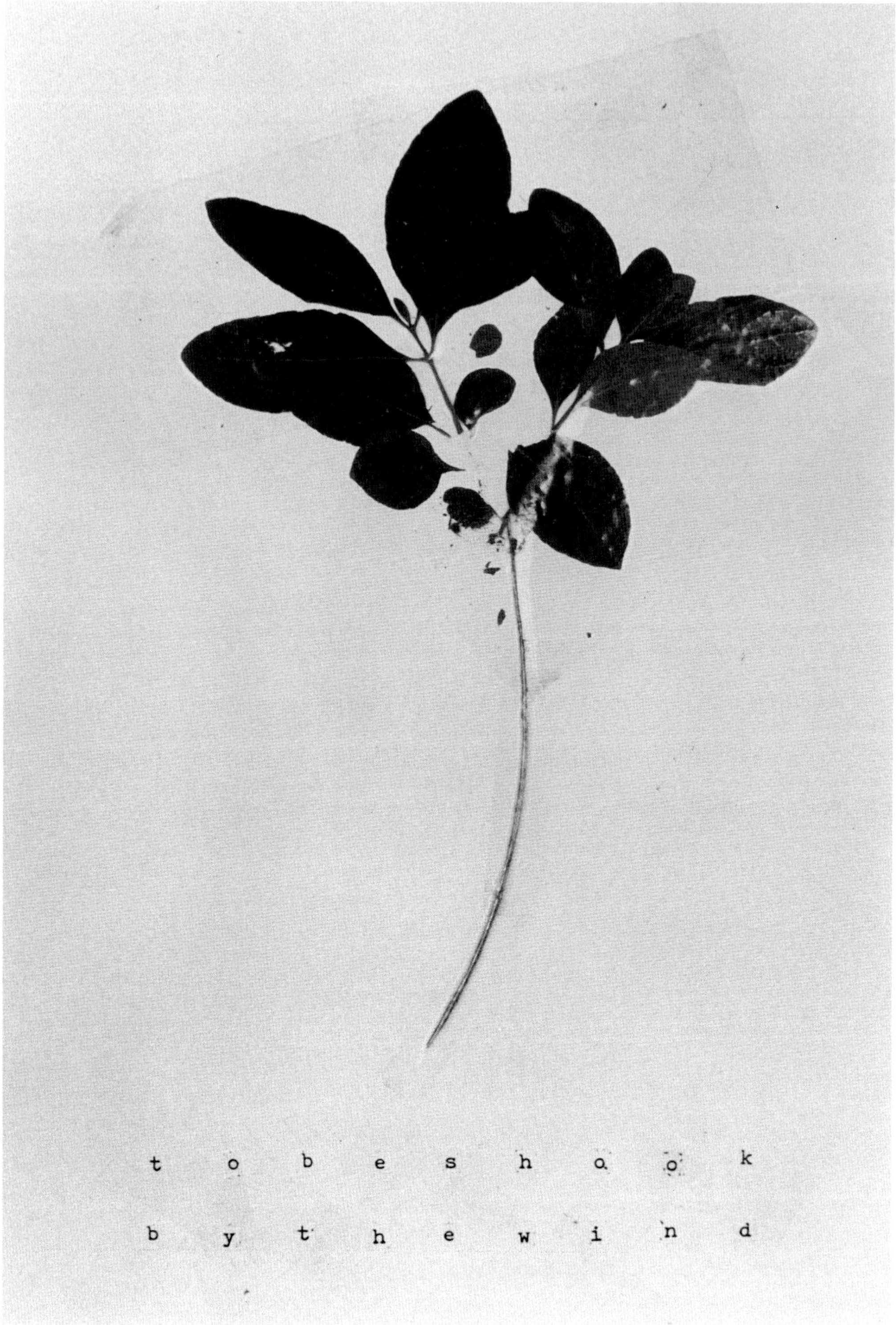


Douglas MacWithey
**The Noisome Corpse**
(Detail) 1991–93, Mixed media on paper, 20" x 12".
Courtesy of Barry Whistler Gallery, Dallas

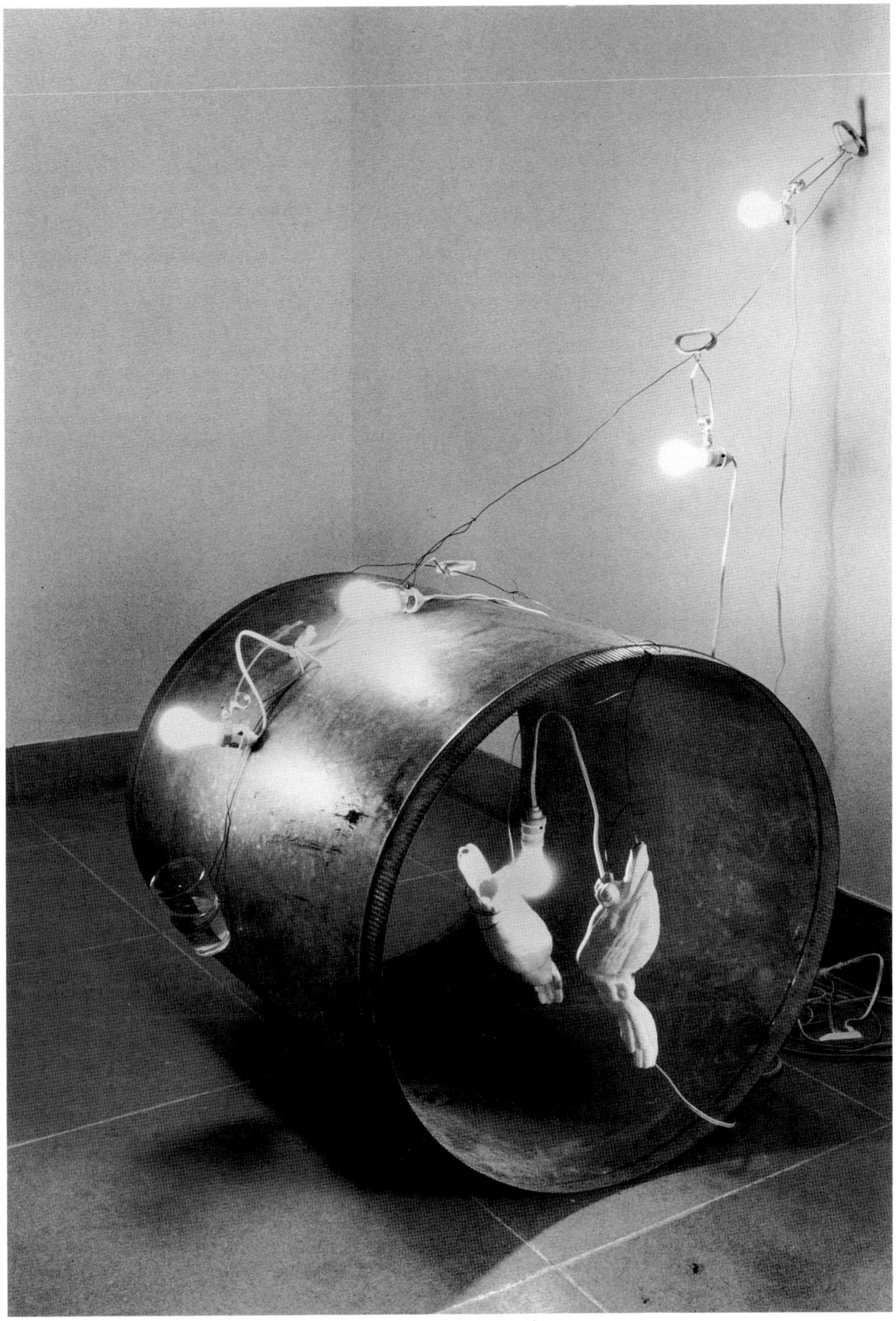

Douglas MacWithey
**Untitled**
1992–93, Mixed media, variable size, 5' x 3½' x 4' approx.
Courtesy of Barry Whistler Gallery, Dallas

# James
# Magee

James Magee gathers materials from dumps across the Rio Grande, from his garden and his kitchen, to forge dark abstractions. He combines sheets of metal and metal-workers' tools, shards of glass and other objects he has fabricated or found, with substances like crankcase oil, rust and paprika in sombre, high reliefs. The works' crusty textures and rich coloration are earthy, intimating passion but also decay in the perpetual battle of Eros and Thanatos. Framed in heavy steel and sealed behind glass, they are arcane reliquaries, oddly sensual and seductive, ultimately impenetrable and mysterious. He assigns them titles, parts of lengthy free-form poems he has written, which do not explain so much as add another dimension to the hermetic work.

His studio is in a warehouse one bridge away from Mexico, where a single work may take him three, four or more years to complete. "It's very much an evolutionary process," he says. "I'm not necessarily certain when I begin, but I'm sure when I finish."

Born in Michigan in 1946, Magee had several careers before finding El Paso at age 35 and dedicating himself to making art. He majored in history and French, then pursued a law degree from the University of Pennsylvania. He painted throughout his college years, never taking an art class, and apprenticed himself to a sculptor in Paris after graduating. When he returned to the United States in the mid seventies, he went to New York where he worked with mentally disabled children and built sets for off-off-off Broadway theater. He limited his law practice to arguing the cause of conscientious objectors before the general assembly of the United Nations, at the same time that he was a roughneck in the oil fields of Midland-Odessa in Texas. Finally, Magee settled in El Paso in 1977 for reasons he says he can't articulate except to say that the strong feelings he had for the city then have not diminished.

There's another side to Magee named Annabel Livermore. She is a spirit unencumbered by Magee's existential questions, whose naif paintings on canvas proffer colorful landscapes and people who seem to rejoice. She has her own methods and her own exhibitions, and although he has a difficult time discussing who or why Annabel is, Magee's respect and admiration for her freedom is fully evident in his awkward acknowledgment of her.

"I have no masters, I had no art courses. When I was a kid, I was sort of taken in by an architect who was a carver and a painter. I had that. And the easel that Annabel paints on, I've had since I was twelve years old."

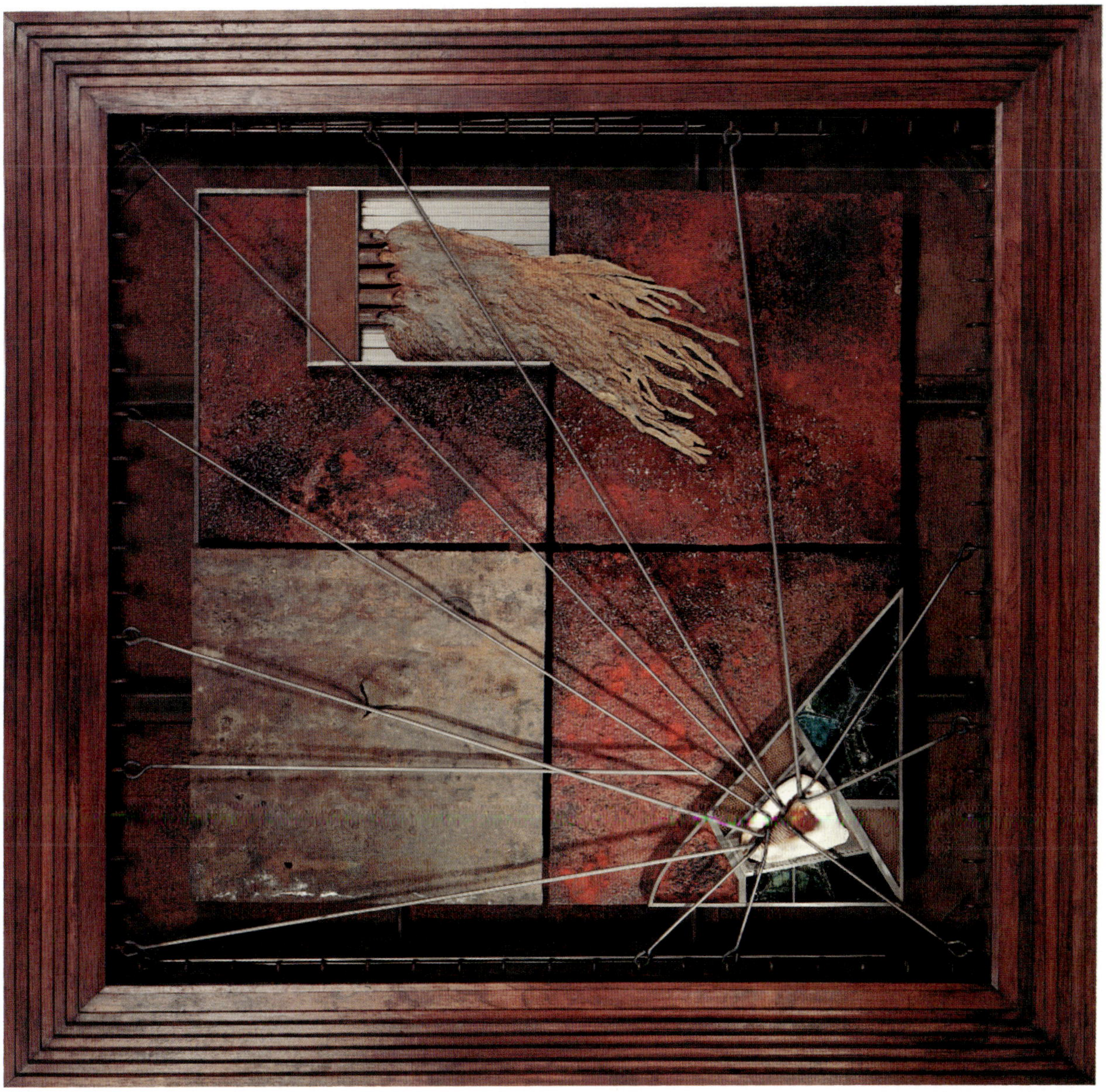

James Magee
**Untitled**
1992, Mixed media, 72" x 72" x 10". Courtesy of
Adair Margo Gallery, El Paso

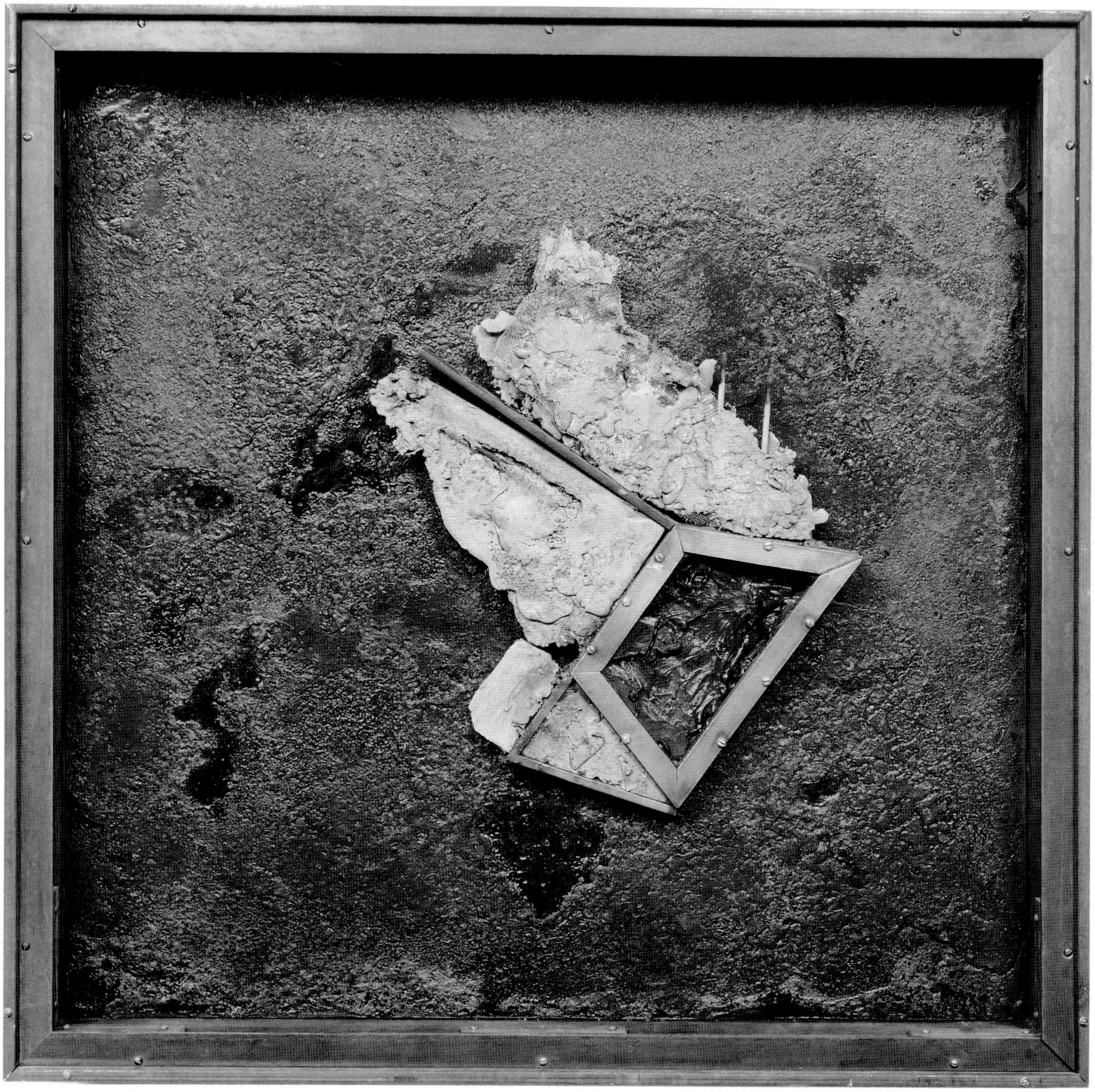

James Magee
**Falling Star**
**(from the "Vaccination Series")**
1988–90, Mixed media: grease, steel, glass,
6" x 6" x 3⅛". Photograph: Tom Jenkins.
Courtesy of the artist

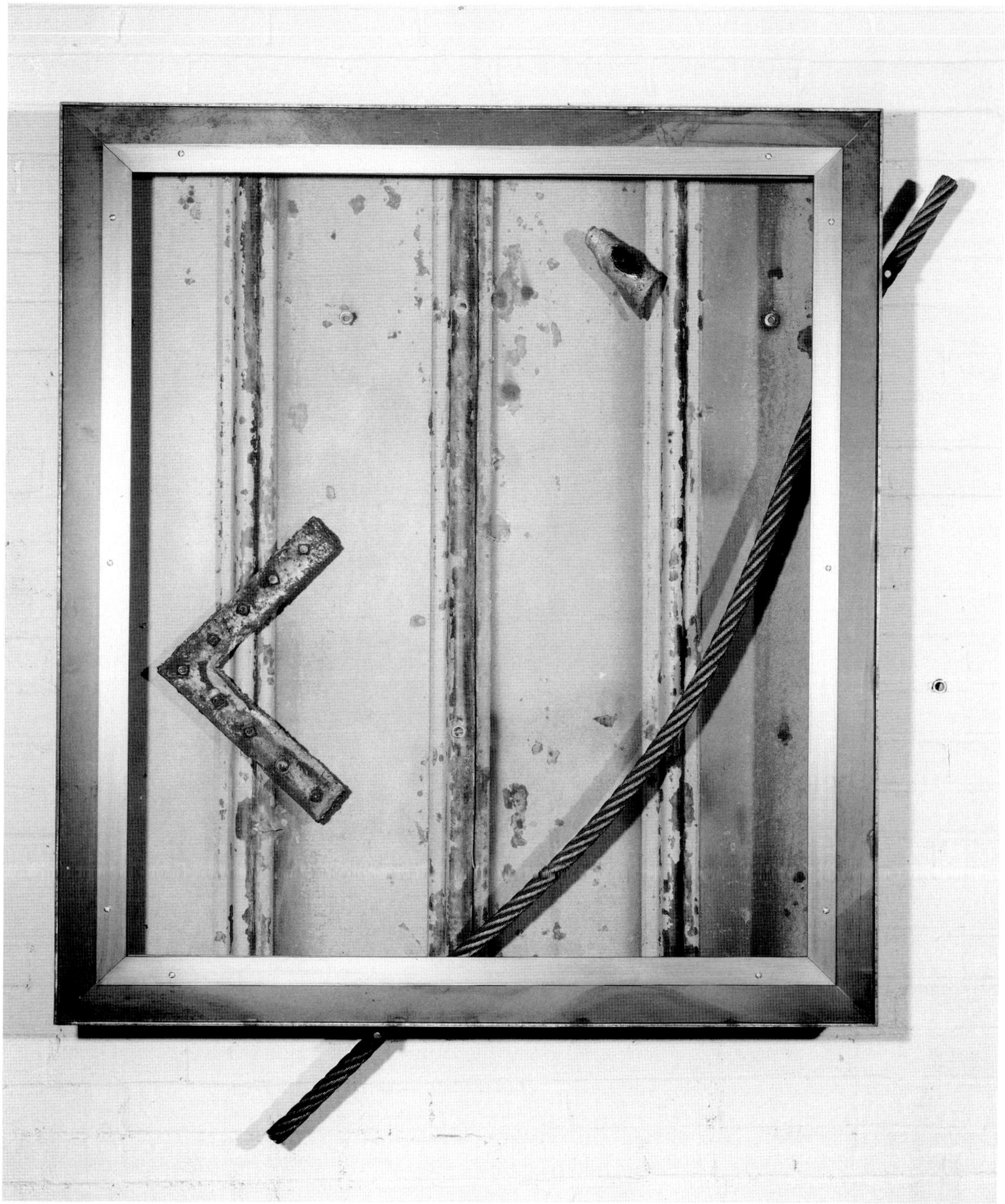

James Magee
**Untitled**
1991, Mixed media: terracotta, tin, steel, etc,
32" x 18" x 4". Photograph: Tom Jenkins. Courtesy of the artist

# MANUAL:
# **Hill & Bloom**

In 1994, Ed Hill and Suzanne Bloom celebrate 20 years as the collaborative team they named MANUAL. The artists, who are also husband and wife, made Houston their home in 1976 when they joined the faculty of the University of Houston's photography department in its infancy. Internationally recognized today as pioneers in the medium of digital imaging, Hill and Bloom chose their name for its gender-neutral but loaded connotations: humble labor and art history's reverence for the artist's hand, and especially for its pragmatism as instructional materials, too. In some ways, the name may appear to be approaching the status of oxymoron. The images MANUAL creates through microchips are as distant from being handiwork as a tree in the forest is from a gilded Queen Anne chair. But it's precisely that tension that lies at the heart of MANUAL's color saturated, computerized digital photography.

"We have an uneasy feeling that the *Eros* of the binary code is also the *Thanatos* of the 'natural' world — not its salvation. Call it a reasoned hunch, but since the 17th Century, Western civilization has been set on a course of technological domination of Nature and it would seem as though there is no turning back."

"Someone once told us Americans think irony is something best left to the dry cleaners. Notwithstanding such a literally warped possibility, there certainly is a large quantity of irony in the fact that over the past seven years we (MANUAL) have chosen to employ computers in our confrontation with pressing environmental issues."[1]

Hill, born in Springfield, Massachusetts in 1935, and Bloom, born in Philadelphia in 1943, were painters by training. His interest in photography, he told an interviewer in 1979, was latent until 1967 when he saw Antonioni's *Blow-Up* — three times over a weekend — and bought a camera the following Monday. In the same interview, Bloom said she bought her first camera in 1970, like any first time tourist to Europe. The two met in 1972 when they were teaching at Smith and Amherst, and Hill taught her how to process her film. Two years later, they bought their first video camera together.

"It may be worth mentioning — in fact, reminding ourselves — that the impetus for our collaboration as well as our turn to electronic technology was born out of the liberating and reforming spirit of the 1960s. Both of us felt it was time to take up alternative methods of conception and production — to leave the church of received aesthetic truths behind and not look back lest we be turned into pillars of salt."[2]

The clarity of their writing underscores the precision logic demanded by their chosen medium, since, as the truism goes, a computer is only as smart as its programmer.

1. Statement by the artists in the catalogue, *Digital Photography*, Centre National de la Photographie, October 1992
2. Statement by the artists in the catalogue, *Digital Photography: Computer Images/Volatile Memory/New Montage*, 1988

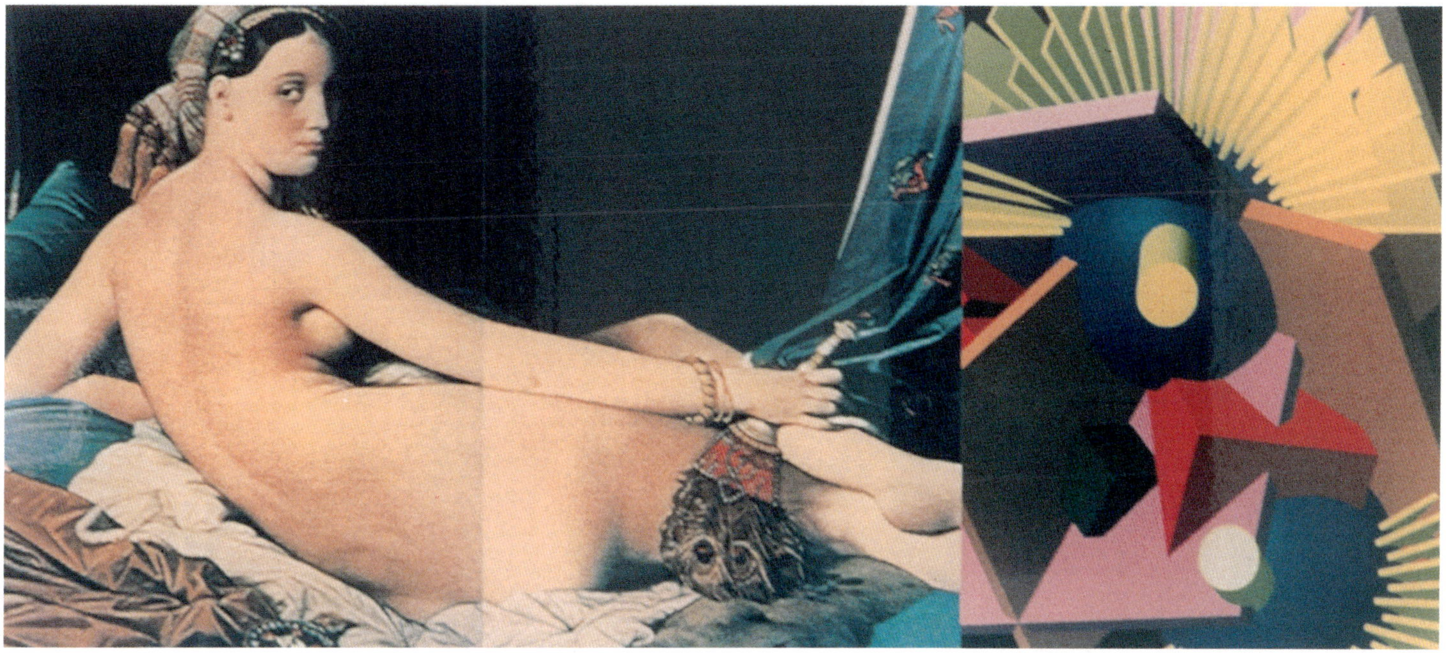

MANUAL: Ed Hill and Suzanne Bloom
**Perfect World**
1990, Type C Photographs, 47" x 104¼". Collection: San Antonio Museum of Art. Courtesy of Moody Gallery, Houston

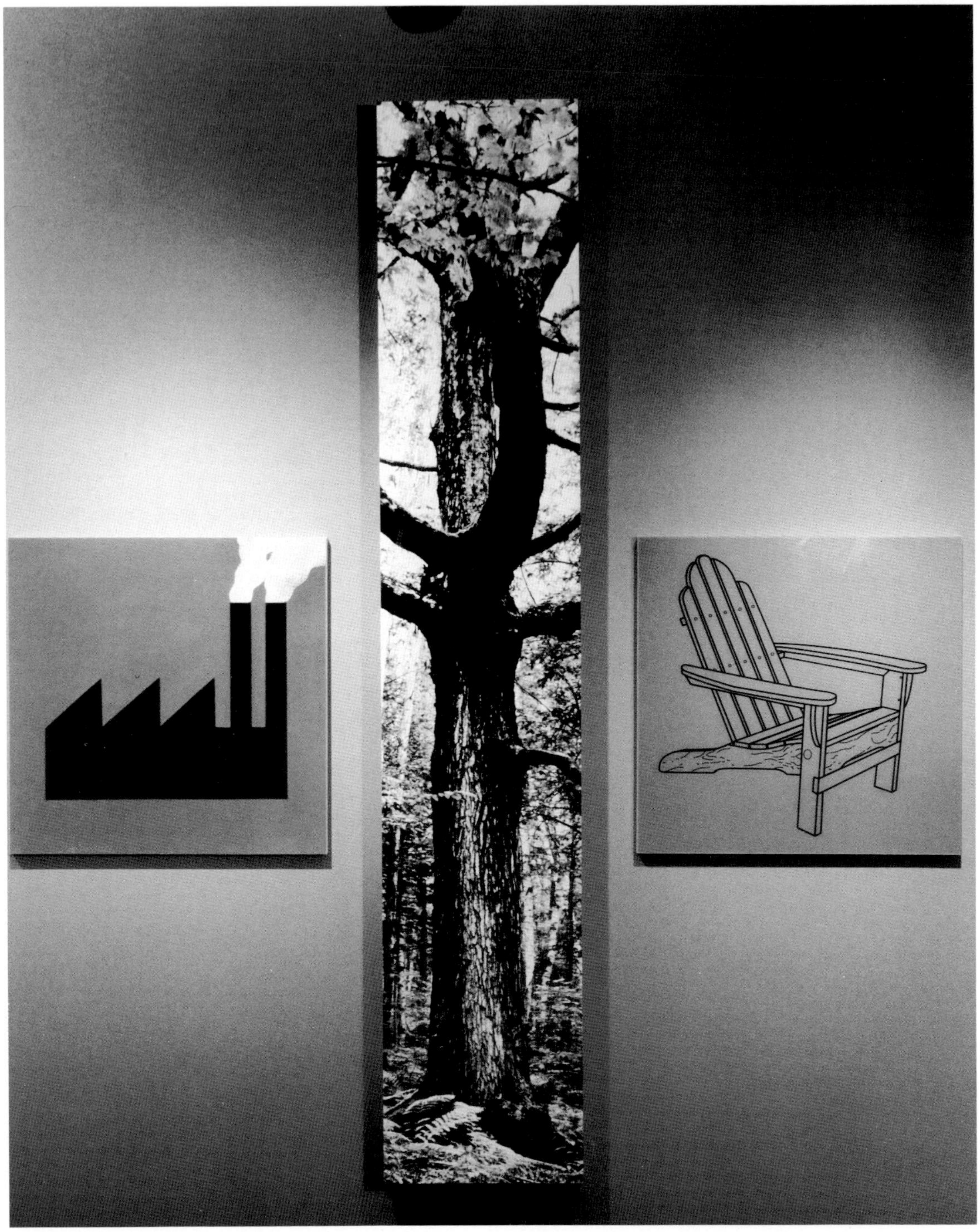

MANUAL: Ed Hill and Suzanne Bloom
**Installation "Forest\Products"**
"Pulp Factory": 1991, Type C print, mounted, 32" x 32"; "Mother Tree": 1991, Type C print, mounted, 108" x 20"; "Adirondack Chair", 1991, gelatin silver print, face mounted, 32" x 32". Courtesy of Moody Gallery, Houston

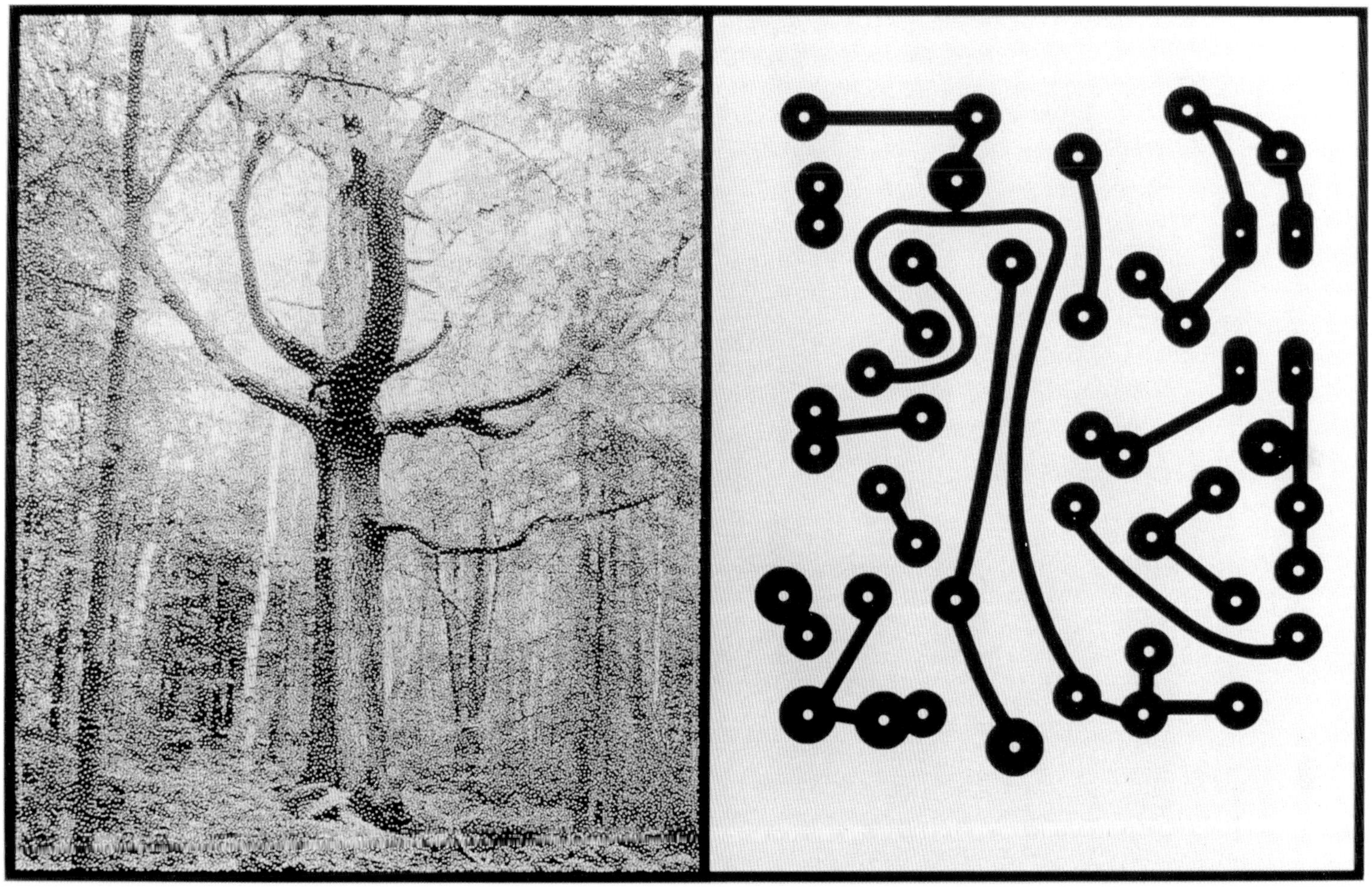

MANUAL: Ed Hill and Suzanne Bloom
**Maple/PCB**
1992, Gelatin silver on plexiglass, 17½" x 28".
Courtesy of Moody Gallery, Houston

# César Augusto **Martínez**

Sifting his heritage through a perceptive eye and discerning intellect, César Martínez explores expressive avenues to bridge his cultural specificity of a Mexican-American from Texas and the universal questions about human identity.

He does not recall discrimination in Laredo, where he was born in 1944, but he was a teenager before realizing that not every place had an "other side" and he began to understand his hybrid heritage. His degree in art education from Texas Arts & Industry University served him well. He settled in San Antonio where he joined the Texas Institute for Educational Development. Under its auspices, Martínez traveled across the state with Carlos Guerra, the founding director of the institute and activist, to organize local voter registration. He discovered art could be the unifying element to the frequently strident mix of cultures and politics which he inherited. Where the battles over tactics and ideology were acrimonious and divisive, Martínez says, images and song held the community together.

"I never planned to be a political artist, but there has been a political spin to what I do because it's always culturally oriented. For me, in order to universalize something, it must be viewed and hopefully, it will lead to understanding."

Martínez works in several modes, including abstract landscapes he fashions with found materials, and stunningly symbolic mixed medias such as *Canonization in South Texas*, painted on a car hood. But his principal interest and deserved renown is based on his stylized portraits of *pachucos* (Mexican-American rebels), both male and female. They are emblematic, rendered rigidly but with enormous humor. Set against planes of saturated color, the figures are frontal and formal in a way reminiscent of Coptic portraiture. Martínez says he owes his use of flat color field backgrounds (though not the color itself) to Jules Olitski, while the individual physiognomy speaks clearly of the complex mix of people and society of which they are born.

"The *pachuco* is an endless source of curiosity and fascination and mythologized to folk hero status. I treat them as both individuals and as a social phenomenon to explore a range of human attitudes within a social context and perhaps give a more accurate perspective than what popular culture can provide."

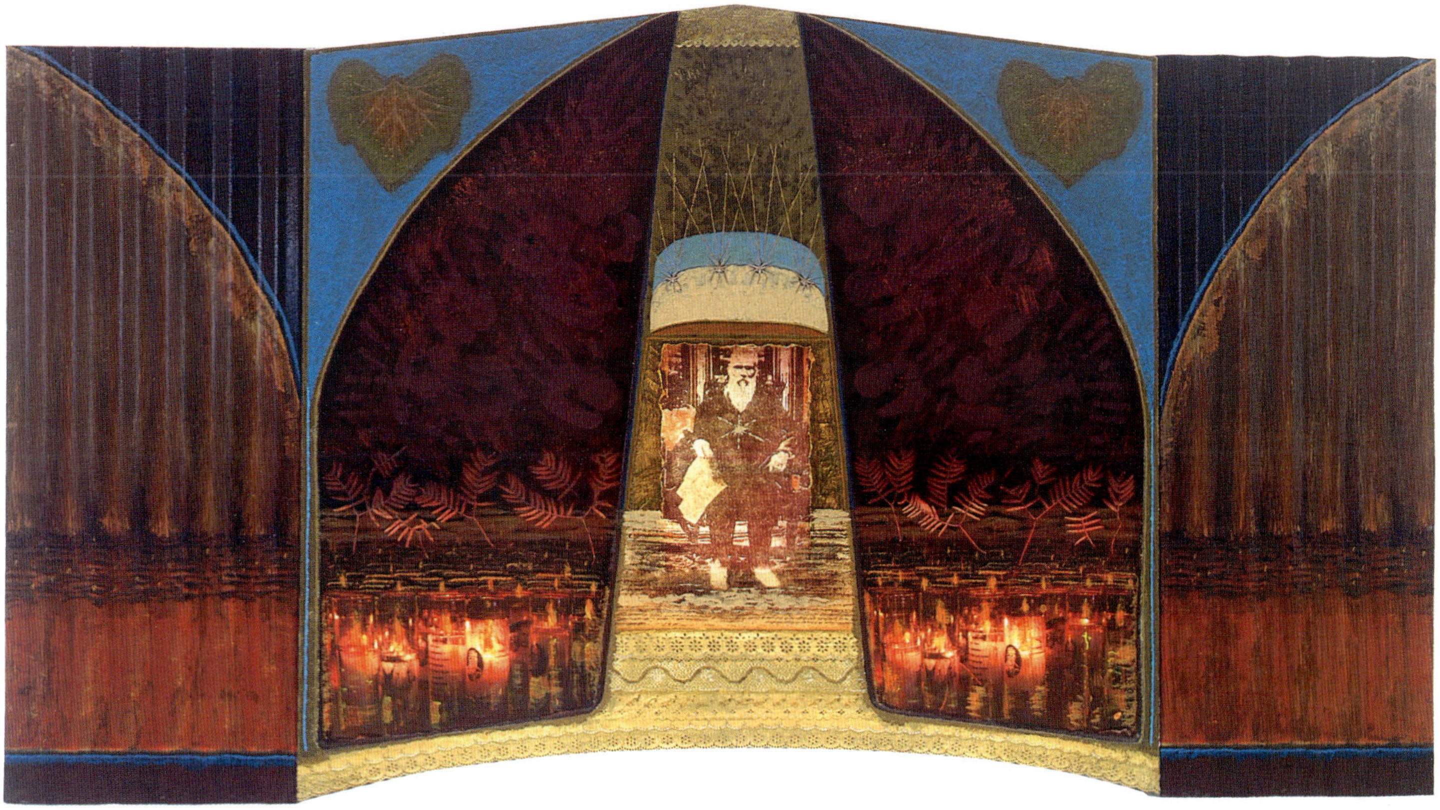

Cesar Augusto Martinez

**Canonization in South Texas (by an Imaginary Pope)**

1990, Mixed media: acrylic, collage on car hood, corrugated metal, 48" x 85". Photograph: Mary Kristen, San Diego. Collection: John Marmaduke, Amarillo, Texas. Courtesy of the artist

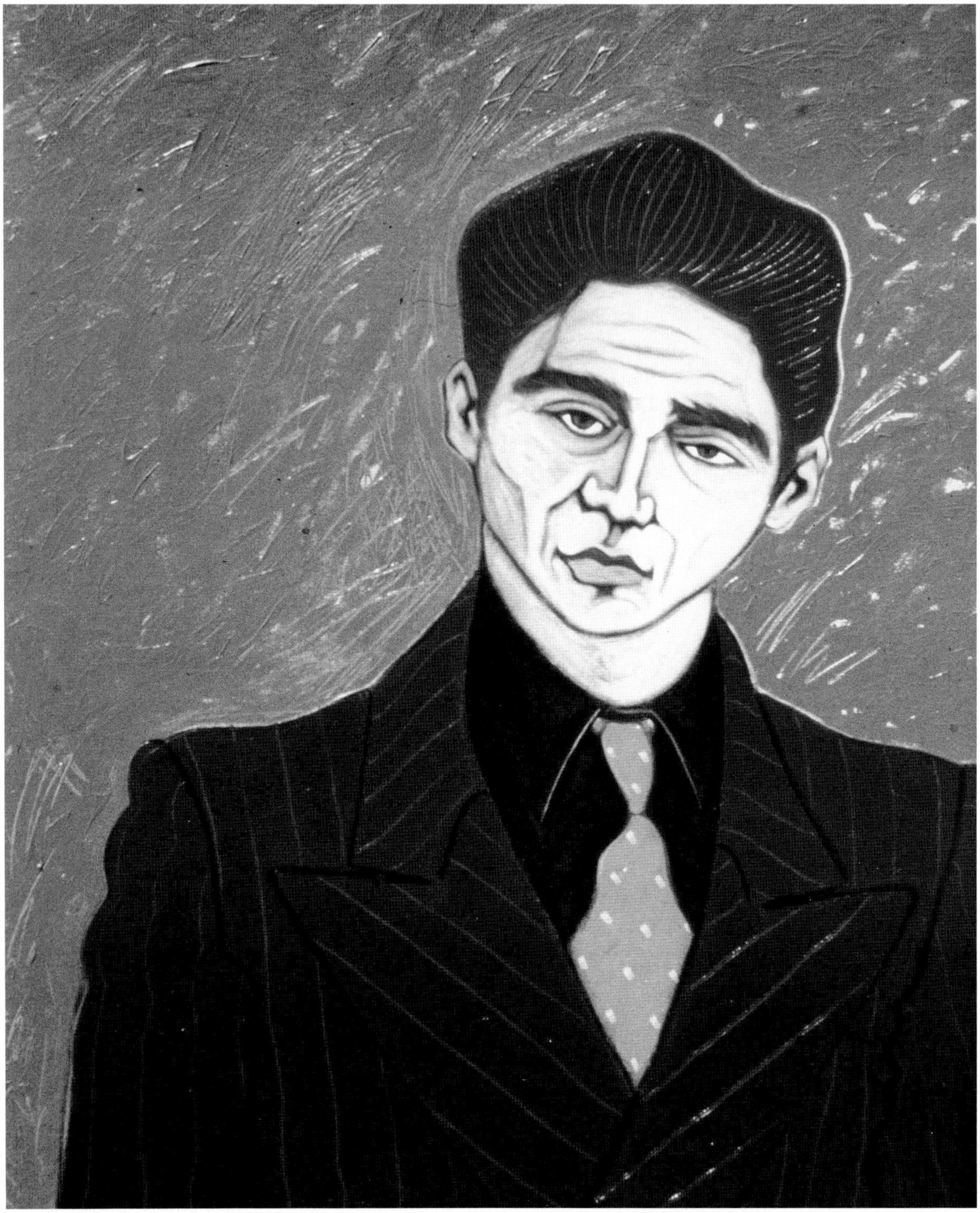

Cesar Augusto Martinez
**El Güero (The Blonde One)**
1987, Acrylic on canvas, 54" x 44". Collection: Cheech Marin, Los Angeles, California. Courtesy of the artist

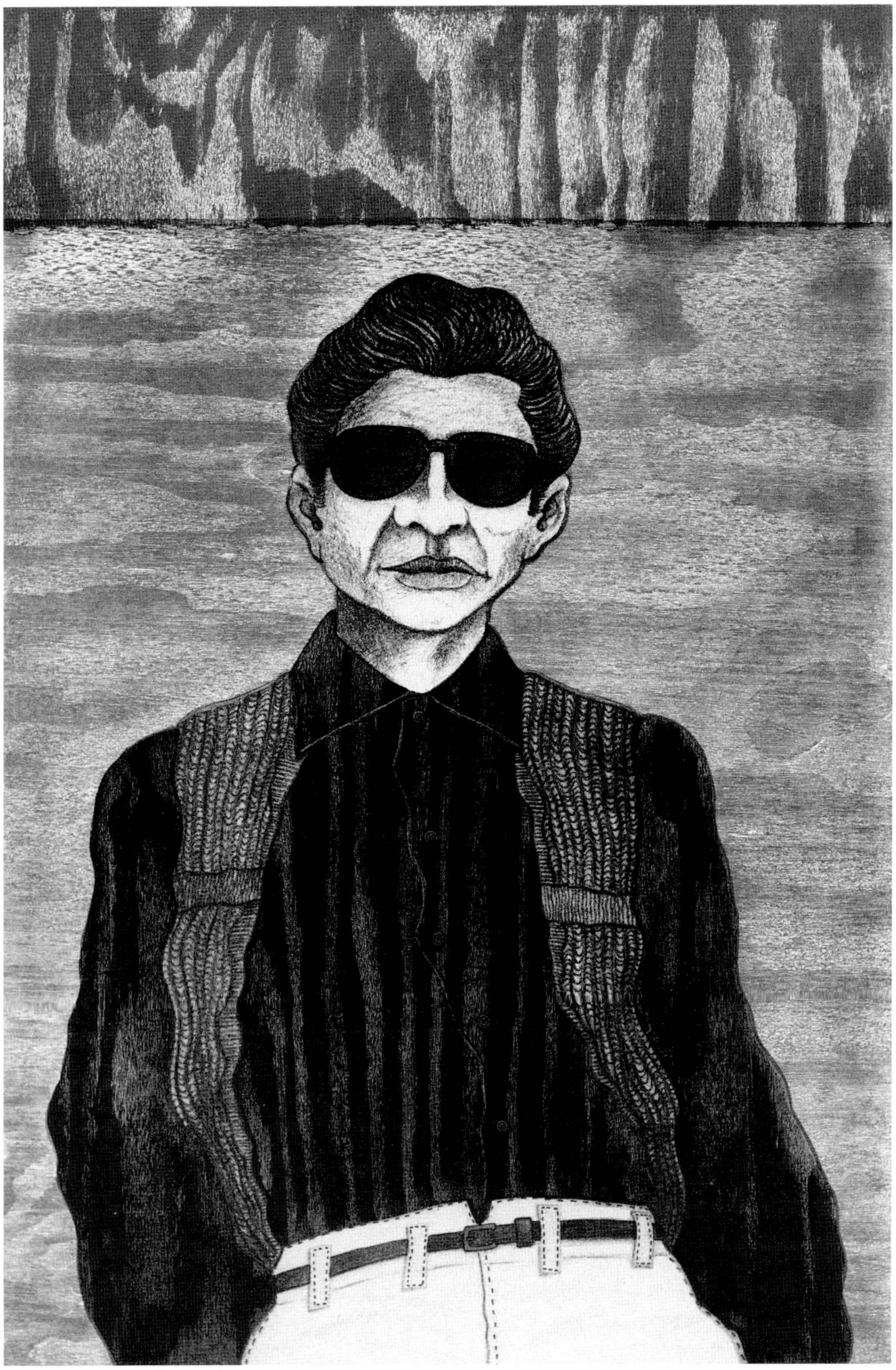

Cesar Augusto Martinez
**El Pantalón Rosa (Pink Trousers)**
1992, Nine-color lithograph, 35" x 23". Courtesy of the artist

# Melissa **Miller**

Melissa Miller's exuberant fables seduce the eye with joyous color and sumptuous surfaces. She paints slowly, taking as long as 18 months to complete a single work. She envisions the full composition before approaching the canvas, then begins by sketching the primary areas and relative positions of the main figures in sepia washes. More detailed and colorful descriptions of secondary shapes and other elements follow on which she gradually builds her opulent metaphors.

Born in Houston in 1951, Miller got her bachelor's degree in painting from the University of Texas in Austin in 1971, and followed it with a six-month fellowship at Yale. She had not been the star student and found she was not as well prepared as her Ivy League colleagues. That challenge, she says, more than any teacher or artist, motivated her to work. She discovered the Fauves and Philip Guston. Moving "backwards" in art history, she gleaned technical and theoretical understanding, too, in a range from traditional Japanese painting to Giotto.

In a time and place when declarations that painting was dead, and minimalism's austere gestalt was the intellectual's response to the commodification of art, Miller chose the heroic brushwork and emotions of American abstract expressionism. The spirit of independence she grew up with in Houston of the fifties and sixties, were crucial to her art.

"There was a pervasive attitude of state independence and pride. New was better. All things were possible, Houston wasn't going to let the "old" North tell it how to do things. The generations of Houstonians in my family felt that my siblings and I should adopt this attitude too; so we did. It really wasn't such a bad attitude to grow up with. The energy and self-respect it nurtured … affected my decision to stay in Texas, giving me courage to believe that quality art could be produced on one's home turf."[1]

Her allegories of the human condition have become increasingly complex over the years. The emotional tension postulated in the earlier work arose primarily from the instinctual fight or flight, life or death decisions faced by her animal characters. More recently, the struggle for survival is far more subtle as she shifts it from the physical to the spiritual arena. The enemy is not the predator but one's own lack of courage; the victims are not the weaker creatures of the world, but the soul. The stakes are much higher, and her paintings no less lush.

1. Artist's statement, *Fresh Paint*, p. 154.

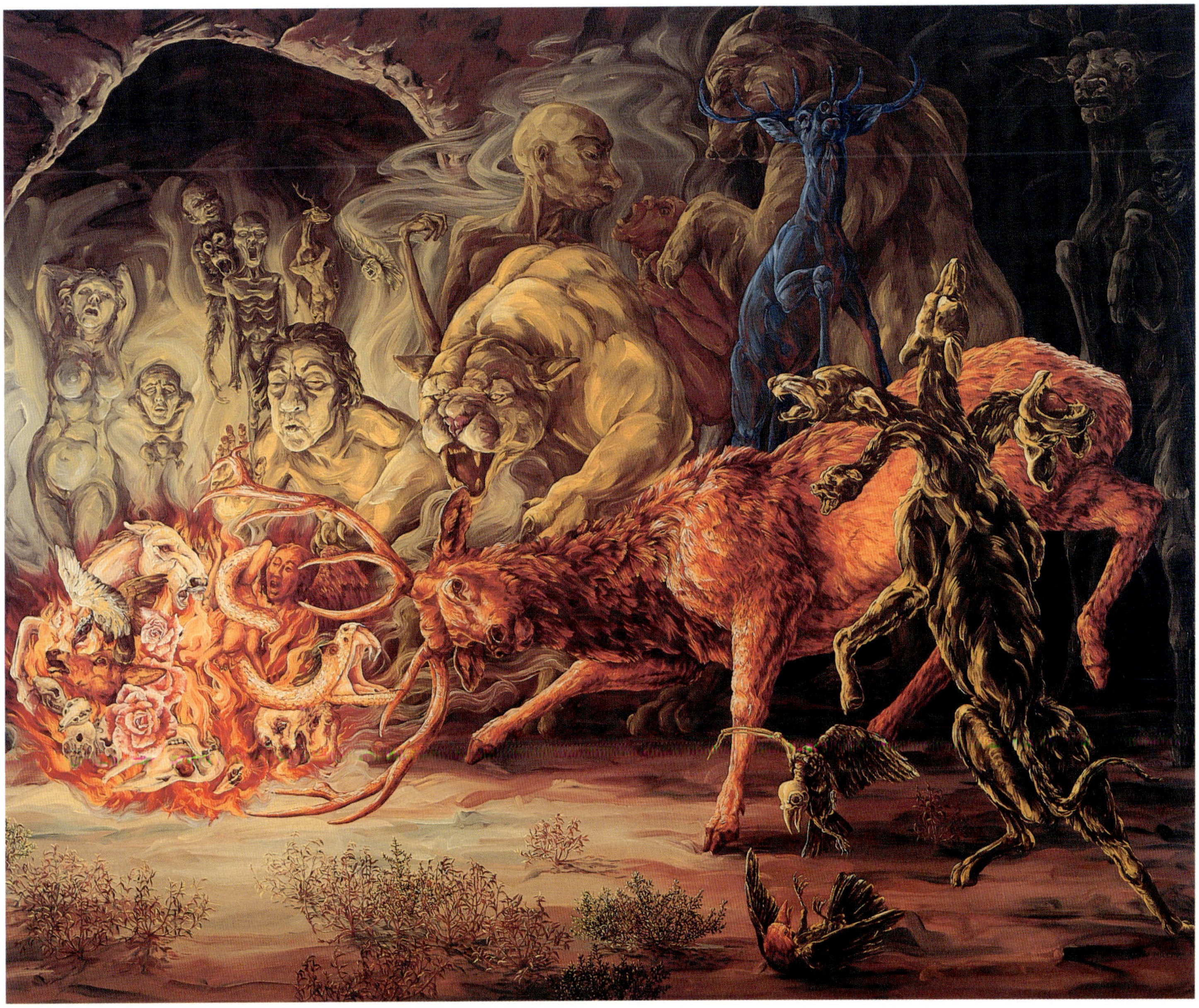

Melissa Miller

**The Temptation of St Anthony**

1993, Oil on linen, 68" x 80". Collection: The Barrett Collection, Dallas. Courtesy of Texas Gallery, Houston

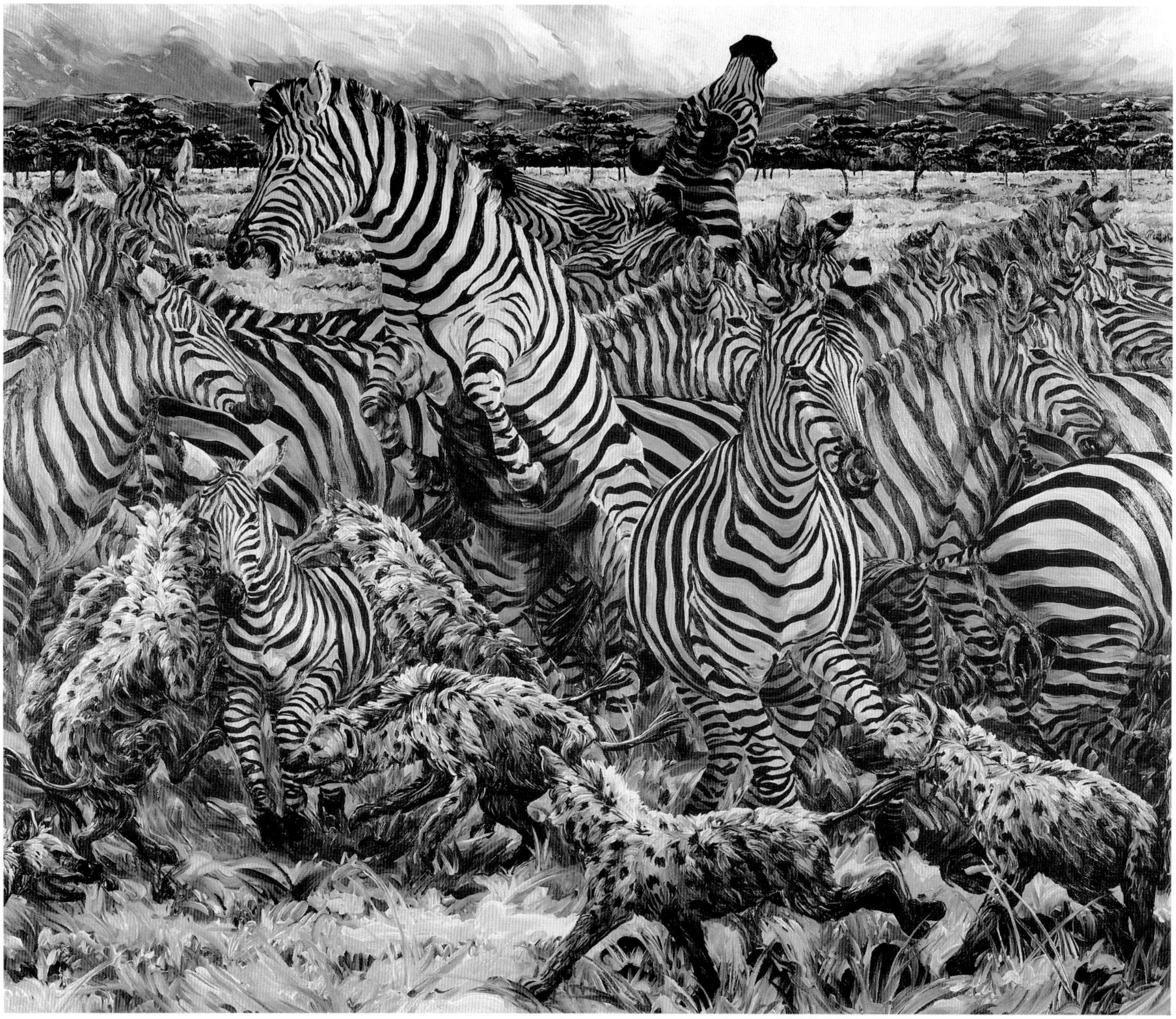

Melissa Miller
**Zebras and Hyenas**
1985, Oil on linen, 72½" x 84". Photograph: Bill Kennedy. Collection: Archer M. Huntington Art Gallery, The University of Texas, Austin, Michener Collection Acquisition Fund, 1986. Courtesy of Texas Gallery, Houston

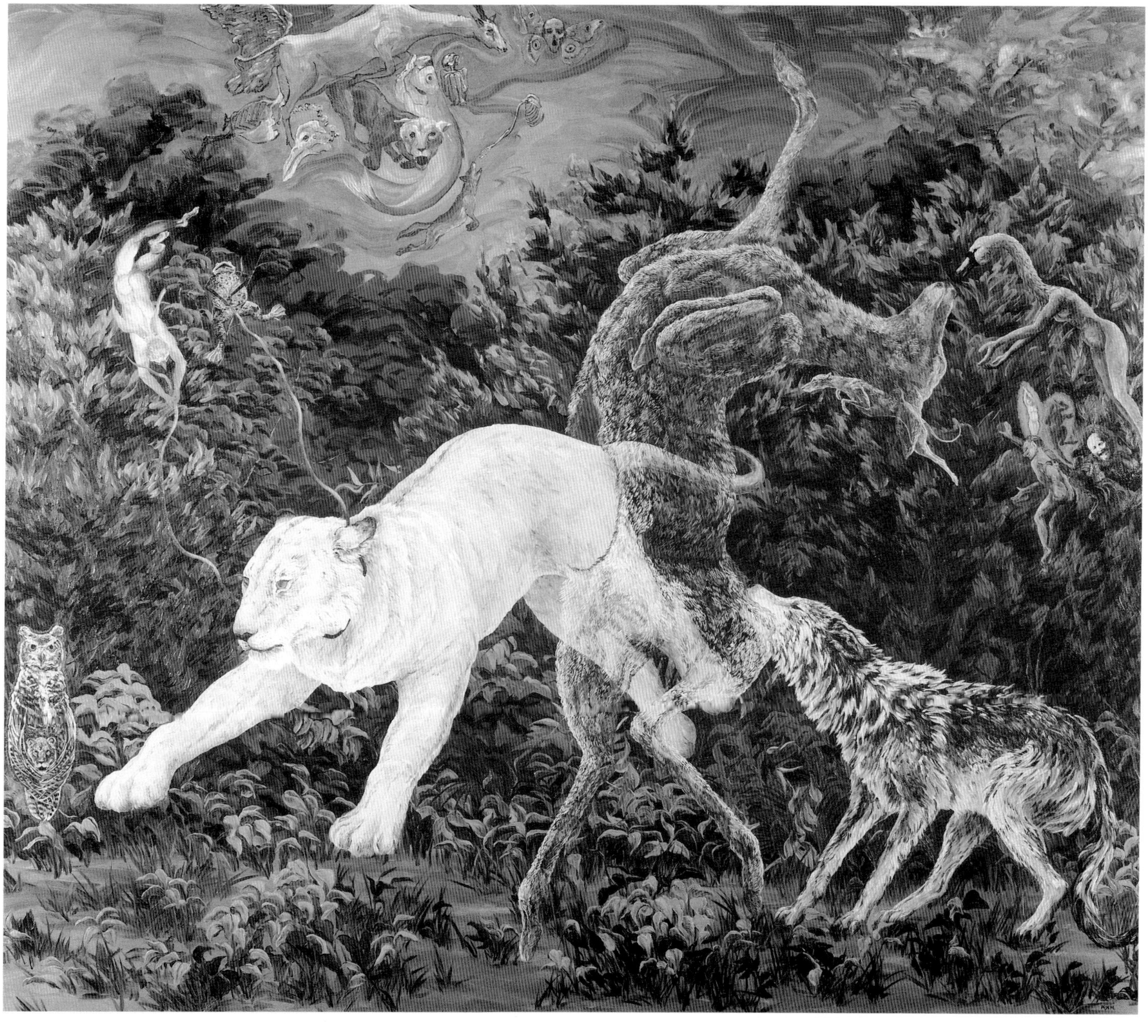

Melissa Miller
**New Skin**
1988, Oil on linen, 64" x 72". Photograph: Bill Kennedy. Collection: Dr Jerry Sherman, Baltimore. Courtesy of Texas Gallery, Houston

# Jesus Bautista **Moroles**

Jesus Moroles loves stone. He is unabashed about the pleasure he derives from "tearing" it, polishing its surfaces, "weaving" the slivers into archetypal monoliths that allude to the ancient temples of Western Europe, which he's studied, and those of Meso-America, which he's never visited. At age 43, a dozen years since his first exhibition, Moroles' architectonic granite poems are in museum and corporate collections from Santa Barbara to Tokyo. He's come a very long way from the kid in the *barrios* of north Dallas where he grew up.

Born in Corpus Christi in 1950, the entrepreneurial Moroles was earning his living from the time he was 14, selling designs for high school logos and eventually making the logos himself. From teenage businessman to the respected sculptor, the constant has been an indefatigable desire to do first class work.

He enrolled at North Texas State University in Denton after serving four years in the U.S. Army. Upon graduating in 1978, he spent a year as an apprentice to sculptor Luis Jimenez in El Paso, "one of the most significant experiences in my life", Moroles says. In odd contradiction, however, Moroles chose the language of European classicism, not that of the Mexican-American heritage he shares with the Latino artist. Moroles spent 1980 in Pietrasanta, Italy, close to the quarries of Carrara, the source of what he knew as "all the great sculpture in the world". Returning to Texas after one year, he settled in Rockport, a small seaside community that shares the coastline with Aransas Bird Refuge. He built a compound on roughly three city blocks that is home to his parents and siblings who assist him, and where the saws, grinders and sanders in the studio never seem to stop.

Moroles loves the hardness of stone, especially granite, but handles it as if it were clay. He cuts it into wafer thin slivers joined at the core to suggest a geometric DNA spiral. He leaves giant hunks of it untouched, embracing the roughness created when torn away from the mountain, and polishes sections of it so that the contrasting textures enhance one another in a dance of light and tactile richness. He pushes granite to the extreme of its tensile strength, where a fraction of a millimeter less would transform the thin slab into shattered stone confetti. Even when the piece is measured in tonnage, its appearance is graceful, even fragile.

"What excites me is the stone suggests its own series. All my sculpture has stared from turning it over and over. Stone carries its own history, it's own cultural baggage, and that's what comes through."[1]

1. Cited in "Officers memorial takes shape", by Patricia C. Johnson, *The Houston Chronicle*, Zest Magazine, November 8, 1992, p. 13

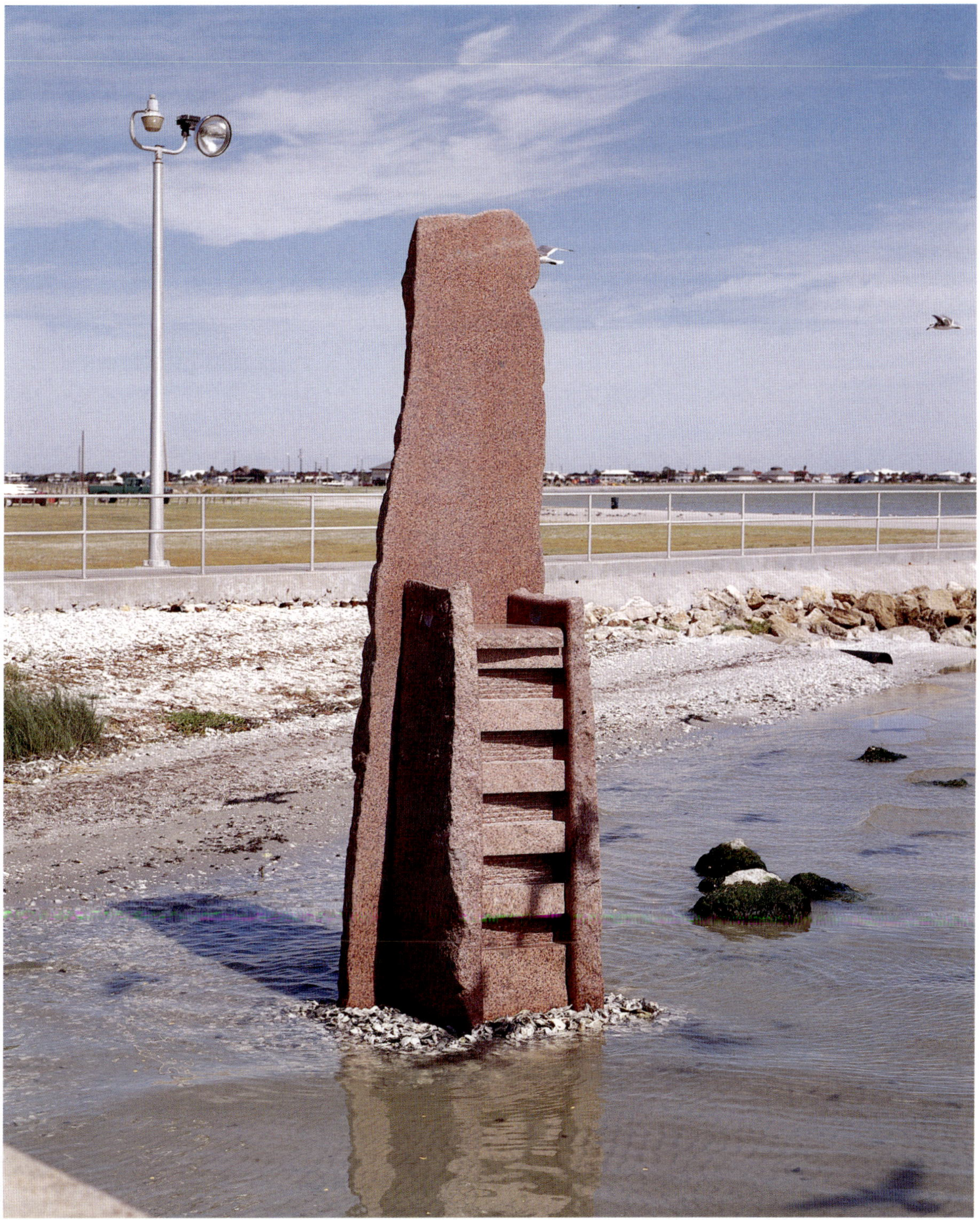

Jesus Bautista Moroles
**High Chair**
1993, Oklahoma granite, 13½'h x 55"w x 35"d.
Photograph: Brad Steiner. Courtesy of
Davis/McClain Gallery, Houston

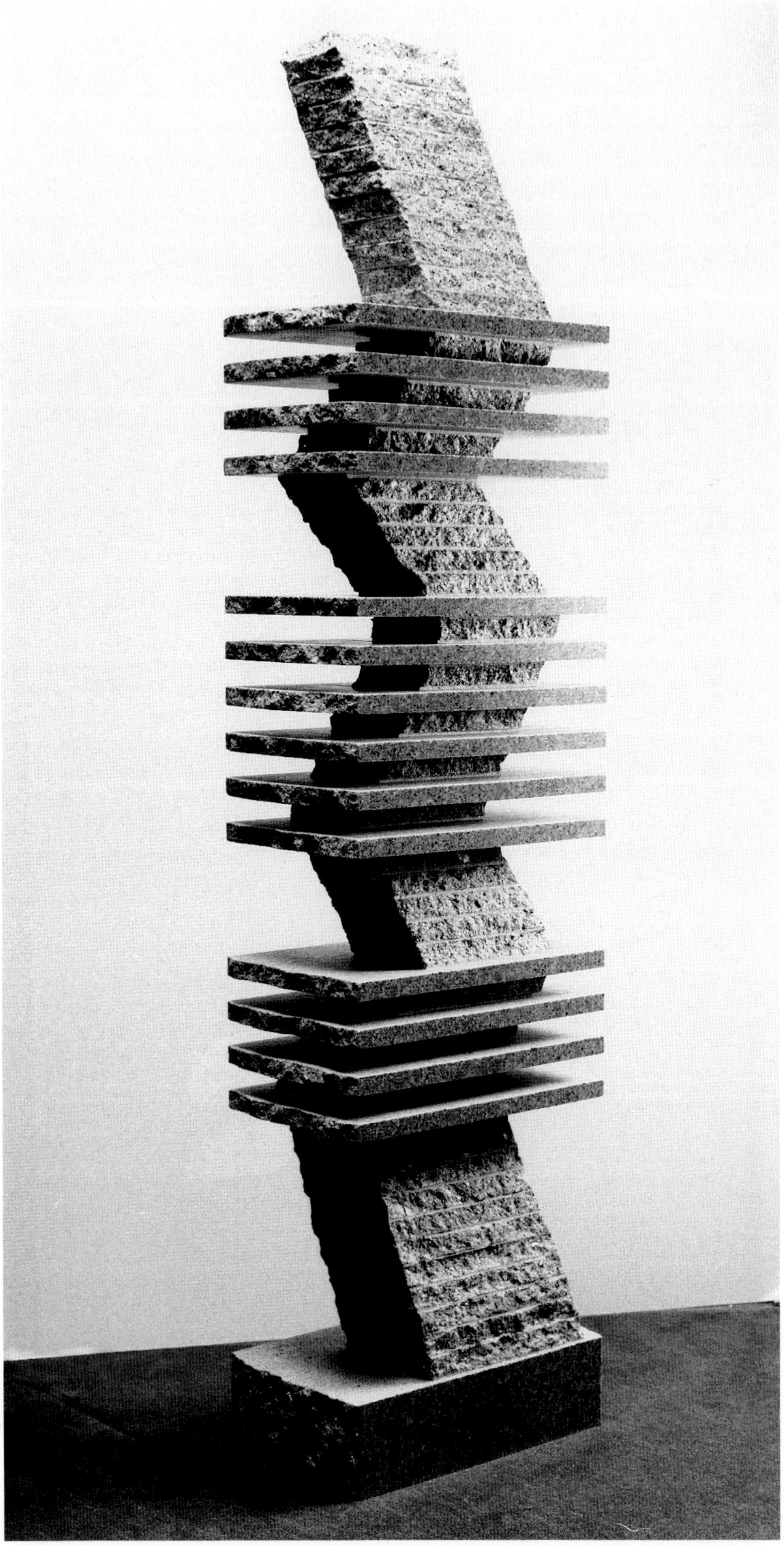

Jesus Bautista Moroles
**Zig Zag Las Mesas**
1984, Texas granite, 78"h x 12"w x 8"d.
Private collection. Courtesy of
Davis/McClain Gallery, Houston

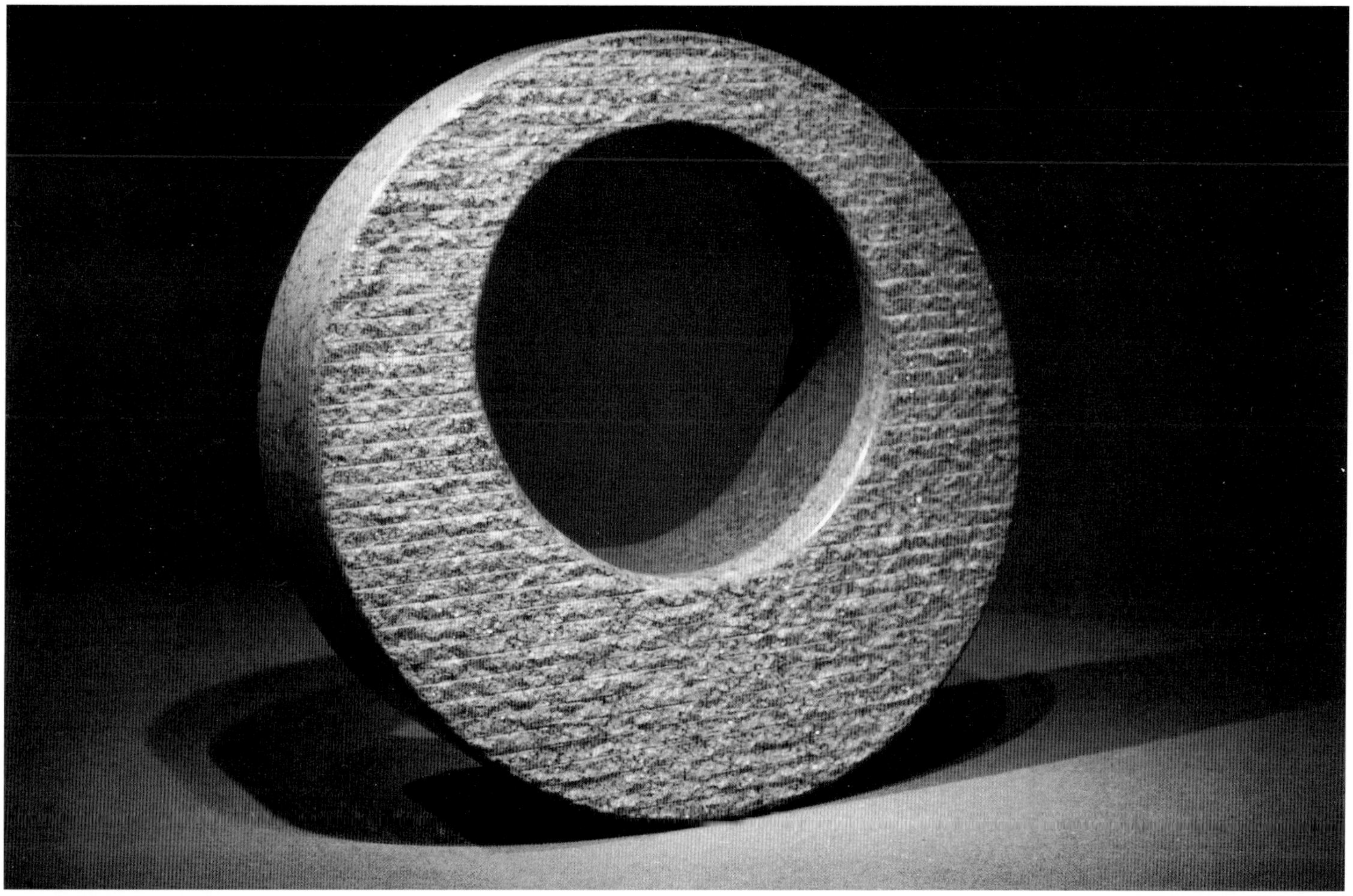

Jesus Bautista Moroles
**Moonscape Ring**
1993, Texas pink granite, 62⅜"h x 62½"w x 22"d.
Courtesy of Davis/McClain Gallery, Houston

# Celia Alvarez **Muñoz**

Celia Muñoz, like many women of her generation and background, was expected to marry and have children. What she wanted was an education, postponing one, then the other to achieve both. When she graduated with a master's degree from the University of North Texas in 1982, she shared a core grounding in post-modernism with her colleagues. But for her, the issues it presented, especially the layering of information, were far more than theory, they were autobiography.

"I think the post-modern issues are concurrent to leading a life that has multiple layers. Being on the border, being in El Paso exposed to three cultures, Mexico, Texas and New Mexico, prepared me."

Born in El Paso in 1937, she followed tradition except for postponing marriage until she had her bachelor's degree. Then she traveled across the country. Her husband was a trouble shooter for the U.S. Government whose investigation of cases of discrimination took the family from one coast to the other in the 1960s and early 1970s. Traveling from the migrant farm workers in California to the antiwar protest marches in Washington D.C., was a learning process for Muñoz. When the family settled in Arlington, half-way between Dallas and Fort Worth, she enrolled at UNT to finally pursue her master's degree. Vernon Fisher's work (among others') with its savvy, wry approach to narrative, were a major influence.

Photography became her medium. "I knew print making, but it was labor intensive and time consuming for me. I had an education in advertising art which uses a lot of photography and I was very ready to use everything as a means to an end. Photography is a way to expedite an image."

When Muñoz first began to exhibit in the mid-1980s, her work typically consisted of black-and-white photographs, like stills from a movie, complemented by a short narrative poem, sometimes written in Spanish. In the years since, she has expanded her ideas of feminism from the personal to more universal concerns while contracting the story telling impulse to single words. Muñoz has simultaneously broadened her visual language to include installation works. The principal component is still photographic, though removed from a photograph's object-ness. She projects images she's made with a large-format 4-by-5 camera onto the exhibition walls to recreate them with an airbrush. To these flat and mediated images, Muñoz adds three-dimensional components, such as textiles, to create an environment that is both specific and ambiguous.

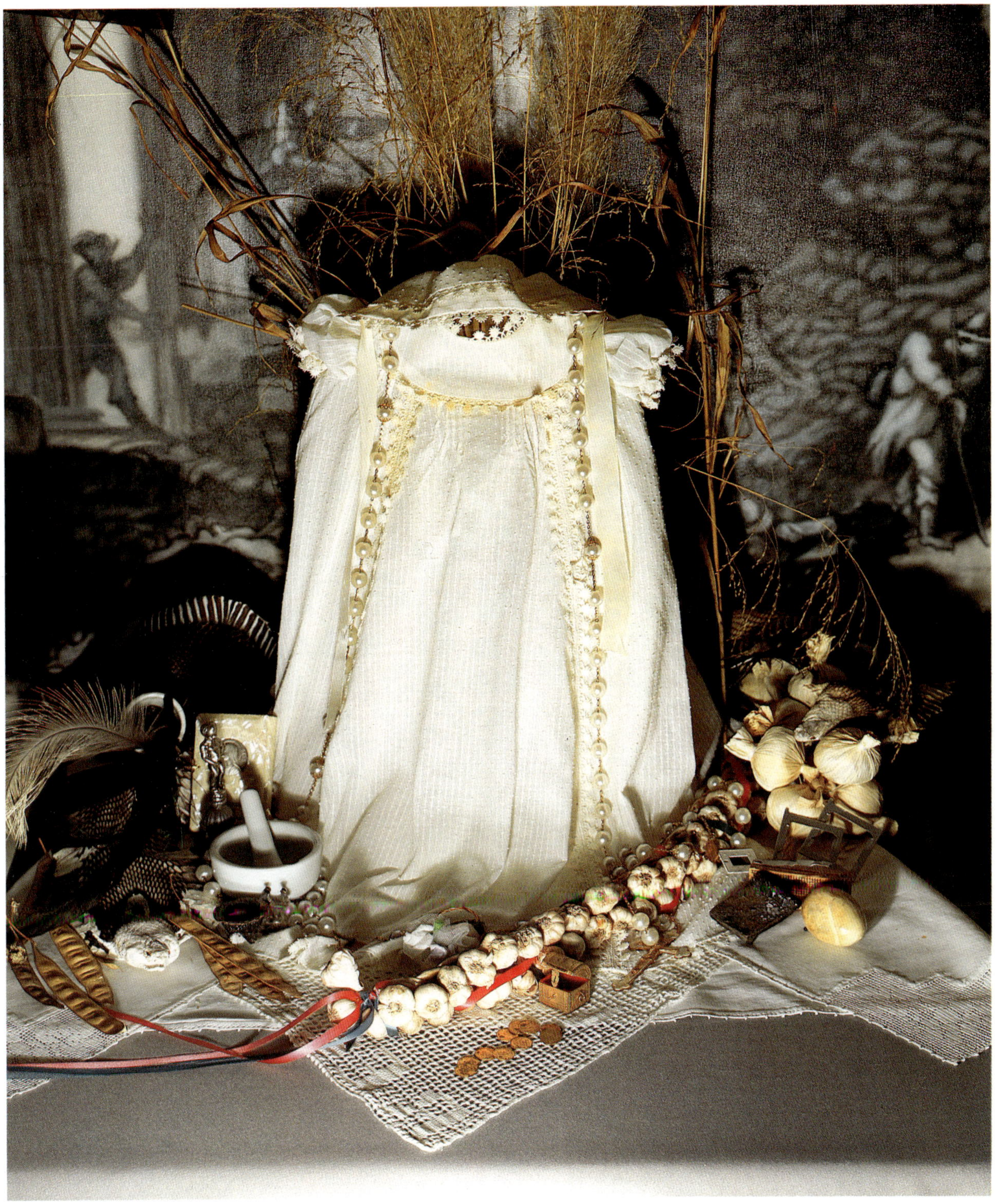

Celia Alvarez Muñoz
**Yo**
Fujichrome, 20" x 16". Photograph: Celia Alvarez Muñoz. Courtesy of the artist

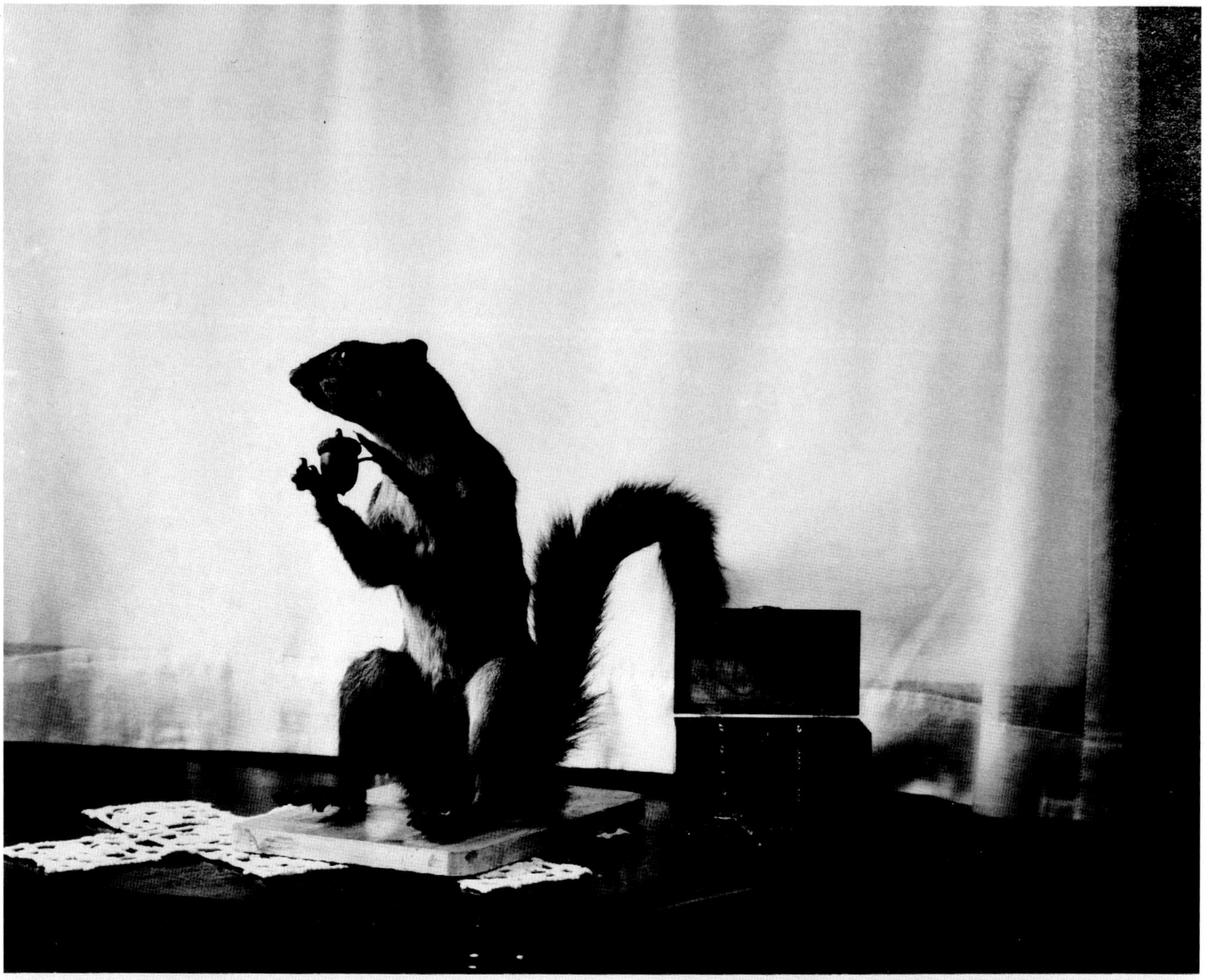

Whenever she sensed a storm approaching, grandmother would cover all the mirrors to ward off the lightning, sprinkle every room with holy water, and gather the family to pray *La Magnifica.*

Celia Alvarez Muñoz
**La Tempestad (The Tempest)**
(Detail: left side) 1985, Mixed media,
52"h x 24"w x 1¾". Courtesy of the artist

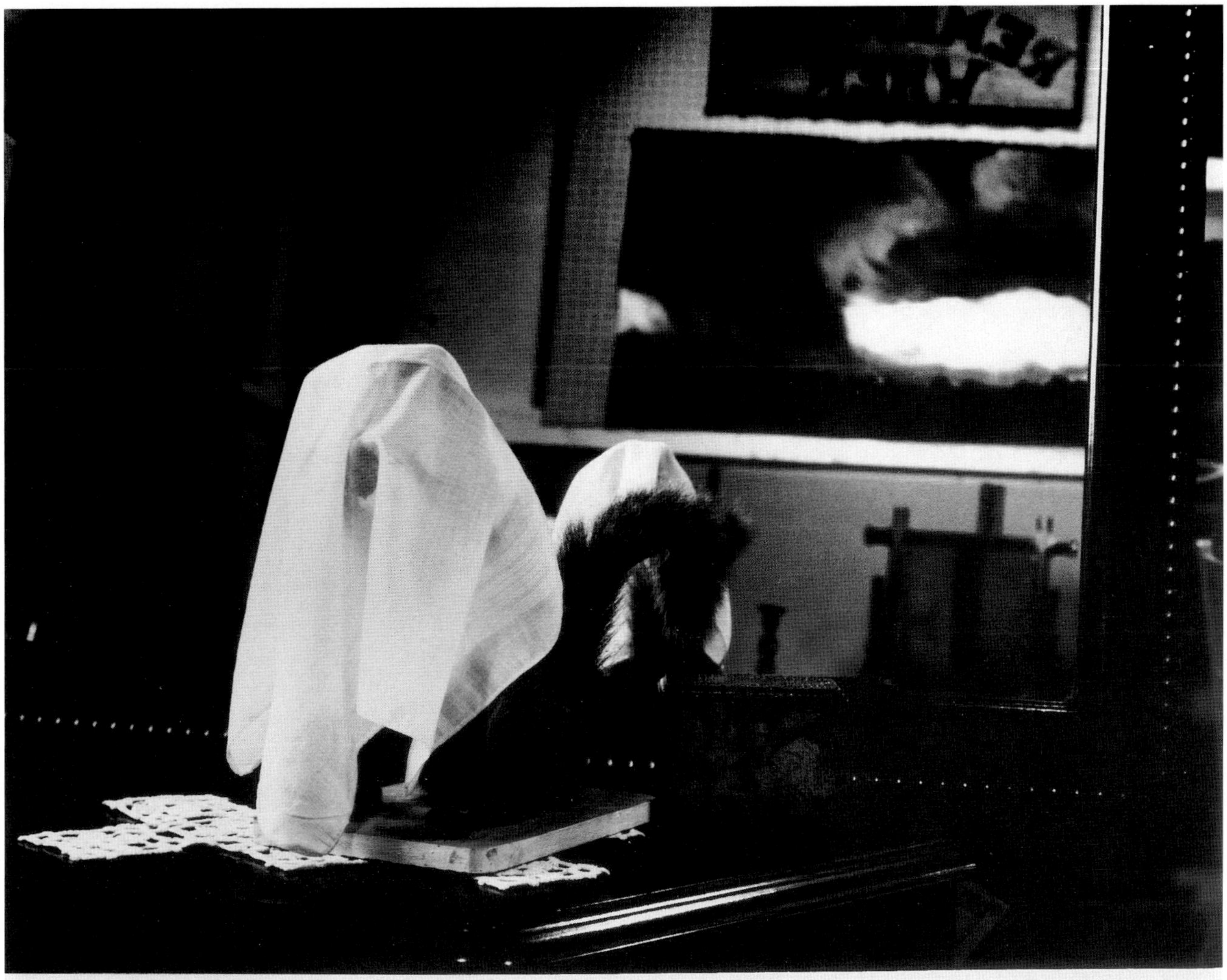

After a heated family argument, grandfather would stuff a clean handkerchief in his back pocket, a rosary in his front pocket, and check himself in the mirror before stepping out to the nearest *cantina.*

Celia Alvarez Muñoz
**La Tempestad (The Tempest)**
(Detail: right side) 1985, Mixed media,
52"h x 24"w x 1¾". Courtesy of the artist

# Nic
# Nicosia

Nic Nicosia approaches photography like a film maker, taking stills of situations he has instigated and choreographed, each preceding and following instant implicit within the one frozen frame. He works in series in which he explores human behavior, not as a sequential event but in separate, revealing moments. Born in Dallas in 1951, Nicosia graduated with a degree in radio, television and film from North Texas State University. Five years later, in 1979, he went back for a master's degree in the university's newly established photography department.

Nicosia rejected the "decisive moment" expounded by Henri Cartier-Bresson, opting instead for the fabricated situation which he could control in its entirety, from sets to costumes. His earliest series, titled "Domestic Dramas and Modern Disasters", portrayed familial conflicts of the suburbs and the corporate office. The large (36 inches by 36 inches) format Cibachrome images resembled commercial story boards. His sets looked like comic book versions of Mondrian geometry — all flat, primary colors, with no illusions of real space — and he posed his actors within them in the exaggerated reactive poses of mime and parody.

He switched from color photography to black and white in 1986–87 after sensing that his audience was not paying attention to the content of his images. The transition was not smooth. Nicosia attempted to recreate the familiar colorful sets in duochrome, but discovered they didn't work. The pictures, he said, looked totally fake and he realized he needed a different approach, and his attitude changed.

"I don't feel it is necessary to be so obviously staged. My thinking became fundamentally different because I found no reward in just staging the stuff anymore. The content changed to become more of a personal view of things as opposed to responding to the media. The images began to have more substance."

The series "Real Pictures", from 1990, were his first successes. Assuming a journalistic point of view, Nicosia photographed his scenes of urban conflict on location. Though as staged as ever, they were believable. "Love & Lust" followed and it signaled a breakthrough. Again, the situation was directed and controlled, but a new ambiguity had entered the scene.

His most recent series, dated 1992–93 and untitled, represents another level in Nicosia's career. More than ever, these pictures of loneliness and alienation, composed with great care and subtlety, have a cinematrographic quality to them. The ambiguity which he resisted at the beginning of his career is now integral to the image. Through nuance in both medium and emotional range, he entices his audience to focus on the content of his art.

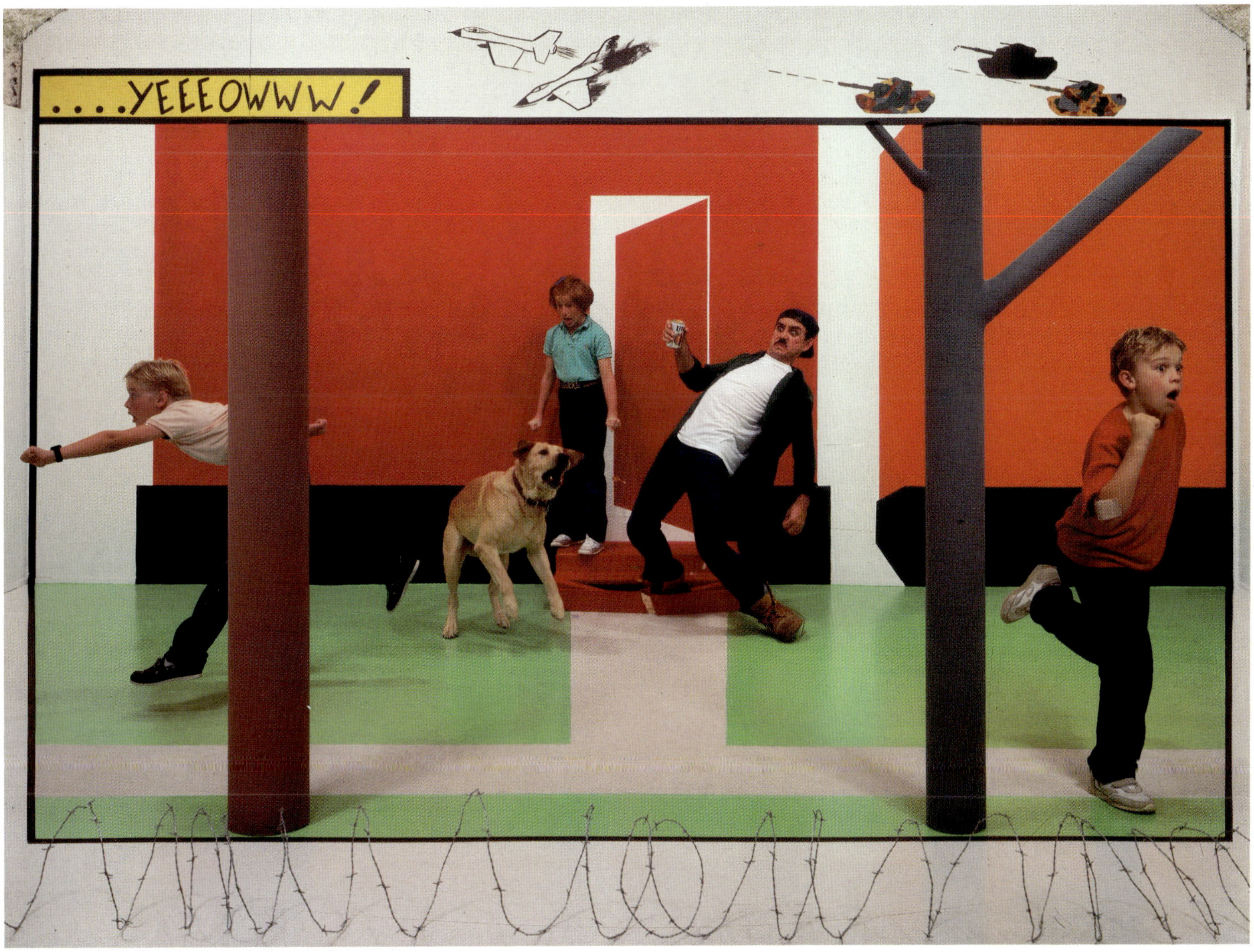


Nic Nicosia

**Near Modern Disaster #7**

1983, Cibachrome, 40" x 60". Courtesy of the artist and Texas Gallery, Houston

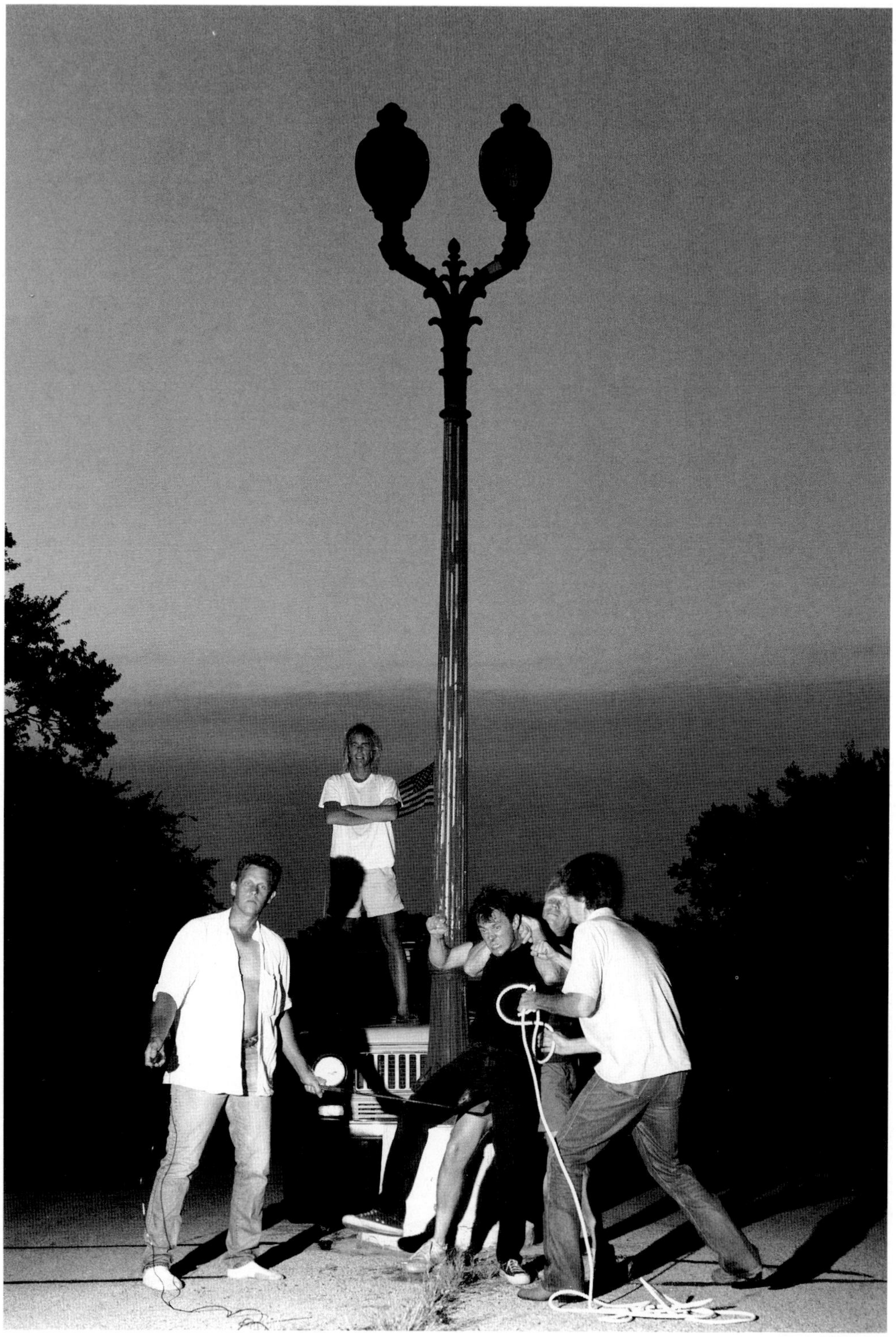

Nic Nicosia
**Real Pictures #4**
1987, Black & white photograph, 72" x 48". Courtesy of the artist and Texas Gallery, Houston

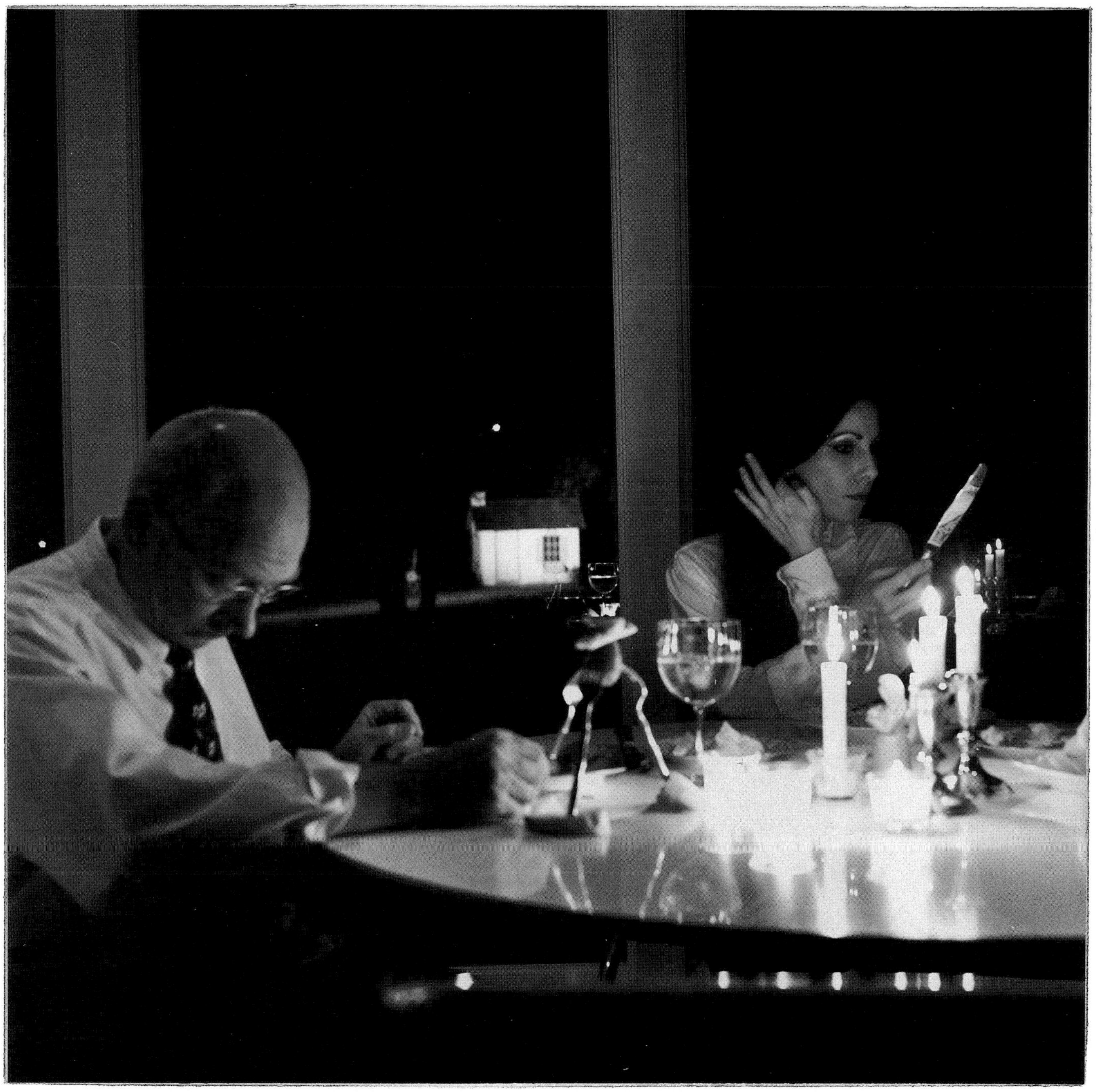

Nic Nicosia
**Untitled #5**
1991, Oil on black & white photograph, 36" x 36".
Courtesy of the artist and Texas Gallery, Houston

# James Reaben

Part concrete poet and part existentialist mystic, James Reaben selected from among the detritus materials that intrigued him visually and that also carried the possibilities of symbolism. The claws of an iguana became the drawer pulls of a little box. Dry beans and tiny pebbles added a shamanistic rattle to a hermetic object. The exterior surfaces of his small sculptures are polished wood painted with helixes and eyes. Each promises secrets within, to be revealed if only one can find the key.

Born in Houston in 1956, Reaben was diagnosed as dyslexic and "hyperactive" as a child, was sent to military school in San Antonio and finally to finish high school in Houston. He attended the University of St. Thomas for one year, then sporadically enrolled in courses at the Glassell School of Art. Essentially, he taught himself to cut, glue and paint the mysterious little objects and talismans, which appear as traces of where he wandered in his search for peace and knowledge.

When he died in 1989, Reaben had only just begun to receive recognition. An exhibit in New Orleans, a few months before his death, was his first out of Texas. But in Texas, and especially in Houston where he lived, he had a dedicated following.

Reaben sought spiritual solutions and read voraciously about Eastern religions and about his own Catholic upbringing. He was dissatisfied with most answers given. The metaphysics of personal salvation are central to Reaben's work. Through action and thought, he proposed the investigation of the human spirit. He aligned himself with the impassioned words of poet and dramatic theorist Antonin Artaud, whose words Reaben often interwove in his meticulous painted works on paper. His work, like that of the late Forrest Bess with whom Reaben felt kinship, are a kind of exorcism in which dreams, fear and desires are transformed into mystical symbols.

"[The art has] been very slowly forming itself into a cohesive body of work, for quite a while I never forced the work, I waited for it to speak to me. It's a process of revelation, it exists by itself, apart. I'm quite sure that a force other than me has been guiding the course."[1]

1. Cited in William Steen, "Conversations with a Mad Man", *11x14* [magazine], 1987

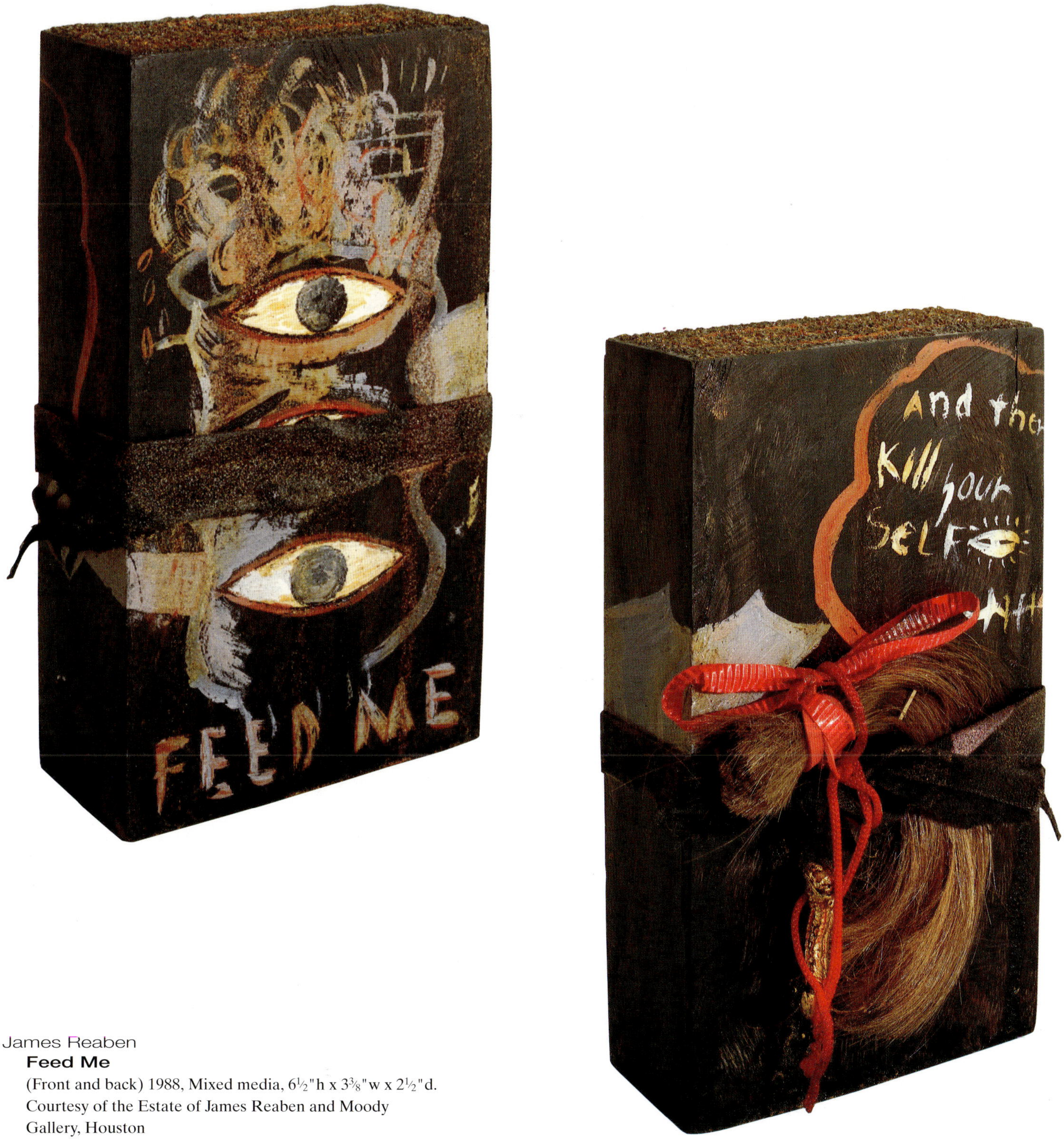


James Reaben

**Feed Me**

(Front and back) 1988, Mixed media, 6½"h x 3⅜"w x 2½"d. Courtesy of the Estate of James Reaben and Moody Gallery, Houston

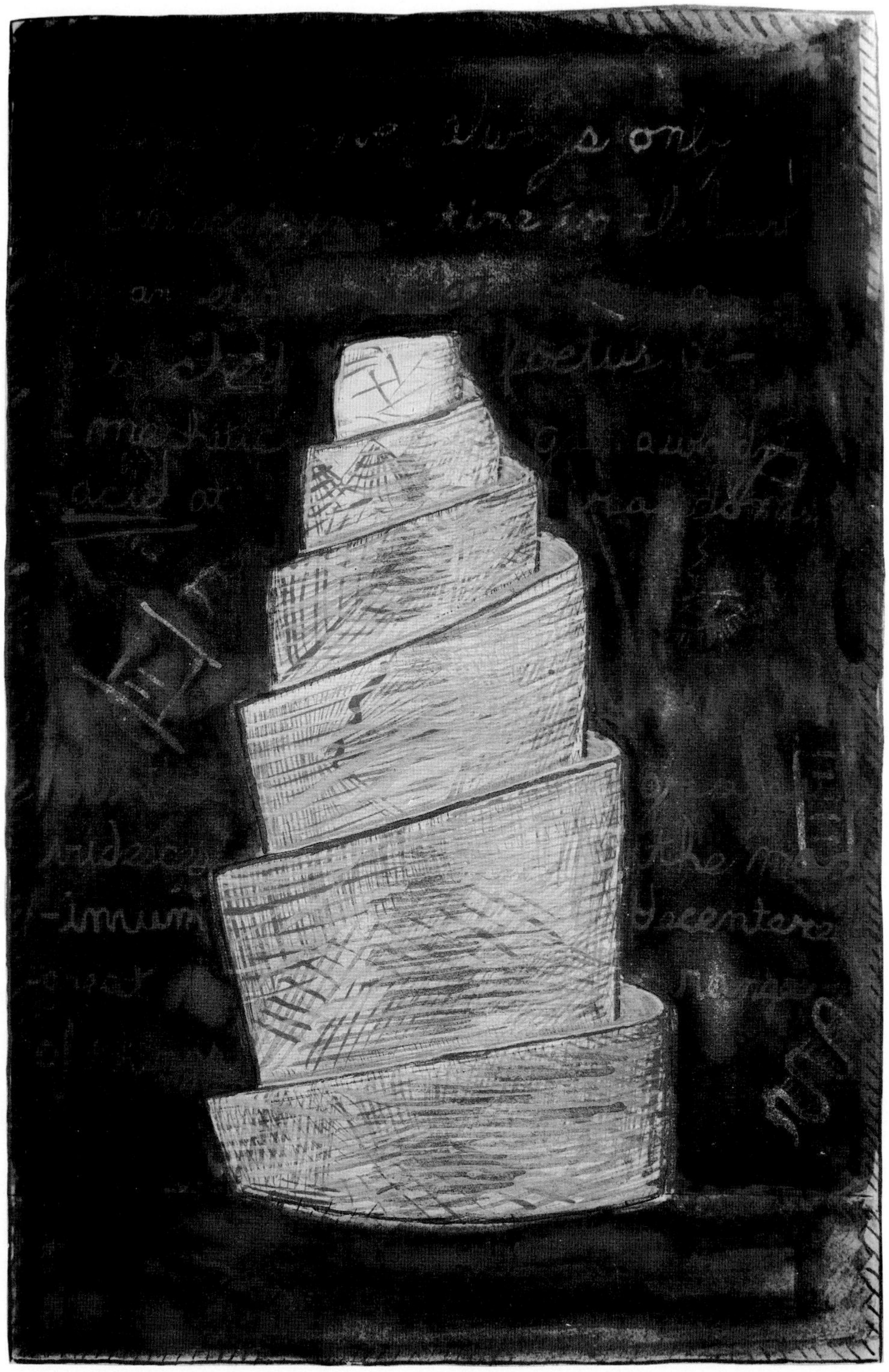

James Reaben
**A Windy Acid at Random**
1986, Gouache and watercolor on paper. Courtesy of the Estate of James Reaben and Moody Gallery, Houston

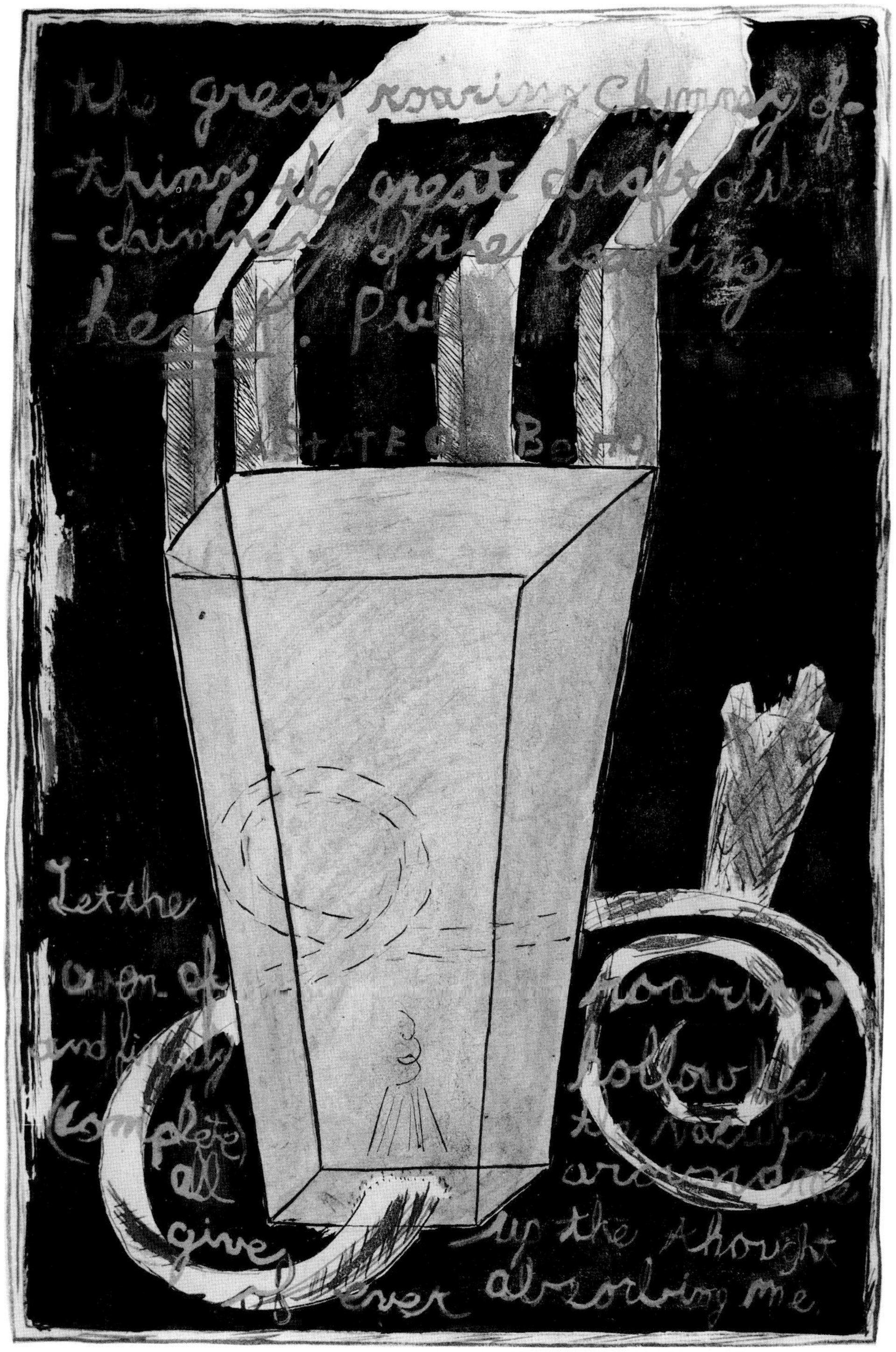


James Reaben

**A State of Being**

1986, Gouache and watercolor on paper. Courtesy of the Estate of James Reaben and Moody Gallery, Houston

# Lee N
# Smith III

Lee Smith lives on the same street where he grew up on the Dallas city limits. He is just one block away from the elementary school he attended and adjacent to the enormous field and drive-in theater on the edge of his boyhood home that are the stages for many of his paintings. He recalls the games played and the adventures lived and imagined there, made real once more through his descriptive brush. His intense colors reflect the total absorption of childhood pastimes, and heighten the emotional tenor of the memory of camping trips, games of pretend and sheer mischief.

Born in New Orleans in 1950 and raised in Dallas from the age of six, Smith wanted to be a musician. For several years he lived an adolescent dream by playing in country-western, rock and roll, and jazz bands, supporting himself by working part time at a silkscreen shop. The background in graphics, and the remembered excitement from seeing images in books and on museum walls, led the self-taught artist to paint full time in the mid 1970s.

His earlier work combined three-dimensional assemblages with painted illusions. Smith reinvented a suburban world of back-yard barbecues, disaster stories of car crashes and full air wars in precisely scaled and detailed miniature figures and props he mostly made himself. These diminutive cosmos (usually 1/87 scale) would then be integrated to painted compositions, a world within the world of his youthful protagonists.

The most recent work is strictly two-dimensional. It all begins with a sketch no more than two inches square where the key components and color are described from different perspectives. Smith doesn't use models of any kind, and transfers his sketches onto the panel surfaces freehand, moving elements around, then building his neon-hued colors with multiple layers of oil glazes.

Since living in Paris for a year in 1988, Smith's work changed in subtle but significant ways. Painting "straight" landscapes sitting by the Loire, he became aware of the natural life around him but mostly of "putting one color next to the other trying to capture light." He also started to allow the girls in his pictures to move from passive roles as spectators, to embark on adventures of their own.

"My pictures are portraits of events more than they are of people. My work is very musical somehow and very intuitive. I want things to be believable, but I don't care if the perspective is off and the colors obviously aren't 'right'. I think a really early influence was looking at these huge paintings of battle scenes in books. They were just fabulous, with so much stuff going on. It was like a dance, all these bodies in space. That's what I'm interested in, how these bodies fill this space."

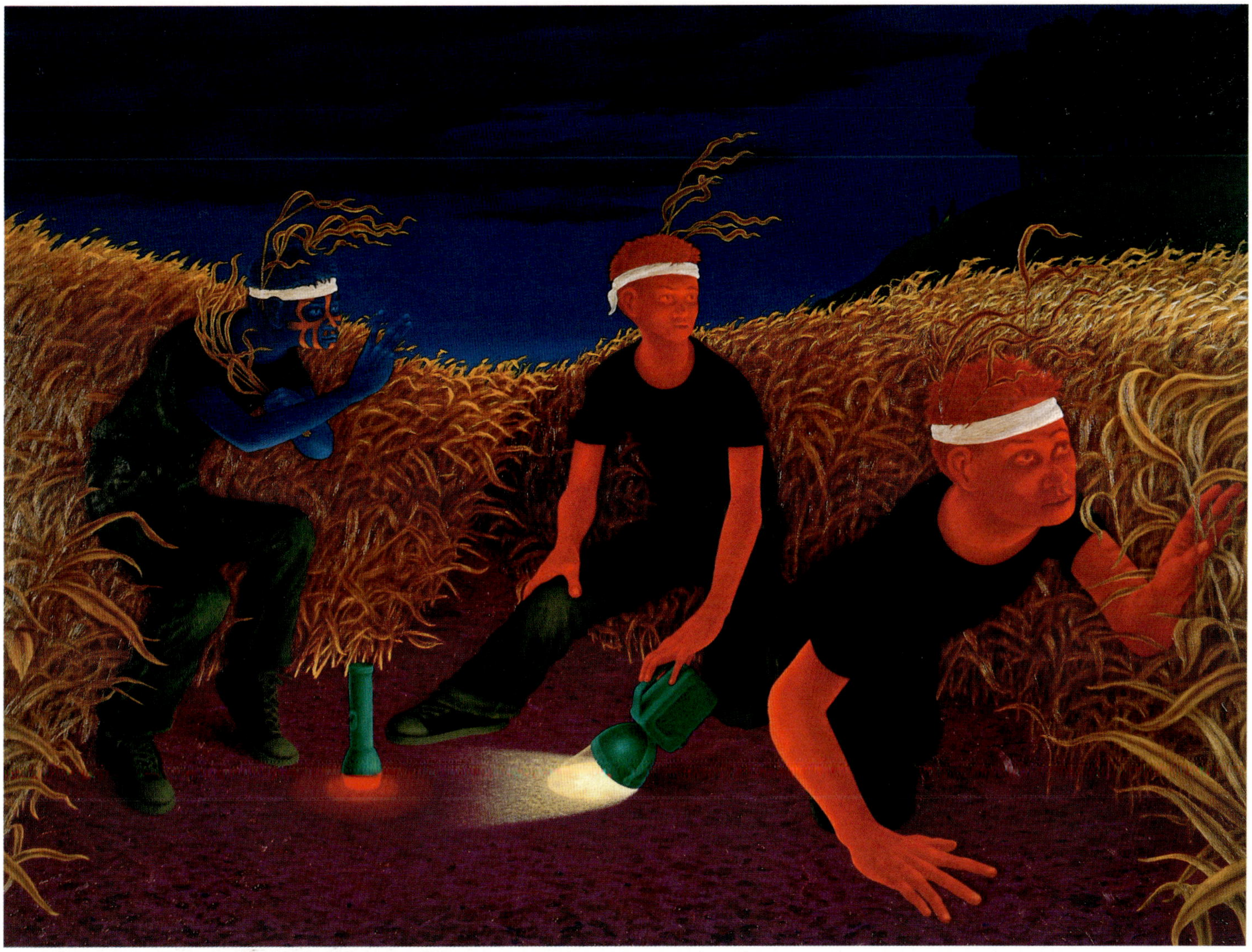

Lee N Smith III
**Edge of Invisibility**
1990, Oil on canvas, 38¼" x 51¼". Private collection.
Courtesy of Barry Whistler Gallery, Dallas

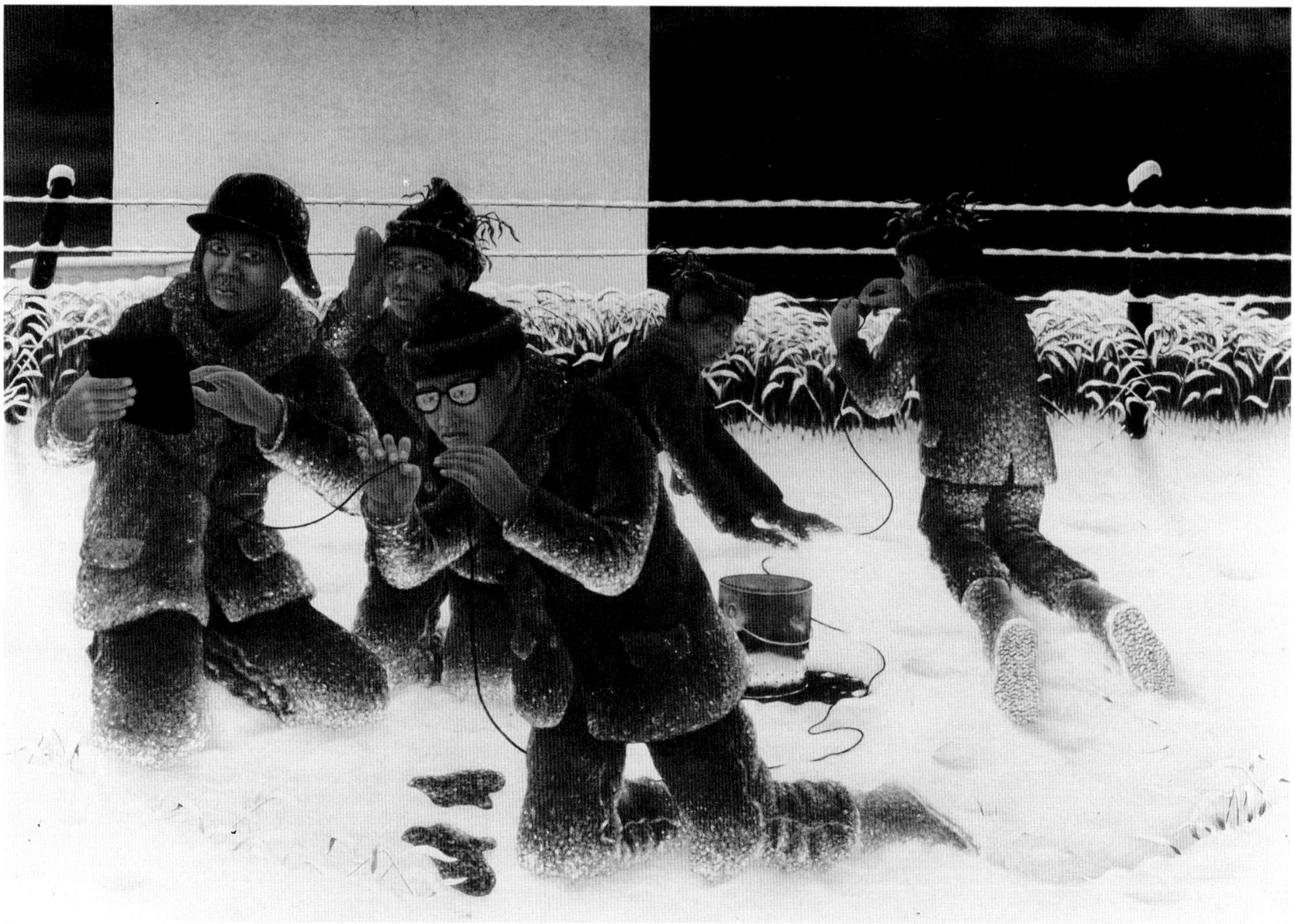

Lee N Smith III

**Sound Stealers**

1989, Oil on canvas, 45" x 59⅛". Collection: The Barret Collection, Dallas. Courtesy of Barry Whistler Gallery, Dallas

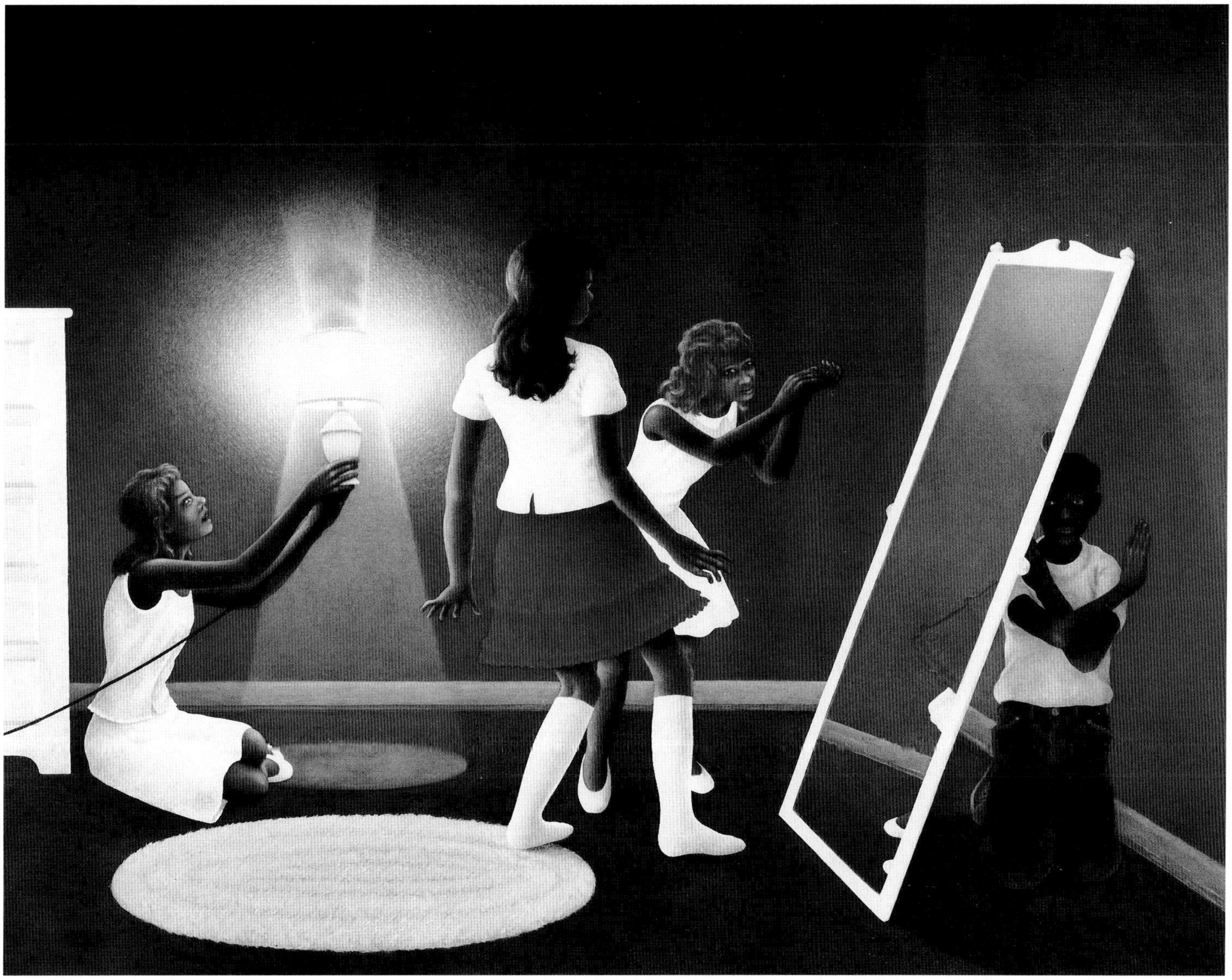

Lee N Smith III

**The Red Petticoat**

1991, Oil on canvas, 45" x 57½". Collection of the artist. Courtesy of the artist and Barry Whistler Gallery, Dallas

# Gael **Stack**

Gael Stack is a difficult artist to get to know. She guards her privacy with the ferocity of a mother bear, a quality transmitted in her brooding, canvases. Like Cy Twombly, Stack makes marks on a flat surface that resemble words and specific objects, but which are essentially elusive. Unlike the masterful abstractionist, though, Stack wants to tell a story. The gossamer threads of a narrative pulsate in the tangle of lines and shapes. The impulse to divulge her knowledge, the gesture of her wrist, and promptings of her subconscious, result in multi-layered compositions. On one hand, veils of pure color wash over the figures which might otherwise reveal too much; on the other, the figures prevent the painterliness from becoming an end in itself.

She alternates between adding figures then rubbing them out, creating complex spatial relationships in the process. The ambiguity between figure and ground draws the viewer in and repels deep probing simultaneously, like a warm but shy embrace.

"Art is the perfect thing for me. It allows me to indulge in everything I like — philosophy, literature, painting."

Born in Chicago in 1941, Gael Stack moved to Houston in 1973, "with a carload of plants, two babies (her sons, age nine and six) and no job", packed in the back of an ancient station wagon. She got a teaching job at the arts magnet school, and a year later at the University of Houston where she is now a tenured professor of painting. Her training, however, was in print making at the University of Illinois in Carbondale. Painting was never at the forefront until 1977 when she exhibited her works on canvas for the first time.

Her outlined human figures and decorative objects like Chinese porcelains or pre-Columbian gods, appear as graffiti against dense layers of moody color, often peppered with miscellaneous information. A shopping list or a rapidly scrawled telephone message appear spontaneously, inscribed on a surface like mislaid clues. Deciphering them demands concentration. There are no guarantees the viewer will know any more about Stack than he would after a casual glance, but he will have discerned rhythms that echo his own.[1]

1. Cited in "Gael Stack: artist-teacher who doesn't easily fit into a mold", by Patricia C. Johnson, *The Houston Chronicle*, October 4, 1981, p. 14

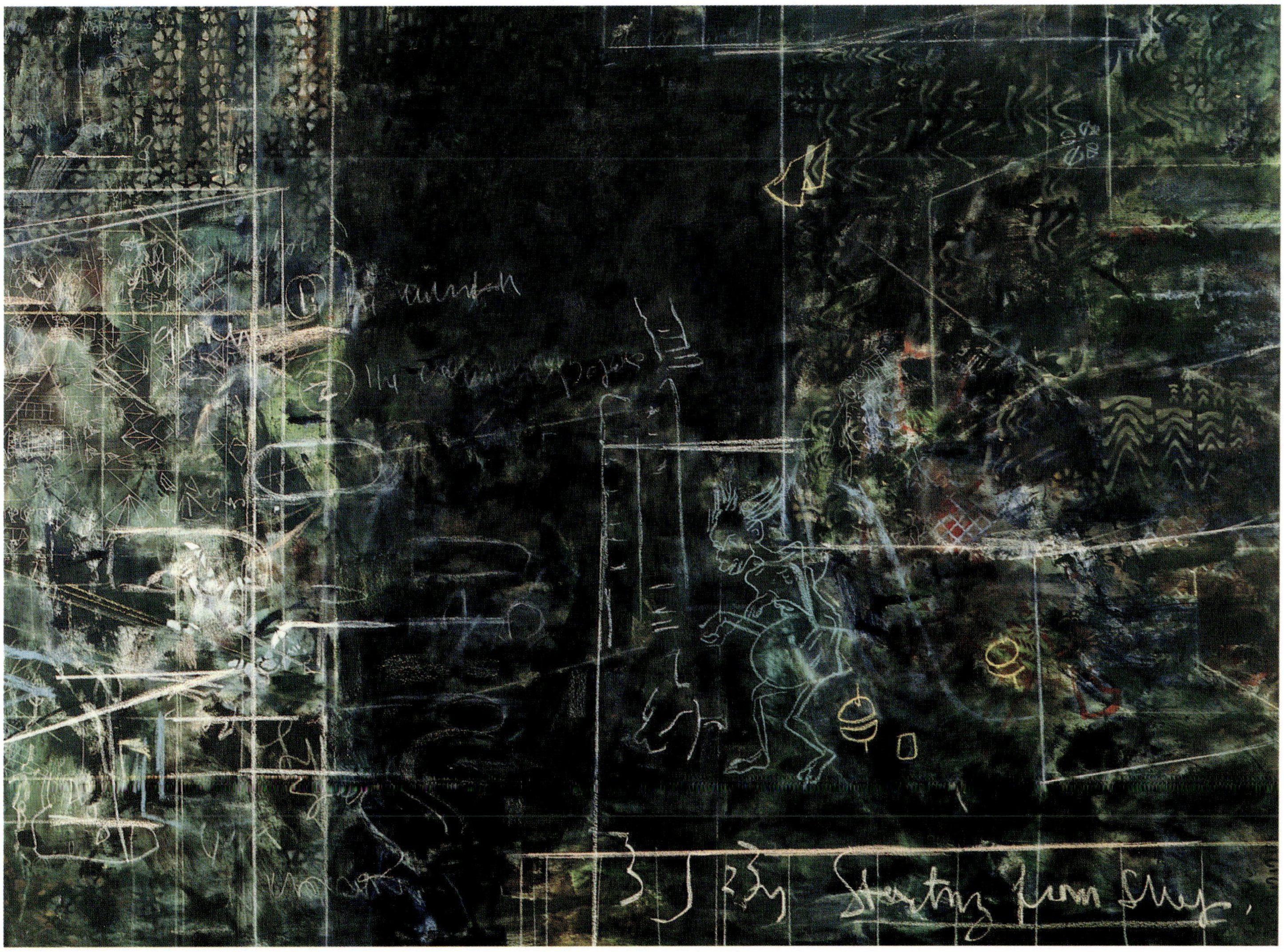

Gael Stack

**Starting from Sleep**

1992, Oil on canvas, 64" x 84". Collection: Helen Elizabeth Hill Trust, Houston. Courtesy of Moody Gallery, Houston

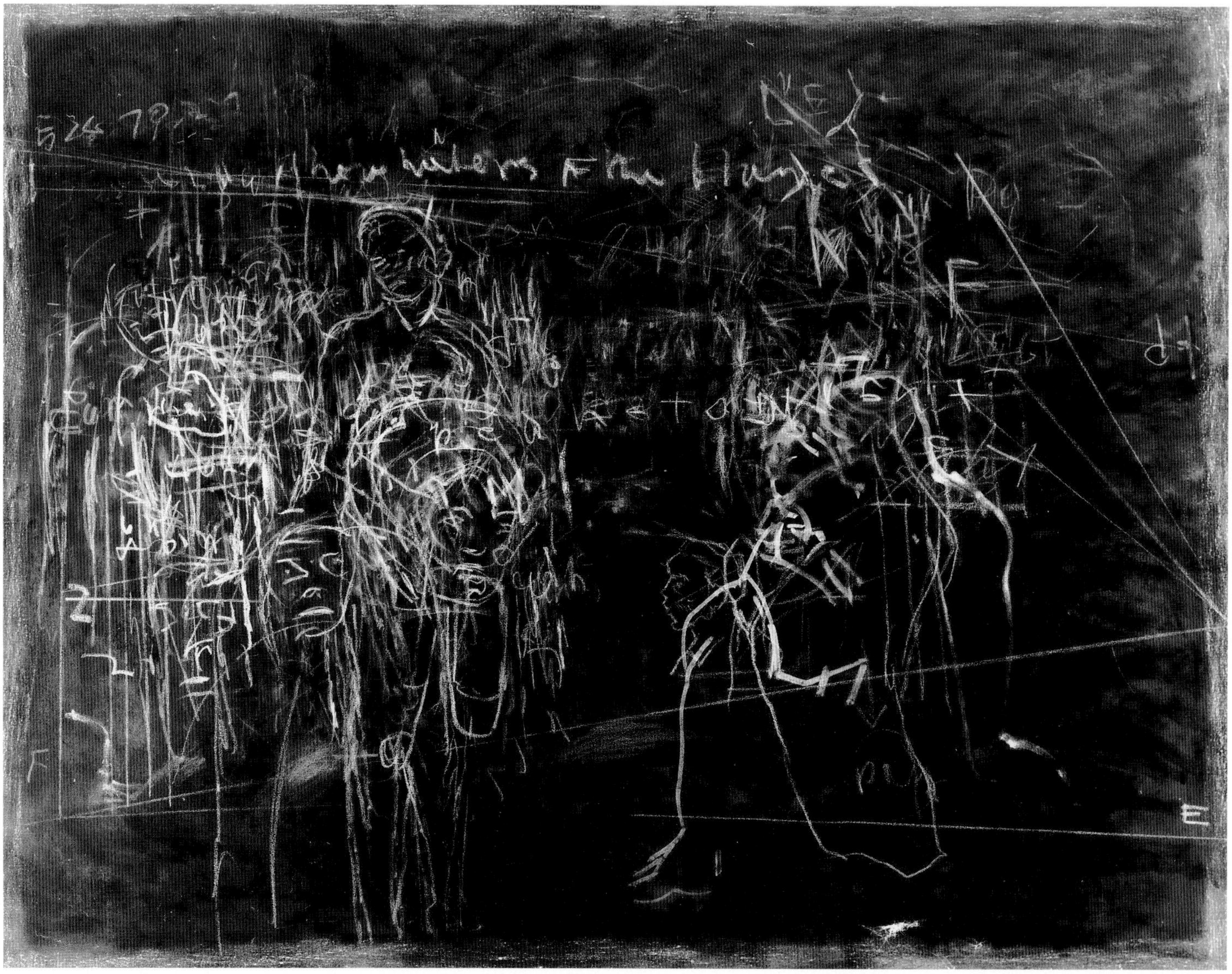

Gael Stack
**Untitled**
1985, Oil on canvas, 48" x 60". Photograph: Zhotograph, Houston. Private collection. Courtesy of Moody Gallery, Houston

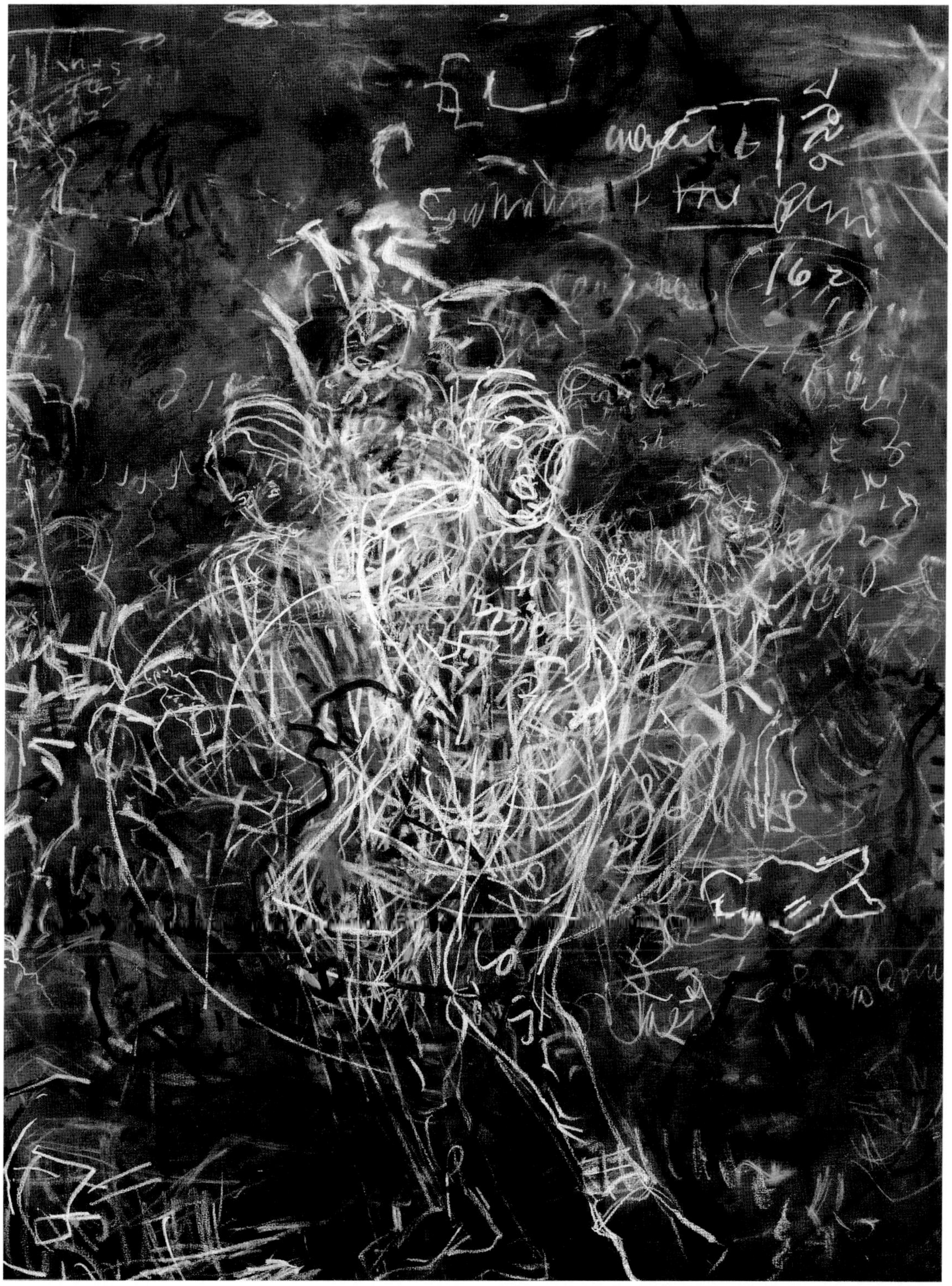

Gael Stack

**Other Graces**

1987, Oil on canvas, 65¾" x 48". Private collection.
Courtesy of Moody Gallery, Houston

# Earl **Staley**

It would not be an exaggeration to say Earl Staley has rolled several artists' careers into his own. He's been painting for more than three decades, exploring myriad styles and subject matter in a range from formal abstraction to the funk aesthetic of the 1970s and the realism of 19th century genres. He delves into the plasticity of paint and the stories it is capable of telling. He also engages in experimental and craft techniques, from using tinsel and dirt as painting components, to modeling ceramics and tooling leather, adopting and adapting medium, scale and stylistic approach to suit his needs of the moment. Using traditional techniques of painting and print making, Staley seeks the "perfect way" to render his subject. "You can't paint the Virgin of Guadalupe in the same way you paint a desert landscape," he has frequently stated.

Driven to work, Staley is remarkably prolific and non-judgemental, and rejects the idea of originality. "I'll steal from anybody" is his constant refrain.

"I use everybody. Leonardo, Raphael, Donatello, Degas — all the boys. They're what I learned from. I didn't think I was original. I don't like the idea of 'original', what it forces on an artist. I just paint what I like [and] I like it all."[1]

He is a voracious appropriator and a populist, unabashedly aiming to please his audience. From antiquity, he steals myths and a realist mode of depiction bathed in dramatic light. His hunger for images is satisfied by the skulls and skeletons of Mexico's Day of the Dead celebrations and the colorful pageantry of border towns and religious ceremony. He renders these in intense colors, studded with glitter and described with animated gestures. In the southwest of Texas, he focuses on the panoramic glory of Big Bend National Park, describing it with smooth brush strokes dipped in colors bleached by the white Texas sun.

Born in Oak Park, Illinois in 1938, Staley received his master's degree from the University of Arkansas in 1963 and three years later settled in Houston. He taught at the University of St. Thomas and Rice University under the shared studio an art history programs established by John and Dominique de Menil, eventually becoming chairman of UST's art department (1973–80). But though Staley had been exhibiting all along in group and solo exhibitions around the country, he feels he only truly began to paint in the late 1970s. His first recognition on the national scene came in 1978 when he was included in the New Museum in New York exhibit titled "Bad Painting". Three years later, he was in the Hirshhorn's Museum's "Directions 81" exhibition. That same year, Staley was awarded a Prix de Rome that took him to Italy for two years. He settled in New York City upon his return, but by 1990, was back in Houston and teaching, this time at a community college.

1. Cited in "Staley: energy and ego", by Patricia C. Johnson, *The Houston Chronicle*, July 12, 1981, p. 18

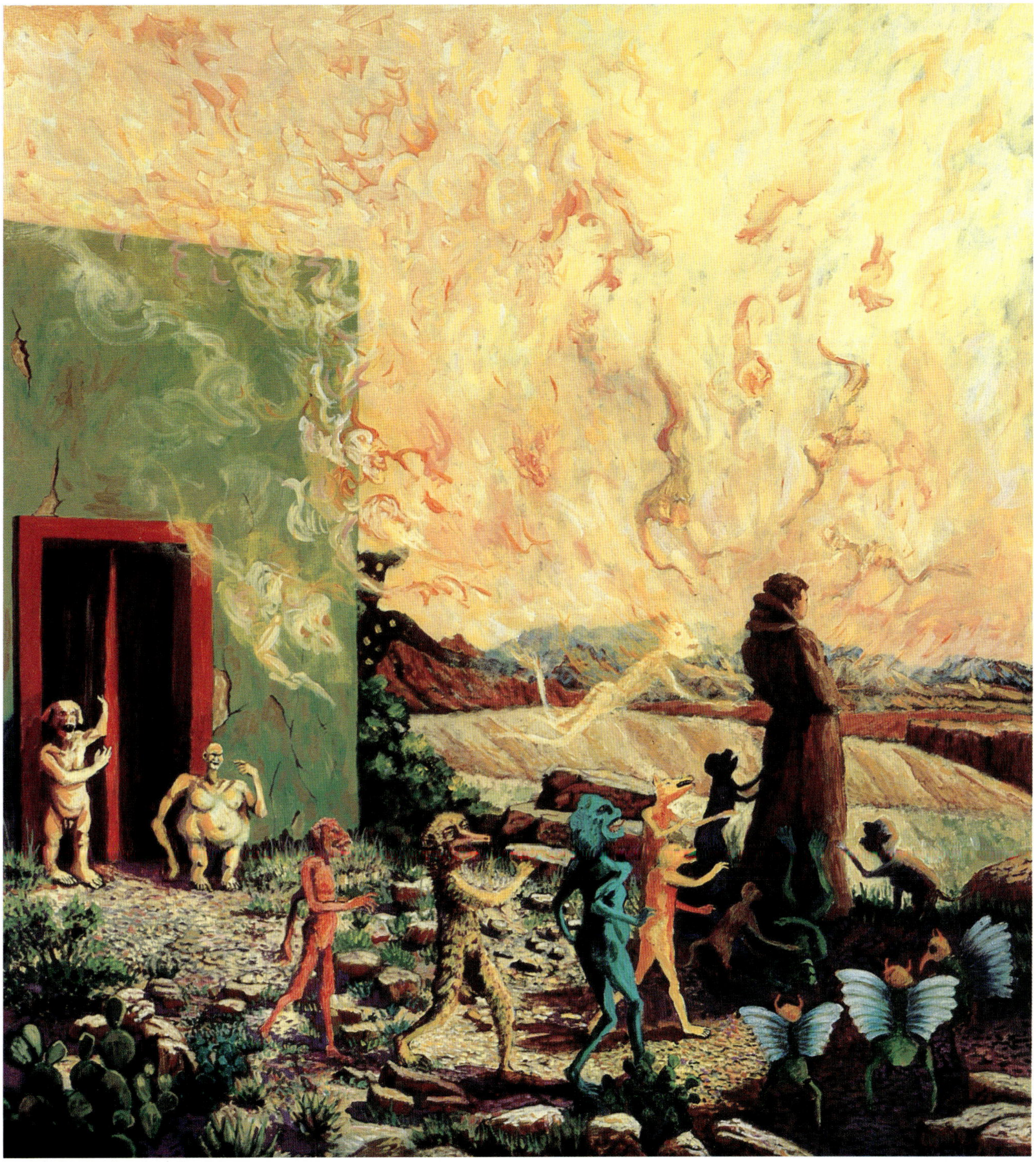

Earl Staley

**Temptation of St Anthony**

1992, Acrylic on canvas, 54" x 48". Courtesy of Moody Gallery, Houston

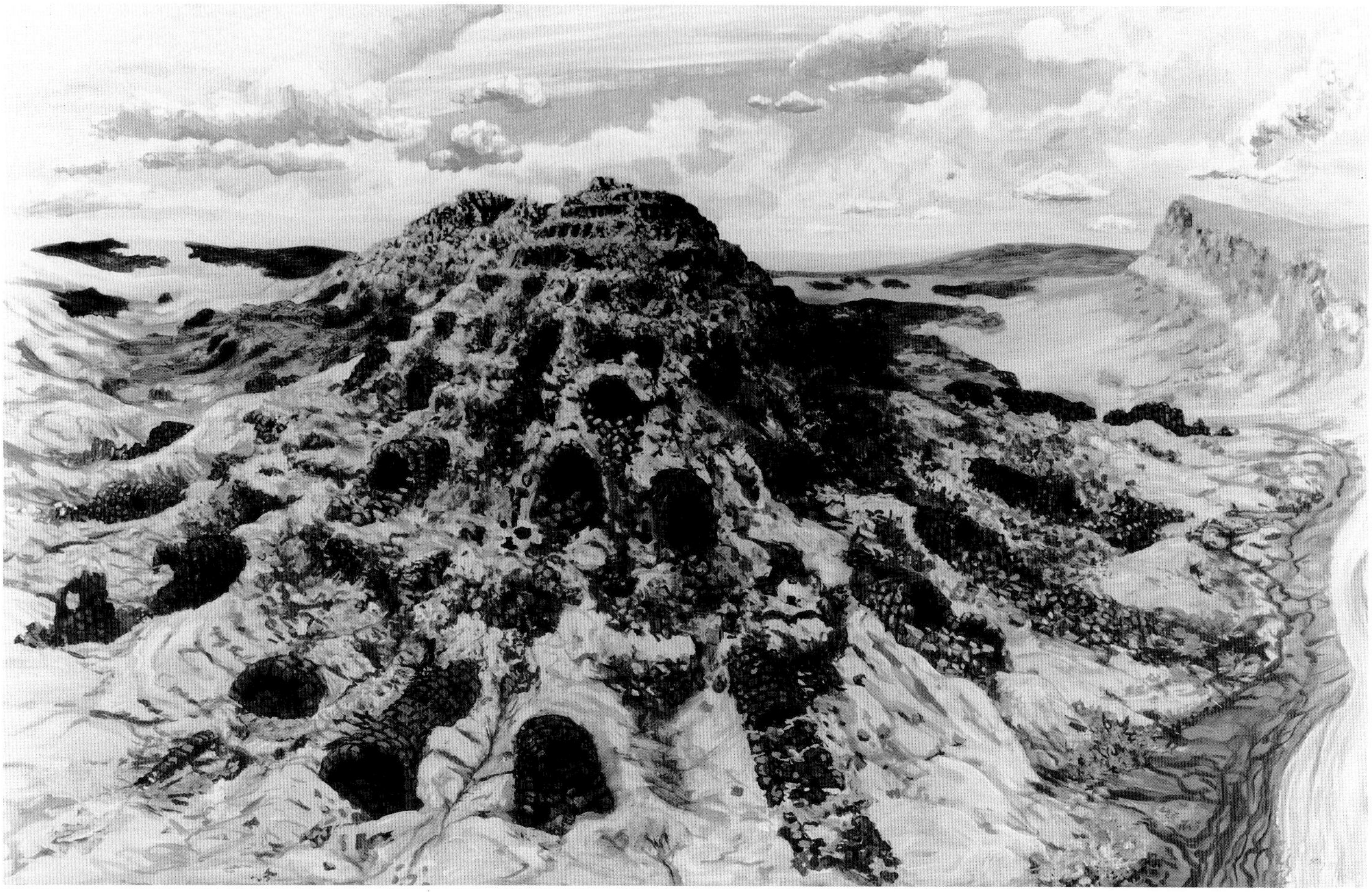

Earl Staley
**Tower of Babel**
1985, Acrylic on canvas, 60" x 96". Courtesy of Moody Gallery, Houston

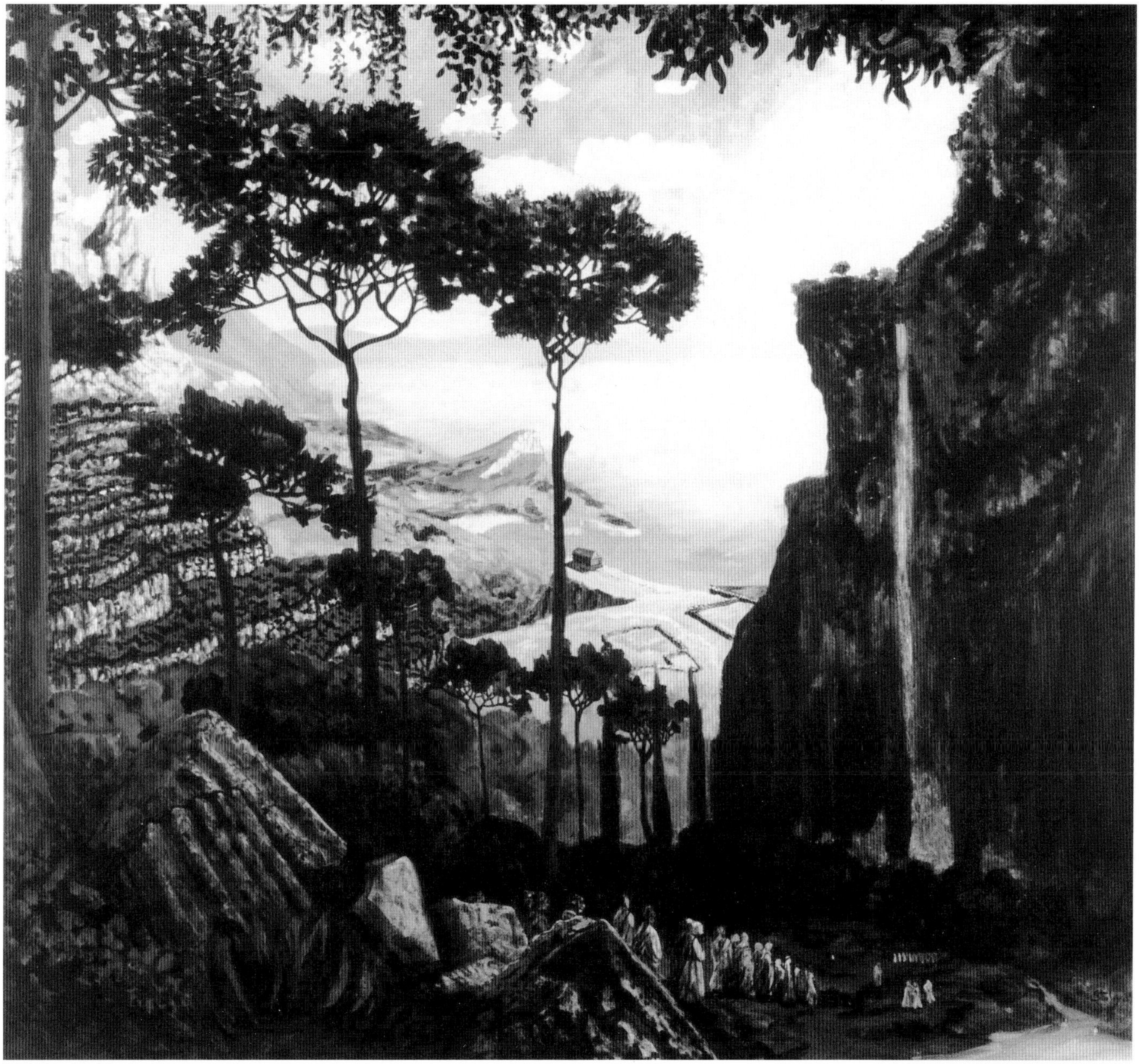

Earl Staley

**Classic Landscape**

1989, Acrylic on canvas, 58¾" x 62¼". Courtesy of Moody Gallery, Houston

# Richard **Stout**

For Richard Stout, painting is about bringing order to the sensations of the world. His stance is rigorously modernist, working within the parameters of the inviolate flatness of the picture plane. He explores those shallow spaces systematically, using thin veils of paint to construct images ranging from geometry's edges to nearly realist landscapes.

Since 1985, Stout has organized the pictorial space on his surfaces to envelop the physical spaces of his life. At first, he approached the composition like a collagist, layering one small descriptive element over another. He arranged things like the small objects found in a drawer — a forgotten letter, a button, old photographs — in careful patterns. These inadvertent still lifes gave way to actual still lifes as his gaze shifted to the controlled chaos of domestic juxtapositions, an end table, for example, where a book, a glass lamp and a pre-Columbian figurine coexist unobserved.

In the most recent paintings, his vision has expanded further to encompass entire rooms. If on the one hand they are mere planes of pigment on a canvas worthy of Greenbergian praise — "I like flat", Stout says — on another, these interiors are as psychologically charged as Edouard Vuillard's sitting rooms. Stout formulates complex ideograms composed of walls, light and unremarkable furniture, but loaded with intimations of life. Solitude, joy, pain and most of all, contemplation, are contained within his delineated spaces.

"In order for either abstraction or figuration to succeed, the other must be present in some measure. There should be no struggle between them, as they are a natural consequence of human life and thought. Art is the bridge to our life."[1]

Born in Beaumont in 1934, Stout is in the minority among Texas artists insofar as he pursued a classical education in fine arts in the 1950s — one year at the Art Academy of Cincinnati, and the full four-year program at the school of Art Institute of Chicago where he got his bachelor's degree in 1957. At age 60, Stout is preparing to retire from the University of Houston where he's been teaching since 1969.

1. Artist's statement, *Fresh Paint*, p. 176

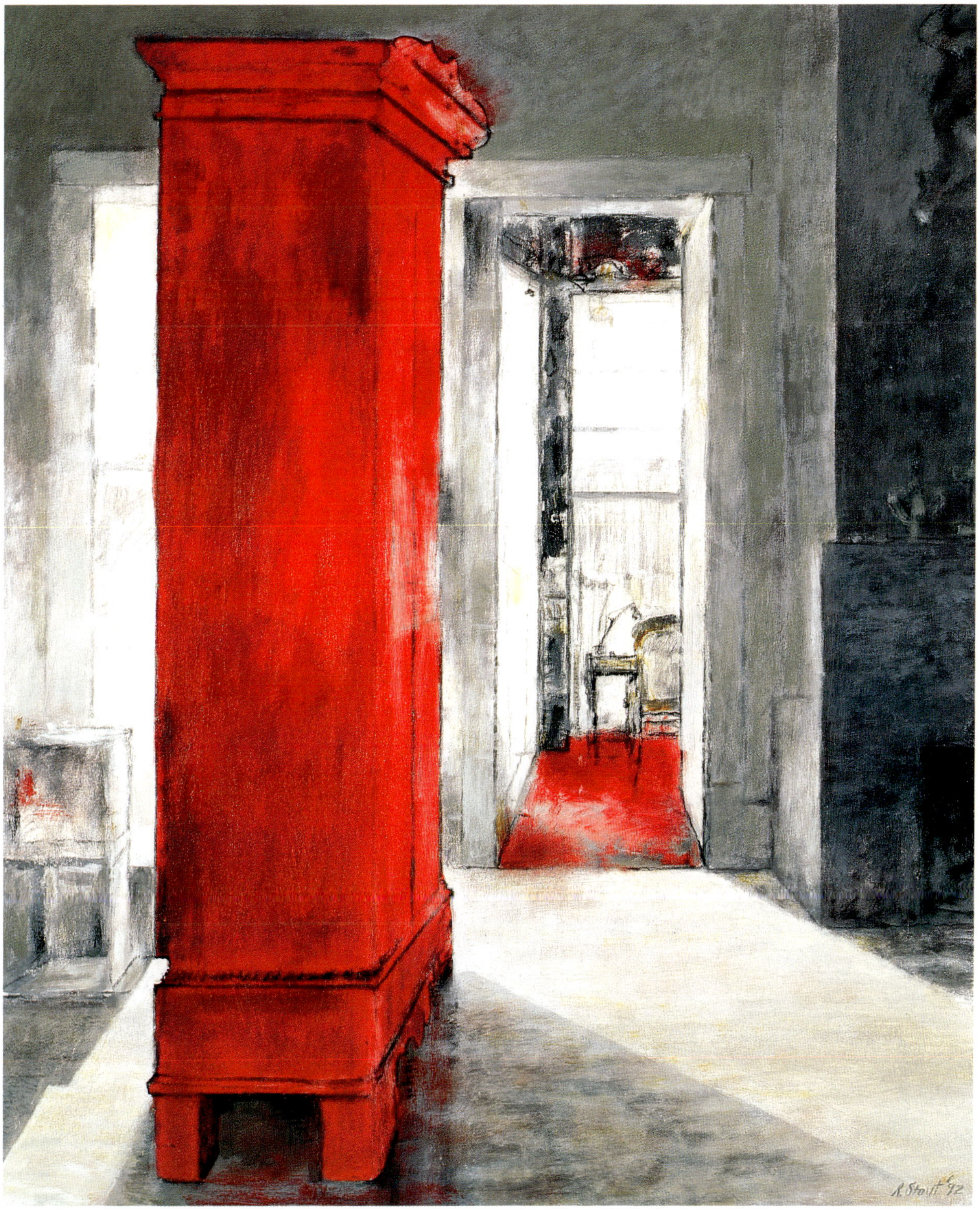

Richard Stout
**Winter Light**
1992, Acrylic on canvas, 50" x 40". Courtesy of Davis/McClain Gallery, Houston

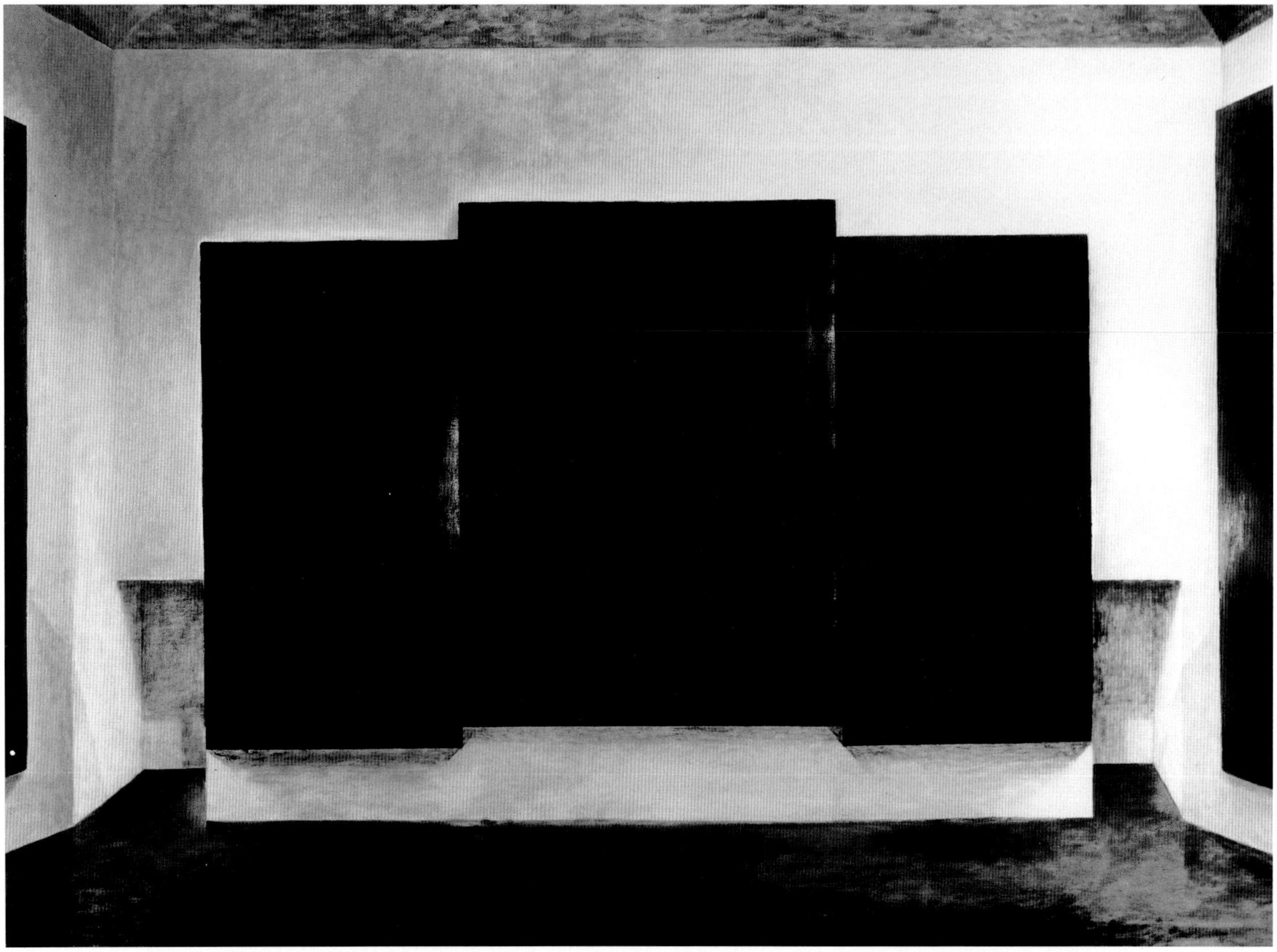

Richard Stout
**Untitled (Rothko Chapel)**
1993, Acrylic on canvas, 75" x 100". Courtesy of Davis/McClain Gallery, Houston

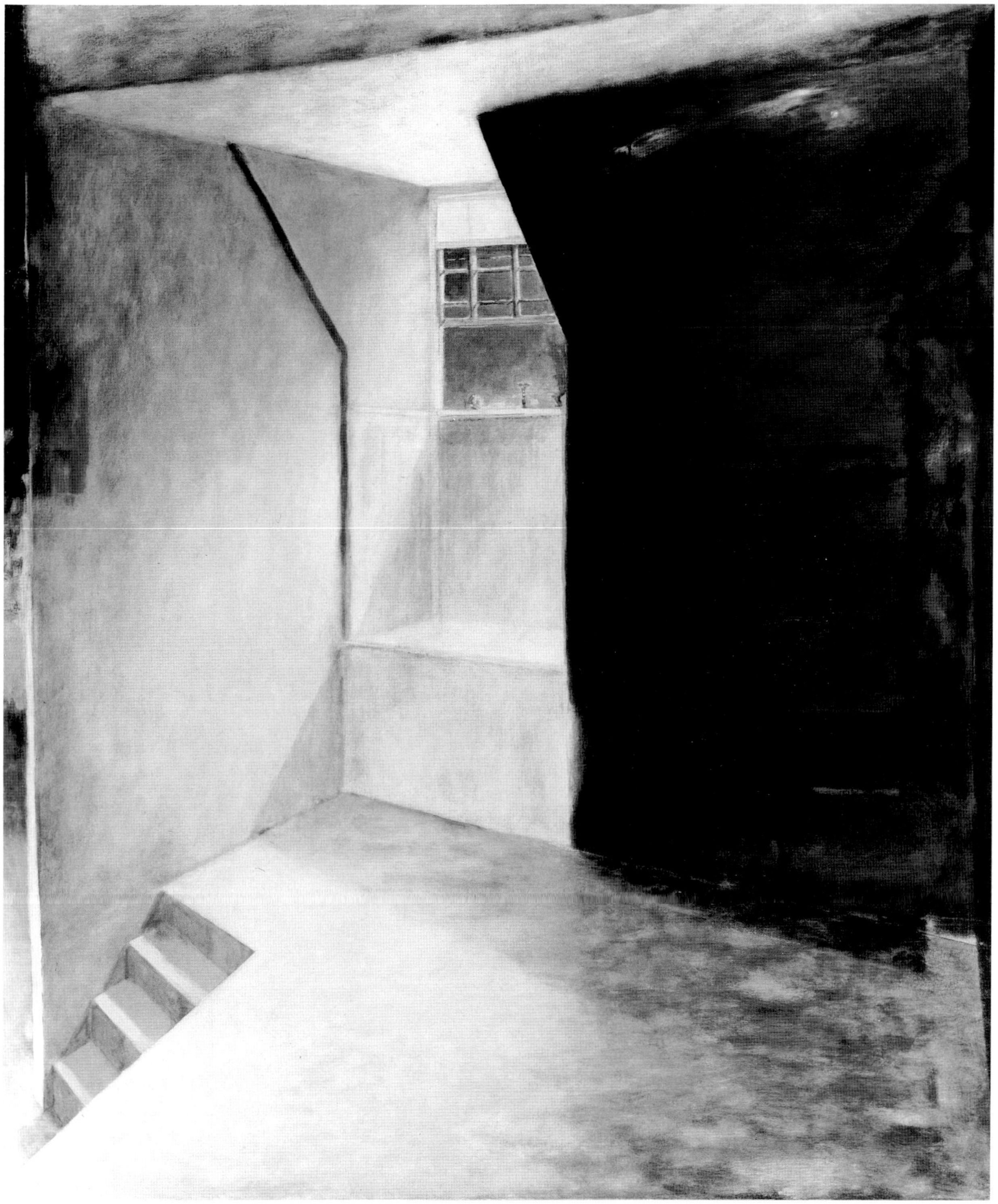

Richard Stout
**Attic Room**
1993, Acrylic on canvas, 60" x 50". Courtesy of Davis/McClain Gallery, Houston

# James **Surls**

James Surls aims to make whole the contradictions inherent to human existence in his sculpture. The heart of his work, whether small or monumental and public, is the essential duality of life — feminine/masculine, nature/technology, spirit/matter. At first he tried making the geometric and minimalist art being promoted in the late 1960s, but "it didn't feel right". Then he discovered the chunk of wood he was working with would suggest forms his will could chisel into being. It was a moment of epiphany.

Wood is Surls' material. Born in Terrell near Dallas in 1943, he's wielded the tools of the carpenter and the lumberjack since childhood building his own toys. He uses them now to bring vitality to the oak, pine and mesquite he envisions as mythic beings. Working from both a folk or primitive art tradition and full modernity, his abstracted figures variously suggest spirit beings, both demonic and angelic, and animal or botanical specimens, spiny as blowfish and delicate as the seed of a dandelion. Another body of less known but crucial work is his drawings. His narrative, stream-of-consciousness imagery, executed in single, continuous lines, incorporates human figures, often self-portraits and symbolic portraits of his family in dreamlike transformations.

He claims he became an artist by chance, but his personal charisma and embrasive approach to making art have been defining elements of contemporary art in the state. As he tells it, he had just been discharged from the armed forces and needed to enroll in college. He chose Sam Houston State University in Huntsville, near Houston. Not knowing what he was interested in, he looked through the course book. "Art was the first listing, so I signed," he said. He got his bachelor's degree, then a masters at Cranbrook Academy of Art (Michigan) in 1969.

Surls had established a reputation in the northern part of Texas when he joined the University of Houston. As chairman of its sculpture department (1979–82), he instigated a spirit of collaboration and mutual support among artists whose most visible expression was the Lawndale Annex. It was the first alternative art center in the city, and it was hot just as national attention was focusing on the state. That high voltage energy and Surls' personality attracted artists and students from within and outside Texas, which in turn helped transform the larger art community.

In 1984, Surls completed his studio in Splendora, about 60 miles northeast of Houston. In the compound he's constructed on 42 acres of woods, he is able to concentrate on his art. But the tug to be involved with his community has also led him and his wife, sculptor Charmaine Locke, to create another alternative art space — this time, for the children in their home town, and to open their great studio to non-profit groups and experimental art.

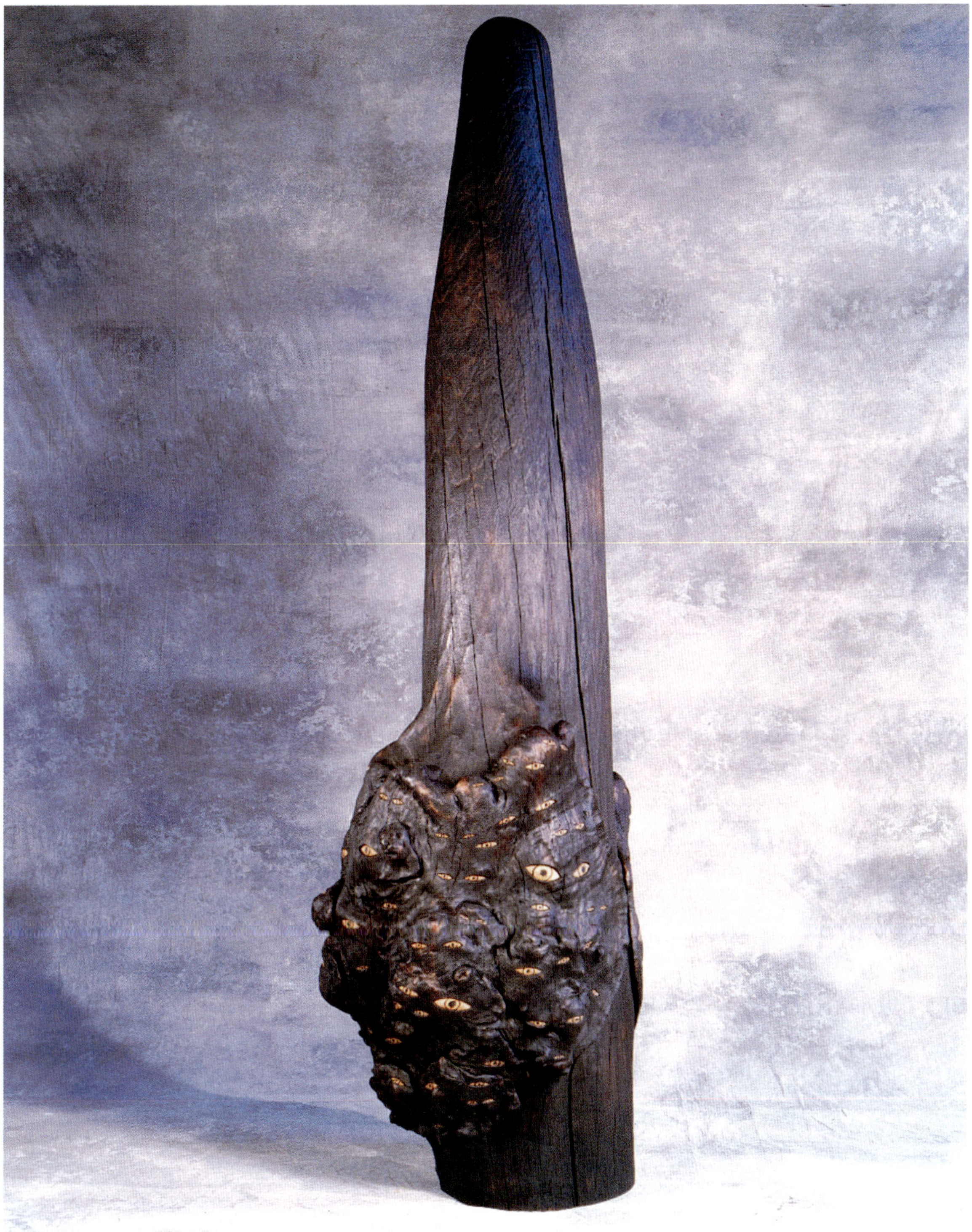

James Surls
**The Death of St Sebastian**
1993, White oak (burned), 117"h. Photograph: Redding Communications. Courtesy of the artist

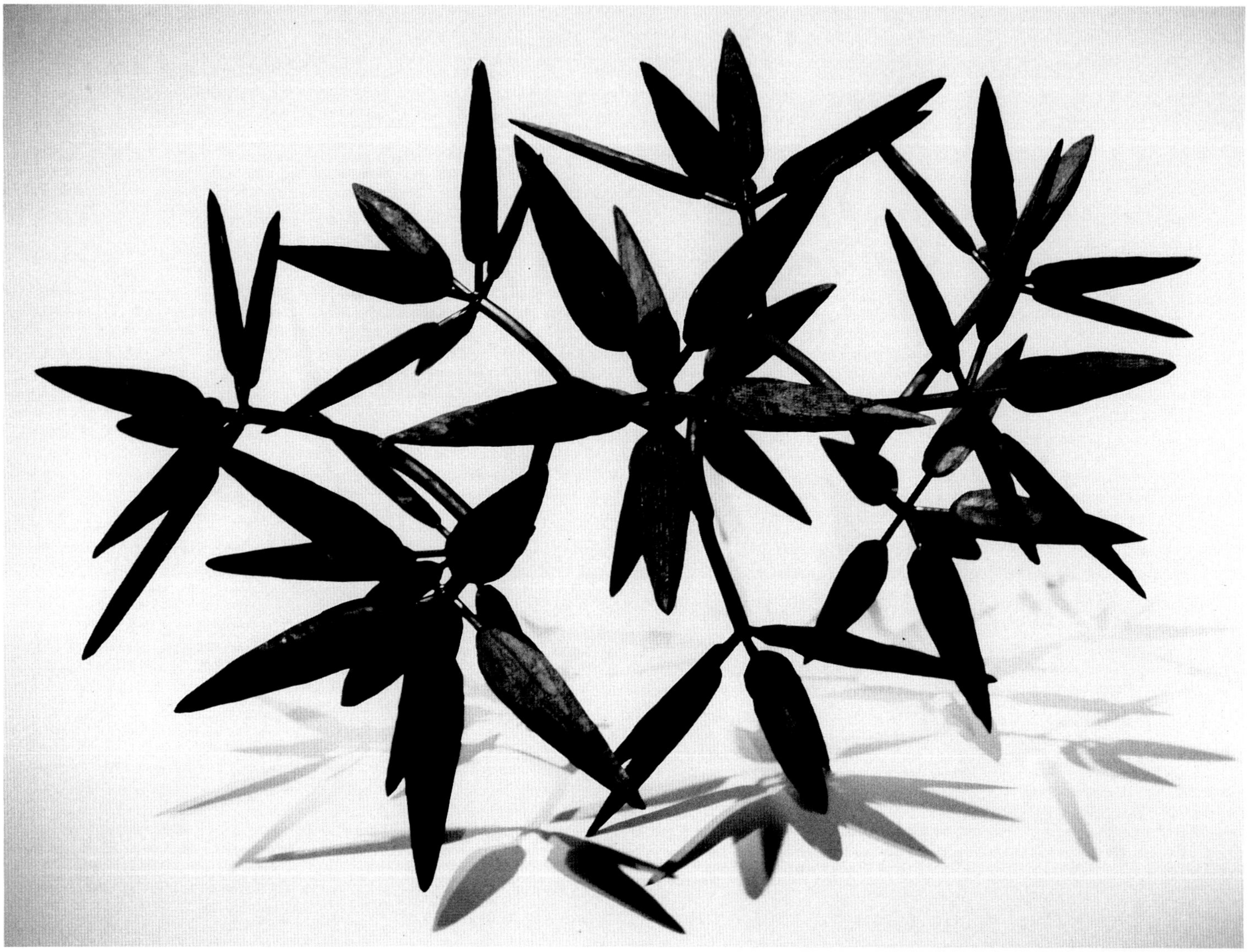

James Surls
**Night Blooming**
1993, Oil, steel, 36"h x 55"w x 37"d. Photograph: Bill Kelley. Courtesy of the artist

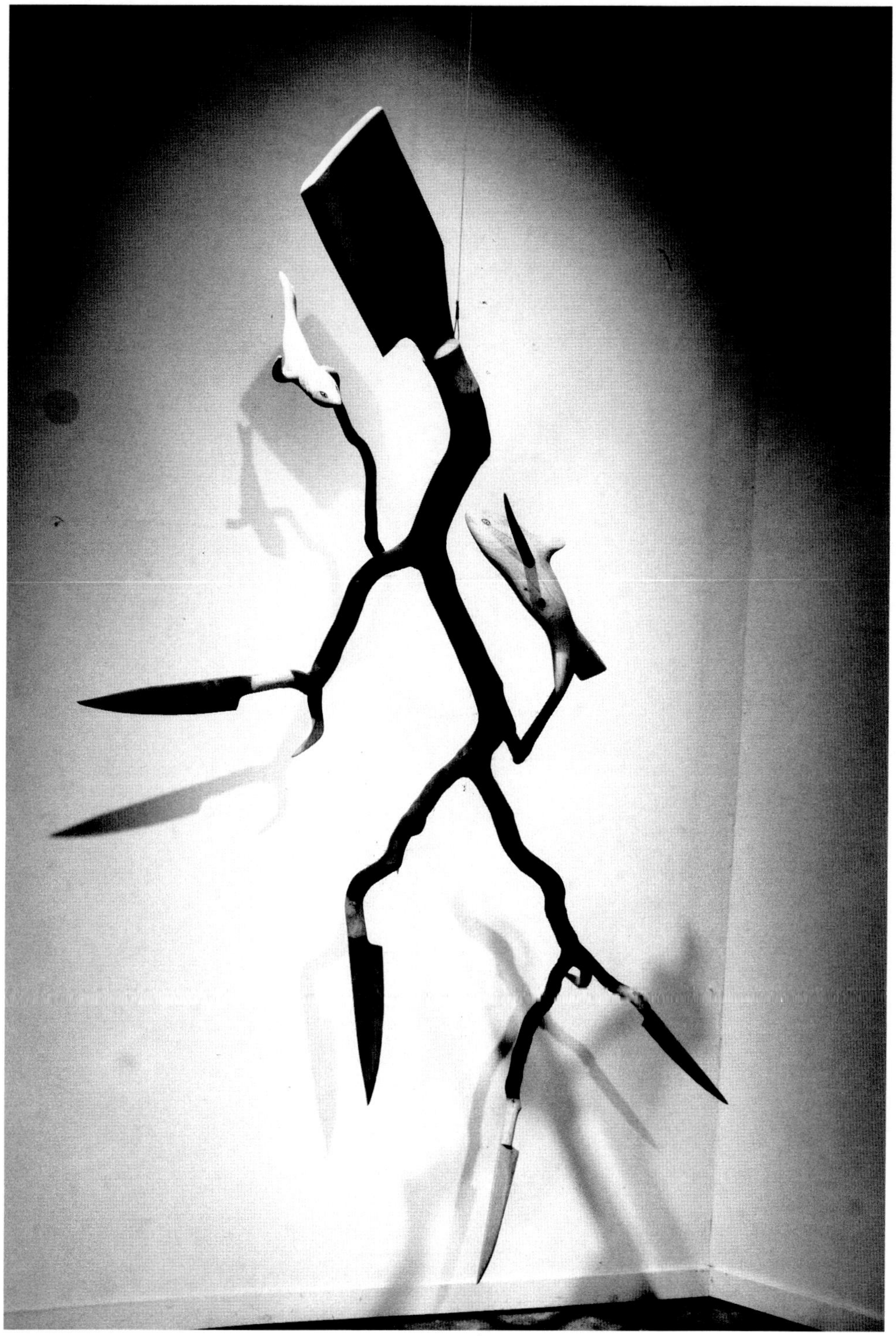

James Surls
**Again the Meat Man and the Bait Fish**
1993, Oak, pine, holly, 113"h x 39"w x 72"d.
Photograph: Bill Kelley. Courtesy of the artist

# Michael **Tracy**

Michael Tracy has explored painting, photography and sculpture for more than two decades. To the traditional materials of paint, paper and the found objects of assemblage, he adds body fluids and dirt. Since moving to San Ygnacio on the Texas-Mexico border in 1978, he has also embraced natural phenomena as collaborator, allowing the searing heat and occasional violent rainstorm to interact with the surfaces. The constant in his multifaceted oeuvre is passion. It is both emotional and intellectual, spiritual and sexual, born of absolute conviction and expressed in a baroque aesthetic that takes equally from the Italian Renaissance, colonial Mexico, and American abstract expressionism.

Born in Ohio in 1943, Tracy began taking art classes at the Cleveland Institute of Art while still in high school. He earned his bachelor's degree there, then pursued his master's at the University of Texas in Austin. Extended trips in Europe, Egypt and Mexico conditioned his discerning eye. Everything he does, including his choice of domicile on the Rio Grande, is symbolic and traverses many layers of politics, art and religion, enveloped in liturgical color and iconic form.

The processional crosses and small altar shapes reflect his Catholic childhood, but more poignantly in the present, point to his identification with the ecclesiastical ceremonies. The encrusted surfaces pierced with spikes, kissed with flowers and adorned with ribbons, evoke the sumptuous trappings of Holy Mass. In the violence evident on the surfaces, however, the tearing and bleeding of the layered pieces become an expression of his rage against human injustice. For Tracy, making art is not an abstract activity but a ritual and a political act. His works are, Tracy said, "the objectified residue of private rituals [conducted] some in the form of mediations, some in the form of actions."[1]

In those terms, the importance of the work of art resides in its having been created, and not in its continued existence in the world of matter. On two occasions Tracy destroyed works of art in ceremonies of sacrifice witnessed by a select audience. The first time, he burned a painting in front of a pyramid of raw sugar, in 1976 in Galveston. The second sacrifice, in 1991, was under the auspices of the River Pierce Foundation, a non-profit group he founded in San Ygnacio. On Good Friday, 1991, Tracy burned a processional cross built to honor the "disappeared" of Latin America's repressive systems, on the banks of the Rio Grande. Art as a substitute for self.

1. Cited in Leffingwell, Edward, and McEvilley, Thomas, *Terminal Privileges*, PS1, The Institute for Urban Resources, 1987, p. 7

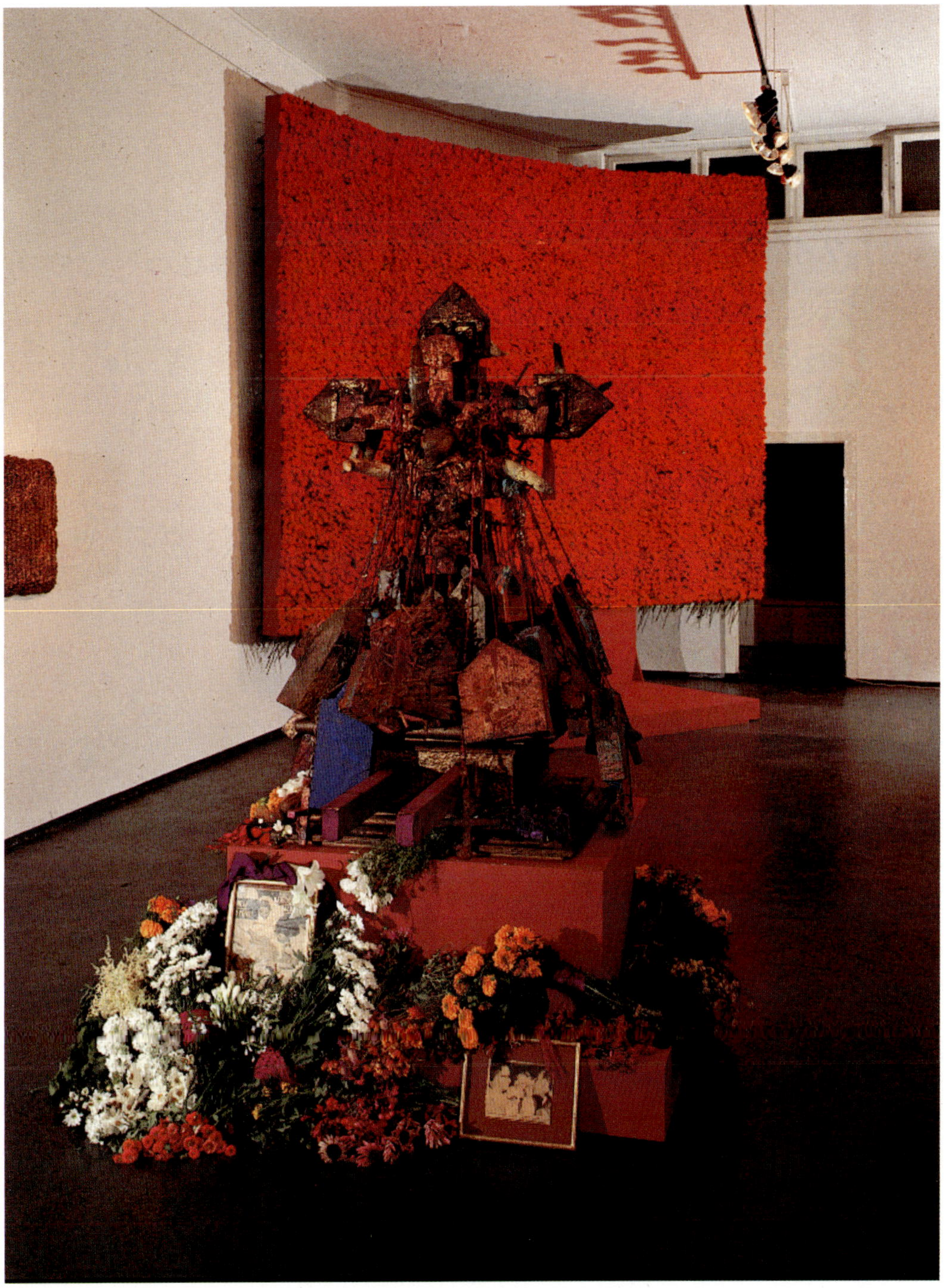

Michael Tracy
**Cruz: to Bishop Oscar Romero, Martyr of El Salvador**
1980–81, Mixed media: acrylic on rayon over wood, horn, spikes, hair, 69"h x 37" x 35". Installation: "The Rio Grande: My Berlin Wall" 1990, with triptych of fresh roses, Raab Gallery, Berlin. Photograph: Angelika Weilding, Berlin. Collection of the artist. Courtesy of the artist

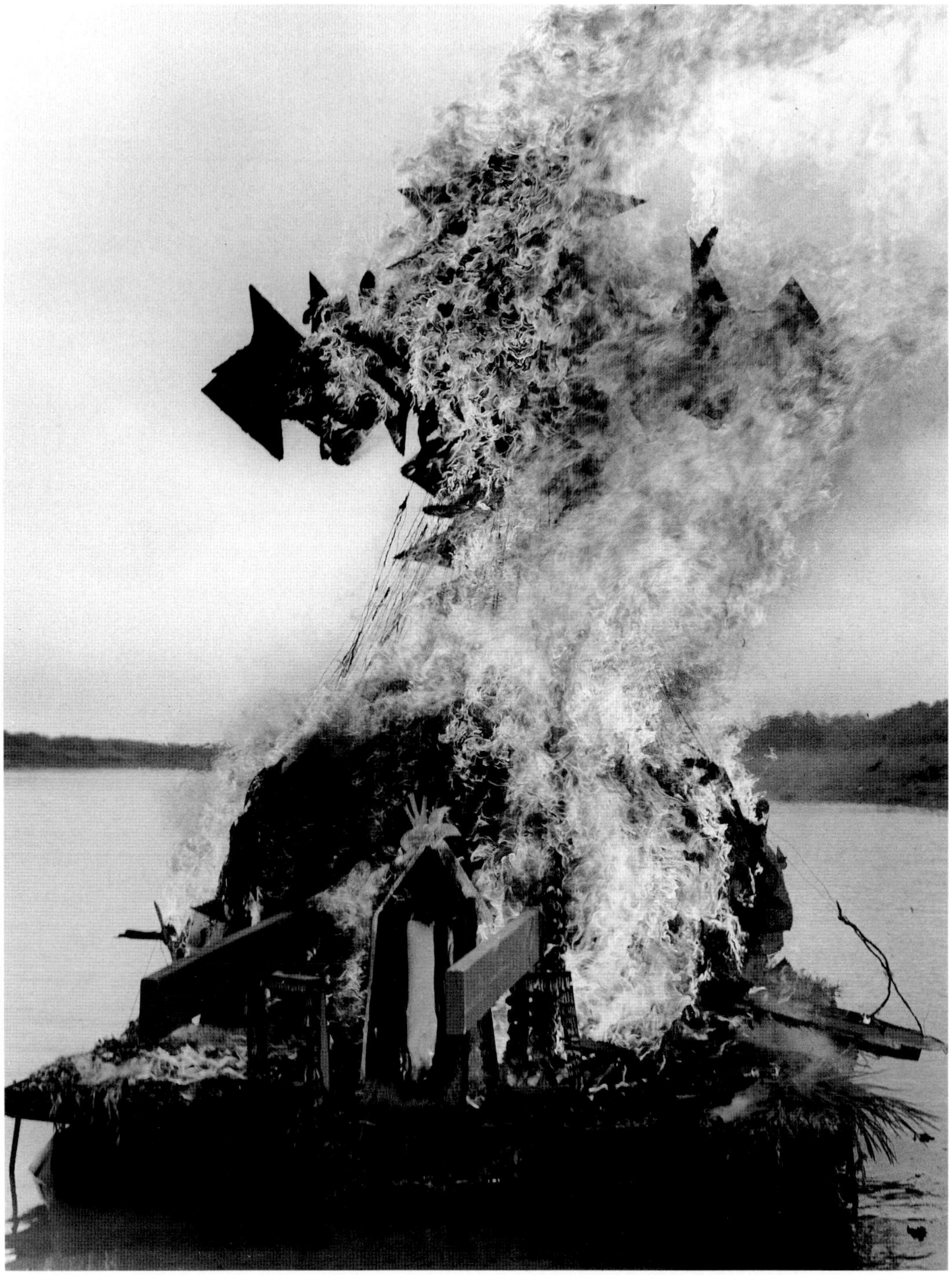

Michael Tracy
**Cruz: La Pasión (Cross: The Passion)**
1982–87, Mixed media: Acrylic, latex on wood, horns, tin, cloth, 140"h x 82" x 76". Destroyed in performance, San Ygnacio, Texas: "Sacrifice II: 13.4.90. The River Pierce". Photograph: Keith Carter, Beaumont, Texas. Courtesy of the artist

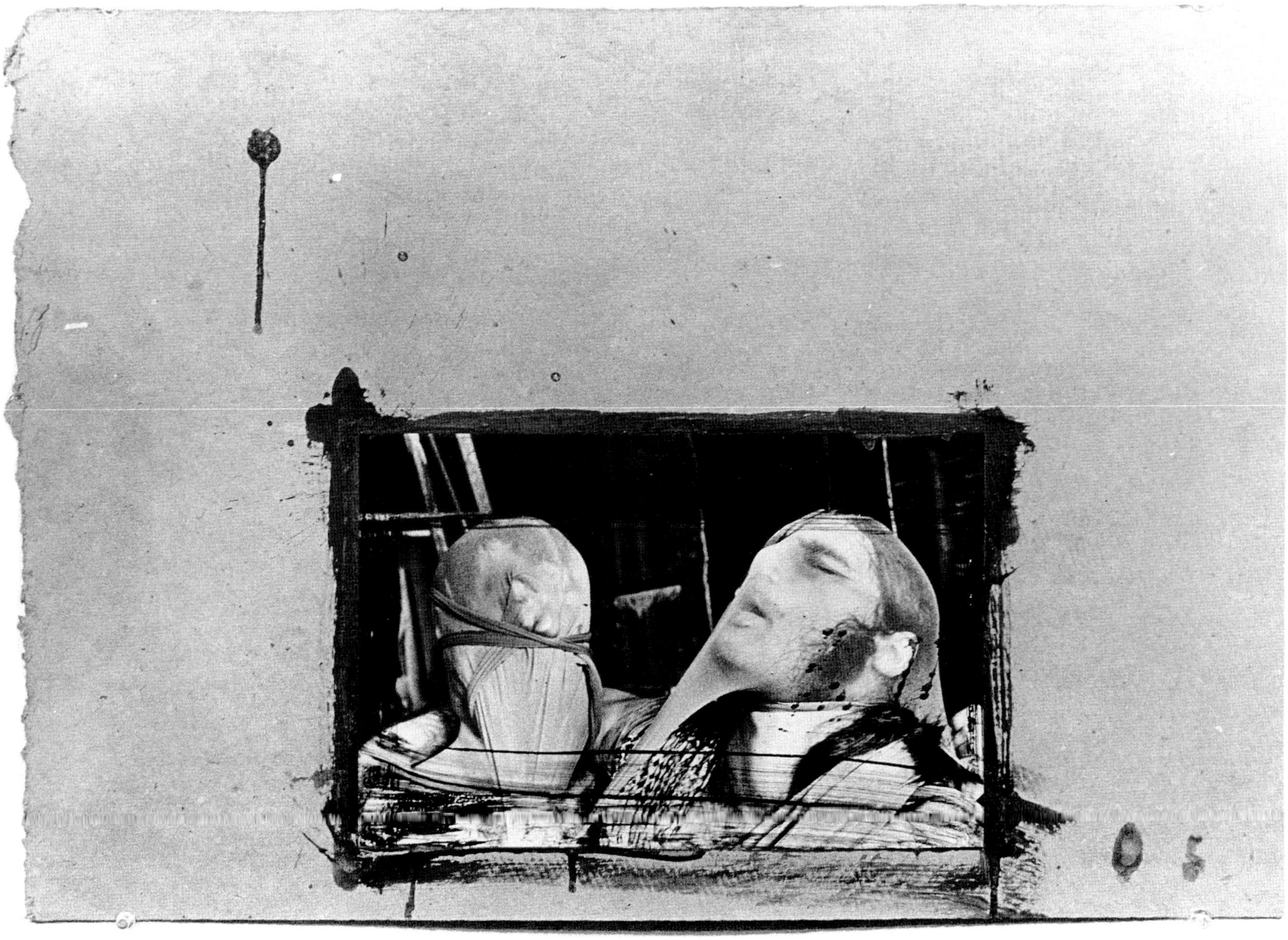

Michael Tracy

**Caravaggio Notations**

(Detail) 1975, Acrylic, sumi ink and blood on photos by Ben Mason, 19¼" x 25¼". Photograph: Richard Geissler. Courtesy of the artist

# Randy
# **Twaddle**

Rarely does an artist make his reputation exclusively on drawings, but since 1985, Randy Twaddle has worked only with charcoal on paper. His subjects range from trees to the universal bar code. He photographs the objects, projects them onto his surface, and outlines their essential shape. Reduced to singular silhouettes, the transformers, satellite dishes, missiles and trees assume an ominous presence. Most intriguing, their profiles reveal surprising affinities between nature and man made structures.

Born in Missouri in 1957, Twaddle received his bachelor's degree from Northwest Missouri State University then moved to Dallas a few years later where he did performance work with Douglas MacWithey, and painted. In 1989, looking for a bigger art community, he settled in Houston. In the earliest drawings, Twaddle centered the isolated object on a page, sometimes repeating it in diptychs and triptychs. Eventually, he started to combine different images in two or three sections, drawing structural parallels between a spider web and a satellite dish, for instance. Throughout, the handling of the powdery material of choice informs the drawing with a warmth not associated with minimalist renderings. In the most recent work, Twaddle draws the image and sands it away to leave a residue ghost. The layering effect enriches not just the surface, but also teases the eye into slowing down.

"People tend to tag my work with Donald Sultan. I admire his work, but mine is a result of my content. I'm interested in technology as an expression of our culture. One reason I like charcoal is because in the smudges there is evidence of the human hand, especially in contrast to the technological subject. I also like the immediacy of the medium."

A one-year residency in France in 1991 proved crucial to Twaddle's understanding of himself and his work. He became very aware of his American-ness, and the specificity of his work as being the product of American society. He was frustrated, too, because he felt he could not relate to the much older culture of France.

"I did some landscapes and the UPC drawings were a direct result of that because of my self-confessed inability to see nuance. I was 'scanning' the landscape. Visually, too, the bar codes reminded me of the way they plant trees there, tall, straight and slender poplars all in neat rows."

The conceptual connection led further to other syllogisms between word and image. He points to the similarity of language in technology and religion, for example: Transformer, saving, conversion.

"My tutor in France was a woman 73 years old. She told me something that really stuck. She said, 'I know why you work in black and white: Because you are an American Puritan.' I knew she was absolutely right. American puritanism doesn't allow for nuance. Everything is black or it is white. So I have begun my investigation."

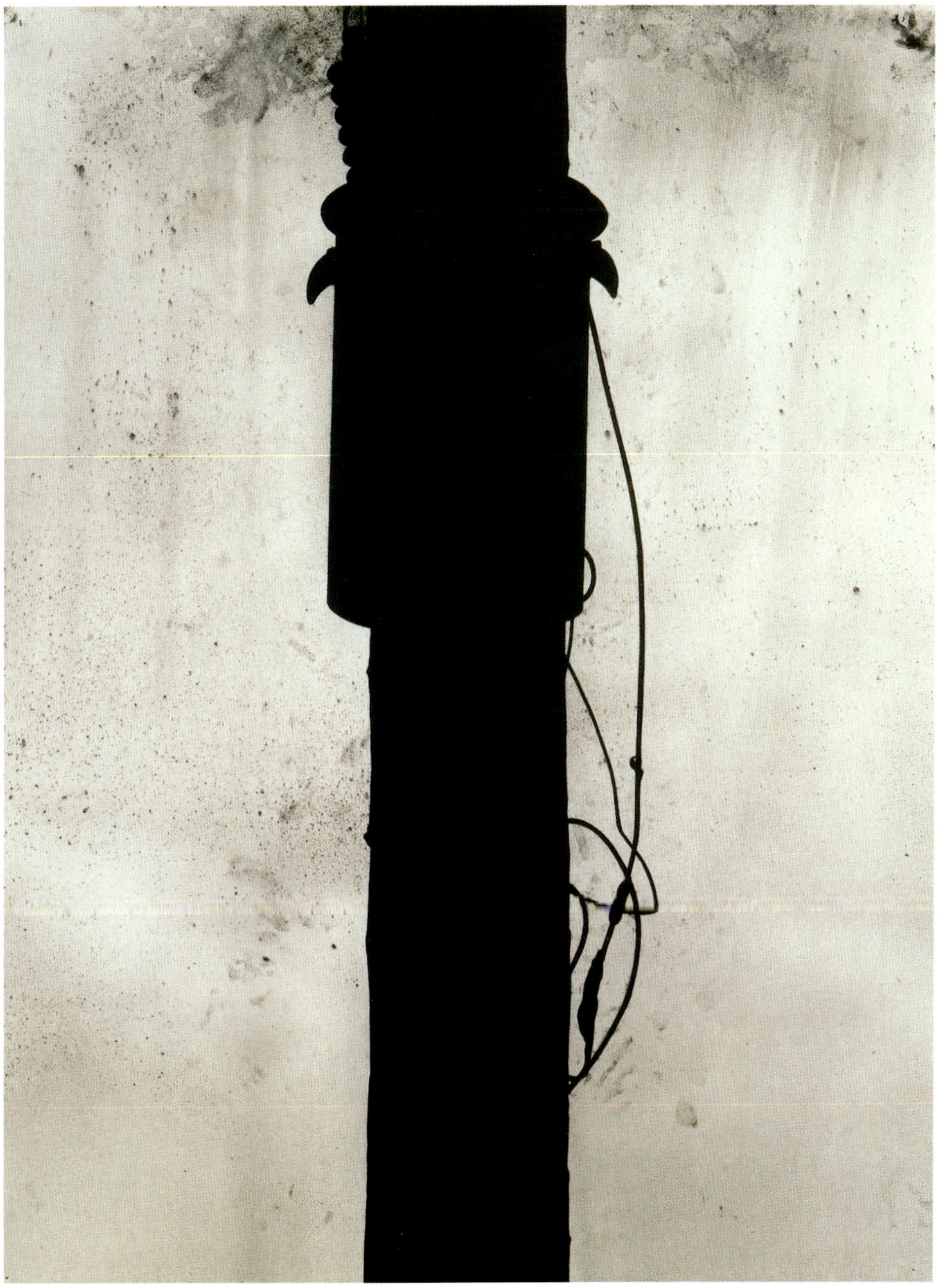

Randy Twaddle

**Sapling**

1990, Charcoal on paper, Triptych, 60½" x 43½".
Courtesy of Moody Gallery, Houston

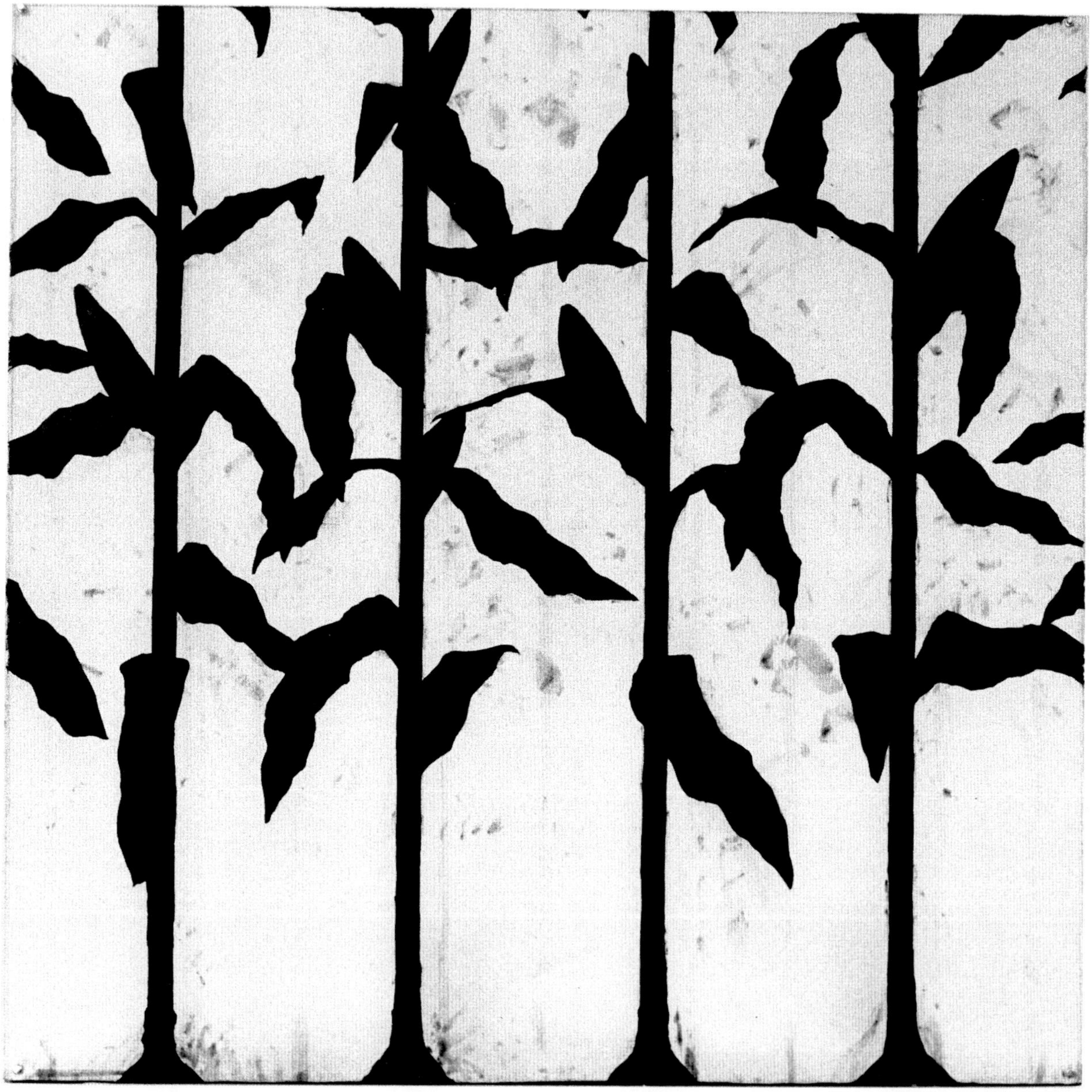

Randy Twaddle
**Crop**
1984, Charcoal on paper, 44" x 44". Private collection. Courtesy of Moody Gallery, Houston

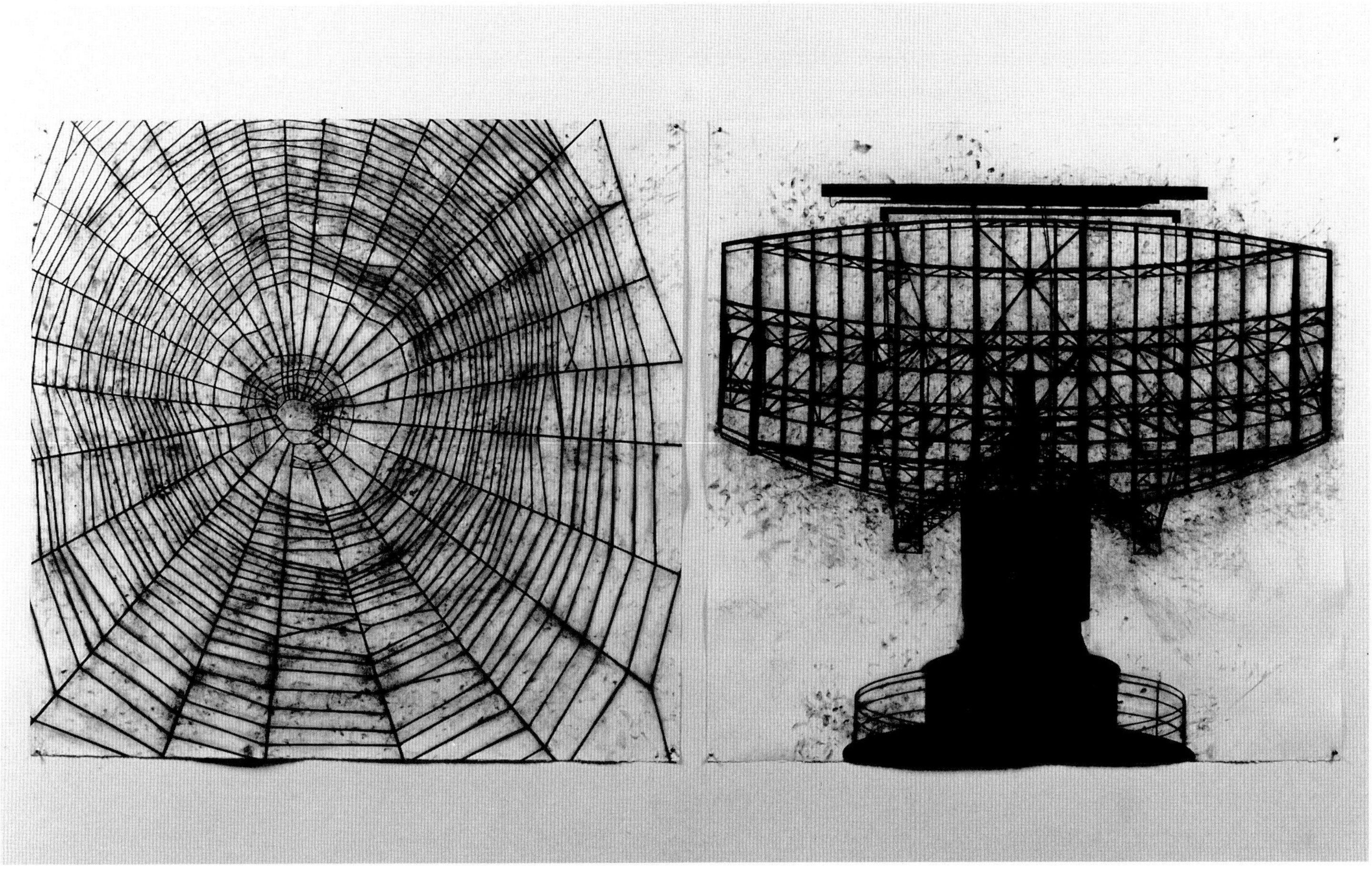

Randy Twaddle
**The Abstraction of Capture**
1987, Charcoal on paper, Diptych, 53" x 53" each.
Courtesy of Moody Gallery, Houston

# Dick **Wray**

Dick Wray paints. He is one of the rare Texans who is a classical artist in the heroic tradition of American abstract expressionism. The supremacy of the surface and the inherent tension of color, play out on his works with grand gesture and chromatic clarity. His work seems all the more remarkable given the context of his life. Born in Houston in 1933, he grew up in a time and a place where being an artist was not merely impractical, but generally considered a "sissy thing" to do, best left to women and children. He was one of those children.

Wray remembers taking art classes in the Museum of Fine Arts School and sneaking peeks at the models in life drawing. Classes were held inside the museum and in rented buildings in the surrounding neighborhood until the museum built The Alfred C. Glassell School of Art in 1979. By then Wray — who had resisted the desire to paint for three years in the University of Houston's school of architecture and two years of work in an architect's office in Denmark — had been one of the school's most influential instructors for a decade and he would remain so until 1986.

He is a restless seeker of means with which to create an image. He experiments with media and techniques that sometimes appear to negate the effulgence of his palette and vigorous brushwork. His first prints were a suite of 22 black and white lithographs created at the Tamarind Lithography Workshop in 1964. They challenged Wray to master a technique new to him and the printers to devise the means to capture the subtlety of his washes. Twenty years later, he explored monotypes in a process that seems particularly suited to his insistence on immediacy and freshness.

The linearity of his architectural training insinuates itself occasionally on his canvas providing order against which to let loose with paint. He also produces drawings with assurance of line and tone, sometimes bringing a creature he name Mr. Crow into the picture as a sassy character lest anyone take figuration too seriously.

In his most recent group of works (1993) Wray explored the possibilities of the photocopying machine with surprisingly lyrical results. He created these collage-like works by gluing hundreds of black and white photocopied images — of his own drawings or illustrations from newspapers and technical manuals, each 8-by-11 inches — onto canvas supports measuring up to 221 inches. As the integrity of the individual components dissolve in the context of the monumental compositions, different patterns emerge. An orderly grid formed by the individual pages is the most obvious. The bold, abstract gesture is the afterimage that lingers.

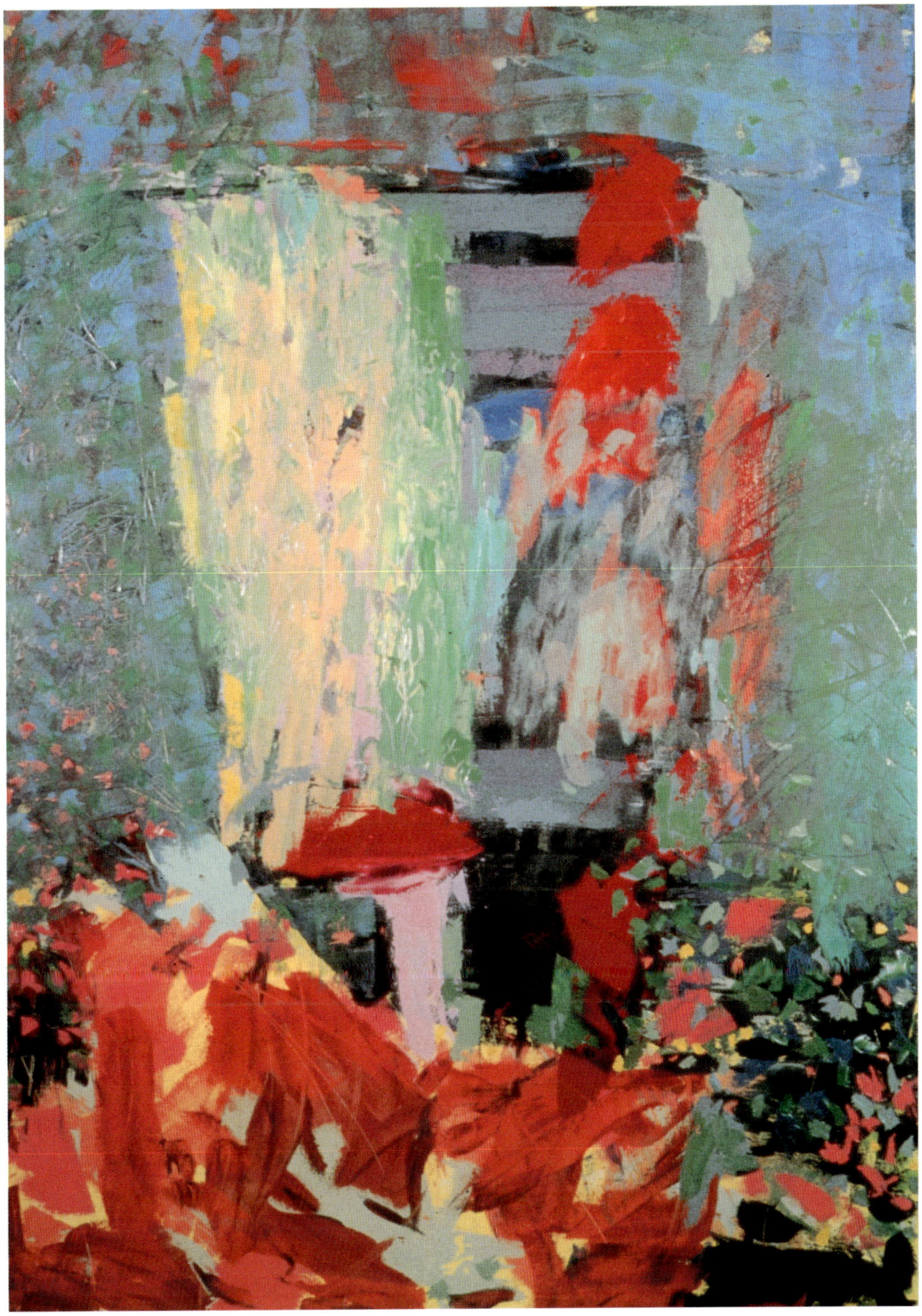

Dick Wray

**Untitled**

1985–86, Oil on canvas, 96" x 66". Courtesy of Moody Gallery, Houston

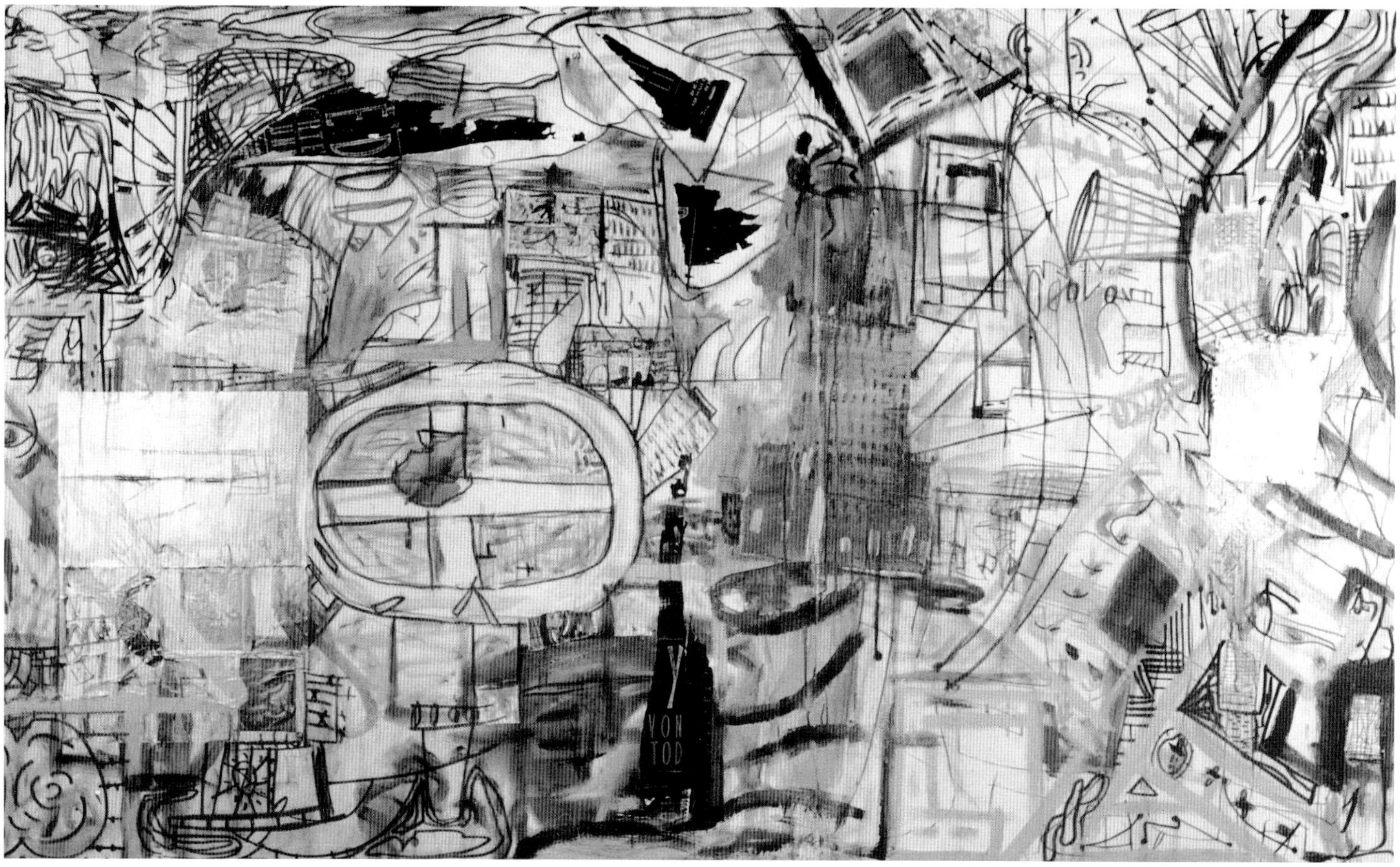


Dick Wray

**The Globe of Warsaw**

1989, Mixed media including oil and acrylic on cotton tarpaulin, 68½" x 110". Courtesy of Moody Gallery, Houston

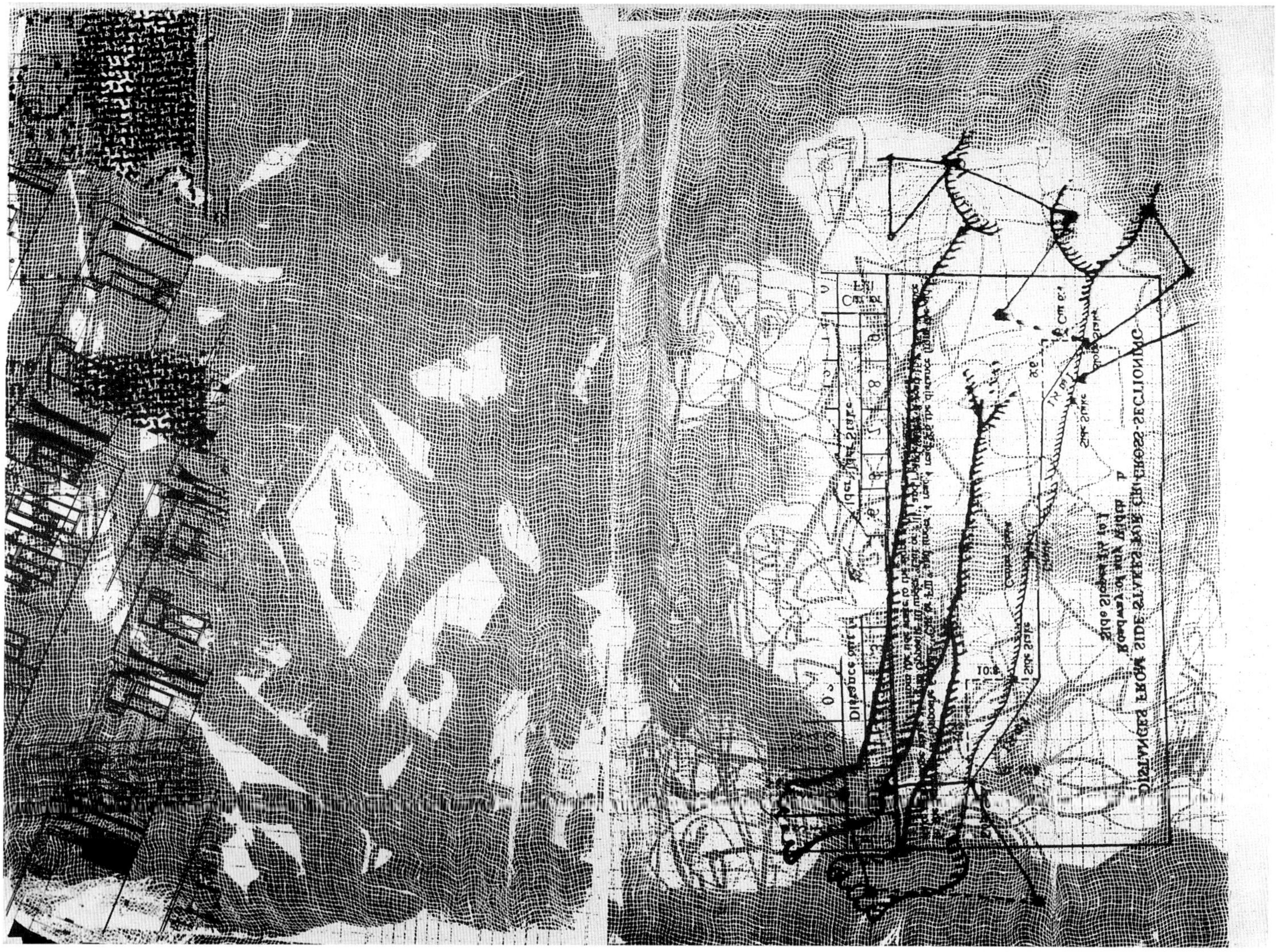

Dick Wray

**Untitled**

1993, Mixed media including photocopy and acrylic medium on canvas, 18" x 24". Courtesy of Moody Gallery, Houston

# Artist Biographies

## The Aaart Guys

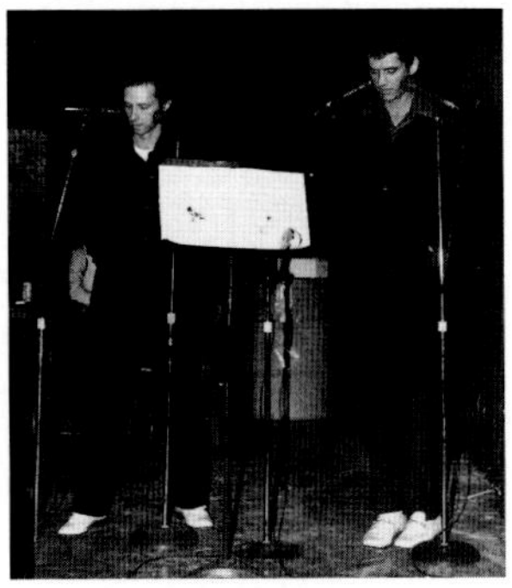

*The Aaart Guys, Jack Massing (left) and Michael Galbreth (right), 1988. Photograph: Ben De Soto. Courtesy of the artists.*

### Michael Galbreth

1956 Born in Philadelphia, Pennsylvania
1980 Memphis State University, Tennessee, BFA
1984 University of Houston, MFA

### Jack Massing

1959 Born in Buffalo, New York
1984 University of Houston, BFA

The artists live in Houston, Texas

**Selected Exhibitions**

1993 *TEXAS/Between Two Worlds*, Contemporary Arts Museum, Houston; Museum of Modern Art of Fort Worth; Museum of South Texas, Corpus Christi
1993 *Texas Contemporary Acquisitions of the 90s*, Museum of Fine Arts, Houston
1993 *Houston in Hope*, The Faith And Charity in Hope Gallery, Hope, Idaho
1992 *Avenues of Departure: Twelve Houston Artists*, Contemporary Arts Center, New Orleans
1992 *FluxAttitudes*, The New Museum of Contemporary Art, New York
1992 *Group Show (Art Guys Only)*, 0-1 Gallery, Los Angeles
1992 *Re-Creation, Recreation, Re:Creation*, Laguna Gloria Art Museum, Austin
1991 *AAAArt Guys*, Barry Whistler Gallery, Dallas
1991 Gallery 3, Huntington, West Virginia
1991 *JETS, Video Installation*, Dallas Museum of Art
1991 *House*, Laguna Gloria Art Museum, Austin
1991 *Matter of Concern*, Diverse Works, Houston
1991 *Creative Partners*, Sewall Art Gallery, Rice University, Houston
1990 *Art Guys*, Barry Whistler Gallery, Dallas
1990 *Landscapes: Outdoor Sculpture Competition*, Houston International Festival
1989 *Talking Pictures: The Art Guys at Full Tilt*, Sonic Arts Gallery, San Diego, California
1989 *Sipping Cokes, a 3 hour and 33 second stunt*, San Jacinto College, Houston
1989 *Stunts and Skits*, Memphis Center for Contemporary Art, Tennessee
1988 *Art Dudes Dine At Denny's in December*, Houston
1988 *Stunt Nite*, The Orange Show, Houston
1988 *Soul Patches for Kansas City*, Kansas City Artists' Coalition
1986 *Mustaches for Seattle*, and *The Sea/Hou-Hou/Sea*, 911 Gallery, Seattle
1985 *Installation*, Hiram Butler Gallery, Houston
1985 *Particles*, Midtown Art Center, Houston
1985 *Music for BBs*, and *Jumping Jack Video*, Public Broadcasting System, Houston

**Selected Public Collections**

Museum of Fine Arts, Houston

## John Alexander

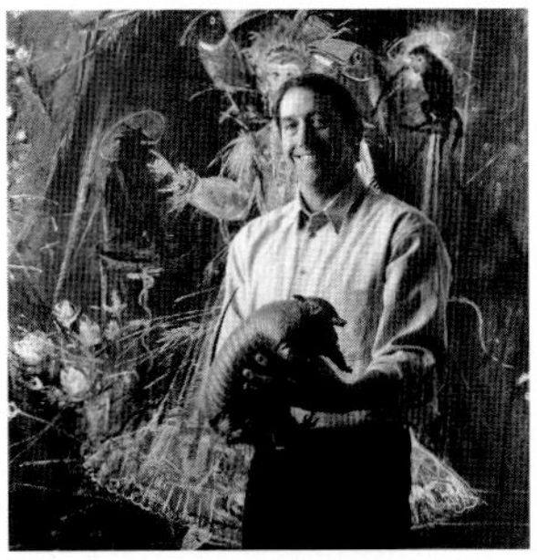

*John Alexander. Courtesy of the artist.*

1945 Born in Beaumont, Texas

Lives in New York City

**Education and Awards**

1968 Lamar University, Beaumont, BFA
1970 Southern Methodist University, Dallas, MFA
1981 National Endowment for the Arts, Individual Artists Fellowship
1984 Solomon R Guggenheim Memorial Foundation Grant

**Selected Solo Exhibitions**

1993 Erika Meyerovich Gallery, San Francisco, California
1992 Marlborough Gallery, New York, New York
1992 Galeria Alred Wild, Bogotá, Colombia
1992 Everard Read Gallery, Johannesburg, South Africa
1991 Jan Turner Gallery, Los Angeles, California
1991 Gerald Peters Gallery, Dallas
1990 Marlborough Gallery, New York, New York
1989 Art Museum of Southeast Texas, Beaumont
1989 Alpha Gallery, Boston
1989 Galeria Freites, Caracas, Venezuela
1988 Contemporary Arts Center, Cincinnati, Ohio; Meadows Museum, Southern Methodist University, Dallas
1987 Marlborough Gallery, London
1986 Marlborough Gallery, New York
1986 Jan Turner Gallery, Los Angeles
1985 Marlborough Gallery, New York
1985 FIAC, Grand Palais, Paris
1985 Zolla/Lieberman Gallery, Chicago
1984 Janie C Lee Gallery, Houston
1983 Marlborough Gallery, New York
1983 Lawrence Oliver Gallery, Philadelphia
1983 Institute of Contemporary Art, Boston
1982 Janie C Lee Gallery, Houston
1982 Diane Brown Gallery, Washington DC
1981 Doebrick Gallery, Chicago
1980 Corcoran Gallery of Art, Washington DC
1978 Max Hutchinson Gallery, New York and Houston
1977 Museum of Art, Long Beach, California
1977 Delahunty Gallery, Dallas
1977 Kornblatt Gallery, Baltimore
1976 University Museum, New Mexico State University, Las Cruces
1976 Meredith Long & Co, Houston
1976 Kornblatt Gallery, Baltimore
1975 Contemporary Arts Museum, Houston
1975 Meredith Long & Co, Houston

**Selected Group Exhibitions**

1993 *The Fine Art of Patronage: Contemporary Painting and Sculpture from Local Collections*, Cranbrook Academy of Art, Bloomfield Hills, Michigan
1993 *The Mask in Contemporary Art*, Sewall Art Gallery, Rice University, Houston
1992 *An Ode to Gardens and Flowers*, Nassau County Museum of Art, Roslyn Harbor, New York
1991 *The Landscape in 20th Century American Art, Selections from the Metropolitan Museum of Art, New York*; Philbrook Museum of Art, Tulsa, Oklahoma; Center for the Fine Arts, Miami, Florida; Joslyn Art Museum, Omaha, Nebraska; other venues in Florida, South Carolina, Wisconsin and Michigan
1991 *Expressive Drawings: European and American Art Through the 20th Century*, New York Academy of Art, New York
1990 *Tradition and Innovation*, Museum of Fine Arts, Houston
1990 *The Common Wealth: 20th Century American Masterpieces from Virginia Collections*, Roanoke Museum of Fine Arts, Virginia
1989 *Private Art/Public Visions*, Western Washington University, Bellingham, Washington
1988 *Direction and Diversity*, Museum of Fine Arts, Houston
1988 *Amarillo to Zebra: An American Artists' Bestiary*, Amarillo Art Center, Amarillo

1988 *The 1990s: A New Generation*, Metropolitan Museum of Art, New York
1988 *Visions/Revisions: Contemporary Representation*, Marlborough Gallery, New York
1987 *Surrealismi*, Retretti Art Centre, Suomi, Finland
1987 *The Frederick R Wesiman Collection: An International Survey*, San Antonio Art Institute
1987 *American Masters: Works on Paper from the Corcoran Gallery of Art*, Corcoran Gallery of Art, Washington DC; The Burling Library, Grinnell, Iowa; Cincinnati Art Musuem, Ohio; Midland Art Council, Midland, Michigan
1986 *The Texas Landscape: 1900–1986*, Museum of Fine Arts, Houston
1985 *Fresh Paint: The Houston School*, Museum of Fine Arts, Houston
1985 *Selections II: 20th Century Art*, Metropolitan Museum of Art, New York
1985 *The New Figure*, Birmingham Museum of Art, Alabama
1984 *New Narrative Paintings from the Collection of the Metropolitan Museum of Art*, Museum of Art, Fort Lauderdale, Florida
1983 *Sacred Artifacts and Objects of Devotion*, Alternative Museum, New York
1983 *New Work, New York*, Phoenix Museum of Art, Arizona
1982 *New, New York*, Fine Arts Gallery, Florida State University, Tallahassee
1982 *Recent Acquisitions*, Corcoran Gallery of Art, Washington DC
1982 *Southern Fictions*, Contemporary Arts Museum, Houston
1981 *Southern Monumental Exhibition*, University Gallery, Memphis State University, Tennessee
1981 *New York Gallery Showcase*, Oklahoma Art Museum, Oklahoma City
1979 *Art of Texas*, Renaissance Society of the University of Chicago
1979 *Painting and Sculpture Today*, Indianapolis Museum of Art, Indiana
1979 *The Art of Texas*, John Michael Kohler Art Center, Sheboygan, Wisconsin
1977 *Six Painters of the Southwest*, Museum of Art, University of Oklahoma, Norman
1977 *1977 Artists Biennial*, New Orleans Museum of Art
1977 *35th Biennial Exhibition of Contemporary American Painting*, Corcoran Gallery of Art, Washington DC
1976 *Philadelphia-Houston Exchange*, Institute of Contemporary Art, University of Pennsylvania
1976 *Annual Exhibition*, American Academy of Arts and Letters, New York

**Selected Public Collections**

Archer M Huntington Art Gallery, Austin
Arkansas Arts Center, Little Rock
Art Museum of Southeast Texas, Beaumont
Birmingham Museum of Art, Birmingham
Chrysler Museum, Norfolk
Corcoran Gallery of Art, Washington DC
Dallas Museum of Art, Dallas
Hirshhorn Museum and Sculpture Garden, Washington DC
Long Beach Museum of Art, Long Beach
The Metropolitan Museum of Art, New York
Modern Art Museum of Fort Worth
Museum of Contemporary Art, Chicago
Museum of Fine Arts, Houston
Nelson-Atkins Museum of Art, Kansas City
San Antonio Museum of Art

## Terry Allen

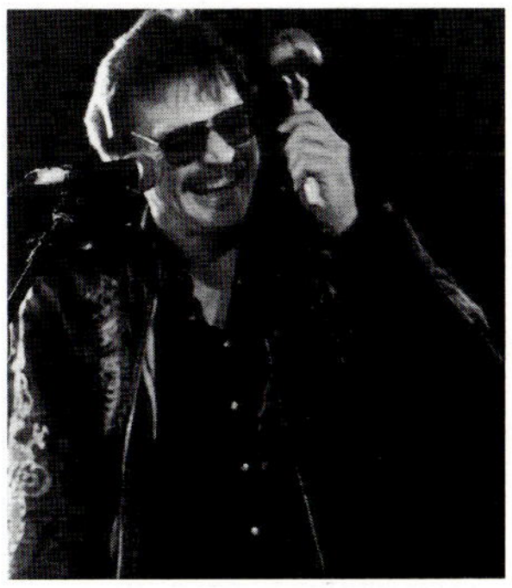

*Terry Allen, 1986. Courtesy of the artist.*

1943 Born in Wichita, Kansas
Lives in Santa Fe, New Mexico

**Education and Awards**

1966 Chouinard Art Institute, Los Angeles, BFA
1986 National Endowment for the Arts, Fellowship
1986 Guggenheim Fellowship
1986 Bessie Award, New York
1989 Adaline Kent Award, San Francisco

**Selected Solo Exhibitions and Installations**

1992 *Youth in Asia*, Southeastern Center for Contemporary Art, Winston-Salem, North Carolina
1992 *Juarez* (installation), Wexner Center for the Visual Arts, Columbus, Ohio
1992 Moody Gallery, Houston
1992 Gallery Paule Anglim, San Francisco
1991 *Terry Allen: New Work*, LA Louver, Venice, California
1991 *The Artist's Eye: Terry Allen*, Kimbell Art Museum, Fort Worth
1989 *Big Witness (living in wishes)* San Francisco Art Institute
1989 *Them Ol' Love Songs*, Cranbrook Art Museum, Bloomfield Hills, Minnesota
1989 *Installation and Concert*, Laumiere Sculpture Park, St Louis, Missouri
1989 Moody Gallery, Houston
1988 *Big Witness (living in wishes)*, LA Louver Gallery, Venice; Santa Barbara Contemporary Arts Forum, Santa Barbara, California; Moore College of Art, Philadelphia; Madison Arts Center, Wisconsin; University of Arizona Museum of Art, Tucson
1988 *Treatment (Angel With Dirty Tracks)*, John Weber Gallery, New York
1988 *Terry Allen: Youth in Asia Series*, Pittsburgh Center for the Arts, Pennsylvania
1988 Gallery Paule Anglim, San Francisco
1986 *Revelations*, Southwest Center for Arts & Crafts, San Antonio
1986 *China Night*, Florida State University Fine Arts Gallery, Tallahassee
1986 John Weber Gallery, New York
1986 Gallery Paule Anglim, San Francisco
1985 *China Night* (installation), Fresno Art Center, Fresno, California
1985 Barbara Gladstone Gallery, New York
1985 Moody Gallery, Houston
1984 *Sprawl/Prowl/Growl*, Espace Lyonnais D'Art Contemporain, Lyon, France
1984 Barbara Gladstone Gallery, New York
1983 *Rooms and Stories*, La Jolla Museum of Contemporary Art, La Jolla
1983 Madeville Gallery, University of California, San Diego
1983 Morgan Art Gallery, Kansas City, Missouri
1983 *Youth in Asia* (installation), Center on Contemporary Art, Seattle, Washington; Espace Lyonnais d'Art Contemporain, Lyon
1981 Portland Center for the Visual Arts, Oregon
1981 *Ring*, Nelson-Atkins Gallery, Kansas City
1981 *Ornithopera (The Devil's Condo)*, (installation), Modern Art Museum of Fort Worth; La Jolla Museum of Contemporary Art; Espace Lyonnais d'Art Contemporain, Lyon
1980 Baxter Art Gallery, California Institute of Technology, Pasadena, California
1979 Lubbock Lights Gallery, Lubbock, Texas
1979 Miami-Dade Community College, Florida
1979 Morgan Art Gallery, Kansas City, Missouri
1978 Hansen Fuller Gallery, San Francisco
1978 Nancy Lurie Gallery, Chicago
1978 Landfall Press Gallery, Chicago
1976 *The Paradise* (installation), Modern Art Museum of Fort Worth
1976 Morgan Art Gallery, Kansas City, Missouri
1975 *Juarez Series*, Contemporary Arts Museum, Houston
1971 Museum of Contemporary Art, Chicago
1968 Pasadena Art Museum, California
1966 Gallery 66, Los Angeles

**Selected Group Exhibitions**

1994 *Poison/Amor: Collaboration, Terry Allen and James Drake*, Blue Star Art Space, San Antonio; Sarah Campbell Blaffer Gallery, University of Houston
1992 *Profiles II: On Paper*, Adair Margo Gallery, El Paso; Weber State University, Ogden Utah; Arlington Museum of Art, Arlington, Texas
1991 *The Political Arm*, John Weber Gallery, New York; Washington University, St Louis, Missouri
1991 *Text Context*, San Jose Institute of Contemporary Art, San Jose, California
1991 *Singular Visions*, Museum of Fine Arts, Santa Fe
1991 *Selections form the Permanent Collection: 1975–1991*, Museum of Contemporary Art, Los Angeles
1990 *CCAI2*, Center for Contemporary Arts of Santa Fe, Second Invitational, New Mexico

1990 *Northwest x Southwest — Painted Fiction*, Palm Springs Desert Museum, California; Yellowstone Art Center, Montana; Bellingham Museum, Washington; Sarah Campbell Blaffer Gallery, University of Houston

1989 *Heroics Recast*, School of the Museum of Fine Arts, Boston

1989 *Forty Years of California Assemblage*, Wight Art Gallery, University of California, Los Angeles; Joslyn Art Museum, Omaha, Nebraska

1989 *A Different War*, Whatcom Museum of History and Art, Bellingham, Washington, a traveling exhibition

1987 *Documenta 8*, Kassel, Germany

1987 *Avant Garde in the Eighties*, Los Angeles County Museum of Art

1987 *War & Memory*, Washington Project for the Arts, Washington DC

1986 *The Allen/Ely Project*, Southwest Craft Center, San Antonio

1986 *The Texas Landscape, 1900–1986*, Museum of Fine Arts, Houston

1986 *Honky-Tonk Visions (On West Texas Music: 1936–1986)*, Texas Tech University, Lubbock; a traveling exhibition

1985 Sao Paolo Biennial, Sao Paolo, Brazil

1984 *Content, A Contemporary Focus, 1974–1984*, Hirshhorn Museum and Sculpture Garden, Washington DC

1984 *Return of the Narrative*, Palm Springs Desert Museum, California

1983 *Site Strategies*, The Oakland Museum, California

1983 *Language Drama Source & Vision*, The New Museum, New York

1982 Sydney Biennale, Art Gallery of New South Wales, Australia

1982 Awards in the Visual Arts, National Gallery of Art, Washington DC; other venues

1982 Exchange Between Artists, 1981–1982, Poland-USA, Museum of Modern Art, Paris

1981 *The Southern Voice: Terry Allen, Vernon Fisher, Ed McGowin*, Modern Art Museum of Fort Worth

1979 *Image & Object in Contemporary Sculpture*, Detroit Institute of Art, Michigan; PS1, Long Island City, New York

1977 *Whitney Biennial*, Whitney Museum of American Art, New York

1977 10th Biennale de Paris, Paris

1977 *American Narrative: Story of Art, 1976–1977*, Contemporary Arts Museum, Houston

1977 *The Record as Artwork*, Modern Art Museum of Fort Worth; venues in the US and Canada

1976 *The Great American Rodeo Show*, Modern Art Museum of Fort Worth; venues in the US in conjunction with rodeos

1976 *Painting and Sculpture in California: The Modern Era*, San Francisco Museum of Modern Art; National Collection of Fine Arts, Smithsonian Institution, Washington DC

**Selected Recordings**

1987 *Amerasia*, film soundtrack

1986 *The Sounds From True Stories*, soundtrack; single *Cocktail Desperado*, co-written with David Byrne

1984 *Bloodlines*, album

1980 *Smokin' The Dummy*, album

1978 *Lubbock (on Everything)*; double album

1975 *Juarez*, album

**Selected Public Collections**

Cleveland Museum of Art

Dallas Museum of Art

Detroit Institute of Arts

Espace Lyonnais d'Art Contemporain, Musee Saint Pierre, Lyon

La Jolla Museum of Contemporary Art

Metropolitan Museum of Art, New York

Museum of Modern Art, New York

Nelson-Atkins Gallery of Art, Kansas City

San Francisco Museum of Modern Art

University Art Museum, Berkeley, California

## Helen Altman

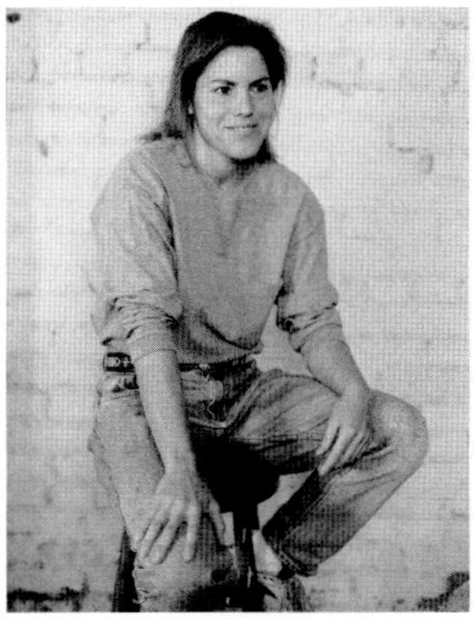

*Helen Altman, 1993. Courtesy of the artist.*

1958 Born in Tuscaloosa, Alabama

Lives in Fort Worth, Texas

**Education and Awards**

1981 Univeristy of Alabama, Tuscaloosa, BA

1986 University of Alabama, Tuscaloosa, MA

1989 University of North Texas, Denton, MFA

1991 Engelhard Award

1993 Mid-America Arts Alliance Award

**Selected Solo Exhibitions**

1992 *Burning Down The House*, Barry Whistler Gallery, Dallas

1992 *Watching Pots*, Ida Green Gallery, Sherman, Texas

**Selected Group Exhibitions**

1993 *TEXAS/Between Two Worlds*; Contemporary Arts Museum, Houston; Museum of Modern Art, Fort Worth; Art Museum of South Texas, Corpus Christi

1993 *Light*, Barry Whistler Gallery, Dallas

1993 *Sculptors & Paper*, Hiram Butler Gallery, Houston

1992 *Housewares on Level 6*, Randolph Street Gallery, Chicago

1992 *New Texas Art*, San Antonio Museum of Art; Cheney Cowles Museum, Spokane, Washington; Boise Art Museum, Idaho

1992 *Re-creation/Recreation, re:Creation*, Laguna Gloria Art Museum, Austin

1992 *Beyond Glory: Re-Presenting Terrorism*, Maryland Institute College of Art, Baltimore

1991 *The Perfect World*, San Antonio Museum of Art

1991 *Metamorphosis of a Butterfly*, Pennsylvania State University, University Park

1990 *Domestic Disorder*, DiverseWorks, Houston

1990 *New American Talent: The Sixth Edition*, Laguna Gloria Art Museum, Austin

## Jesse Amado

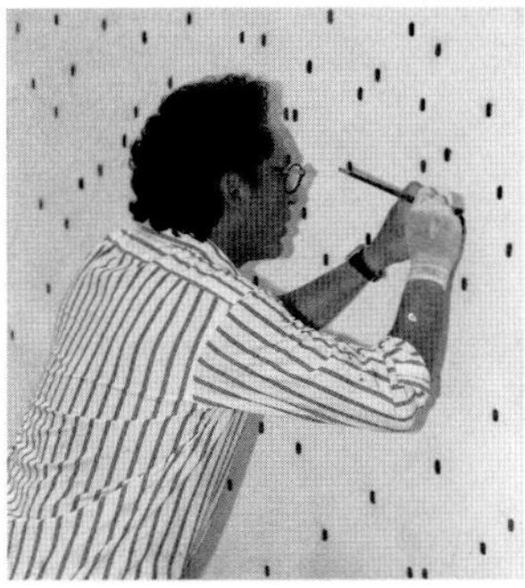

*Jesse Amado, c.1992. Courtesy of the artist.*

1951 Born in San Antonio, Texas

Lives in San Antonio, Texas

**Education and Awards**

1976 University of Texas, Austin, BA

1987 University of Texas, San Antonio, BFA

1990 University of Texas, San Antonio, MFA

1990 National Endowment for the Arts, Individual Artists Fellowship

1990 The Fabric Workshop, Artist in Residence, Philadelphia

1992 Visual Arts Fellowship Grant, Art Matters, Inc, New York

**Selected Solo Exhibitions**

1993 *TEXAS/Between Two Worlds*, Contemporary Arts Museum, Houston; Museum of Modern Art, Fort Worth; Art Museum of South Texas, Corpus Christi

1993 *Introductions*, Davis/McClain Galleries, Houston

1992 *Just Selections*, Galveston Arts Center, Galveston, Texas

1992 *Drawings and Sculptures*, Jansen-Perez Gallery, San Antonio

1991 *New Works*, Fabric Workshop, Philadelphia

**Selected Group Exhibitions**

1993 *Darkness + Light*, Sarah Campbell Blaffer Gallery, University of Houston

1992 *Spanish Remnants: Borders Real and Imagined*, Arlington Museum of Art, Arlington, Texas; Blue Star Art Space, San Antonio

1991 *The Perfect World*, San Antonio Museum of Art

1991 *Colorado Contemporary Art Biennial*, Sangre de Cristo Art Center, Pueblo, Colorado

1991 *Tejanos: artistas mexicanos-norteamericanos*,

Museo de Arte Alvar y Carmen Carrillo Gil, Mexico City
1990 *Texas Dialogue: San Antonio-El Paso*, Blue Star Art Space, San Antonio; Bridge Center for Contemporary Art, El Paso, Texas
1989 *New American Talent*, Laguna Gloria Art Museum, Austin
1988 *Prints from San Antonio*, Instituto Cultural Peruano-Norteamericano, Lima, Peru

**Selected Public Collections**

Matthew and Branscomb, Attorneys, San Antonio
Sunbelt Corporation, San Antonio

## John Biggers

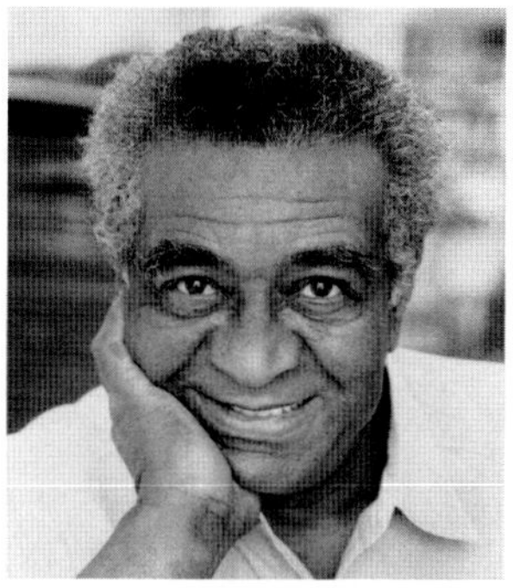

*John Biggers, c.1990. Photograph: Donnie Roberts.*

1924 Born in Gastonia, North Carolina
Lives in Houston, Texas and North Carolina

**Education and Selected Awards**

1941–43 Hampton Institute, Hampton, Virginia
1946 Hampton Institute, Hampton, Virginia
1948 Pennsylvania State University, BS and MS
1950 Purchase Prize, Museum of Fine Arts, Houston
1951 Schlumberger Prize, Museum of Fine Arts, Houston
1952 Neiman Marcus Prize for Drawing, Dallas Museum of Art
1952–53 Purchase Prize, Atlanta University Annual Exhibition
1954 Pennsylvania State University, PhD
1957 UNESCO Fellowship
1963 Excellence of Design, Chicago Book Clinic Award and Southern Book Competition, for *Ananse: The Web of Life in Africa*
1964 Piper Professor Award, Minnie Stevens-Piper Foundation
1972 Distinguished Alumnus Award, Pennsylvania State University

**Selected Solo Exhibitions**

1993 *John Biggers: A Cultural Legacy, Retrospective 1950–1992*, Whatley Center for the Performing Arts, Northeast Texas Community College, Mt Pleasant, Texas
1987 *Patchwork Quilts and Shotguns*, Transco Energy Co, Houston
1983 *Bridges*, California Museum of Afro-American History and Culture, Los Angeles
1963 *Ceremonies and Vision*, Laguna Gloria Art Museum, Austin. Traveled to Africa under the auspices of the United States Information Agency
1963 Lubbock Museum of Fine Arts, Lubbock, Texas
1963 Dallas Public Library, Dallas
1962 Museum of Fine Arts, Houston
1955 Pennsylvania State University, University Park

**Selected Group Exhibitions**

1989 *Black Art/Ancestral Legacy:The African Impulse in African-American Art*, Dallas Museum of Art; High Museum of Art, Atlanta, Georgia; Milwaukee Art Museum, Wisconsin; Virginia Museum of Fine Arts, Richmond
1985 *Fresh Paint: The Houston School*, Museum of Fine Arts, Houston
1976 *Two Centuries of Black American Art: 1750–1950*, Los Angeles County Museum of Art
1972 *Reflections: The Afro-American Artist*, Winston-Salem Fine Arts, North Carolina
1969 *12 Black American Artists*, University of Wisconsin, Madison
1959 *Ford Foundation Invitational Art Exhibit*, Fort Worth Art Center, Texas
1958 *Ford Foundation Invitational Art Exhibit*, Fort Worth Art Center
1952 *Texas Contemporary Artists*, M Knoedler and Co, New York
1945 Baltimore Museum of Art
1944 Virginia Museum of Fine Arts, Richmond
1944 Museum of Modern Art, New York

**Selected Public Commissions and Collections**

1993 Hampton University Library
1987 Paris Public Library, Paris, Texas
1987 Tom Bass Regional Park, Harris County, Texas
1982 Christia Adair Park, Harris County, Texas
1981 Music Hall, Houston
1976 Sterling Student Life Center, Texas Southern University, Houston
1966 WL Johnson Branch, Houston Public Library
1957 Longshoreman's Association Local 872, Houston
1953 Blue Triangle YWCA, Houston
1951 Eliza Johnson Home for the Aged, Houston
1946 United Transport Workers Labor Temple, CIO, Chicago

Atlanta University
Barnett-Aden Collection, Washington DC
Dallas Museum of Art
Golden State Mutual Life Insurance Co, Los Angeles
Hampton Univeristy Museum, Virginia
Howard University, Washington DC
Lubbock Museum
Museum of Fine Arts, Houston
National Museum of American Art, Smithsonian Institution, Washington DC
Texas Southern University, Houston

## Julie Bozzi

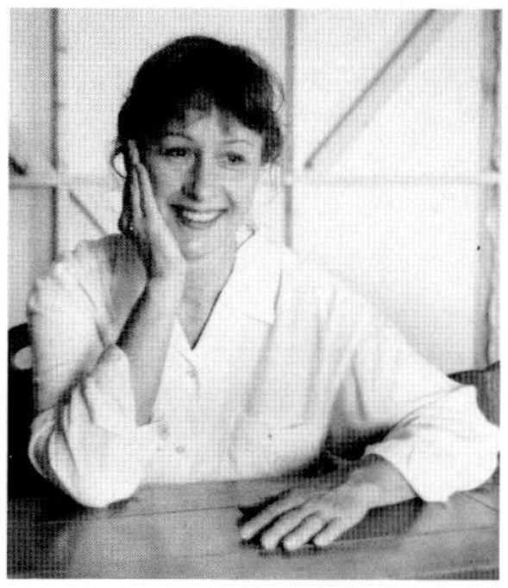

*Julie Bozzi, 1993. Photograph: Christina Patoski. Courtesy of the artist.*

1943 Born in San Jose, California
Lives in Fort Worth, Texas

**Education and Awards**

1989 National Endowment for the Arts, Individual Artists Fellowship
1987 The Louis Comfort Tiffany Foundation
1975 Skowhegan School of Painting and Sculpture
1975–76 Chancellor's Graduate Fellowship, University of California, Davis
1974–76 University of California, Davis, BA and MFA

**Selected Solo Exhibitions**

1992 *American Food*, San Diego Museum of Contemporary Art, San Diego; University of Massachusetts, Amherst; Modern Art Museum of Fort Worth; Indianapolis Museum of Art, Indiana
1990 *Scene of Three Murders. Paintings*, Texas Gallery, Houston
1988 *Recent Landscape Paintings*, Texas Gallery, Houston
1984 *Suburban Landscape*, Texas Gallery, Houston
1983 *Ethnic American Still Life*, Brown-Lupton Gallery, Texas Christian University, Fort Worth
1983 *Still Life with Pairs*, Delahunty Gallery, Dallas

**Selected Group Exhibitions**

1990 *Tradition and Innovation*, Museum of Fine Arts, Houston
1989 *Legacy II: Texas Realism*, Art Museum of Southeast Texas, Beaumont
1989 *A Century of Sculpture in Texas, 1889–1989*, Archer M Huntington Art Gallery, University of Texas, Austin
1989 *The New American Landscape*, Alfred C Glassell School of Art, Houston
1988 *Six Artists/Six Idioms*, Sarah Campbell Blaffer Gallery, University of Houston, Houston
1988 *Land*, ACA Contemporary, New York
1988 *Drawn From Life: The Physical and Cultural landscape of the 1980s*, College of the Mainland Art Gallery, Texas City
1987 *Boundless Realism*, The Rockwell Museum, Corning, New York
1987 *Third Coast Review: A Look at Art in Texas*, The Aspen Art Museum, Aspen, Colorado
1986 *Natural Settings*, Corcoran Gallery of Art, Washington DC

1986 *Texas Landscape: An Historical Survey of Texas Landscape from the 19th Century to the Present*, Museum of Fine Arts, Houston
1985 *Indigestion*, PPOW Gallery, New York
1984 *New Work: New York/Outside New York*, The New Museum of Contemporary Art, New York
1981 *California: State of the Landscape*, Newport Harbor Art Museum, Newport Beach and Santa Barbara Museum of Art, California
1980 *The Tableau Show*, Los Angeles Institute of Contemporary Art, Los Angeles

**Selected Public Collections**
The Brooklyn Museum, New York
Dallas Museum of Art, Dallas
The Lannan Foundation, Los Angeles
Modern Art Museum of Fort Worth
Museum of Fine Arts, Houston

## Karin Broker

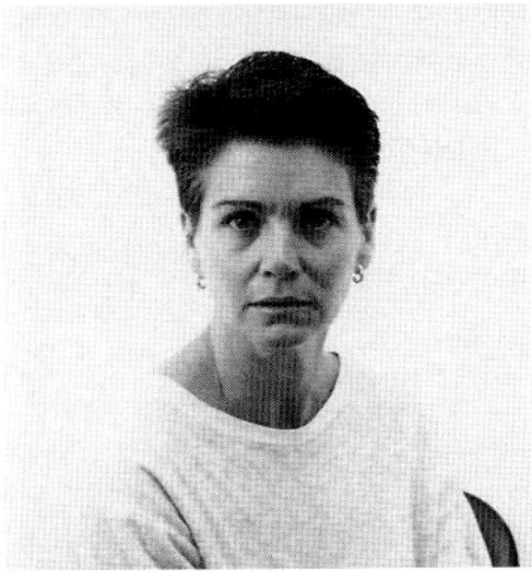

*Karin Broker, 1993. Courtesy of the artist.*

1950 Born in Penn, Pennsylvania
Lives in Houston, Texas

**Education and Awards**
1972 University of Iowa, Iowa City, BFA
1973 Atelier 17, Paris, France
1980 University of Wisconsin, Madison, MFA
1989 Mellon Fellowship
1987 National Endowment for the Arts, Individual Artist Fellowship
1985 National Endowment for the Arts, Individual Artist Fellowship

**Selected Solo Exhibitions**
1992 *Searching for a Saint: Karin Broker, 1980–1992*, Sewall Art Gallery, Rice University, Houston
1992 McMurtrey Gallery, Houston
1989 Susanna Sheffield Gallery, Houston
1988 Corpus Christi State University, Corpus Christi
1986 Hadler-Rodriguez Gallery, Houston
1982 Studio-Galerie, Rasteded, Federal Republic of Germany

**Selected Group Exhibitions**
1992 *Figurative Graphics, Graphic Figures, Kunst Aus Den USA*, USIA and Berufsverband Bildener Kunstler, Koln, Germany
1988 *Colorprint USA*, Texas Tech University, Lubbock
1988 *Off the Wall*, Michigan Gallery, Detroit, Michigan
1987 *1987 International Exchange Exhibition of Prints*, Gallery of Fine Arts Center, Seoul, Korea
1987 *Graphica Atlantica*, Kjarvalsstadir Art Gallery, Reykjavik, Iceland
1986 *Shrines and Altars: Tradition and Innovation*, John Michael Kohler Arts Center, Sheboygan, Wisconsin
1986 *New Orleans Triennial: The Centennial Exhibition*, New Orleans Museum of Art
1986 *Nine Texas Printmakers*, San Antonio Museum of Art, San Antonio
1986 *Point of Departure*, Elvehjem Museum, Madison, Wisconsin; World Print Council, San Francisco; Philadelphia Print Club, Philadelphia
1986 *10 Texas Printmakers*, Abilene Fine Arts Museum, Abilene, Texas
1984 *Artists in the Trenches*, Katherine E Nash Gallery, University of Minnesota, Minneapolis
1984 *Figure and Narratives: National Invitational Print Exhibition*, Visual Arts Center of Alaska, Anchorage
1983 *International Print Exhibition: 1983 ROC*, Taipei City Museum of Fine Arts, Taipei, Taiwan
1983 *Bienal Internacional de Gravura e Arte Grafico de Cabo Frio*, Cabo Frio, Brazil
1983 *Showdown*, Alternative Museum, New York

**Selected Public Collections**
Brooklyn Museum of Art
Curitiba Cultural Foundation, Brazil
Grunwald Center for the Graphic Arts, University of California, Los Angeles
Library of Congress, Washington DC
Mint Museum, Milwaukee Museum of Art
Museum of Fine Arts, Boston
Museum of Fine Arts, Houston
National Museum of American Art, Smithsonian Institution, Washington DC
New York Public Library, New York
Harvard University Fogg Museum, Boston
Elvehjem Museum of Art, Madison

## Keith Carter

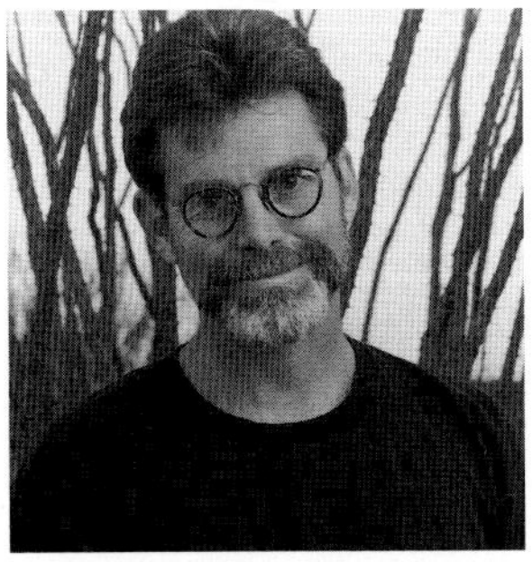

*Keith Carter, 1993. Photograph: James Evans. Courtesy of the artist.*

1948 Born in Madison, Wisconsin
Lives in Beaumont, Texas

**Education and Awards**
1970 Lamar University, BBA, Beaumont
Alfred Eisenstadt Seminar, New School of New York
1981 National Endowment for the Arts, Photographers' Visual Arts Grant
1991 Mid-America Arts Alliance Fellowship Grant
1991 The Lange-Taylor Prize, Center for Documentary Studies, Duke University
1992 Outstanding Achievement by an Artist Award, Southwest Texas Arts Council
1993 Stanley Marcus Award for Excellence in Design, *Mojo*, Texas Institute of Letters

**Selected Solo Exhibitions and Publications**
1993 Photo-Eye Gallery, Santa Fe
1993 Witkin Gallery, Inc, New York
1993 Houston Center for Photography, Houston
1993 Kathleen Ewing Gallery, Washington DC
1993 Catherine Edleman Gallery, Chicago
1993 Afterimage Gallery, Dallas
1992 *Mojo*, Rice University Press, Text by Rosellen Brown
1992 Tyler Museum of Art, Tyler
1992 Vision Gallery, San Francisco
1992 McMurtrey Gallery, Houston
1992 McNeese State University, Lake Charles, Louisiana
1991 Dum Umeni Mesta Brna, Brno, Czechoslovakia
1991 Allen Street Gallery, Dallas
1990 *The Blue Man*, Rice University Press; Afterword by Anne W Tucker
1990 Witkin Gallery, Inc, New York
1990 Texas Tech University, Lubbock
1990 McMurtrey Gallery, Houston
1990 Tyler Museum of Art
1988 *From Uncertain to Blue*, Texas Monthly Press, Text by Horton Foote
1988 Art Museum of Southeast Texas, Beaumont
1981 Beaumont Art Museum
1978 Art Museum of South Texas, Corpus Christi
1975 Galveston Arts Center
1973 Afterimage Gallery, Dallas

**Selected Group Exhibitions**
1993 *Wings of Change: Images of Contradiction and Consensus*, The Directors' Guild, Los Angeles
1992 *Facing South*, Galveston Arts Center
1992 *Profiles III: On Photography*, Arlington Museum of Art, Arlington, Texas
1992 *Past/Present: Photographs from the Collection of the Museum of Fine Arts*, Museum of Fine Arts, Houston
1991 *Reinventing the World: Fox Harris*, Houston Center for Photography
1991 *Two From the South: Keith Carter, Debbie Caffery*, Arizona State University, Tempe
1990 *Photography: 1980s Discovery and Invention*, Basel Art Fair, Switzerland
1990 *Three Generations of Southern Photographers*, University of Houston, Clear Lake
1989 *The Deep South*, a slide presentation, Arles Recontres, Arles, France
1989 *Keith Carter and Geoffrey Brune*, McMurtrey Gallery, Houston
1986 Southwest Craft Center, San Antonio
1986 *Texas 150: New Work from Texas*, Houston Center for Photography
1981 *Ties That Bind: Photographers Look at the Family*, Dougherty Cultural Arts Center, Austin
1978 *Works on Paper: Southwest 1978*, Dallas Museum of Art

1977	Tyler Museum of Art
1975	Beaumont Art Museum

**Selected Public Collections**

Amon Center Museum, Fort Worth
Art Museum of Southeast Texas, Beaumont
Carpenter Center for the Visual Arts, Harvard University, Cambridge
Halmark Collection, Kansas City
Humanities Research Centre, University of Texas, Austin
The Menil Collection, Houston
Museum of Fine Arts, Houston
Phoenix Arts Commission
San Antonio Museum of Art
San Francisco Museum of Modern Art
Santa Barbara Museum of Fine Arts
Tyler Museum of Art, Tyler
Yale University Museum, New Haven

## Mel Chin

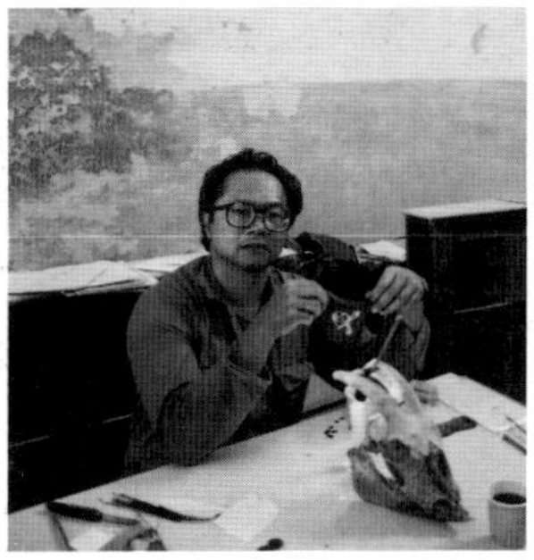

*Mel Chin, 1993. Photograph: Tam Miller. Courtesy of the artist.*

1950	Born in Houston
Lives in New York City

**Education and Awards**

1975	Peabody College, Nashville, Tennessee, BA
1982	Visual Arts Commission, Houston Festival
1988	Founder's Day Grant, Uranian Phlanstery: The First NY Gnostic Lyceum
1988	National Endowment for the Arts, Fellowship
1989	Pollock/Krasner Foundation Fellowship
1989	Louis Comfort Tiffany Foundation Grant
1989–90 New York State Council for the Arts, Projects Award
1990	Mid Atlantic Arts Foundation
1990	Art Matters, Inc, Artists' Fellowship
1990	National Endowment for the Arts, Artist's Projects
1991	Engelhard Award
1991	Penny McCall Foundation Award

**Selected Solo Exhibitions, Projects and Installations**

1993	*Revival Field Project*, Site: Palmerton, Pennsylvania
1992	*Soil and Sky*, The Fabric Workshop and Swarthmore College, Philadelphia
1992	*Gallery*, simultaneous installation at Capp Street Project, San Francisco, and Three Rivers Arts Festival, Pittsburgh
1992	*Revival Field/Netherlands: Simultaneous Replicated Field Test*, Site: Floriadepark, Zoetermeer, The Netherlands
1991	*Degrees of Paradise*, Storefront for Art and Architecture, New York
1991	*Mel Chin*, The Menil Collection, Houston
1991	*Revival Field Project*, Site: Pig's Eye Landfill, St Paul, Minnesota
1990	*Viewpoints: Mel Chin*, Walker Art Center, Minneapolis
1990	*Ghost*, installation, Real Art Ways, Hartford
1989	*Directions: Mel Chin*, Hirshhorn Museum and Sculpture Garden, Washington DC
1989	*Forgetting Tiananmen Square, Kent State, Tlatelolco*, performance and production with Corcoran School of Art, Washington DC
1988	*Selected Weapons*, Frumkin/Adams Gallery, New York
1988	*The Edge That Cuts Also Instructs*, William A Graham Gallery, Houston; Frumkin/Adams Gallery, New York
1987	*The Operation of the Sun Through the Cult of the Hand*, Loughelton Gallery, New York
1986	*Myrrha PIA*, Bryant Park, New York; Max Hutchinson Sculpture Fields, Kenoza Lake, New York
1985	*Modus Operandi: 1974–1985*, DiverseWorks, Houston
1976	Robinson Galleries, Houston
1976	*The Earth Works: See/Saw*, Hermann Park, Houston

**Selected Group Exhibitions**

1993	*Differentes Natures*, La Defense, Paris, France
1992–94 *Fragile Ecologies*, Smithsonian Institution Traveling Exhibitions, various venues
1992	*Putt Modernism*, Artists Space, New York, New York
1992	*Allocations: Art for a Natural and Artificial Environment*, Floriadepark, Zoetermeer, The Netherlands
1992	*Beyond Glory: Re-Presenting Terrorism*, Maryland Institute College of Art, Baltimore
1990	*Diverse Representation*, Morris Museum, Morristown, New Jersey
1990	*Garbage Out Front: A New Era of Public Design*, Municipal Art Society, New York
1990	*International Memorial Arts Festival: China, June 4*, Institute for Contemporary Art, Long Island City, New York
1990	*Tradition and Innovation: A Museum Celebration of Texas Art*, Museum of Fine Arts, Houston
1989	*China, June 4*, Blum Helman Warehouse, New York
1989	*Sculpture Part II*, Frumkin/Adams Gallery, New York
1988	*Texas Art: Selections*, Richmond Hall, The Menil Collection, Houston
1988	*Art Against AIDS*, Benefit Exhibition and Auction, Houston
1986	*The Texas Landscape, 1900–1986*, Museum of Fine Arts, Houston
1986	*Inaugural Exhibition*, Max Hutchinson Sculpture Fields, Kenoza Lake, New York
1983	Benefit for Amnesty International, USA, DiverseWorks, Houston
1982	*Prisoners of Conscience*, Amnesty International, traveling exhibition

**Selected Public Collections**

Contemporary Arts Museum, Houston
The Menil Collection, Houston
Museum of Fine Arts, Houston
Walker Art Center, Minneapolis

## James Drake

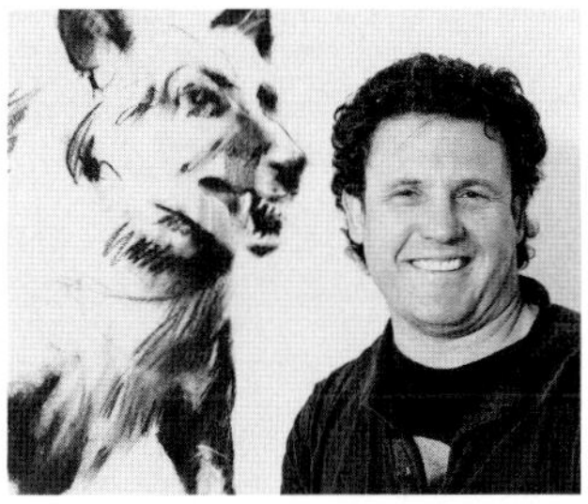

*James Drake, 1993. Courtesy of the artist.*

1946	Born in Lubbock, Texas
Lives in El Paso, Texas

**Education and Awards**

1969	Art Center College of Design, Los Angeles, BFA
1970	Art Center College of Design, Los Angeles, MFA
1988	Award in the Visual Arts, Southeastern Center for Contemporary Art
1988	Mid-America Arts Alliance
1989	National Endowment for the Arts, Grant and Travel Fellowship
1989–	Artist in Residence, La Napoule Foundation, France

**Selected Solo Exhibitions**

1993	*Recent Drawings*, Adair Margo Gallery, El Paso
1992	*The Border of Desire*, Art Museum of Southeast Texas, Beaumont
1992	*The Valley of the World*, Arthur Roger Gallery, New York
1991	*Force Fields/Pure Light/Voices*, Center for Research of Contemporary Art, University of Texas, Arlington
1991	*Heart of Gold*, Shea/Bornstein Gallery, Santa Monica, California
1990	*James Drake: Place and Passage*, Corcoran Gallery of Art, Washington DC
1990	*James Drake: The Border/La Frontera*, Contemporary Arts Museum, Houston; Anderson Gallery, Virginia Commonwealth University, Richmond; Palmer Museum of Art, Pennsylvania State University, University Park; Gardiner Art Gallery, Oklahoma State University, Stillwater
1990	*James Drake: New Work from the Border*, Adair Margo Gallery, El Paso
1990	*James Drake Sculpture*, Arthur Roger Gallery, New Orleans
1990	*James Drake Prints and Drawings*, Fendrick Gallery, Washington DC
1989	*New Work*, Texas Gallery, Houston
1989	La Jolla Museum of Contemporary Art, Downtown, La Jolla
1988	*James Drake: Border Incident*, Alternative Museum, New York

1988 *James Drake: Sculpture and Drawings*, The University of Texas, San Antonio
1987 Adair Margo Gallery, El Paso
1985 Texas Gallery, Houston
1985 Arthur Roger Gallery, New Orleans
1983 Texas Christian University, Fort Worth
1982 Galveston Arts Center, Galveston
1982 The University of Texas, El Paso
1982 Robert Speaker Gallery, Los Angeles
1981 *New Vision*, Amarillo Art Center, Amarillo, Texas; Abilene Fine Arts Museum; El Paso Museum of Art; Wichita Falls Museum and Art Center, Wichita Falls, Texas
1976 Museo de Arte e Historia, Ciudad Juarez, Mexico
1976 The Pavilion Art Gallery, Scottsdale, Arizona
1971 The University of Texas, El Paso

**Selected Group Exhibitions**

1994 *Poison/Amor: Collaboration: Terry Allen and James Drake*, Blue Star Art Space, San Antonio; Sarah Campbell Blaffer Gallery, University of Houston
1992 *The Passionate Eye*, Laguna Gloria Art Museum, Austin
1992 *Drawing: An Invitational*, New Mexico State University, Las Cruces
1992 *Who Discovered Whom?* Islip Art Museum, East Islip, New York
1991 *Roswell Invitational: James Drake, Luis Jimenez, Ken Little*, Roswell Museum of Art, New Mexico
1991 *Caporitada: Eight El Paso Artists*, El Paso Museum of Art
1991 *The 4th International Shoebox Exhibition*, University of Hawaii, Manoa
1991 *The Perfect World*, San Antonio Museum of Art
1990 *Tradition and Innovation: A Museum Celebration of Texas Art*, Museum of Fine Arts, Houston
1990 *Texas Figurative Drawings*, Dallas Museum of Art
1990 *Center for Contemporary Arts Invitational*, Center for Contemporary Arts, Santa Fe
1990 *Graphica Creative 90, The 6th International Print Triennial*, Alvar Aalto Museum, Jyvaskyla, Finland
1989 *A Century of Sculpture in Texas*, Archer M Huntington Gallery, University of Texas, Austin
1989 *Painted Stories & Other Narrative Art*, Laguna Gloria Art Museum, Austin
1989 *Legacy II, Texas Realism*, Art Museum of Southeast Texas, Beaumont
1989 *Lanna Acquisitions*, La Jolla Museum of Contemporary Art
1989 *Awards in the Visual Arts*, High Museum of Art, Atlanta, Georgia; La Jolla Museum of Contemporary Art; University of Washington, Seattle
1988 *The Mid-America Biennial*, Nelson-Atkins Museum, Kansas City, Missouri
1988 *Selections from the Permanent Collection, Part II*, La Jolla Museum of Contemporary Art
1988 *Texas Narrations*, Connecticut College, New London
1987 *Third Coast Review: A Look at Art in Texas*, Aspen Art Museum, Aspen, Colorado
1987 *Contemporary Texas Figurative Drawing*, Art Museum of South Texas, Corpus Christi
1986 *New Orleans Triennial*, New Orleans Museum of Art
1986 *Western States Biennial*, Brooklyn Museum, New York; Contemporary Art Center, New Orleans; Art Museum of South Texas, Corpus Christi; Colorado Springs Fine Arts Center; San Antonio Museum of Art; Yellowstone Fine Arts Center, Billings, Montana; Palm Springs Desert Museum, and San Jose Museum of Art, California
1986 *Personal Environments*, Museum of Fine Arts, Santa Fe
1983 *Southern Fictions*, Contemporary Arts Museum, Houston
1983 *New Orleans Triennial*, New Orleans Museum of Art
1982 *International 1982*, Longview Museum & Art Center, Waco, Texas
1980 *Copper II*, University of Arizona Museum of Art, Tucson
1980 *Southwest Sculpture*, Galveston Arts Center
1979 *Made in Texas*, Archer M Huntington Art Gallery, University of Texas, Austin
1979 *International Designer Craftsmen*, El Paso Museum of Art
1977 *7th Annual Print & Drawing Exhibition*, Minot State College, Indiana
1976 *Art Exhibition Peace*, Slovenj Gradec, Yugoslavia
1976 *Primo Internazionale Biella Per L'Incisione*, Biella, Italy
1975 *International Biennial of Graphic Art*, Museum of Modern Art, Ljublijana, Yugoslavia
1974 *33rd Annual Exhibit*, Jersey City Art Museum, New Jersey
1974 *5th Annual Colorprint USA*, Texas Tech University, Lubbock
1973 *Society of Art Center for Alumni*, Art Center College of Design, Los Angeles
1971 Long Beach Museum of Art
1967 *Annual Sun Carnival Exhibition*, El Paso Museum of Art

**Selected Public Collections and Commissions**

Birmingham Museum of Fine Art, Alabama
Corcoran Gallery of Art, Washington DC
El Paso County Courthouse
El Paso Museum of Art
Federal Reserve Bank, Washington DC
Kelly Ingram Park, Birmingham
Museo de Arte e Historia, Ciudad Juarez, Mexico
Museum of Fine Arts, Houston
New Mexico State University, Las Cruces
New Orleans Museum of Art
Pascagula County Library
Phoenix Museum of Art
San Diego Museum of Contemporary Art
University of New Mexico, Albuquerque
Washington University, St Louis, Missouri

## Sharon Engelstein

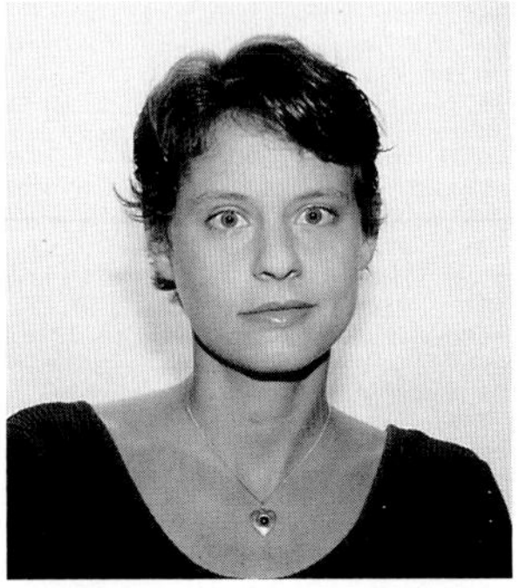

*Sharon Engelstein, 1993. Courtesy of the artist.*

1965 Born in Montreal, Canada
Lives in Houston, Texas

**Education and Awards**

1987 University of South Florida, Tampa, BA
1990 Claremont Graduate School, Claremont, California, MFA
1989 Graduate Fellowship, Claremont Graduate School
1991–92 Core Fellowship, Alfred C Glassell School of Art
1992 Visual Arts Grant, Canada Council for the Arts
1993 Mid-America Arts Alliance Fellowship Award

**Solo Exhibitions**

1990 *Introductions*, William A Graham Gallery, Houston

**Selected Group Exhibitions**

1993 *Texas Contemporary Acquisitions of the 90s*, Museum of Fine Arts, Houston
1993 *Engelstein and Tileston*, Women and Their Work, Austin
1993 *Sharon Engelstein and Rachel Hecker*, Texas Gallery, Houston
1993 *3-D Rupture*, Contemporary Arts Museum, Houston
1993 *Conventional Forms/Insidious Visions*, Alfred C Glassell School of Art, Houston
1992 *Texas Art Celebration*, Assistance League of Houston
1992 Core Fellows 1992, Alfred C Glassell School of Art, Houston
1991 Core Fellows 1991, Alfred C Glassell School of Art, Houston
1990 *The New Fabricants*, Richard Green Gallery, Santa Monica, California
1990 *VEX*, Otis Parsons School of Design, Los Angeles
1990 San Diego Art Institute Annual Exhibition, San Diego

**Selected Public Collections**

Museum of Fine Arts, Houston

## Vernon Fisher

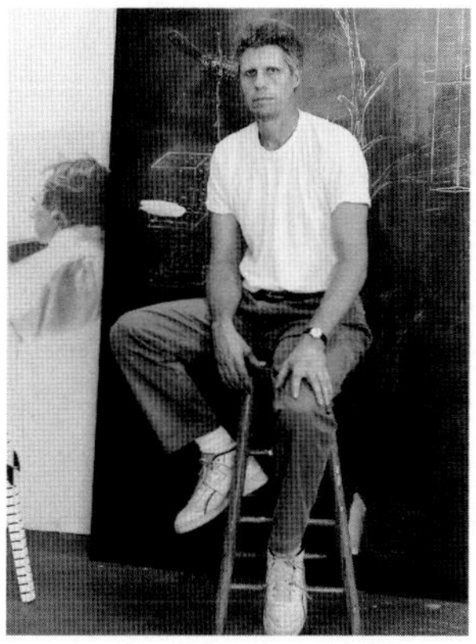

*Vernon Fisher, 1993. Courtesy of the artist.*

1943 Born in Fort Worth
Lives in Fort Worth, Texas

**Education and Awards**

1967 Hardin-Simmons University, Abilene, Texas, BA
1969 University of Illinois, Champaign-Urbana, MFA
1974 National Endowment for the Arts, Individual Artists Fellowship
1980 National Endowment for the Arts, Individual Artists Fellowship
1981 National Endowment for the Arts, Individual Artists Fellowship
1984 Louis Comfort Tiffany Foundation
1988 Southeastern Center for Contemporary Art, Awards in the Visual Arts
1992 College Art Association, Distinguished Teaching of Art Award

**Selected Solo Exhibitions**

1993 *Vernon Fisher at Landfall Press, 1983–1993*, Landfall Press, Chicago
1993 Hiram Butler Gallery, Houston
1993 *Framing Water*, Modernism, San Francisco
1992 *Art in the Armory: Occupied Territory (Pac War Diary)*, Museum of Contemporary Art, Chicago
1992 *Moonrise, Hernandez, New Mexico, 1951*, (installation), The Center for Creative Photography, University of Arizona, Tucson
1992 *Drawings*, Hiram Butler Gallery, Houston
1991 *Blank Slate Sky*, (installation), Yellowstone Art Center, Billings, Montana
1991 *Hills Like White Elephants*, Barry Whistler Gallery, Dallas; Fred Hoffman Gallery, Los Angeles; The Center for Contemporary Art, Sacramento
1990 *Movements Among the Dead* (installation) Museum of Modern Art, New York
1990 *Dead Reckoning* (installation) Smith College Museum of Art, Northampton, Maryland
1990 Installation, University of Texas, Arlington
1990 Hiram Butler Gallery, Houston
1989 *Vernon Fisher*, La Jolla Museum of Contemporary Art; Albright-Knox Art Gallery, Buffalo; Contemporary Arts Museum, Houston; Modern Art Museum of Fort Worth; Center for the Fine Arts, Miami
1989 *Niagara: Welcome to US* (installation), Albright-Knox Art Gallery, Buffalo
1988 *Lost for Words* (installation), Dallas Museum of Art
1988 *Screaming: Installation of Recent Work*, Barry Whistler Gallery, Dallas
1988 *Parallel Lines* (installation), Hirshhorn Museum and Sculpture Garden, Washington DC
1987 *Complementary Pairs* (installation), Hiram Butler Gallery, Houston
1987 *Perdido en El Mar* (installation), Lannan Museum, Lake Worth , Florida
1987 Barbara Gladstone Gallery, New York
1985 Hiram Butler Gallery, Houston
1984 Barbara Gladstone Gallery, New York
1983 Installation, Madison Art Center, Madison, Wisconsin
1982 Galerie T'Venster, Rotterdam, Holland
1982 *Vernon Fisher: New Work*, Delahunty Gallery, Dallas
1981 *Breaking the Code*, Franklin Furnace, New York
1980 *Vernon Fisher: Story Paintings and Drawings*, Contemporary Arts Museum, Houston
1979 Delahunty Gallery, Dallas
1977 *Paintings, Drawings, Photographs*, Delahunty Gallery, Dallas
1976 William Sawyer Gallery, San Francisco
1975 Delahunty Gallery, Dallas
1973 Smither Gallery, Dallas

**Selected Group Exhibitions**

1993 *Texas Contemporary Acquisitions of the 90s*, Museum of Fine Arts, Houston
1993 *Darkness + Light, Twentieth Century Works from Texas Collections*, Sarah Campbell Blaffer Gallery, University of Houston
1993 *Reading Print*, Museum of Modern Art, New York
1992 *Beyond Just Words: I*, Modernism, San Francisco
1991 *The State I'm In: Texas Art at the DMA*, Dallas Museum of Art
1991 *Little Things (Slice it Down to Size) Mean A Lot*, Momentary Modern, Amsterdam, Holland
1990 *Word As Image: American Art 1960–1990*, Milwaukee Art Museum, Wisconsin
1989 *Painting Beyond the Death of Painting*, Kuznetsky Most Exhibition Hall, Moscow, USSR
1987 *New York, New York*, Spencer Museum of Art, University of Kansas, Lawrence; Seattle Art Museum, Washington
1987 *Awards in the Visual Arts 7*, Los Angeles County Museum of Art,; Carnegie-Mellon University, Pittsburgh; Virginia Museum of Fine Arts, Richmond
1987 *Not for the Living Room*, DiverseWorks, Houston
1987 *Past Imperfect: Eric Fischl/Vernon Fisher/Laurie Simmons*, Walker Art Center, Minneapolis; Spirit Square Center for the Arts, Charlotte, North Carolina; Contemporary Arts Center, Cincinnati; Institute of Contemporary Art, University of Pennsylvania, Philadelphia
1987 *Comic Iconoclasm*, Institute of Contemporary Arts, London; Douglas Hyde Gallery, Dublin; Cornerhouse Gallery, Manchester; Círculo de Bellas Artes, Madrid; Kunstmuseum, Berne
1987 *Avant-Garde in the Eighties*, Los Angeles County Museum of Art
1986 *Memento Mori*, Centro Cultural Arte Contemporáneo, Mexico City
1986 *Seventy-fifth American Exhibition*, Art Institute of Chicago
1984 *Narrative Forms*, Museo Rufino Tamayo, Mexico City
1984 *Content: A Contemporary Focus, 1974–1984*, Hirshhorn Museum and Sculpture Garden, Washington DC
1984 *Words Pictures*, Bronx Museum of the Arts, New York
1983 *Language, Drama, Source and Vision*, The New Museum, New York
1983 *The Comic Art Show*, Whitney Museum of American Art, New York
1983 *38th Corcoran Biennial Exhibition of American Painting*, Corcoran Gallery of Art, Washington DC
1983 *Southern Fictions*, Contemporary Arts Museum, Houston
1982 *Fifth India Triennial*, New Delhi, India
1982 *Painting and Sculpture Today, 1982*, Indianapolis Museum of Art
1982 *Mediums of Language*, Hayden Gallery, MIT, Cambridge, Massachusetts
1981 *The Southern Voice: Terry Allen, Vernon Fisher, Ed McGowin*, The Fort Worth Art Museum
1981 *Directions 81* , Hirshhorn Museum and Sculpture Garden, Washington DC
1981 *1981 Biennial Exhibition*, Whitney Museum of American Art, New York
1981 *19 Artists — Emergent Americans: 1981 Exxon National Exhibition*, Guggenheim Museum, New York
1980 *Investigations: Probe — Structure — Analysis*, The New Museum, New York
1977 *American Narrative/Story Art, 1967–1977*, Contemporary Arts Museum, Houston; Contemporary Art Center, New Orleans, University of California Art Museum, Santa Barbara and Berkley
1975 *Exchange DFW/SFO*, Fort Worth Art Museum, Fort Worth; San Francisco Museum of Modern Art

**Selected Public Collections**

Albright-Knox Gallery of Art, Buffalo
Art Institute of Chicago
Baltimore Museum of Art
Corcoran Gallery of Art
Dallas Museum of Art
Guggenheim Museum, New York
Hirshhorn Museum and Sculpture Garden
La Jolla Museum of Contemporary Art
Milwaukee Museum of Art

Museum of Contemporary Art, Chicago
Museum of Fine Arts, Houston
Museum of Modern Art, New York
Museum of Modern Art of Fort Worth
New Orleans Museum of Art

## Roy Fridge

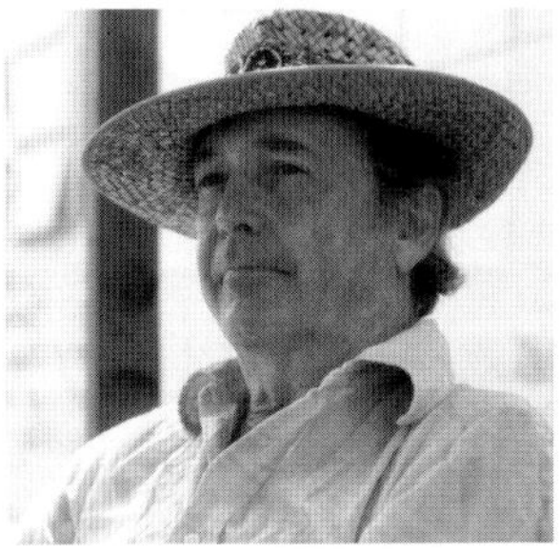

*Roy Fridge, c.1985. Photograph: Roberta Hammond. Courtesy of the artist.*

1927 Born in Beeville, Texas
Lives in Port Aransas, Texas

**Education and Awards**

1950 Baylor University, Waco, Texas, BA
1957 Recognition Award for Film, Waco Art Forum Annual, Waco
1962 International Theater Conference, Sao Paolo, Brazil, award for 16 mm film, *Dallas Theater Center*
1969 Fourth Annual Independent Filmmakers Competition, Lawrence University, Washington, *Concert Tonight*, and *Reflections of St Bambola*
1970 Ninth Annual Independent Filmmakers Festival, Foothills College, California, *Concert Tonight*, and *Reflections of St Bambola*
1970 Purchase Award, Film Festival '70, University of South Florida, *Concert Tonight*, and *Reflections of St Bambola*
1971 Film Festival '71, Seattle, Washington, *Reflections of St Bambola*
1972 Third Annual Southwest Film Festival, Tulsa, Oklahoma, *Reflections of St Bambola*

**Selected Solo Exhibitions**

1985 *Heroes, Hermits, Shamans and Boats: Roy Fridge, Selected Works, 1959–1985*, Art Museum of South Texas, Corpus Christi
1984 *Visions and Rituals*, Moody Gallery, Houston
1982 *Conversations from the Woods*, Moody Gallery, Houston
1980 *Souvenirs of the Voyage*, Moody Gallery, Houston
1978 *Reflections of an Amateur Hermit*, Art Museum of South Texas, Corpus Christi
1977 DW Co-op Gallery, Dallas
1976 Robinson Gallery, Houston
1966–69 David Gallery, Houston
1959 Waco Museum, Waco
1957 Baylor Theater, Waco

**Selected Group Exhibitions**

1988 *The Poetic Object*, San Antonio Museum of Art; Boise Museum of Art, Idaho; Art Museum of South Texas, Corpus Christi
1988 *Visions of Fate*, Minneapolis College of Art and Design
1987 *Found*, DiverseWorks, Houston
1987 *Art that Moves*, Laguna Gloria Art Museum, Austin
1986 *Artists' Response to Architecture*, Nave Museum, Victoria, Texas; Amarillo Art Center, Amarillo; The Museum, Texas Tech University, Lubbock
1986 *Shrines and Altars*, Kohler Arts Center, Sheboygan, Wisconsin
1986 *The Texas Landscape, 1900–1986*; Museum of Fine Arts, Houston
1986 *The Photograph, C Print: Extending the Limits*; Houston Center for Photography, Houston
1985 *Boats: Artists and Artisans*; Galveston Art Center
1985 *Texas Currents Part I*; San Antonio Art Institute, San Antonio
1984 *Return of the Narrative*; Palm Springs Desert Museum, Palm Springs, California
1983 *Southern Fictions*; Contemporary Arts Museum, Houston
1983 *Totems, Fetishes and Devotional Objects*, Alternative Museum, New York
1982 *Poetic Objects*, Washington Project for the Arts, Washington DC
1981 *Inside Out-Self Beyond Likeness*, Newport Harbor Art Museum, Newport Beach, California; Portland Art Museum, Oregon; Joslyn Art Museum, Omaha
1979 *Fire!*, Contemporary Arts Museum, Houston
1979 *Wood in Art*, Museum of Fine Arts, Houston
1976 *Altered Image*, Texas A & I University, Corpus Christi
1975 *Artists Make Toys*, Art Museum of South Texas, Corpus Christi
1971 *One i at a time*, Southern Methodist University, Dallas
1967 *Roy Fridge, Jim Love, David McManaway*, Trinity University, San Antonio
1961 *The Art that Broke the Looking Glass*, Dallas Museum for Contemporary Art
1961 *The Art of Assemblage*, Dallas Museum for Contemporary Art
1961 *Three Sculptors of the Southwest*, Dallas Museum for Contemporary Art
1958 *Made in Texas by Texans*, Dallas Museum for Contemporary Art

**Theater and Film Pieces**

1955–56 Sets for *Waiting for Godot, The Maids*, and *Don Juan in Hell*, productions by the Dallas Little Theater
1962 *Injun*, (Claes Oldenburg happening)
1963 *Concert Tonight*
1968 *Reflections of St Bambola*
1970 *The Big Man*
1971 *Jomo*

**Selected Public Collections**

Art Museum of South Texas, Corpus Christi
The Menil Collection, Houston
Museum of Fine Arts, Houston
Museum of Modern Art (film)
San Antonio Museum of Art

## Joseph Glasco

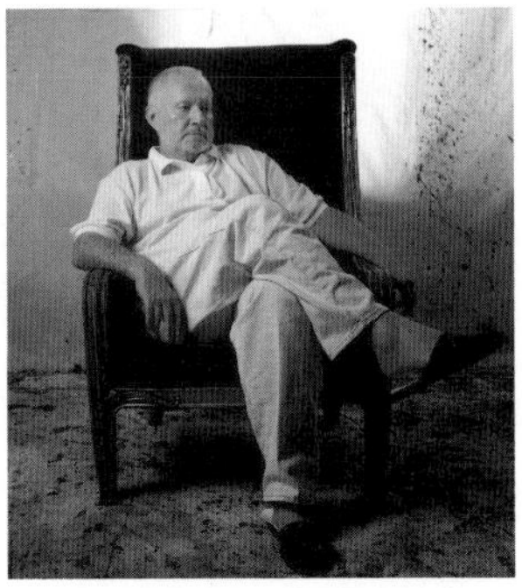

*Joseph Glasco, 1993. Courtesy of the artist.*

1925 Born in Paul's Valley, Oklahoma
Lives in Galveston, Texas

**Education and Awards**

1942 University of Texas, Austin
1946 Art Center School, Los Angeles
1948 Academia de San Carlos, Mexico City
1949 Art Students League, New York

**Selected Solo Exhibitions**

1993 *Recent Work*, Meredith Long & Co, Houston
1990 University of Oklahoma Museum of Art, Norman
1989 Waddington Gallery, London
1986 *Joseph Glasco, 1948–1986*, Contemporary Arts Museum, Houston
1986 Gimpel and Weitzenhoffer Gallery, New York
1986 Meredith Long & Co, Houston
1983 Gimpel and Weitzenhoffer Gallery, New York
1979 Gimpel and Weitzenhoffer Gallery, New York
1976 Arnold Gallery, Atlanta, Georgia
1976 Louisiana Gallery, Houston
1975 Louisiana Gallery, Houston
1973 Louisiana Gallery, Houston
1970 Catherine Viviano Gallery, New York; also 1951–1965
1968 Kiko Gallery, Houston
1967 Rizzoli Gallery, New York
1950 Perls Gallery, New York

**Selected Group Exhibitions**

1993 *Darkness + Light: 20th Century Works From Texas Collections*, Sarah Campbell Blaffer Gallery, University of Houston
1991 *Whitney Biennial of American Art*, Whitney Museum of American Art, New York
1985 *Fresh Paint: The Houston School*, Museum of Fine Arts, Houston; PS1, Long Island City, New York
1982 *The Americans: The Collage*, Contemporary Arts Museum, Houston
1965 *A Decade of American Drawings: 1955–1965*, Whitney Museum of American Art, New York
1965 *Three Distinguished Artists From Oklahoma* (Glasco, Lee Mullican, Leon Polk Smith), Museum of Art, University of Oklahoma, Norman
1964 *Elements of Modern Art III: From the Solomon R Guggenheim Museum*, A national traveling exhibition
1964 *The Friends Collect*, Whitney Museum of

American Art, New York
1963 *The 28th Biennial Exhibition of Contemporary American Paintings*, Corcoran Gallery of Art, Washington DC
1963 *Contemporary American Painting and Sculpture*, Krannert Art Museum, University of Illinois, Urbana
1962 *The 157th Annual Exhibition of Paintings and Sculpture*, Pennsylvania Academy of Fine Arts, Philadelphia
1962 *Forty Artists Under Forty*, Whitney Museum of American Art, New York, A traveling exhibition
1961 *64th American Exhibitions: Painting and Sculpture*, Art Institute of Chicago
1961 *The Theater Collects American Art*, Whitney Museum of American Art, New York
1961 *Annual Exhibition 1961: Contemporary Painting and Sculpture*, Whitney Museum of American Art, New York
1961 *Modern American Drawings, The Festival of Two Worlds*, Spoleto, Italy
1960 *100 Drawings from the Museum Collection*, Museum of Modern Art, New York
1958 *Contemporary American Painters*, Montreal Museum of Fine Arts, Canada
1958 *American Sculpture*, The Arts Club of Chicago; Milwaukee Art Center
1957 *Golden Years of American Drawings, 1905–1956*, The Brooklyn Museum, New York
1957 *Contemporary Art Acquisitions, 1954–1957*, Albright Art Gallery, Buffalo, New York
1957 *Recent Loans and Acquisitions*, Guggenheim Museum, New York
1956 *1956 Annual Exhibition of Contemporary American Sculpture*, Whitney Museum of American Art, New York
1955 *Two Hundred Years of American Painting*, The Vancouver Art Gallery, Canada
1955 *The 24th Biennial Exhibition of Contemporary American Painting*, Corcoran Gallery of Art, Washington DC
1955 *Three Young Americans* (Glasco, Joseph McCullough and Richard Diebenkorn); Allen Memorial Art Museum, Oberlin College, Ohio
1955 *The New Decade: 35 American Painters and Sculptors*, Whitney Museum of American Art, New York
1955 *Young Painters*, Congress for Cultural Freedom, a traveling exhibition to Rome, Brussels
1954 *Reality and Fantasy: 1900–1945*, Walker Art Center, Minneapolis
1954 *Younger American Painters: A Selection*, Guggenheim Museum, New York
1954 *61st American Exhibitions: Paintings and Sculpture*, Art Institute of Chicago
1953 *International Watercolor Exhibition: 17th Biennial*, The Brooklyn Museum, New York
1953 II Bienal do Museu de Arte Moderna, Sao Paulo, Brazil
1952 *15 Americans*, The Museum of Modern Art, New York
1951 *60th Annual American Exhibition: Paintings and Sculpture*, Art Institute of Chicago
1950 *Recent Acquisitions*, Museum of Modern Art, New York

**Selected Public Collections**
Albright-Knox Gallery of Art
Hirshhorn Museum and Sculpture Garden, Washington DC
Museum of Fine Arts, Houston
Museum of Modern Art, New York
Solomon R Guggenheim Museum, New York
Whitney Museum of American Art

## Virgil Grotfeldt

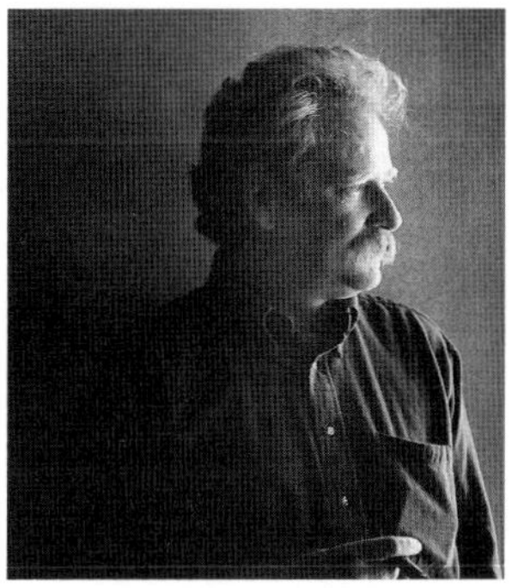

*Virgil Grotfeldt. Photograph: Jeffrey Nixon. Courtesy of the artist.*

1948 Born in Decatur, Illinois
Lives in Houston, Texas

**Education and Awards**
1971 Eastern Illinois University, Charleston, BS
1974 Tyler School of Art, Temple University, Philadelphia
1976 Illinois Council Grant
1991 Engelhardt Grant, Boston

**Selected Solo Exhibitions**
1990 Hiram Butler Gallery, Houston
1990 Trable Arts Center, Eastern Illinois University, Charleston
1988 Hiram Butler Gallery, Houston
1987 Gallery D'Theebom, Amsterdam, The Netherlands
1974 Tyler School of Art, Temple University, Philadelphia
1974 The George School, Newton, Pennsylvania
1971 Eastern Illinois University, Charleston

**Selected Group Exhibitions**
1993 *Virgil Grotfeldt, Joseph Havel, and James Surls*, Hiram Butler Gallery, Houston
1992 *Art & Nature*, Hiram Butler Gallery, Houston
1992 *Selections from the Twentieth Century Collection*, Museum of Fine Arts, Houston
1989 *Texas Realism*, Art Museum of Southeast Texas, Beaumont
1989 *Paper, Papier, Papel*, Lawndale Art and Performance Center, Houston
1988 *The Fish Show*, Brent Gallery, Houston
1986 *Texas Annual*, Laguna Gloria Art Museum, Austin
1986 *Austin Annual*, Mexic-Arte, Austin
1986 *Exposed*, Commerce Street Artists Warehouse, Houston
1986 *On Waugh Invitational*, On Waugh Gallery, Houston

**Selected Public Collections**
The Menil Collection
Museum of Fine Arts, Houston
Tyler Museum of Art, Tyler, Texas
University of Oklahoma Art Museum, Norman

## Joe Guy

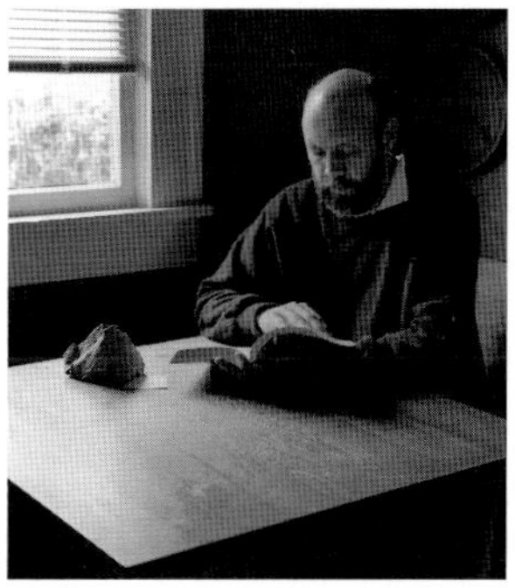

*Joe Guy, 1988. Photograph: Jenney Conn. Courtesy of the artist.*

1943 Born in Deposit, New York
Lives in Fort Worth, Texas

**Education and Awards**
1961–63 University of Georgia, Athens
1971 University of Florida, Tampa
1977 Texas Christian University, Fort Worth, BFA
1987 Louis Comfort Tiffany Grant
1988 University of Texas, Arlington, Creative Achievement Award
1990 Mid-America Arts Alliance Fellowship

**Selected Solo Exhibitions**
1989–91 *Joe Guy: Waiting. Listening*, Adams-Middleton Gallery, Dallas; Bridge Center for Contemporary Art, El Paso; Amarillo Art Center, Texas; Center for Contemporary Art, Santa Fe; Laguna Gloria Art Museum, Austin; Art Museum of Southeast Texas, Beaumont
1988 *Joe Guy*, San Antonio Art Institute, San Antonio
1987 *Joe Guy*, Adams-Middleton Gallery, Dallas
1985 *Concentrations 12: Joe Guy*, Dallas Museum of Art, Dallas
1983 *Joe Guy: Waiting. Listening*, Waco Art Center, Waco, Texas; Midwestern State University, Wichita Falls, Texas
1982 *Joe Guy: Waiting. Listening*, University of Texas, Arlington
1980 *An Aesthetic Inquiry: A Probe in Space, Time and Language*, Texas Christian University, Fort Worth

**Selected Group Exhibitions**
1993 *Selections From the Permanent Collection*, Modern Art Museum of Fort Worth
1992 *Face of the Holy, Space of the Holy*, Haggar University Gallery, University of Dallas
1992 *Presence*, University of Texas, Arlington
1992 Modern Art Museum of Fort Worth
1991 *Art in the Metroplex '91*, Texas Christian University Gallery, Fort Worth
1991 *1991 Mid-American Biennial*, Nelson Atkins Museum of Art, Kansas City, Missouri
1990 *Everyday Miracles: Retablos, Ex-votos and*

*Contemporary Art in Texas*, Contemporary Arts Museum, Houston
1990 *The CCA Second Annual Invitational*, Center for Contemporary Art, Santa Fe
1989 *Another Reality*, Hooks-Epstein Galleries, Houston; Marion Koogler McNay Art Institute, San Antonio
1988 *Columbus Collects: American Paintings, Sculpture, Photography*, Columbus Museum of Art, Ohio
1987 *Third Coast Review: A Look at Art in Texas*, Aspen Art Museum, Colorado
1987 *The Faux Arts: Illusionistic Finishes and Simulated Surfaces*, La Jolla Museum of Contemporary Art, California
1986 *Texasberlin*, Amerika House, Berlin
1985 *Recent American Painting: Francis, Frankenthaler, Guy, Held, Noland, Pepper, Rotterdam*, Adams-Middleton Gallery, Dallas
1984 *6 Artists With Paper*, University of Texas, Dallas
1984 Old Jail Foundation Museum, Albany, Texas
1983 *Invitational '83*, Longview Museum of Art, Longview, Texas
1982 *National Works on Paper Invitational Exhibit*, Stephen F Austin University, Nacogdoches, Texas
1979 *Paperworks: An Invitational Show of Texas Artists*; Witte Museum, San Antonio; Laguna Gloria Art Museum, Austin; Museo de Monterrey, Mexico; Wichita Falls Museum, Wichita Falls, Texas
1978 *Works On Paper: Southwest 1978*, Dallas Museum of Art

**Selected Public Collections**
Modern Art Museum of Fort Worth

## Joseph Havel

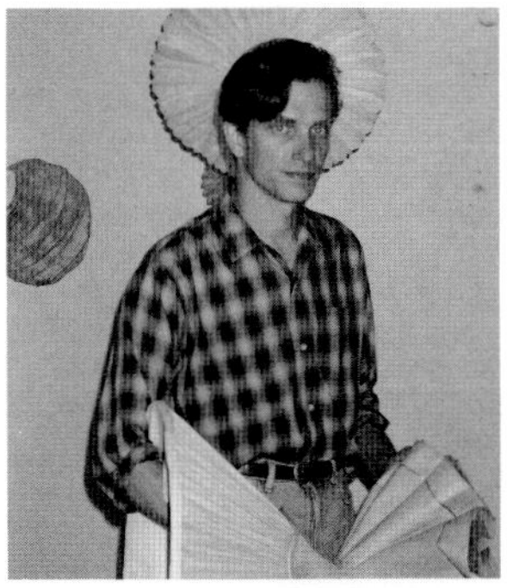

*Joseph Havel, 1993. Courtesy of the artist.*

1954 Born in Minneapolis, Minnesota
Lives in Houston, Texas

**Education and Awards**
1976 University of Minnesota, Minneapolis, BFA
1979 Pennsylvania State University, University Park, MFA

**Selected Solo Exhibitions**
1992 *New Sculpture and Drawings*, Linda Farris Gallery, Seattle
1992 *New Sculpture*, Davis/McClain Gallery, Houston
1991 *Recent Sculpture*, Barry Whistler Gallery, Dallas
1989 *Sculpture and Drawing*, Barry Whistler Gallery, Dallas
1989 *Introductions 89*, Davis/McClain Gallery, Houston
1987 DW Gallery, Dallas
1985 Texas Women's University, Denton
1985 500X Gallery, Dallas
1984 Texas Women's University, Denton
1984 500X Gallery, Dallas
1982 East Texas State University, Commerce
1980 Austin College, Sherman, Texas
1979 North Texas State University, Denton

**Selected Group Exhibitions**
1993 *3-D Rupture*, Contemporary Arts Museum, Houston
1993 *Virgil Grotfeldt, Joseph Havel, James Surls*, Hiram Butler Gallery, Houston
1993 *Light*, Barry Whistler Gallery, Dallas
1993 *Collage and Assemblage*, Hooks-Epstein Gallery, Houston
1992 *Out of Bounds: Contemporary Sculpture*, Museum of Fine Arts, Houston
1992 *Urban/Suburban*, Arlington Museum of Art, Arlington, Texas
1992 *re: Creation, Re-Creation, Recreation: Art from Found Objects*, Laguna Gloria Art Museum, Austin
1992 *Vernon Fisher, Joseph Havel, Doug MacWithey*, Barry Whistler Gallery, Dallas
1991 *The State I'm In: Texas Art*, Dallas Museum of Art
1991 *Creative Partners*, Sewall Art Gallery, Rice University, Houston
1991 *Ship Shape*, Galveston Art Center, Galveston
1991 *Material as Message*, Alfred C Glassell School of Art, Houston
1990 *Ordinary Objects as Extraordinary Subjects*, Galveston Art Center
1990 *Working with Harry [Geffert]*, University of North Texas, Denton
1990 *Wood Work*, Arlington Museum of Art
1989 *A Century of Sculpture in Texas, 1889–1989*, Archer M Huntington Art Gallery, University of Texas, Austin
1989 *Tracking Information: Drawings by Texas Sculptors*, Amarillo Art Center, Amarillo
1989 *Another Reality*, Hooks-Epstein Gallery, Houston
1989 *The Artist's Eye*, Kimbell Art Museum, Fort Worth
1988 *Working Papers*, Brookhaven College, Dallas
1988 *Drawings by Texas Artists*, College of William and Mary, Williamsburg, Virginia
1987 *40th Anniversary Exhibition*, Rochester Art Center, Minnesota
1987 *Excellence of 87*, Plaza of the Americas, Dallas
1987 *Found*, DiverseWorks, Houston
1986 *Texas Sculpture Association International Exhibition*, Plaza of the Americas, Dallas
1985 *Art in the Metroplex*, Texas Christian University, Fort Worth
1984 *American Coffee Cup*, Rochester Art Center
1984 *Nine Sculptors*, Midtown Art Center, Houston
1984 *Outdoor Sculpture Exhibition*, San Antonio Art Institute
1983 *Showdown: Sculptors of the Southwest*, Sculpture Center Gallery, New York
1983 *Houston Showdown*, DiverseWorks, Houston
1983 *Survey of Texas Clay*, Objects Gallery, San Antonio
1982 *Texas Sculptors Invitational*, Pensacola, Florida
1981 *Large Scale*, MCECA Exhibition, Wichita Museum of Art, Wichita Falls, Texas
1981 *Directions in Clay by Young Artists*, Central Michigan University, Mt Pleasant
1978 *Craftsmen 78*, Philadelphia Civic Center Museum, Pennsylvania

**Selected Public Collections**
Dallas Museum of Art, Dallas
Museum of Fine Arts, Houston

## Rachel Hecker

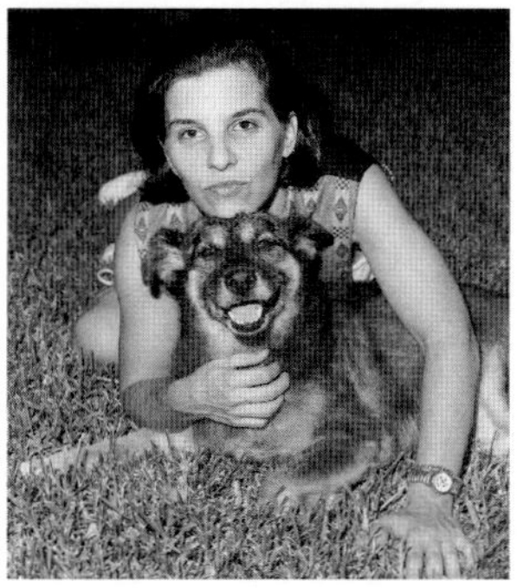

*Rachel Hecker, 1993. Photograph: Amy Blakemore. Courtesy of the artist.*

1958 Born in Providence, Rhode Island
Lives in Houston, Texas

**Education and Awards**
1980 Moore College of Art, Philadelphia, BFA, Summa Cum Laude
1982 Rhode Island School of Design, Providence
1989 National Endowment for the Arts, Visual Arts Fellowship

**Selected Solo Exhibitions**
1992 Texas Gallery, Houston
1988 Texas Gallery, Houston

**Selected Group Exhibitions**
1993 *Texas Contemporary Acquisitions of the 90s*, Museum of Fine Arts, Houston
1993 *Sharon Engelstein and Rachel Hecker*, Texas Gallery, Houston
1992 *Freedom of Expression*, University of Houston, Clear Lake
1991 *OUT! Voices From a Queer Nation*, DiverseWorks, Houston
1991 *Pop Art: The Object Transformed*, Museum of Fine Arts, Houston
1990 *Tradition and Innovation: A Museum Celebration of Texas Art*, Museum of Fine Arts, Houston
1990 *Women View Women*, Women and Their Work and RKG Foundation, Austin
1990 *Octagon: Eight Houston Artists*, University of

West Florida Art Gallery, Pensacola
1989 *Painted Stories and Other Narrative Art*, Laguna Gloria Art Museum, Austin
1988 *6 Artists/6 Idioms*, Sarah Campbell Blaffer Gallery, University of Houston
1988 *First Texas Triennial*, Contemporary Arts Museum, Houston
1987 *From the Object: Still Life Themes and Variations*, Alfred C Glassell School of Art, Houston
1984 *Introductions*, Texas Gallery, Houston
1984 Faculty Exhibition, Alfred C Glassell School of Art, Houston

**Selected Public Collections and Commissions**
DiverseWorks, Houston, 1990
8.0 Restaurant, Houston, 1990
Museum of Fine Arts, Houston
University of Houston, 1993

## Ron Hoover

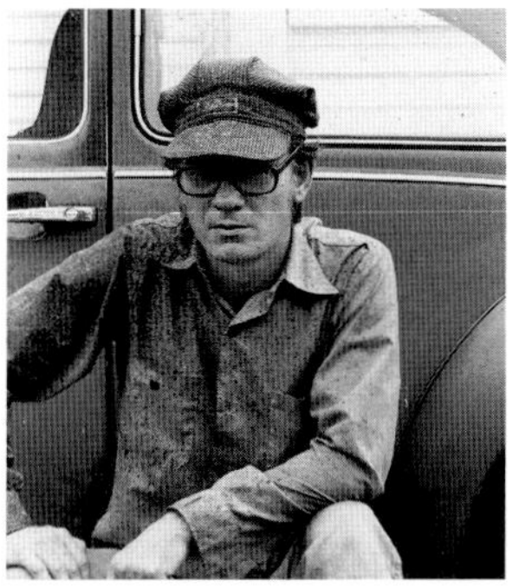

*Ron Hoover, 1981. Courtesy of the artist.*

1944 Born in Liberty, Texas
Lives in Houston, Texas

**Education and Awards**
1970 Lee College, Baytown, Texas, associate of art
1975 University of Houston, BFA
1977 University of Oklahoma, Norman, MFA

**Selected Solo Exhibitions**
1990 William A Graham Gallery, Houston
1989 *Ron Hoover: Paintings*, Art Museum of Southeast Texas, Beaumont
1988 William A Graham Gallery, Houston
1986 William A Graham Gallery, Houston
1985 William A Graham Gallery, Houston
1984 William A Graham Gallery, Houston
1982 William A Graham Gallery, Houston
1981 William A Graham Gallery, Houston

**Selected Group Exhibitions**
1991 *On Line: Drawings by Texas Artists*, Amarillo Art Center
1991 *The War Show*, Lanning Gallery, Houston
1990 *Northwest x Southwest: Painted Fictions*, Palm Springs Desert Museum, California; Yellowstone Art Center, Montana; Bellingham Museum, Washington; Sarah Campbell Blaffer Gallery, University of Houston
1987 *Blood Ties and Other Knotty Issues*, DiverseWorks, Houston
1985 *Fresh Paint: The Houston School*, Museum of Fine Arts, Houston; PS1, Long Island City, New York
1984 *Three Painters*, Midtown Art Center, Houston
1984 *Houston Figurative Art*, College of the Mainland, Texas City
1983 *38th Biennial Exhibition of American Painting and the Second Western States Exhibition*, Corcoran Gallery of Art, Washington DC
1983 *Certain Realities*, University of New Mexico Art Gallery, Albuquerque
1982 *Art from Houston in Norway*, Stavanger Kunstforening
1982 *Thirteen Artists: A Look at Houston*, Georgia State University, Atlanta
1981 *Invitational Drawing Show*, Lawndale Annex, University of Houston
1980 *Five Houston Painters*, Texas A&M University, College Station
1979 *Fire!*, Contemporary Arts Museum, Houston
1979 *Made in Texas*, University of Texas, Austin
1978 *Pow Wow*, Lawndale Annex, University of Houston

## Perry House

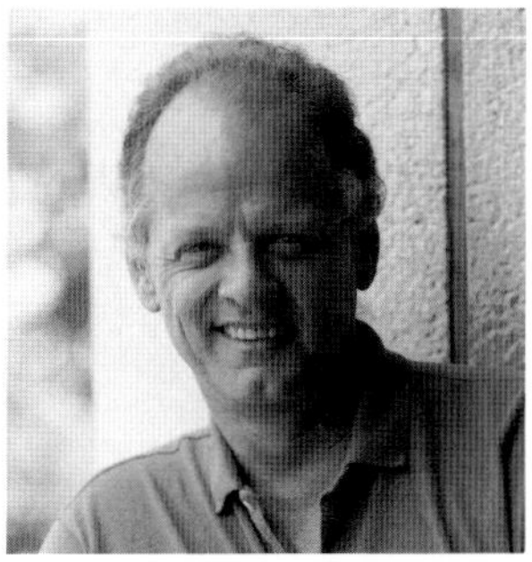

*Perry House, 1993. Courtesy of the artist.*

1943 Born in Orange, Texas
Lives in Houston, Texas

**Education and Awards**
1969 California College of Arts and Crafts, Oakland, BFA
1971 California College of Arts And Crafts, Oakland, MFA
1990 Mid-America Arts Alliance Fellowship Award

**Selected Solo Exhibitions**
1993 Gray Matters, Dallas
1992 Davis/McClain Gallery, Houston
1989 Davis/McClain Gallery, Houston
1986 Davis/McClain Gallery, Houston
1984 Davis/McClain Gallery, Houston
1983 William A Graham Gallery, Houston
1978 University of St Thomas, Houston
1978 Humbolt State College, Arcadia, California
1974 California State College, Bakersfield
1974 Nicholls State College, Thibodeaux, Louisiana

**Selected Group Exhibitions**
1993 *Darkness + Light*, Sarah Campbell Blaffer Gallery, University of Houston
1993 *Conventional Forms/Insidious Visions*, Alfred C Glassell School of Art, Houston
1992 *The Big Show*, Lawndale Art and Performance Center, Houston
1992 *Political Stamps*, Small Gallery, University of Houston
1992 *Texas Dialogue (Houston)*, Bridge Center for Contemporary Art, El Paso
1991 *Mid-America Biennial*, Nelson-Atkins Museum of Art, Kansas City, Missouri
1989 *Perry House, David MacKenzie*, Angles Gallery, Venice, California
1988 *The Abstract Impulse*, Davis/McClain Gallery, Houston
1987 *Houston Area Abstraction: An Update*, Lawndale Art and Performance Center, Houston
1985 *Fresh Paint: The Houston School*, Museum of Fine Arts, Houston; PS1, Long Island City, New York
1985 *Texas Visions*, Art League of Houston; Museum of Art of the American West, Houston
1985 *Houston Drawing*, Alfred C Glassell School of Art, Houston
1984 *Texas Only*, Laguna Gloria Art Museum, Austin
1983 *A Salute to Houston Artists*, Midtown Art Center, Houston
1983 *Introductions 81*, Robinson Gallery, Houston
1980 *Los Bizzarros*, Lawndale Art and Performance Center, Houston
1974 *Postcards*, Fine Arts Ltd, London, England

**Selected Public Collections**
Museum of Fine Arts, Houston

## Luis Jimenez Jr

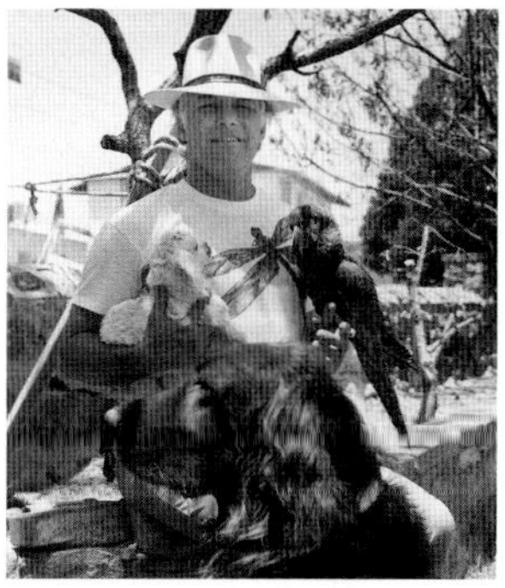

*Luis Jimenez Jr, 1984. Photograph: Gay Block. Courtesy of the artist.*

1940 Born in El Paso, Texas
Lives in Hondo, New Mexico

**Education and Awards**
1964 University of Texas, Austin, BS
1964 Universidad Nacional Autónoma de México, Mexico City
1977 National Endowment for the Arts, Artists Fellowship Grant
1985 Awards in the Visual Arts
1987 Greenberger Foundation Award, New York
1990 La Napoule Art Foundation, Residency Fellowship, La Napoule, France

**Selected Solo Exhibitions**
1994 *Man on Fire*, Albuquerque Museum; National Museum of American Art, Washington DC

1992 Wichita Museum of Art, Kansas
1992 Spenser Museum of Art, Lawrence, Kansas
1992 Art Museum of Southeast Texas, Beaumont
1992 LewAllen Gallery, Santa Fe
1992 Social & Public Art Resource Center, Venice, California
1991 Adair Margo Gallery, El Paso
1991 Scottsdale Center for the Arts, Arizona
1991 Moody Gallery, Houston
1991 Brookhaven Forum Gallery, Brookhaven College, Dallas
1991 Lisa Sette Gallery, Scottsdale
1991 LewAllen Gallery, Santa Fe
1990 Scottsdale Center for the Arts
1989 Art Institute of the Permian Basin, Odessa, Texas
1989 Maloney Butlery Gallery, Santa Monica, California
1988 Nave Museum, Victoria, Texas
1988 Adair Margo Gallery, El Paso
1987 Moody Gallery, Houston
1986 University of Texas, El Paso
1986 University of Arizona Museum of Art, Tucson
1986 Adair Margo Gallery, El Paso
1985 Dallas Museum of Art
1984 Roswell Museum & Art Center, Roswell
1984 Sculpture Plaza, New York
1984 Hammarskjold, Plaza, New York
1984 Alternative Museum, New York
1983 Laguna Gloria Art Museum, Austin
1980 Joslyn Art Museum, Omaha, Nebraska
1979 Museum of Fine Arts, Santa Fe
1979 Plains Art Museum, Moorehead, Minnesota
1979 Landfall Press Gallery, Chicago
1977 University of North Dakota, Grand Forks
1975 OK Harris Works of Art, New York
1974 OK Harris Works of Art, New York
1974 Contemporary Arts Museum, Houston
1973 Long Beach Museum of Art
1973 OK Harris Works of Art, New York
1972 OK Harris Works of Art, New York
1970 Graham Gallery, New York
1969 Graham Gallery, New York

**Selected Group Exhibitions**

1992 *20th Anniversary Exhibition, 1972–1992*, The Art Center, Waco, Texas
1991 *Whitney Biennial*, Whitney Museum of American Art, New York
1991 *The State I'm In: Texas Artists at the DMA*, Dallas Museum of Art
1990 *Rodeo in Fact and Fantasy*, The Philbrook Museum of Art, Tulsa
1990 *Printmaking in Texas: The 1980s*, Modern Art Museum of Fort Worth
1990 *The New Decade*, The New Museum, New York
1990 *Gardens Real and Imagined*, University of Colorado, Boulder; Mathes Cultural Center, Escondido, California; Atlanta College of Art, Georgia; Ball State Art Gallery, Muncie, Indiana; University Art Gallery, SUNY, Albany, New York
1989 *A Century of Sculpture in Texas, 1889–1989*, Archer M Huntington Gallery, University of Texas, Austin; Amarillo Art Center, Amarillo; San Angelo Museum of Fine Art; El Paso Museum of Fine Arts; Art Museum of South Texas, Corpus Christi
1989 *The Demon of Angels*, Departamento de Cultura de la Generalitat de Catalunya, Barcelona; also venues in Nantes, Brussels, Stockholm, and Marseilles
1989 *Painted Stories and Other Narrative Art*, Laguna Gloria Art Museum, Austin
1989 *The American Cowboy: Reality and Reactions*, Art Museum of Southeast Texas, Beaumont
1989 *41st Annual Purchase Exhibition*, American Academy & Institution of Arts an Letters, New York
1989 *Committed to Print*, Museum of Modern Art, New York
1988 *Images on Stone: Two Centuries of Artists' Lithographs*, Sarah Campbell Blaffer Gallery, University of Houston
1988 *Different Drummers*, Hirshhorn Museum and Sculpture Garden, Washington DC
1988 Museum of Modern Art, New York
1987 *Hispanic Art in the United States: Thirty Contemporary Painters and Sculptors*, Museum of Fine Arts, Houston; Corcoran Gallery of Art, Washington DC, Los Angeles County Museum of Art, other venues in Miami, Brooklyn and Santa Fe
1987 *The Latin American in the United States: 1920–1970*, The Bronx Museum of the Arts, New York, El Paso Museum of Art; San Diego Museum of Art; Institute of Puerto Rican Culture, San Juan, Puerto Rico; Center for the Arts, Vero Beach, Florida
1986 *Honky Tonk Visions*, Museum of Art, Texas Tech University, Lubbock
1984 *Collision*, Lawndale Annex, Houston
1984 *Arts New Mexico*, Santuario de Guadalupe, Santa Fe; Museum of Art of Latin America, Washington DC, Instituto Nacional de Etnografia e Historia, Mexico City; Roswell Museum & Art Center, New Mexico
1984 *Automobile and Culture*, Los Angeles County Museum of Art
1983 *Language, Drama Source & Vision*, New Museum of Contemporary Art, New York
1983 *Tejano! Three Artists from Texas*, Fondo del Sol Visual Art & Media Center, Washington DC
1983 *Texas Figurative Drawing*, San Antonio Art Institute
1983 *Myth of the Cowboy*, Library of Congress, Washington DC
1983 *Showdown*, Alternative Museum, and The Sculpture Center, New York
1982 *In Our Time*, Contemporary Arts Museum, Houston
1982 *Recent Trends in Collecting*, National Museum of American Art, Washington DC
1982 *First Annual Wild West Show*, Alberta College of Art, Canada
1981 *Alternative Realities in Contemporary America*, University of Minnesota
1980 *The First Western States Biennial Exhibition*, Denver Art Museum, Colorado; National Collection of Fine Arts, Washington DC; other venues in San Francisco, Santa Fe, Hawaii, Illinois, and California
1979 *Fire!*, Contemporary Arts Museum, Houston
1979 *Made in Texas*, Archer M Huntington Art Gallery, University of Texas, Austin
1979 *Ancient Roots/New Visions*, Tucson Museum of Art, Arizona; National Collection of Fine Art, Washington DC; other venues in New Mexico, California, Colorado, New York, Texas, Illinois
1977 *Dale Gas*, Contemporary Arts Museum, Houston
1977 *Three Texas Artists*, Centre Cultural Americaine, Paris
1977 *Bison in Art: A Graphic Chronicle of the American Bison*, Amon Carter Museum of Western Art, Fort Worth
1976 *A Survey of New Mexico Sculpture*, Museum of Fine Arts, Santa Fe
1975 *New Work, New Mexico*, Roswell Museum & Art Center
1975 *Monumental Sculpture*, Museum of Fine Arts, Houston
1974 *12/Texas*, Contemporary Arts Museum, Houston
1973 *The First International Motorcycle Art Show*, Phoenix Art Museum, Arizona
1973 *The Male Nude*, Hofstra University, Long Island, New York
1973 *1973 Biennial Exhibition*, Whitney Museum of American Art
1972 *Recent Figure Sculpture*, Fogg Art Museum, Boston
1969 *Human Concern/Personal Torment*, Whitney Museum of American Art, New York
1968 Brandeis University, UNESCO, Washington DC

**Selected Public Collections**

Art Institute of Chicago
Bronx Museum
Centro Cultural/Arte Contemporáneo, Mexico City
Denver Art Museum
Hirshhorn Museum and Sculpture Garden, Washington DC
Long Beach Museum
Metropolitan Museum of Art, New York
Modern Art Museum of Fort Worth
Museum of Fine Arts, Houston
Museum of Modern Art, New York
National Collection of Fine Art, Smithsonian Institution, Washington DC
National Museum of American Art, Washington DC
Rockefeller Foundation, New York
Roswell Museum and Art Center

## Lucas Johnson

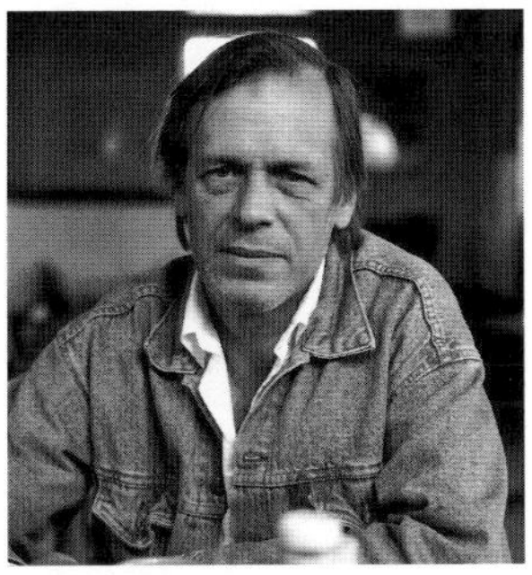

*Lucas Johnson, 1992. Photograph: Frank Golden. Courtesy of the artist.*

1940 Born in Hartford, Connecticut
Lives in Houston, Texas

**Selected Solo Exhibitions**

1994 *Drawings from the Underworld*, Contemporary Arts Museum, Houston
1993 *Recent Etchings*, Moody Gallery, Houston
1991 *Recent Paintings*, Moody Gallery, Houston
1990 *Dibujos*, Museo Ex-Convento del Carmen, Guadalajara, Mexico
1988 *Drawings: The Estuary Series*, Serpentine Gallery, London
1985 *Paintings and Drawings*, Moody Gallery, Houston
1982 *Paintings and Monotypes*, Moody Gallery, Houston
1977 *Recent Drawings*, University of Houston, Clear Lake
1974 Galeria de Arte Misrachi, Mexico City
1972 Galeria de Arte Misrachi, Mexico City
1971 David Gallery, Houston
1971 Gotham Book Mart Gallery, New York
1970 Galeria de Arte Misrachi, Mexico City
1970 David Gallery, Houston
1967 Galeria Sagitario, Mexico City
1967 Instituto Mexicano-Norteamericano, Mexico City
1967 William Sawyer Gallery, San Francisco
1966 Instituto Mexicano Norteamericano, Mexico City
1966 David Gallery, Houston
1965 Instituto de Cultura Hispánica, Mexico City
1965 Galeria Chapultepec, Mexico City
1964 Instituto Mexicano-Norteamericano, Monterrey and San Luis Potosi, Mexico

**Selected Group Exhibitions**

1993 *Texas Contemporary Acquisitions of the 90s*, Museum of Fine Arts, Houston
1993 *Talleres en Fronteras: Contemporary Art from South Texas and Baja California*; Corpus Christi State University; University of Texas, El Paso; Universidad Autónoma de Baja California, Mexicali; Centro Cultural, Tijuana, Mexico
1993 *Houston in Hope*, Faith and Charity in Hope Gallery, Hope, Idaho
1993 *Seeing the Forest Through the Trees*, Contemporary Arts Museum, Houston
1993 *Conventional Forms/Insidious Vision*, Alfred C Glassell School of Art, Houston
1992 *New Texas Art*, Cheney Cowles Museum, Spokane, Washington; Boise Art Museum, Idaho
1990 *1960–1990, Anniversary Exhibition*, Galeria de Arte Misrachi, Mexico City
1990 *15 Year Anniversary Exhibition*, Moody Gallery, Houston
1990 *Tradition and Innovation: A Museum Celebration of Texas Art*, Museum of Fine Arts, Houston
1990 *The Inspiration of Music*, Scottsdale Center for the Arts, Arizona
1989 *Another Reality*, Hooks-Epstein Gallery, Houston; Arkansas Arts Center, Little Rock; McNay Art Institute, San Antonio
1989 *Texas Realism*, Art Museum of Southeast Texas, Beaumont
1989 *Messages from the South*, Sewall Art Gallery, Rice University, Houston
1989 *Drawing Conclusions*, Southwest Texas State University, San Marcos
1988 *Drawn from Life: Contemporary Interpretive Landscape*, Sewall Art Gallery, Rice University, Houston
1988 *Twentieth Century Art in the Museum Collection: Direction and Diversity*, Museum of Fine Arts, Houston
1988 *One + One: Collaborations by Artists and Writers*, Alfred C Glassell School of Art
1987 *Images on Stone: Two Centuries of Artists' Lithographs*, Sarah Campbell Blaffer Gallery, University of Houston
1987 *Third Coast Review: A Look at Art in Texas*, Aspen Art Museum, Colorado
1987 *Line and Form: Contemporary Texas Figurative Drawing*, Art Museum of South Texas, Corpus Christi
1986 *Dead Days 1986*, Blue Star Art Space, San Antonio
1986 *Prisoners of Conscience*, DiverseWorks, Houston
1986 *Cinq x Cinq Houston, Texas*, Stedman/Hubbard Gallery, Paris
1986 *Collaborations: Artists Working Together in Houston, 1969–1986*, Alfred C Glassell School of Art, Houston
1985 *Fresh Paint: The Houston School*, Museum of Fine Arts, Houston; PS1, Long Island City, New York
1984 *Painterly Texas Monoprints*, Amarillo Art Center
1982 *Thirteen Artists: A Look at Houston*, Georgia State University Art Gallery, Atlanta
1982 *New American Graphics 2*, Madison Art Center, Wisconsin
1982 *Art from Houston in Norway*, Stavanger Museum
1982 *Colorado: State of the Arts, Selections from Shark Lithography Ltd*, Denver Art Museum
1982 *A Peaceable Kingdom: Animals in Art*, Museum of Fine Arts, Houston
1982 *Altars/Labyrinths/Installations for Day of the Dead*, Zero Alternative Space/Tejano Artists Gallery, Houston
1979 *Ten From Houston*, The Art Center, Waco, Texas
1979 *Fire!*, Contemporary Arts Museum, Houston
1979 *Twenty-First National Print Exhibition*, Brooklyn Museum, New York
1977 *Six Painters Southwest*, Museum of Art, University of Oklahoma, Norman
1975 *Graphic Collective*, ISSSTE, Mexico City
1975 *Artists Make Toys*, Art Museum of South Texas, Corpus Christi
1974 *Bienal de Morelia*, Morelia, Michoacan, Mexico
1971 Gotham Book Mart Gallery, New York
1971 *Salon Independiente*, Universidad Nacional Autónoma de México, Mexico City
1970 *Salon Independiente*, Universidad Nacional Autónoma de México, Mexico City
1969 *Manscape: Collection of Selden Rodman*, Fair Lawn Public Library, New Jersey
1968 *Salon Independiente*, Universidad Nacional Autónoma de México, Mexico City
1968 *Olympic Collective*, Collection of the Mexican-American Institute, Mexico City
1968 *Graphic Exhibition*, Ponce Museum, Ponce, Puerto Rico
1967 Traveling Group Exhibition, Smithsonian Institution, Washington DC
1967 Boston Print Show, Massachusetts
1967 Philadelphia Print Show, Pennsylvania
1966 *Graphic Collective Exhibition*, Pratt Institute, New York
1966 *Collective Exhibition*, MIT, Cambridge, Massachusetts
1965 Delgado Museum (New Orleans Museum of Art), New Orleans
1965 *Realism from Four Studios*, May Brooks Gallery, Mexico City
1964 New Orleans Art Association
1964 *All Southern Collective Exhibition*, Biloxi, Mississippi
1963 New Orleans Art Association

**Drawings in Poetry Books**

*The Loss of Rivers*, CW Truesdale, Azalel, 1967
*Moon Shots*, CW Truesdale, New Rivers, St Paul, Minnesota, 1967
*Early Poems: Pablo Neruda*, New Rivers Press, 1969
*Minnesota Review*, Volume IX, 1969, and Volume X, 1970
*Master of Knives*, CW Truesdale, Hamman Publishing Co, Houston, 1970
*Letters from Siberia and Other Poems*, Roger Mitchell, New Rivers Press, 1971
*Toward Winter*, anthology, Latitudes Press, Austin, 1972
*Antaeus*, Volumes 5, 6, 7, 8, 9, 1972
*Antaeus*, Volume 24, 1976
*Moving*, Roger Mitchell, New Rivers Press, 1976
*Antaeus*, Volumes 36, 38 1980
*Cold Harbors*, CW Truesdale, Latitudes Press, Austin, 1972
*Life Among Others*, Daniel Halpern, Viking Press and Penguin Press, New York and Canada, 1978

**Selected Public Collections**

Amarillo Art Center, Amarillo, Texas
Archer M Huntington Library, Austin
Art Museum of Santa Cruz County, California

Benjamin Franklin Library, Mexico City
Brooklyn Library
Brooklyn Museum
Greenville County Museum of Art, South Carolina
Instituto Mexicano-Norteamericano, Mexico City
Los Angeles County Museum of Art
Massachussetts Institute of Tehcnology, Cambridge
Mexican Museum, San Francisco
Museo Jose Luis Cuevas, Mexico City
Museo de Arte Francisco Toledo, Oaxaca, Mexico
Museo de Ponce, Ponce, Puerto Rico
Museum of Fine Arts, Houston
Museum of Modern Art, Tel Aviv
National Museum of Art, Warsaw
New Orleans Museum of Art
San Antonio Museum of Art
San Francisco Museum of Art
Smithsonian Institution, American Graphics Collection, Washington DC
University of Houston Print Collection
United States Embassy Permanent Collection, Mexico City
Univeristy of Southern Illinios, Carbondale
Wichita Falls Museum, Texas

## Donald Judd

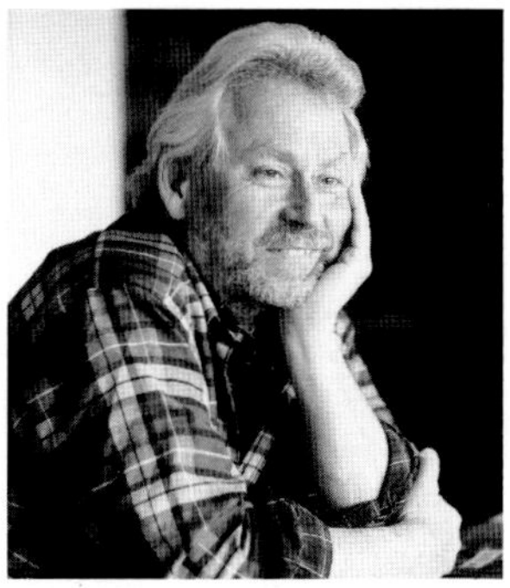

*Donald Judd, c.1992. Photograph: © B. Mancia/ F. Bodmer. Courtesy of the artist.*

1928–1994

**Education and Awards**

1958–53 Art Students League, New York
1953 Columbia Universiy, New York, BS in philosophy
Graduate courses in art history, Columbia University
1965 Travel grant, Swedish Insitute
1987 Skowhegan Medal for Sculpture; Skowhegan School of Painting and Sculpture, Maine
Brandeis University Medal for Sculpture, Waltham, Massachussetts
1992 Stankowski Prize, Stankowski Foundation, Stuttgart, Germany
1992 Foreign Member of Royal Academy of Fine Arts, Stockholm,Sweden
1993 Sikkens Award, Sikkens Foundation, Sassenheim, Holland

**Selected Solo Exhibitions**

1993 Sculpture, Stedelijk Museum, Amsterdam
1993 Sculpture and Design, Museum Wiesbaden, Germany
1993 Print Retrospective, Haag Germeentemuseum, Den Haag
1993 Furniture Retrospective, Museum Bymans-van Beuningen, Rotterdam
1993 Sculpture, Kitakyushu Municipal Museum of Art, Japan
1992 Sculpture, Shizuoka Prefectural Museum of Art, Japan
1991 Archetectural Works, Osterreichisches Museum fur Angewandte Kunst, Vienna
1987 Retrospective, Whitney Museum of American Art, New York
1968 Mid-career retrsopective, Whitney Museum of American Art, New York

**Selected Public Collections**

Allen Memorial Art Museum, Oberlin College, Ohio
Art Gallery of Ontario, Toronto
Art Museum of South Texas, Corpus Christi
The Chinati Foundation, Marfa
The Cleveland Museum of Art
Dayton Art Institute
Solomon R Guggenheim Museum, New York
Hirshhorn Museum and Sculpture Garden, Washington DC
Indiana University Art Museum, Bloomington
Kaiser Wilhelm Museum, Krefeld, Germany
Kunstmuseum Basel
Milwaukee Art Museum
Modern Art Museum of Fort Worth
Moderna Museet, Stockholm
Musee d'Art ed d'Industrie, Saint-Etienne
Museum Ludwig, Cologne
Museum of Contemporary Art, Los Angeles
Museum of Fine Arts, Houston
Museum of Modern Art, New York
Museum of Modern Art, Shiga, Japan
National Gallery of Canada, Ottawa
Nelson-Atkins Museum of Art, Kansas City
Saint Louis Art Museum
San Francisco Museum of Modern Art
Norton Simon Museum, Pasadena
Staatsgalerie Stuttgart
Stedelijk Van Abbemuseum, Eindhoven
Storm King Art Center Sculpture Park, Moutainville, New York
Tokyo Metropolitan Art Museum
Walker Art Center, Minneapolis
Whitney Museum of American Art, New York

**Books by Donald Judd**

*Book One, Collected Writings 1958–1992*, Die Zweite Pfeil, Cologne, Germany, 1994
*Architektu* Vr: Westfallscher Kunstverein, Munster, Germay, 1989
*Complete Writings 1975–1986*, van Abbemuseum, Eindhoven, The Netherlands, 1987
*Complete Writings 1959–1975*, The Press of Nova Scotia College, New York University Press, 1975

## Paul Kittelson

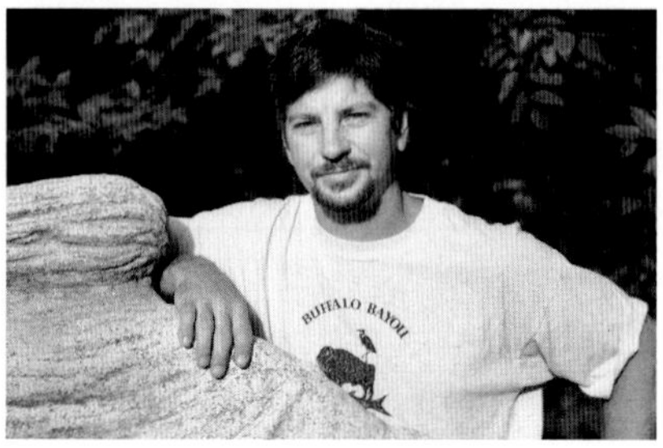

*Paul Kittelson, 1993. Photograph: Carter Ernst. Courtesy of the artist.*

1959 Born in Wheaton, Minnesota
Lives in Houston, Texas

**Education and Awards**

1982 University of California, Santa Barbara, BA
1985 University of Houston, MFA
1987 Project Artist, ARTPARK, Lewiston, New York
1987 Creative Artist Program Fellowship, Cultural Arts Council Houston
1988 Anne Giles Kimbrough Fund, Dallas Museum of Art
1989 Mid-America Arts Alliance Award

**Selected Solo Exhibitions**

1993 *Inside Out: Installation*, Art Museum of Southeast Texas, Beaumont
1991 *Garden of Earthly Delights*, a collaboration with Carter Ernst, Hiram Butler Gallery, Houston
1988 *The Seven Deadly Sins*, Hiram Butler Gallery, Houston

**Selected Group Exhibitions**

1993 *Buffalo Bayou ArtPark: Past, Present and Future*, Mother Dog Museum of Modern Art, Houston
1993 *Exploring Scale in Contemporary Art*, Laguna Gloria Art Museum, Austin
1992 *Silhouettes of the Southwest*, Snug Harbor Cultural Center, Staten Island, New York
1992 *Recreation/Re-Creation: Art From Found Objects*, Laguna Gloria Art Museum, Austin
1992 *Inaugural Exhibition*, Buffalo Bayou Art Park, Houston
1991 *Twelfth Annual Outdoor Sculpture Exhibition*, Abilene, Texas
1991 *Contemporary Issues*, DiverseWorks, Houston
1991 *Creative Partners*, Sewall Art Gallery, Rice University, Houston
1989 *Tenth Annual Outdoor Sculpture Exhibition*, Abilene
1988 *The First Texas Triennial*, Contemporary Arts Museum, Houston
1987 *Off the Wall*, The Michigan Gallery, Detroit
1986 *Collaborators*, with Olin Calk, Alfred C Glassell School of Art, Houston
1985 *Ten Artists*, DiverseWorks, Houston

**Community Projects**

1992 *Travisaurus*, Travis Elementary School, Houston
1991 *Children's Art Wall*, collaboration with Carter

Ernst, Mariposa Park, Corpus Christi
1989 *The Children's Bridge*, collaboration with Carter Ernst, Wortham Theater, Houston
1989 *Art in Public Places*, a collaboration with Carter Ernst, City of Houston Downtown Christmas Display, Houston
1988 *Children's Art Wall*, collaboration with Carter Ernst, Old Sixth Ward Park, Houston
1987 *Whale*, a temporary sculpture installation on city streets. Sponsored by the Cultural Arts Council of Houston and Hiram Butler Gallery
1986 *Stegosaurus*, a temporary sculpture installation on city streets. Sponsored by DiverseWorks, Houston

## Sharon Kopriva

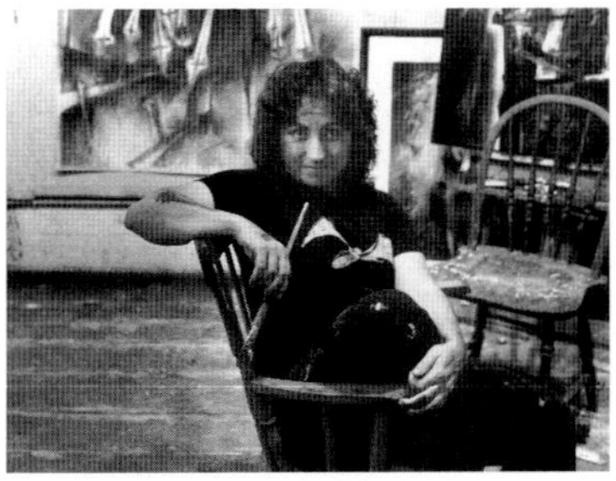

*Sharon Kopriva, c.1992. Courtesy of the artist.*

1948 Born in Houston, Texas
Lives in Houston, Texas

**Education and Awards**

1970 University of Houston, BS
1981 University of Houston, MFA
1991 Cultural Arts Council of Houston, Individual Artists Grant
1992 Artists Residency, Museum of Arts and Sciences, Darwin, Australia
1993 Mid-America Arts Alliance Fellowship

**Selected Solo Exhibitions**

1993 LewAllen Gallery, Santa Fe New Mexico
1993 *Sharon Kopriva*, Southwest Texas State University, San Marcos
1992 *Conflicting Rituals*, Corpus Christi State University
1991 *Rite of Passage*, The Art Center, Waco, Texas
1989 J Rosenthal Fine Arts, Chicago
1989 William A Graham Gallery, Houston
1986 William A Graham Gallery, Houston
1981 Brazosport Fine Arts Center, Lake Jackson, Texas

**Selected Group Exhibitions**

1993 *Hope in Houston/Houston in Hope*, Moody Gallery, Houston; Faith and Charity in Hope Gallery, Hope, Idaho
1993 *Texas Contemporary Acquisitions of the 90s*, Museum of Fine Arts, Houston
1993 *Houston Narrative*, Martin-Rathburn Gallery, San Antonio
1993 *Texas Biennial*, DARE, Dallas
1993 *Talleres en Fronteras: An Exhibition of Contemporary Art from South Texas and Baja California*; Corpus Christi State University; other venues in Texas and Mexico
1993 *Fur, Fins, Feathers and More*, Galveston Art Center, Galveston
1993 *In the Beginning*, Art Museum of Southeast Texas, Beaumont
1992 *Dreams and Shield*, Salt Lake City Art Center, Utah
1992 *Texas Dialogues*, Bridge Center for Contemporary Art, El Paso
1992 *Popular Delusions and the Madness of Crowds*, Lanning Gallery, Houston
1991 *Healing Hands*, Lubbock Fine Art Center, Lubbock; D-Art, Dallas; Center for Research in Contemporary Art, Arlington, Texas
1990 *Ritual and Myth*, Stephen F Austin University, Nacogdoches, Texas
1989 *A Century of Texas Sculpture*, Archer M Huntington Art Museum, University of Texas, Austin
1989 *Another Reality*, Hooks-Epstein Gallery, Houston; Arkansas Art Center, Little Rock; McNay Museum, San Antonio
1988 *Texas Women*, National Museum of Women in the Arts, Washington DC; Laguna Gloria Art Museum, Austin
1987 *Line and Form: Contemporary Texas Figurative Drawing*, Art Museum of South Texas, Corpus Christi
1987 *Found*, DiverseWorks, Houston
1987 *Sculpture: The Spectrum*, Lawndale Art and Performance Center, Houston; Blue Star Art Space, San Antonio
1986 *Memento Mori*, Centro Cultural/Arte Contemporáneo, Mexico City
1986 *Texas Invitational*, Fort Worth Art Festival
1986 *Amnesty International*, DiverseWorks, Houston
1985 *Fresh Paint: The Houston School*, Museum of Fine Arts, Houston; PS1, Long Island City, New York
1985 *One Up*, Lawndale Art and Performance Center, Houston
1983 *50th Annual Exhibition*, Springville Museum of Art, Utah
1982 *Arteder*, Graphic Arts International, Bilbao, Spain
1982 *Thirteen Artists: A Look at Houston*, Georgia State University, Atlanta
1981 *News Event*, Galveston Art Center, Galveston
1981 *Rockford International*, Rockford College, Illinois
1980 *67th Annual Allied Artists of America*, American Academy of Arts and Letters, New York
1980 *Heartland*, Mid-America Art Association Conference, Jung Center, Houston
1979 *8th Annual Texas Fine Arts Association Exhibition*, Laguna Gloria Art Museum, Austin

**Selected Public Collections**

The Menil Collection, Houston
Museum of Fine Arts, Houston
Museum of Fine Arts, Santa Fe

## George Krause

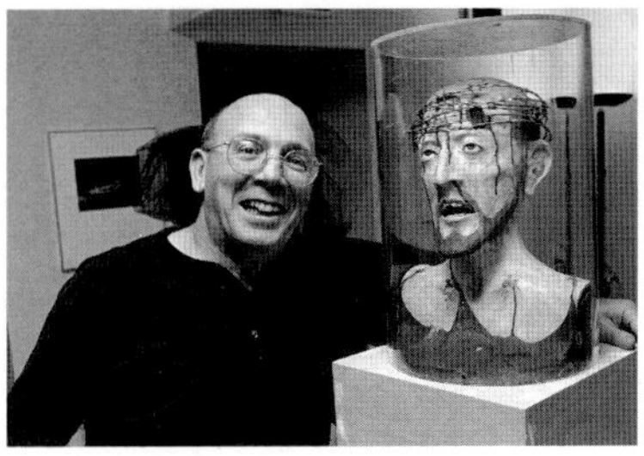

*George Krause, 1993, with work in progress. Photograph: Andrea Petor. Courtesy of the artist.*

1937 Born in Philadelphia, Pennsylvania
Lives in Houston, Texas

**Education and Awards**

1960 Philadelphia College of Art, BA
1986 Cultural Arts Council of Houston, Artists Fellowship
1985 National Endowment for the Arts, Individual Artists Grant
1979 National Endowment for the Arts, Individual Artists Grant
1979 Photographer in Residence, American Academy in Rome
1976 First Prix de Rome in Photography
1976 Guggenheim Fellowship
1972 National Endowment for the Arts, Individual Artists Grant
1967 Guggenheim Fellowship
1963 Fulbright-Hays Fellowship

**Selected Solo Exhibitions**

1993 Philadelphia Arts Alliance, Philadelphia
1992 *George Krause, A Retrospective*, Museum of Fine Arts, Houston
1991 Art Institute of Philadelphia, Philadelphia
1990 New England Photographic Workshops, New Milford, Connecticut
1990 Harris Gallery, Houston
1988 Harris Gallery, Houston
1988 Maine Photographic Workshops, Rockport
1987 Torino Fotografia, Turin, Italy
1987 The Photographer's Gallery, London
1985 Torino Fotografia, Turin
1985 f,32 Foto Galerie, Amsterdam, The Netherlands
1985 Harris Gallery, Houston
1983 *A Retrospective*, Pennsylvania Academy of Fine Arts, Philadelphia; The Chrysler Museum, Norfolk, Virginia
1980 The American Academy in Rome
1979 Rochester Institute of Technology, New York
1979 Witkin Gallery, New York
1979 Museum of Fine Arts, Houston
1975 Philadelphia Print Club, Philadelphia
1974 Museo de Bellas Artes, Caracas, Venezuela
1973 Pennsylvania Academy of Fine Arts, Philadelphia
1972 George Eastman House, Rochester
1970 Museo de Bellas Artes, Caracas

**Selected Group Exhibitions**

1989 *Selections*, International Center for Photography, New York

1988 *Contemporary Photographers: The Present of the Sublime*, San Antonio Museum of Art
1988 *One on One*, Alfred C Glassell School of Art, Houston
1984 *American Photography Today, 1984*, Denver
1984 *Photographic Masterpieces from 70 International Galleries*, AIPAD, New York
1981 *New Directions: The Nude*, Massachusetts Institute of Technology, Cambridge
1980 Annual Exhibition, American Academy in Rome
1978 *Mirrors and Windows: American Photography Since 1960*, Museum of Modern Art, New York
1977 Annual Exhibition, American Academy in Rome
1975 *Photography in America*, Whitney Museum of Art, New York
1971 *Five Young Americans*, Museum of Modern Art, New York
1967 *Photography in the 20th Century*, National Gallery of Canada, Ottawa
1965 *Recent Acquisitions*, Museum of Modern Art, New York
1964 *The Photographer's Eye*, Museum of Modern Art, New York
1964 *Six Photographers*, International Museum of Photography, George Eastman House, Rochester
1963 *Five Unrelated Photographers*, Museum of Modern Art, New York

**Selected Public Collections**

Amon Carter Museum Fort Worth
George Eastman House, Rochester
The Gernsheim Collection, University of Texas, Austin
Library of Congress, Washington DC
Museo de Bellas Artes, Caracas
Museum of Fine Arts, American Academy in Rome
Museum of Fine Arts, Boston
Museum of Fine Arts, Houston
Museum of Modern Art, New York
New Orleans Museum of Art
Philadelphia Museum of Art, Philadelphia

## Jean Lacy

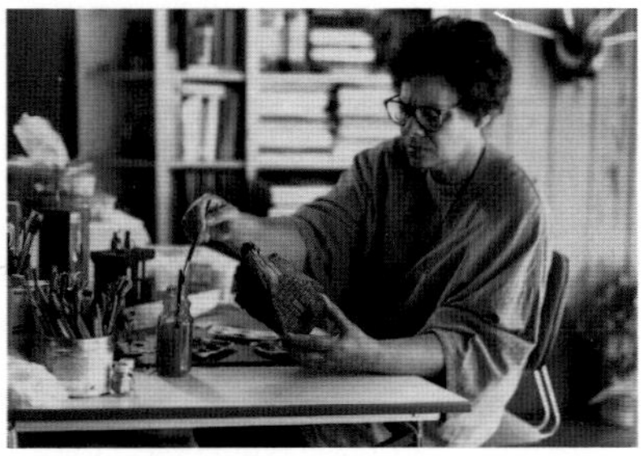

*Jean Lacy, c.1991. Courtesy of the artist.*

1932 Born in Washington DC
Lives in Dallas, Texas

**Education and Awards**

1956 Southern University, Baton Rouge, Louisiana, BA
1956–57 Art Students League, New York City
1977 Southern Methodist University, Dallas
1977 North Texas State University, Denton

**Selected Exhibitions**

1989 *Black Art: Ancestral Legacy*, Dallas Museum of Art; High Museum of Art, Atlanta; Milwaukee Art Museum, Wisconsin; Virginia Museum of Fine Arts, Richmond
1988 *African-American Artists of Dallas*, Southern Methodist University, Dallas
1979 *National Urban League Art Expo*, Houston
1979 *Black Artists/South*, Huntsville Art Museum, Huntsville, Alabama

**Public Collections and Commissions**

Dallas Museum of Art
St Luke United Methodist Church, Dallas

## Jesse Lott

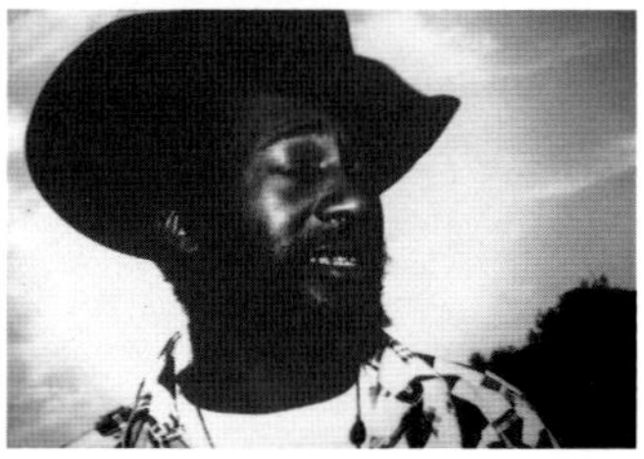

*Jesse Lott. Photograph: Suzie Paul. Courtesy of the artist.*

1943 Born in Simmesport, Louisiana
Lives in Houston, Texas

**Education**

1963–64 Hampton Institute, Hampton, Virginia
1965 California State University, and Los Angeles City College, Los Angeles
1967–79 Otis Art Institute, Los Angeles

**Solo Exhibitions**

1991 *Lone Star Visions: Jesse Lott*, Art Museum of Southeast Texas, Beaumont
1991 *Relics of the Future, Part Four: Evolution of Imagery*, Midtown Art Center, Houston
1989 *Jesse Lott*, O'Kane Gallery, University of Houston
1989 *Jesse Lott: The Piñatero Method*, Lawndale Art and Performance Center, Houston
1987 Hiram Butler Gallery, Houston
1978 Robinson Galleries, Houston

**Selected Group Exhibitions**

1993 *Texas Contemporary Acquisitions of the 90s*, Museum of Fine Arts, Houston
1993 *Black and White*, Midtown Art Center and Barnes-Blackman Gallery, Houston
1992 *Black Creativity in Texas*, Lubbock Fine Arts Center and The Lubbock Black Cultural and Heritage Center
1991 *The Perfect World*, San Antonio Museum of Art
1990 *Next Generation: Southern Black Aesthetics*, Southeastern Center for Contemporary Art, Winston-Salem, North Carolina
1990 Lawndale Art and Performance Center
1989 *Forerunners and Newcomers: Houston's Leading African-American Artists*; University of Houston, Clear Lake
1988 *The First Texas Triennial*, Contemporary Arts Museum, Houston; Texas A&M University, College Station; Art Museum of South Texas, Corpus Christi; Lubbock Fine Arts Center; San Angelo Museum of Fine Arts, Texas; Center for Research in Contemporary Art, Arlington; Bridge Center For Contemporary Art, El Paso
1986 *Artists of the Southwest*, Studio Museum, New York
1986 *Saludo to the Mexican Independence*, Sarah Campbell Blaffer Gallery, University of Houston
1984 *Collision*, Lawndale Art and Performance Center, Houston
1983 *Showdown*, Alternative Museum, New York
1983 *Recreating the World*, University of St Thomas, Houston
1983 *Sense of Spirit*, Lawndale Annex
1992 *Impressions of Houston*, University of Houston, Downtown

**Public Collections**

Museum of Fine Arts, Houston

## Jim Love

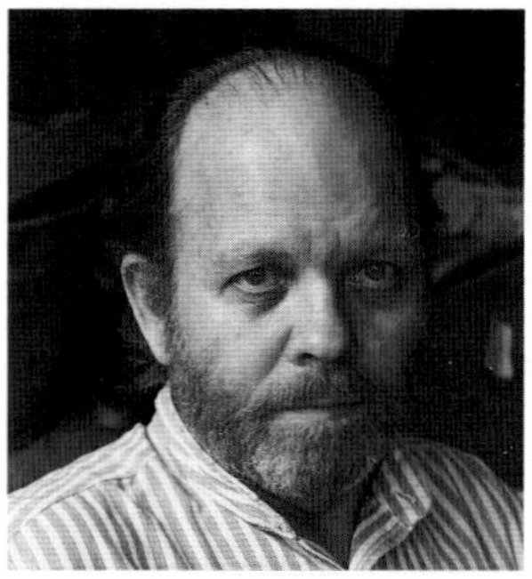

*Jim Love, 1984. Photograph: Gay Block. Courtesy of the artist.*

1927 Born in Amarillo, Texas
Lives in Houston, Texas

**Education and Awards**

1952 Baylor University, Waco, Bachelor of Business Administration

**Selected Solo Exhibitions**

1994 *New Work*, Moody Gallery, Houston
1992 *Recent Sculpture*, Janie C Lee Gallery, Houston
1988 *Recent Sculpture*, Janie C Lee Gallery, Houston
1984 *Tomorrow is no Solution*, Janie C Lee Gallery, Houston
1981 *Recent Sculpture*, Janie C Lee Gallery, Houston
1980 *Jim Love Up To Now*, The Institute for the Arts, Rice University, Houston; Amarillo Art Center, Texas; San Francisco Museum of Modern Art; Hudson River Museum, Yonkers, New York
1976 Jim Love and Dave McManaway, Janie C Lee Gallery, Houston
1973 *Jim Love: In Pursuit of the Bear*, Contemporary Arts Museum, Houston; Fort Worth Art Center; Tyler Museum of Art
1971 Louise Ferrari Gallery, Houston
1965 Studio Exhibition, Houston

1964 Alexander Iolas Gallery, New York
1961 New Arts Gallery, Houston
1959 New Arts Gallery, Houston
1958 New Arts Gallery, Houston

**Selected Group Exhibitions**

1993 *Exploring Scale in Contemporary Art*, Laguna Gloria Art Museum, Austin
1992 *New Texas Art*, Cheney Cowles Museum, Spokane, Washington; Boise Art Museum, Idaho
1990 *Tradition and Innovation: A Museum Celebration of Texas Art*; Museum of Fine Arts, Houston
1989 *A Century of Sculpture in Texas*, Archer M Huntington Art Gallery, University of Texas, Austin; Amarillo Art Center; San Angelo Museum of Art; El Paso Museum of Art; Art Museum of South Texas, Corpus Christi, Texas
1988 *One + One: Collaborations by Artists and Writers*, Alfred C Glassell School of Art, Houston
1988 *The Poetic Object*, San Antonio Museum of Art; Boise Art Museum, Idaho; Art Museum of South Texas, Corpus Christi
1987 *Found*, Diverse Works, Houston
1987 *The Menil Collection*, The Menil Collection, Houston
1986 *The Texas Landscape: 1900–1986*, Museum of Fine Arts, Houston
1986 *Adjustments Must be Made Continually*, Nave Museum, Victoria, Texas; Tyler Art Museum, Tyler; Laguna Art Museum, Laguna Beach, California
1984 *Le rime at la raison (les collections Menil, Houston-New York)*, Grand Palais, Paris
1984 *A Museum of Fun, Part II*; Asahi Shimbun, Tokyo
1983 *Inaugural Exhibition*, Gateway Gallery, Dallas Museum of Art
1983 *A Century of Modern Sculpture: 1882–1982*, Museum of Fine Art, Houston
1979 *Fire!*, Contemporary Arts Museum, Houston
1979 *Made in Texas*, Archer M Huntington Art Gallery, University of Texas, Austin
1974 *Modern Sculpture from Houston Collections*; Museum of Fine Arts, Houston
1971 *One i at a time*; Southern Methodist University, Dallas
1968 *1968 Annual Exhibition*, Whitney Museum of American Art, New York
1968 *Permanent Collection of the University of St Thomas*, Museum of Fine Arts, Houston
1968 *Jermayne MacAgy, A Life Illustrated by an Exhibition*; University of St Thomas, Houston
1966 *A Benefit for Marcel Duchamp's Chess Foundation*, Cordier & Eckstrom Gallery, New York
1963 *Some Recent Acquisitions*, Museum of Fine Arts, Houston
1961 *Three Southwest Sculptors*, Dallas Museum for Contemporary Art
1957 *Humor in Art*, Dallas Museum for Contemporary Art

**Selected Public Collections**

Alley Theatre, Houston
Hobby Airport, City of Houston
The Menil Collection, Houston
Museum of Fine Arts, Houston
Museum of Modern Art, New York
Rice University, Houston
University of Houston
University of Texas at Dallas
Whitney Museum of American Art, New York

## David McManaway

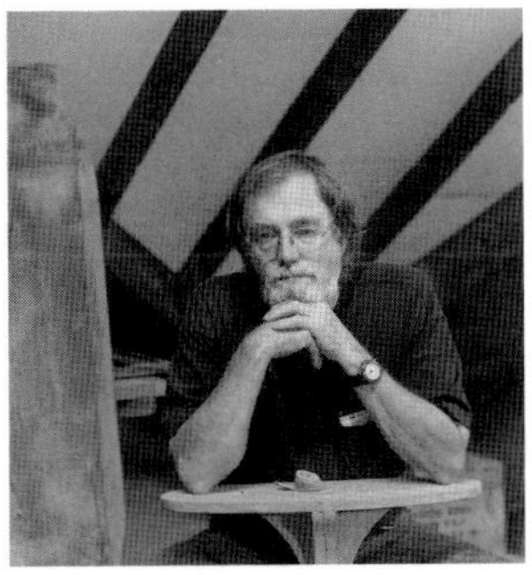

*David McManaway. Photograph: Charles DeBus. Courtesy of the artist.*

1927 Born in Chicago, Illinois
Lives in Dallas, Texas

**Education and Awards**

1953–58 University of Arkansas, Fayetteville
1961 South Coast Art Show, Purchase Award, Ringling Museum, Sarasota, Florida
1977 National Endowment for the Arts, Individual Artists Fellowship
1991 Engelhard Award, The Institute of Contemporary Art, Boston

**Selected Solo Exhibitions**

1994 *Dave McManaway*, Moody Gallery, Houston
1986 Eugene Binder Gallery, Dallas
1979 *David McManaway: Works of Twenty Years*, Southern Methodist Univeristy, Dallas
1973 *David McManaway*, Contemporary Arts Museum, Houston
1969 Recent Work, Atelier Chapman Kelly, Dallas
1967 Recent Work, Atelier Chapman Kelly, Dallas
1965 *Symbols in Art*, Atelier Chapman Kelly, Dallas

**Selected Group Exhibitions**

1992 *Re: Creation/Re-Creation/Recreation: Art From Found Objects*, Laguna Gloria Art Museum, Austin
1989 *A Century of Sculpture in Texas, 1889–1989*, Archer M Huntington Gallery, University of Texas, Austin; Amarillo Art Center; San Angelo Museum of Art; El Paso Museum of Art
1988 *The Poetic Object*, San Antonio Museum of Art, Texas; Boise Art Museum, Idaho; Art Museum of South Texas, Corpus Christi
1987 *Found*, DiverseWorks, Houston
1986 *The Texas Landscape: 1900–1986*, Museum of Fine Arts, Houston
1984 *Once Upon a Time*, Gateway Gallery, Dallas Museum of Art
1982 *Fun and Games*, The Art Center, Waco, Texas
1979 *Fire!*, Contemporary Arts Museum, Houston
1978 *Cowboys, Indians, Settlers*, The Art Center, Waco
1975 *Artists Make Toys*, Art Museum of South Texas, Corpus Christi; Nave Museum, Victoria, Texas
1973 *1973 Biennial Exhibition*, Whitney Museum of American Art, New York
1971 *One i at a time*, Southern Methodist University, Dallas
1969 *Human Concern/Personal Torment*, Whitney Museum of American Art, New York
1961 *11th Southwestern Exhibition of Prints and Drawings*, Dallas Museum of Art
1959 *Dallas County Exhibition of Painting and Sculpture*, Dallas Museum of Art

## Douglas MacWithey

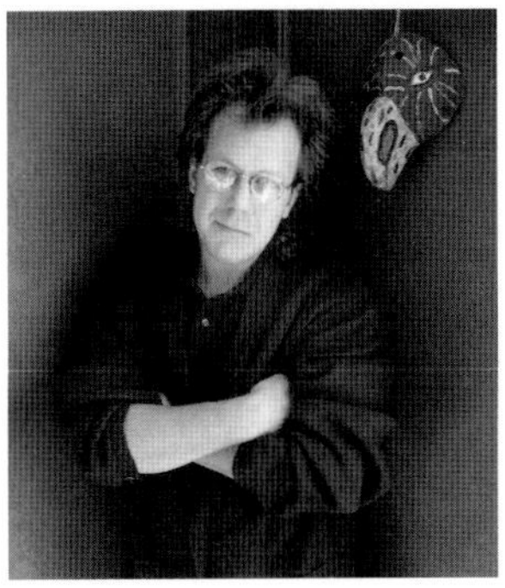

*Douglas MacWithey. Photograph: Alison Victoria. Courtesy of the artist.*

1952 Born in Ames, Iowa
Lives in Dallas, Texas

**Education and Awards**

1989 Southern Methodist University, Dallas, MFA
1988–89 Artistic Merit Scholarship Award, Meadows School of the Arts, Dallas
1985–86 Meadows Foundation Scholarship, Dallas

**Selected Solo Exhibitions**

1993 *Douglas MacWithey: Encounters 3*, Dallas Museum of Art
1992 Rena Bransten Gallery, San Francisco
1991 Hiram Butler Gallery, Houston
1990 Barry Whistler Gallery, Dallas
1988 *Selections from the "The Book of Hours"*, Barry Whistler Gallery, Dallas
1986 *Drawings and Performance from "The Book of the City of Sighs"*, DiverseWorks, Houston
1986 Barry Whistler Gallery, Dallas
1982 Carol Taylor Art, Dallas

**Selected Group Exhibitions**

1993 Galveston Art Center
1993 *Light*, Barry Whistler Gallery, Dallas
1993 *Works on Paper: Permanent Collection*, Dallas Museum of Art
1992 *Paintings/Sculpture/Drawing: Vernon Fisher, Joe Havel, Douglas MacWithey*, Barry Whistler Gallery, Dallas
1992 *Art and Nature*, Hiram Butler Gallery, Houston
1992 *Introspect*, NRH Gallery, North Richland Hills
1991 *Texas Dialogues*, Blue Star Art Space, San Antonio

1990 *The Vessel*, Hickory Street Annex, Dallas
1990 *Woodwork*, Arlington Museum of Art, Arlington, Texas
1989 *The New American Landscape: Selections from the Permanent Collection*, Museum of Fine Arts, Houston
1989 MFA Exhibition, The Meadows Museum, Southern Methodist University, Dallas
1988 *SMU Salon: Students, Faculty and Alumni*, The Crescent Gallery, Dallas
1988 *Working Paper*, Brookhaven College, Dallas
1988 *Performance Art Preview II: Visual Art Theatre*, Caravan of Dreams Theater, Fort Worth
1987 *Small Wonders*, Barry Whistler Gallery, Dallas
1987 *A Drawing Exhibition: The Continuity of Man*, Haggerty Art Center, University of Dallas, Irving
1986 *Works on Paper/Inside Texas*, Barry Whistler Gallery
1986 *Day of the Dead*, Blue Star Art Space, San Antonio, Texas
1986 *Performance Art Preview I: Visual Art Theater*, Caravan of Dreams Theater, Fort Worth
1986 *The Book of the City of Sighs*, Performance with Martin Rayner and Alyson Reim, The Clearview Building, Dallas
1983–89 *Recent Music*, Collaboration with Tom Sleeper, The Bath House Cultural Center, Dallas
1981 *Pidgin English*, Performance in two acts, The Greenville Avenue Theater, Dallas

**Selected Public Collections**
Dallas Museum of Art
Museum of Fine Arts, Houston
Lannan Foundation, Los Angeles
The Prudential, Newark
Frito-Lay Inc, Plano

## James Magee

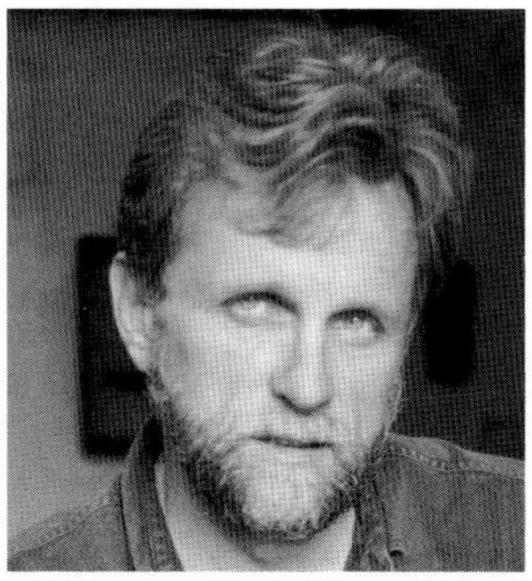

*James Magee. Photograph: Tom Jenkins. Courtesy of the artist.*

1946 Born in Fremont, Michigan
Lives in El Paso, Texas

**Education and Awards**
1968 Alma College, Alma, Michigan, BA
1971 University of Pennsylvania Law School

**Selected Exhibitions**
1992 *James Magee: Recent Works*, El Paso Museum of Art
1992 *James Magee*, San Antonio Museum of Art; DiverseWorks, Houston
1991 *State of the Art*, Dallas Museum of Art
1990 *Texas Dialogue: San Antonio/El Paso*, Blue Star Art Space, San Antonio
1990 *Everyday Miracles: Retablos, Ex Votos and Contemporary Art in Texas*, Contemporary Arts Museum, Houston
1989 *The Alcove Show*, Museum of Fine Arts, Santa Fe
1989 *James Magee*, Adair Margo Gallery, El Paso
1989 *The Texas Landscape, 1900–1986*, Museum of Fine Arts, Houston
1982 Deerfield Academy, Deerfield, Massachusetts
1975 Azuma Gallery, New York

**Public Collections**
Dallas Museum of Art

## MANUAL

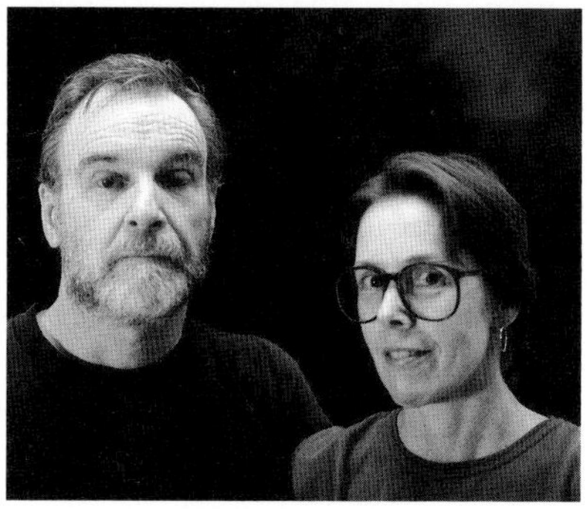

*Manual: Ed Hill and Suzanne Bloom, 1993. Courtesy of the artists.*

### Ed Hill
1935 Born in Springfield, Massachusetts
1957 Rhode Island School of Design, BFA
1960 Yale University, MFA

### Suzanne Bloom
1943 Born in Philadelphia, Pennsylvania
1965 Pennsylvania Academy of Fine Arts and University of Pennsylvania, BFA
1968 University of Pennsylvania, MFA

The artists live in Houston, Texas

**Selected Solo Exhibitions**
1992 The Museum of Contemporary Photography, Columbia College, Chicago
1992 Jayne Baum Gallery, New York
1992 Moody Gallery, Houston
1991 Contemporary Arts Museum, Houston
1989 Didactic Space, Frito-Lay Inc, Dallas
1988 Southwest Craft Center, San Antonio
1988 Laurence Miller Gallery, New York
1988 Moody Gallery, Houston
1987 VSG Gallery, Torino Fotographia '87, Torino, Biennale Internazionale, Italy
1987 Moody Gallery, Houston
1986 Tyler Museum of Art, Tyler, Texas
1985 University of Colorado, Boulder
1985 Orange Coast College, Costa Mesa, California
1985 Arizona State University, Tempe
1984 Hampshire College, Amherst, Massachusetts
1984 Moody Gallery, Houston
1983 Visual Studies Workshop, Rochester, New York
1983 Moody Gallery, Houston
1981 Cronin Gallery, Houston
1980 Museum of Fine Arts, Houston
1978 Cronin Gallery, Houston
1976 Cronin Gallery, Houston
1975 Amherst College, Amherst

**Selected Group Exhibitions**
1992 *Domestic Violence*, Center for Research in Contemporary Art, University of Texas, Arlington
1991 The Perfect World, San Antonio Museum of Art
1991 *Creative Partners*, Sewall Art Gallery, Rice University, Houston
1991 *A Sense of Place: Recent Acquisitions in Contemporary Texas Art*, San Antonio Museum of Art
1990 *Recent Acquisitions: Houston Photographers*, Museum of Fine Arts, Houston
1990 *The Great Photo Show*, Houston FotoFest '90, George R Brown Convention Center, Houston
1990 *Collaboration*, Film in the Cities, St Paul, Minnesota
1989 *Messages from the South*, Sewall Art Gallery, Rice University, Houston
1989 *The Photographic Book*, Houston Center for Photography
1989 *Machines in the Garden of Art*, Minneapolis College of Art & Design, Minnesota
1989 *Digitale Photographie: Perspektief*, Rotterdam, The Netherlands
1989 *Nature and Culture: Conflict and Reconciliation in Contemporary Photography*, Friends of Photography, San Francisco
1989 *The Private Eye*, Museum of Fine Arts, Houston
1989 *Computers and Photography*, Pyramid Arts Center, Rochester
1988 *Photography and Art: Interactions Since 1946*, Museum of Art, Fort Lauderdale, Florida; Queens Museum, Flushing, New York; Des Moines Art Center, Iowa
1988 *Evocative Presence*, Museum of Fine Arts, Houston
1988 *Photography Process*, The Athenaeum, Alexandria, Virginia
1988 *Two to Tango*, International Center for Photography, New York
1988 *Re: Presentation/Conception/Perception*, Fullerton Museum, Fullerton, California
1987 *Third Coast Review: A Look at Texas Art*, Aspen Art Museum
1987 *High Tech — New Pop*, Photographic Resources Center, Boston
1987 *Photo-Technology: An Exploration of the Electronic Imaging Environment*, Houston Center for Photography, Houston
1986 *Collaborations*, Alfred C Glassell School of Art, Houston
1986 *Contemporary Color Photography*, Photokina, Cologne
1986 *Photo-synthesis*, Smith College Museum of Art, Northampton, Massachusetts
1986 *The Texas Landscape, 1900–1986*, Museum of Fine Arts, Houston
1986 *TV Generation*, Los Angeles Contemporary Exhibitions

1986 *The Photographic Print: Extending the Limits*, Houston Center for Photography
1985 *Houston Photographers in the Museum Collection*, Museum of Fine Arts, Houston
1985 *The Photographic Print: Color Processes*, Houston Center for Photography
1984 *Video Installations*, San Antonio Art Institute, San Antonio
1984 AIPAD '84, Annual International Fine Art Photography Exposition, New York
1984 *Constructions/Photographs*, San Antonio Art Institute
1983 *Collaborations*, Los Angeles Center for Photographic Studies
1982 *Target III: In Sequence*, Museum of Fine Arts, Houston
1982 *Photographs from the Permanent Collection*, University of Massachusetts, Amherst
1982 *Art from Houston in Norway*, Stavanger Kunstforening, Denmark
1981 *Color in Photography*, Museum of Art, Rhode Island School of Design, Providence
1981 *Texas Photo Sampler*, Washington Project for the Arts, Washington DC; Camerawork, San Francisco
1980 *Mail Art Exhibition*, Kunstlerhaus, Hannover, Germany
1980 *Response*, Tyler Museum of Art, Tyler
1979 *Photographie als Kunst: Kunst als Photographie, 1949–1979*, Tiroler Landesmusem, Innsbruck, Austria
1979 *Curator's Choice: Contemporary American Photography*, Venezia '79, Venice, Italy
1978 *Photography and the Landscape*, Photopia Gallery, Philadelphia
1978 *Contemporary Art & Modern Living: '48/'78*, Contemporary Arts Museum, Houston
1978 *1977 Artists' Biennial*, New Orleans Museum of Art
1978 *Four Texas Photographers*, Modern Art Museum of Fort Worth
1978 *The Target Collection of American Photography*, Museum of Fine Arts, Houston; Art Museum of South Texas, Corpus Christi; Heckscher Museum, Huntington, Long Island; Joslyn Museum, Omaha, Nebraska; Modern Art Museum of Fort Worth; other venues in Minnesota, Iowa, and New York

**Selected Public Collections**

International Center for Photography, New York
International Museum of Photography, The George Eastman House, Rochester
Museum of Contemporary Photography, Columbia College, Chicago
Museum of Fine Arts, Houston
San Francisco Museum of Modern Art
Smith College Museum of Art, Northampton
University of Massachusetts, Amherst
Virginia Museum of Fine Arts, Richmond

## César Augusto Martínez

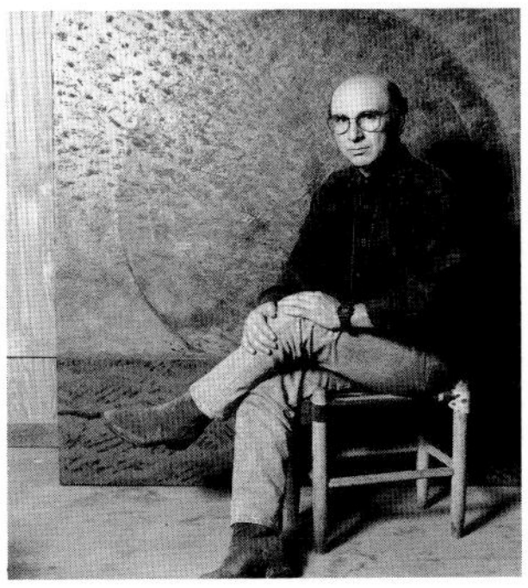

*César Augusto Martínez, 1992. Photograph: Robert Chalk. Courtesy of the artist.*

1944 Born in Laredo, Texas
Lives in San Antonio, Texas

**Education**

1964 Associate Arts Degrees, Laredo Junior College
1968 Texas Arts and Industries University, Kingsville, BS

**Selected Exhibitions**

1993 *Sin Frontera: Chicano Artists from the Border States of the United States*, Greater Manchester Arts Centre Ltd, Manchester, England
1993 *Visual Vanguards: Cinco de Tejas/Five from Texas*, Fine Arts Center, Lubbock
1993 *César Martínez: Recent Work*, Lynn Goode Gallery, Houston
1993 *La Frontera/The Border*, Centro Cultural de Tijuana, Tijuana, Baja California (Mexico); Tacoma Art Museum, Washington
1993 *Can Safo: Los Pintores de San Antonio*, Guadalupe Cultural Arts Center, San Antonio
1993 *Ceremony of Memory II: New Experiences in Spirituality Among Latino Artists*, The Mexican Museum, San Francisco, Touring through 1994
1992 *Chicano Art: Resistance and Affirmation, 1965–1985*, Tuscon Museum of Art, Arizona; National Museum of American Art, Smithsonian Institution, Washington DC; El Paso Museum of Art; San Antonio Museum of Art
1992 *Igual Pero Diferente*, Jansen-Perez Gallery and the Mexican Cultural Institute, San Antonio
1992 *Experiences in a New World Order*, Group exhibition of artists from Texas, Centro Colombo-Americano, Medellín, Colombia
1992 *Ventanas/Windows*, Plains Art Museum, Moorhead, Minnesota
1990 *Everday Miracles: Retablos, Ex-Votos and Contemporary Art in Texas*, Contemporary Arts Museum, Houston
1990 *15 pintores y 3 escultores tejanos: Artistas mexicano-norteamericanos*, Museo de Arte Alvar y Carmen Carrillo Gil, Mexico City
1988 *11 pintores Chicanos*, Palacio de Mineria, Mexico City
1987 *Hispanic Art in the United States: Thirty Contemporary Painters and Sculptors*, Museum of Fine Arts, Houston; Corcoran Gallery of Art, Washington DC; Lowe and Metropolitan Museum of Art, Coral Gables, Florida; Museum of Fine Arts and Museum of International Folk Art, Santa Fe; Los Angeles Museum of Contemporary Art; The Brooklyn Museum, New York
1987 *Influence, Part II*, San Antonio Museum of Art
1987 *Chulas Fronteras*, Midtown Art Center, Houston
1987 *Figurative Artists*, The Multicultural Center, Corpus Christi
1987 *Mira! The Canadian Club Hispanic Art Tour*, Plaza de La Raza, Los Angeles
1983 *Showdown*, The Alternative Museum, New York

**Selected Public Collections**

Museum of Fine Arts, Houston
San Antonio Museum of Art
Mexican Fine Arts Center Museum, Chicago
Federal Reserve Board, Dallas

## Melissa Miller

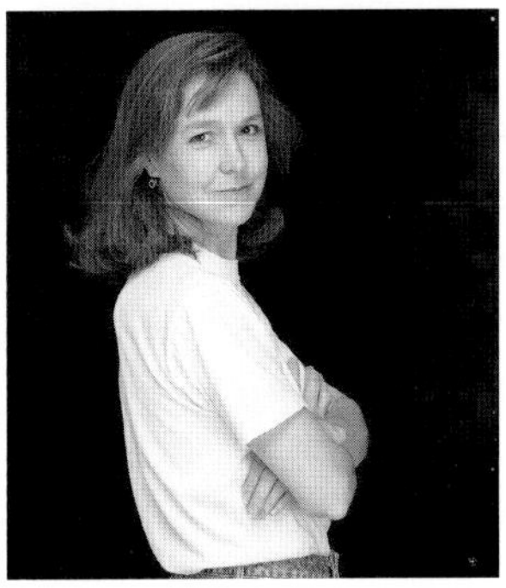

*Melissa Miller, 1993. Photograph: © Bill Kennedy. Courtesy of the artist.*

1951 Born in Houston, Texas
Lives in Austin, Texas

**Education and Awards**

1969–71 University of Texas, Austin
1971 Museum of Fine Arts School, Houston
1974 Yale Summer School of Music and Art, New Haven, Connecticut
1974 University of New Mexico, Albuquerque, BFA
1979 National Endowment for the Arts, Individual Artists Fellowship
1982 National Endowment for the Arts, Individual Artists Fellowship
1985 National Endowment for the Arts, Individual Artists Fellowship
1987 Texas Art Award
1992 Anne Giles Kimbrough Award, Dallas Museum of Art

**Selected Solo Exhibitions**

1991 *Melissa Miller: The Artist's Eye*, Kimbell Art Museum, Fort Worth
1990 *Paintings*, Georgia State University Art Gallery, Atlanta
1989 Yellowstone Art Center, Billings, Montana
1986 *Melissa Miller: A Survey, 1978–1986*, Albright-Knox Art Gallery, Buffalo, New York; Contemporary Arts Museum, Houston; Modern Art Museum of Fort Worth

1985 Texas Gallery, Houston
1985 Holly Solomon Gallery, New York
1984 Holly Solomon Gallery, New York
1983 Texas Gallery, Houston
1981 Projects Gallery, Art Museum of South Texas, Corpus Christi
1981 Perspectives Gallery, Contemporary Arts Museum, Houston
1978 *Young Artists Series*, Amarillo Art Center

**Selected Group Exhibitions**

1993 *Corcoran Gallery of Art 43rd Biennial of Contemporary American Painting*, Corcoran Gallery of Art, Washington DC
1993 *Master Prints from the Rutgers Center for Innovative Printmaking*; The Gallery at Bristol-Meyers Squibb, Princeton, New Jersey; DuBois Gallery, Lehigh University Art Galleries
1992 *Mind and Beast: Contemporary Artists and the Animal Kingdom*, Woodson Art Museum, Wassau, Wisconsin; Art Museum of South Texas, Corpus Christi; Knoxville Museum of Art, Tennessee; Tucson Museum of Art, Arizona; Canton Art Institute, Ohio; Fort Wayne Museum of Art, Indiana
1992 *100th Anniversary Prints*, Modern Art Museum of Fort Worth
1992 *Annual Academy Institute Purchase Exhibition*, American Academy and Institute of Arts and Letters, New York
1990 *Baltimore Collections: Painting and Sculpture Since 1960*, Baltimore Art Museum
1990 *Northwest x Southwest: Painted Fictions*, Palm Springs Desert Museum, California; Yellowstone Art Center, Billings, Montana, Western Washington University, Bellingham, Washington; Sarah Campbell Blaffer Gallery, University of Houston
1990 *Annual Academy Institute Purchase Exhibition*, American Academy and Institute of Arts and Letters, New York
1989 *Deep Woods: Concerning Nature in Recent Painting, Drawing and Sculpture*, University of Minnesota, Duluth
1989 *Making Their Mark: Women Artists Today, 1970–1985*, Cincinnati Art Museum, Ohio; New Orleans Museum of Art; Denver Art Museum, Colorado
1989 *Texas Women*, National Museum of Women n the Arts, Washington DC; Laguna Gloria Art Museum, Austin
1988 *Live Stories*, University of Washington, Seattle
1988 *Twentieth Century Art in the Museum Collection: Direction and Diversity*, Museum of Fine Arts, Houston
1988 *One + One: Collaborations by Artists and Writers*, Alfred C Glassell School of Art, Houston
1987 *Third Coast Review: A Look at Art in Texas*, Aspen Art Museum, Colorado
1987 *Texas*, San Francisco Museum of Modern Art, Art Rental Gallery
1986 *Directions*, Hirshhorn Museum and Sculpture Garden, Washington DC
1986 *Western States Biennial*, Brooklyn Museum of Art, New York
1986 *A Sense of Place: Contemporary Southern Art*, Minneapolis College of Art and Design
1985 *Fresh Paint: The Houston School*, Museum of Fine Arts, Houston; PS1, Long Island City, New York
1985 *Private Treasures, Public View*, San Antonio Museum of Art
1984 *Paradise Lost/Paradise Regained*, The Venice Biennial, Italy
1984 *New Directions for the Michner Collection*, Archer M Huntington Art Gallery, University of Texas, Austin
1984 *Biennial III*, San Francisco Museum of Modern Art
1984 *El arte narrativo*, Museo Rufino Tamayo, Mexico City
1983 *Whitney Biennial Exhibition*, Whitney Museum of American Art, New York
1983 *Southern Fictions*, Contemporary Arts Museum, Houston
1983 *The End of the World: Contemporary Visions of the Apocalypse*, The New Museum, New York
1980 *1980 New Orleans Triennial*, New Orleans Museum of Art
1980 *Visions and Figurations*, California State University, Fullerton
1980 *Texas Fine Arts Association Annual Exhibition*, Laguna Gloria Art Museum, Austin
1980 *Introductions 80*, Robinson Galleries, Houston
1979 *The Amarillo Competition*, Amarillo Art Center, Amarillo
1979 *Women in Sight: New Art in Texas*, Dougherty Cultural Arts Center, Austin
1978 *Works on Paper: Southwest 1978*, Dallas Museum of Art
1977 *Women and Their Work*, Laguna Gloria Art Museum, Austin
1974 *Southwest Fine Arts Biennial*, Museum of Fine Arts, Santa Fe

**Selected Public Collections**

Albright-Knox Gallery of Art, Buffalo
Modern Art Museum of Fort Worth
Museum of Fine Arts, Houston
Museum of Modern Art, New York
San Francisco Museum of Modern Art
The Contemporary Museum, Honolulu

## Jesus Bautista Moroles

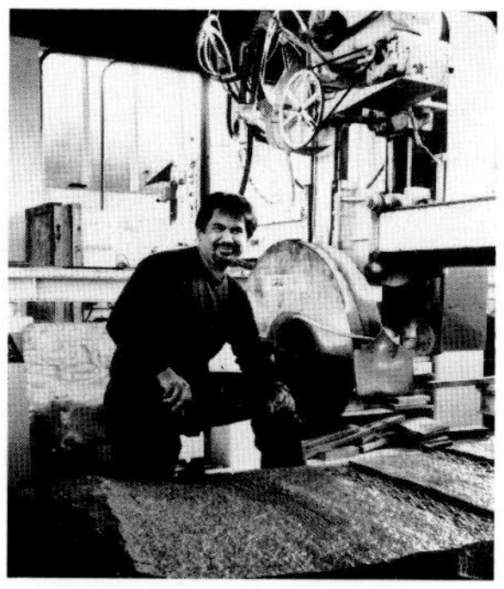

*Jesus Bautista Moroles, 1993. Courtesy of the artist and Davis/McClain Gallery, Houston.*

1950 Born in Corpus Christi, Texas
Lives in Rockport, Texas

**Education and Awards**

1975 El Centro College, Dallas,
1978 North Texas State University, Denton, BFA
1982 Awards in the Visual Arts, Fellowship
1992 University of North Texas Citation Award

**Selected Solo Exhibitions**

1993 Davis/McClain Gallery, Houston
1993 University of Oklahoma, Norman
1993 Morgan Gallery, Kansas City, Missouri
1993 Klein Art Works, Chicago
1993 Art Museum of Southeast Texas, Beaumont
1993 Carl Schlosberg Fine Art, Sherman Oaks, California
1992 Davis/McClain Gallery, Houston
1992 Klein Art Works, Chicago
1991 Richard Green Gallery, Los Angeles
1991 Klein Art Works, Chicago
1990 Davis/McClain Gallery, Houston
1989 Janus Gallery, Santa Fe
1988 Headley-Whitney Museum, Lexington, Kentucky
1986 Baumgarten Galleries, Washington DC
1986 The Wright Gallery, Dallas
1986 Davis/McClain Gallery, Houston
1984 *Moroles: 1981–1983*, Koehler Cultural Center, San Antonio College
1984 Davis/McClain Gallery, Houston
1982 Mattingly Baker Gallery, Dallas
1982 Nave Museum, Victoria, Texas
1982 Amarillo Art Center

**Selected Group Exhibitions**

1993 *Malibu International Sculputre Exhibition*, Carl Schlosberg Fine Arts, California
1989 *A Century of Sculpture in Texas, 1889–1989*, Archer M Huntington Art Gallery, Austin
1989 *For the Collector: Important Contemporary Sculpture*, Meredith Long & Co, Houston
1987 *Hispanic Art in the United States: Thirty Contemporary Painters and Sculptors*, Museum of Fine Arts, Houston; Corcoran Gallery of Art, Washington DC, Los Angeles County Museum of Art, other venues in Miami, Brooklyn and Santa Fe
1986 *New American Talent from Texas*, Texas Fine Arts Association, Laguna Gloria Art Museum, Austin
1986 *The New West*, Colorado Springs Fine Arts Center
1985 Santa Fe Festival of the Arts, New Mexico
1985 *Outdoor Sculputre Installation*, San Antonio Art Institute
1984 *Art in Public Places*, DiverseWorks
1984 *Awards in the Visual Arts 2*; Museum of Contemporary Art, Chicago; other venues
1983 *Showdown*, Alternative Museum, New York
1983 *Contemporary Images, Thirteen South Texas Artists*, Cayman Gallery, New York
1983 *Showdown*, DiverseWorks, Houston
1982 *Another Great Love Affair*, Denver Art Museum, Colorado
1982 Chicago International Art Exposition, Navy Pier, Chicago
1982 Twelfth International Sculpture Conference,

San Francisco
1982 *Fourth Annual Shidoni Outdoor Sculpture Show*, Shidoni Gallery, Tesuque, New Mexico

**Selected Public Collections and Commissions**

Albuquerque Museum, New Mexico
Birmingham Botanical Gardens, Alabama
Dallas Museum of Art
Fondazione Umberto Severi, Capri, Italy
Houston Police Officer's Memorial, Houston, 1992
Mint Museum, Charlotte
Modern Art Museum of Fort Worth
Museum of Fine Arts, Houston
Museum of Fine Arts, Santa Fe
National Museum of American Art, Washington DC
New Orleans Museum of Fine Arts
Palm Springs Desert Museum, California
San Antonio Museum of Art
University of Houston
University of North Texas

## Celia Alvarez Muñoz

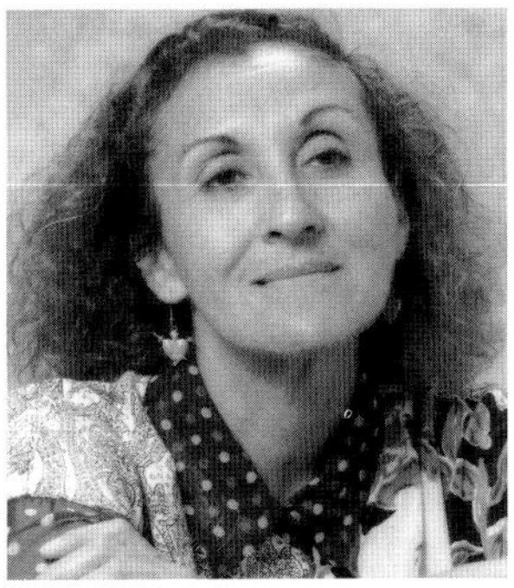

*Celia Alvarez Muñoz. Courtesy of the artist.*

1937 Born in El Paso, Texas
Lives in Arlington, Texas

**Education and Awards**

1964 University of Texas, El Paso, BA
1982 University of North Texas, Denton, MFA
1963 Museum Purchase Award, El Paso Museum of Art
1963 Graphics Award, Annual Regional Exhibition, Laguna Gloria Art Museum, Austin
1988 National Endowment for the Arts, Individual Artists Fellowship
1990 University of North Texas 100 Outstanding Alumni Centennial Award
1991 National Endowment for the Arts, Individual Artists Fellowship

**Selected Solo Exhibitions/Installations**

1993 *Celia Alvarez Muñoz: Piquetitos/Little Pricks*, Center for Contemporary Arts, Santa Fe
1992 *El Límite*, Center for the Fine Arts, Miami
1991 *El Límite*, La Jolla Museum of Contemporary Art, California
1991 *Abriendo Tierra: Breaking Ground*, Dallas Museum of Art
1990 University Museum, University of Texas, El Paso
1990 *Paper Dolls and Patron Saints*, installation, Adair Margo Gallery, El Paso
1989 *Rompiendo la Liga*, installation, Lannan Museum, Lake Worth, Florida
1989 *Postales*, Bridge Center for Contemporary Arts, El Paso
1988 *Lana Sube, Lana Baja*, installation, Lannan Museum, Lake Worth, Florida
1988 *Vistas Series*, installation, San Angelo Museum of Art, Texas
1988 *Celia Muñoz: Postales y Sin Remedio*, Tyler Museum of Art, Tyler, Texas
1983 *Bookworks*, University of Texas, El Paso

**Selected Group Exhibitions**

1993 *Sin Fronteras: Chicano Arts from the Border States of the US*, Cornerhouse Greater Manchester Centre Limited, Manchester, England
1993 *The Return of the Cadavre Exquis*, The Drawing Center, New York
1992 *Wall Drawings*, The Drawing Center, New York
1992 *Gender: Fact or Fiction*, Laguna Gloria Art Museum, Austin
1992 *Slouching Towards 2000: The Politics of Gender*, Women and Their Work, Austin; Lawndale Art and Performance Center, Houston
1992 *Volumination: The Book as Art Object*, Edwin A Ulrich Museum of Art, Wichita State University, Kansas
1992 *The Chicano Codices: Encountering Art of the America*, The Mexican Museum, San Francisco
1992 *Forty + View*, Arlington Museum of Art, Texas
1991 *1991 Biennial Exhibition*, Whitney Museum of American Art, New York
1991 *Border Issues: Negotiations and Identity*, Center for Research for Contemporary Art, University of Texas, Arlington
1991 *Encuentro: Invasion of the Americas and the Making of the Mestizo*, SPARK, Venice, California
1990 *Personal Odysseys*, Intar Gallery, New York; Next Stage Inc, Cambridge Multicultural Center, Massachusetts; Intersection for the Arts, San Francisco
1990 *Family Stories*, Newhouse Center for Contemporary Art, Snug Harbor Cultural Center, Staten Island, New York
1990 *Chicano Art: Resistance and Affirmation*, Wight Art Gallery, University of California, Los Angeles; Denver Art Museum, Colorado; Albuquerque Museum of Art, New Mexico; San Francisco Museum of Modern Art; Tuscon Museum of Modern Art, Arizona; National Museum of American Art, Washington DC
1989 *Book Arts in the USA*, Arts America, Center of Book Arts, New York; travels to seven countries
1989 *Sin Fronteras: Contemporary Mexican American Artists*; University of Colorado, Colorado Springs
1989 *Ceremony of Memory*, Center for Contemporary Arts, Santa Fe; Lannan Museum, Lake Worth, Florida; Museum of Contemporary Hispanic Art, New York; Museum of Art, University of Arizona, Tucson. Also museums in San Diego, Dallas, Austin, New Orleans, and Fullerton, California
1988 *The Texas Triennial*, Contemporary Art Museum, Houston; Texas A&M University, College Station; Art Museum of South Texas, Corpus Christi; Lubbock Fine Arts Centre, San Angelo Museum of Fine Arts, Texas; Center For Contemporary Art, El Paso
1988 *Texas Women*, National Museum of Women in the Arts, Washington DC; Laguna Gloria Art Museum, Austin
1988 *Texas Exploring the Boundaries*, Lawndale Art Center, Houston
1987 *Third Coast Review: A Look at Art in Texas*, Aspen Museum of Art, Colorado; University of Colorado, Boulder; Power Plant Visual Arts Center, Fort Collins, Colorado; Blue Star Art Space, San Antonio
1986 *Artistas Contemporáneos de Tejas*, Lubbock Fine Arts Center, Texas
1986 *Chulas Fronteras*, Midtown Art Center, Houston; Bath House Cultural Center, Dallas; Cultural Activity Center, Temple, Texas; Corpus Christi State University, Texas; Americana Museum, El Paso
1986 *Diverse Idioms*, Lawndale Art Center, Houston
1986 *Members' Summer Exhibition*, Center for Book Arts, New York
1986 *3D-2D: Invitational Alumni Exhibition*, University of North Texas, Denton
1985 *Second Handmade Photographic Book Exhibition*, National Society of Photographic Education Conference, Minneapolis
1985 *Foto Flow III*, University of Texas, Arlington
1985 *Cover to Cover: Experimental Book Works*, Santa Fe Museum of Fine Art
1984 *At Home: A Decade of Women's Art*, Long Beach Museum of Art, California
1984 *Handmade Photographic Books: Third Annual Photo Symposium*, Texas Women's University, Denton, Texas

**Selected Public Collections**

Atlantic Richfield Co, Dallas
Bruce Peel Special Collections, University of Alberta, Edmonton, Canada
The Center for Book Arts Archives, New York
Frito-Lay Inc, Plano, Texas
Getty Center for the History of Art and the Humanities Library, Malibu, California
Harvard University, Cambridge
Lannan Foundation, Los Angeles
Longview Museum and Arts Center, Texas
New Mexico State University, Las Cruces
Sackner Archives, Los Angeles
San Antonio Museum of Art
Stanford University Special Collections, Palo Alto, California

## Nic Nicosia

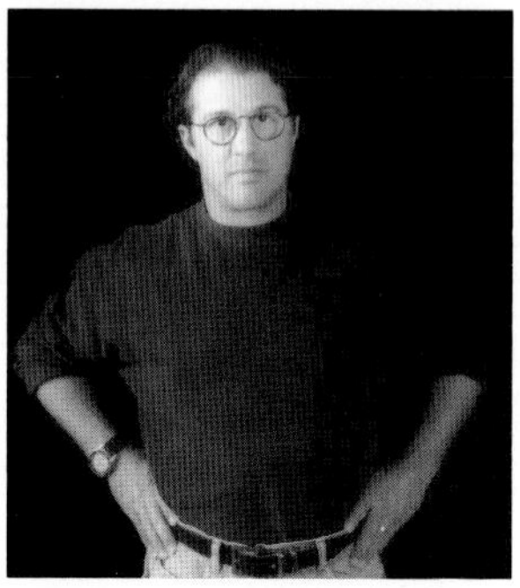

*Nic Nicosia, 1993. Courtesy of the artist.*

1951 Born in Dallas, Texas
Lives in Dallas, Texas

**Education and Awards**

1974 North Texas State University, Denton, BA
1980 Graduate work at North Texas State and the University of Houston
1984 Louis Comfort Tiffany Grant
1992 Southeastern Center for Contemporary Art, Award in the Visual Arts, North Carolina

**Selected Solo Exhibitions**

1993 *Love & Lust*, Raab Gallery, London, England
1992 *Love & Lust*, Texas Gallery, Houston
1991 *Love & Lust*, Linda Cathcart Gallery, New York; Dart Gallery, New Orleans
1990 Linda Cathcart Gallery, Santa Monica, California; Bruno Facchetti Gallery, New York
1989 *Real Pictures*, Dart Gallery, Chicago; Barry Whistler Gallery, Dallas
1988 *Real Pictures*, Texas Gallery, Houston; Bruno Facchetti Gallery, New York
1987 *Life as We Know It*, Albert Totah Gallery, New York; Barry Whistler Gallery, Dallas; University Art Galleries, Wright State University, Dayton, Ohio
1987 *Nic Nicosia: Photographs*, Arthur Roger Gallery, New Orleans
1987 *Nic Nicosia*, Honolulu Academy of Arts, Hawaii
1987 *Real Pictures and Life as We Know It*, Art Museum of Southeast Texas, Beaumont
1986 *Concentrations 13: Nic Nicosia*, Dallas Museum of Art
1986 *Nic Nicosia: Recent Photographs*, Wellesley Jewitt Museum, Wellesley College, Boston
1986 *The Cast*, Texas Gallery, Houston
1986 *Nic Nicosia*, Maurice Keitlman Gallery, Brussels, Belgium
1986 *Nic Nicosia*, Film in the Cities, St Paul, Minnesota
1986 *Nic Nicosia: Photographs*, Evan Mannes Gallery, Atlanta
1985 *Nic Nicosia's Realities*, Milwaukee Art Museum
1985 *Nic Nicosia, Domestic Dramas/Near Modern Disasters*, Houston Center for Photography, Houston
1985 *The Cast*, Marcuse Pfeifer Gallery, New York
1985 *New Photographs — Nicosia*, Dart Gallery, Chicago
1984 *Nic Nicosia*, The Akron Museum, Ohio
1984 *Near Modern Disasters*, Delahunty Gallery, Dallas
1984 *Domestic Dramas/Near Modern Disasters*, Jane Corkin Gallery, Toronto
1983 *Nic Nicosia*, University of Arizona, Tucson
1982 *Nic Nicosia*, Artist Space, New York
1981 *Nic Nicosia: Photographs*, Texas Christian University, Fort Worth

**Selected Group Exhibitions**

1993 *TEXAS/Between Two Worlds*, Contemporary Arts Museum, Houston; Modern Art Museum of Fort Worth; Art Museum of South Texas, Corpus Christi
1993 *Autoportraits Contemporains: Here's Looking at Me*, ELAC, Art Contemporain, Lyon, France
1993 *Love and Other (Fatal) Attractions*, Klausner Gallery, Santa Barbara Contemporary Arts Forum, California
1992 *Documenta 9*, Kassell, Germany
1992 *1992 New Orleans Triennial: New Southern Photography*, New Orleans Museum of Art
1991 *Pleasures and Terrors of Domestic Comfort*, Museum of Modern Art, New York
1990 *Reinventing Reality*, Sarah Campbell Blaffer Gallery, University of Houston
1990 *Meditations*, Center for Research in Contemporary Art, University of Texas, Austin
1989 *Staged Documents*, Camerawork, San Francisco
1989 *Nature and Culture: Conflict and Reconciliation in Recent Photography*, The Friends of Photography, San Francisco
1989 *Konstruite Fotografie*, Kunstverein Museum, Munich
1988 *Contemporary Art from Texas*, Groninger Museum, The Netherlands
1988 *Fabrications*, Sert Gallery, Harvard University, Cambridge
1988 *Evocative Presence*, Museum of Fine Arts, Houston
1988 *Vision/Television*, JIPAM, Montpelier, France
1987 *Arrangements for the Camera: A View of Contemporary American Photography*, Baltimore Museum of Art, Maryland
1987 *Torino Fotographie 87*, Biennale Internazionale, Torino, Italy
1987 *Selections from the Exxon Series: Emerging Artists, 1976–1986*, Guggenheim Museum, New York
1987 *Third Coast Review: A Look at Art in Texas*, Aspen Art Museum, Aspen, Colorado
1986 *A Sense of Place: Contemporary Southern Art*, Minneapolis College of Art and Design, Minnesota
1986 *Intersection: Artists View the City*, Laguna Gloria Art Museum, Austin
1986 *Photographic Fictions*, Whitney Museum of American Art, Stamford, Connecticut
1985 *Texas Currents*, San Antonio Art Institute
1984 *Anxious Interiors*, Laguna Beach Museum of Art, Laguna Beach, California
1984 *New Images in Photography*, Visual Arts Museum, New York
1984 *Visions of Childhood: A Contemporary Iconography*, Whitney Museum of American Art, Downtown, New York
1983 *Whitney Biennial*, Whitney Museum of American Art, New York
1983 *1983 New Orleans Triennial*, New Orleans Museum of Art
1983 *Image Fabrique*, Musée Nationale d'Art Modern, Center Georges Pompidou, Paris
1983 *Southern Fictions*, Contemporary Arts Museum, Houston
1983 *New Perspectives in American Art: 1983 Exxon National Exhibition*, Guggenheim Museum, New York
1981 *Texas Photo Sampler*, Washington Project for the Arts, Washington DC; Camerawork, San Francisco
1981 *The New Photography*, Contemporary Arts Museum, Houston
1980 *Voertman Show*, North Texas State University, Denton
1980 *The Print Club 56th Annual International Competition*, The Print Club, Philadelphia

**Selected Public Collections**

Art Gallery of Ontario, Toronto
The Bayly Museum, Charlottesville, Virginia
Dallas Museum of Art
The Gernsheim Collection, University of Texas, Austin
Groninger Museum, Nederland, The Netherlands
Solomon R Guggenheim Museum, New York
La Jolla Museum of Contemporary Art, California
Milwaukee Art Museum
Museum of Contemporary Art, Montreal
Museum of Fine Arts, Houston
Museum of Modern Art, New Nork
New Orleans Museum of Art

## James Reaben

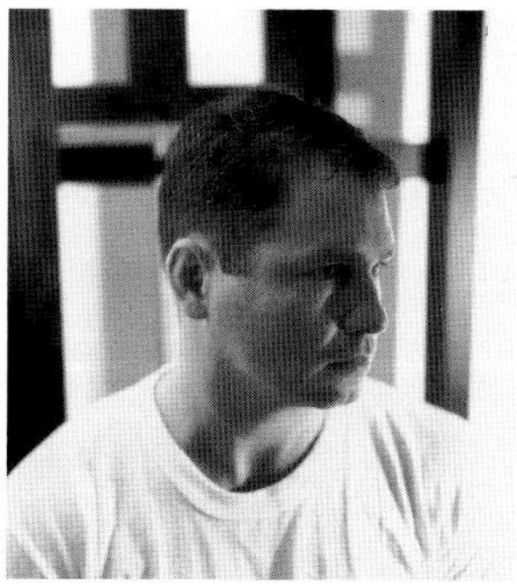

*James Reaben, c.1988. Courtesy of the Estate of James Reaben.*

Houston, 1956–1989

**Selected Solo Exhibitions**

1990 *James Reaben*, The Menil Collection, Houston
1990 *James Reaben: Death Threats*, Museum of Fine Arts, Houston
1989 CG Jung Educational Center, Houston
1989 Simms Fine Art, New Orleans, Louisiana
1988 *Introductions*, Moody Gallery, Houston
1987 *James Reaben: Paintings/Objects*, Brazos Bookstore, Houston

1983 Studio One, Houston

**Selected Group Exhibitions**

1992 *Avenues of Departure: Twelve Houston Artists*, Contemporary Arts Center, New Orleans
1992 *Freedom of Expression*, University of Houston, Clear Lake; Lawndale Art and Performance Center, Houston
1991 *Texas Selections from the Menil Collection*, Galveston Art Center
1990 *Tradition and Innovation: A Museum Celebration of Texas Art*, Museum of Fine Arts, Houston
1990 *Direct References: Drawings by Texas Artists*, Alfred C Glassell School of Art
1990 *15 year Anniversary Exhibition*, Moody Gallery, Houston
1990 *A Sacred Presence*, Simms Fine Art, New Orleans
1989 *Another Reality*, Hooks-Epstein Galleries, Houston
1989 *Messages from the South*, Sewall Art Gallery, Rice University, Houston
1989 *Intimate Collages: An Invitational Exhibition*, Watson Gallery, Houston
1988 *Altars*, Susanna Sheffield Gallery, Houston
1988 *Conscience and Content*, Art League of Houston, Houston
1988 *Inter-Cosmos*, Midtown Art Center, Houston
1987 *The Small Show*, Lawndale Art Center, Houston
1987 *The Collage Show*, Commerce Street Studios, Houston
1986 *Prisoners of Conscience*, DiverseWorks, Houston

**Selected Public Collections**

The Menil Collection, Houston
Museum of Fine Arts, Houston
The Voodoo Museum, New Orleans

## Lee N Smith III

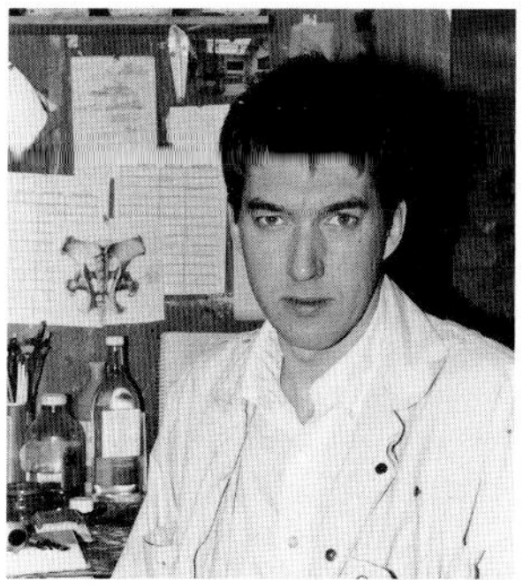

*Lee N Smith III, 1989. Courtesy of the artist.*

1950 Born in New Orleans, Louisiana
Lives in Dallas, Texas

**Education and Awards**

1972 El Centro Junior College, Dallas
1987 National Endowment for the Arts, Individual Artists Grant
1988–89 The American Center Residence Grant, Paris, France

**Selected Solo Exhibitions**

1993 *Lone Star Visions: Lee N Smith III*, Art Museum of Southeast Texas, Beaumont
1992 Koplin Gallery, Santa Monica, California
1989 *New Paintings*, Barry Whistler Gallery, Dallas
1989 *Cité International des Arts*, Paris
1986 *Lee N Smith III: Recent Paintings*, Contemporary Arts Museum, Houston
1985 DW Gallery, Dallas
1984 The Art Center, Waco, Texas
1982 DW Gallery, Dallas
1981 *Focus: Lee N Smith III*, Fort Worth Art Museum
1981 Texas Christian University, Fort Worth
1980 DW Gallery, Dallas
1979 Mountain View College, Dallas
1979 University of Texas, Arlington
1978 Eastfiled College, Mesquite, Texas

**Selected Group Exhibitions**

1993 *Eye on the Figure*, LewAllen Gallery, Santa Fe
1990 *Concentrations: Texas Figurative Drawings*, Dallas Museum of Art
1990 *Real Allusions*, Whitney Museum of Art at the Equitable Center, New York
1990 *Northwest x Southwest: Painted Fictions*, Palm Springs Desert Museum, California; Yellowstone Art Center, Billings, Montana; Western Washington University, Bellingham, Washington; Sarah Campbell Blaffer Gallery, University of Houston
1989 *boys will be boys*, Linda Cathcart Gallery, Santa Monica, California
1989 *Now/Then/Again*, Dallas Museum of Art
1988 *Life Stories: Myth, Fiction and History in Contemporary Art*, University of Washington
1988 *Art for the Museum: A Legacy*, Art Museum of Southeast Texas, Beaumont
1986 *V Bienal Americana de Artes Graficas*, Museo de Arte Moderno, Cali, Colombia
1986 *The Texas Landscape, 1900–1986*, Museum of Fine Arts, Houston
1986 *1986 New Orleans Triennial*, New Orleans Museum of Art
1983 *Southern Fictions*, Contemporary Arts Museum, Houston
1983 *Enigma of the Night*, Art Museum of South Texas, Corpus Christi
1983 *Invitational*, Longview Museum and Art Center, Atlanta
1983 *Touch with Your Eyes, Fell with Your Mind: Surfaces in Contemporary Art*, Laguna Gloria Art Museum, Austin
1982 *Fun and Games*, The Art Center, Waco
1982 *1982 Biennial National Exhibition*, Meadows Museum of Art, Shreveport, Louisiana
1981 *Landscape Show*, DW Gallery, Dallas
1981 *81 West Art and the Law*, Minnesota Museum of Art, St Paul
1980 *1980 New Orleans Triennial*, New Orleans Museum of Art
1980 *Inside Texas Borders*, South Texas Art Mobile, Corpus Christi
1979 *11th Monroe National Art Exhibition*, Masur Museum of Art, Monroe, Louisiana
1979 *6th Annual Midwestern Printmaking and Drawing Competition*, Philbrook Art Center, Tulsa, Oklahoma
1978 *The Eighth National Southwest Texas State University Works on Paper Exhibition*, Southwest Texas State University, San Marcos
1978 *20th Annual Eighth State Exhibition of Painting and Sculpture*, Oklahoma Art Center, Oklahoma City
1978 *Works on Paper: Southwest 1978*, Dallas Museum of Art

**Selected Public Collections**

The American Center, Paris
Atlantic Richfield Company, Dallas
Dallas Museum of Art
Frito-Lay Inc, Plano, Texas
Archer M Huntington Art Gallery, Austin
Modern Art Museum of Fort Worth
Museum of Contemporary Art, Chicago
Museum of Fine Arts, Houston
Nations Bank, Charlotte, North Carolina
West Texas Museum Association, Lubbock

## Gael Stack

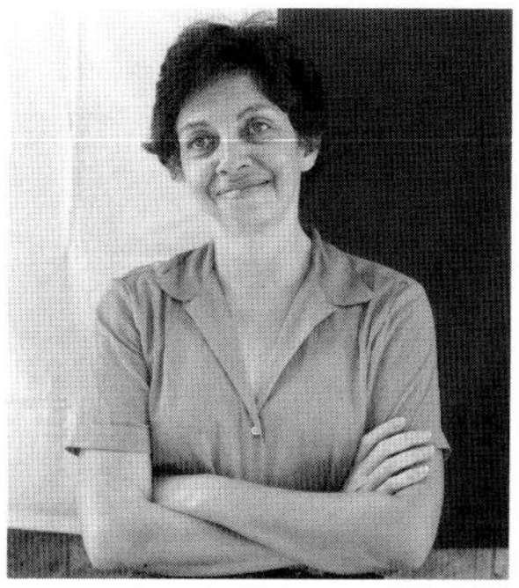

*Gael Stack, 1981. Photograph: Suzanne Bloom. Courtesy of the artist.*

1941 Born in Chicago
Lives in Houston, Texas

**Education and Awards**

1970 University of Illinois, Champaign, BFA
1972 Southern Illinois University, Carbondale, MFA
1982 National Endowment for the Arts, Individual Artists Grant
1985 Cultural Arts Council of Houston Award
1986 Louis Comfort Tiffany Foundation Grant
1989 National Endowment for the Arts, Individual Artists Grant

**Selected Solo Exhibitions**

1993 Condeso/Lawler Gallery, New York
1992 *Gael Stack: Revealing Clues* Amarillo Art Center, Amarillo, Texas
1992 *Recent Paintings*, Moody Gallery, Houston
1990 *Paintings and Works on Paper*, University of Arkansas, Little Rock
1990 *Recent Paintings*, Moody Gallery, Houston
1989 *Gael Stack: A Survey, 1974–1989*, Sarah Campbell Blaffer Gallery, University of Houston; Dallas Museum of Art
1989 *Paintings on Paper and Working Drawings*, Janie C Lee Gallery, Houston
1988 Beitzel Fine Arts, New York
1987 Janie C Lee Gallery, Houston

1985 Brown-Lupton Gallery, Fort Worth
1985 Hadler-Roddriguez Galleries, New York
1985 Janie C Lee Gallery, Houston
1983 Janie C Lee Gallery, Houston
1981 Meredith Long & Co, Houston
1980 Meredith Long & Co, Houston
1979 Meredith Long & Co, Houston
1978 Meredith Long & Co, Houston
1977 Art Museum of South Texas, Corpus Christi
1977 Meredith Long & Co, Houston
1976 Meredith Long & Co, Houston
1975 Meredith Long & Co, Houston
1974 Graphics Gallery, San Francisco
1972 Mitchell Gallery, Carbondale, Illinois

**Selected Group Exhibitions**

1993 *Darkness + Light*, Sarah Campbell Blaffer Gallery, University of Houston
1993 *Recent Acquisitions*, Yale University Art Gallery, New Haven, Connecticut
1992 *Selections From the Permanent Collection*, Museum of Fine Arts, Houston
1992 *From Chaos to Order*, Art Museum of Southeast Texas, Beaumont
1991 *The State I'm In: Texas Artists at the DMA*, Dallas Museum of Art
1991 *A Sense of Place: Recent Acquisitions in Contemporary Texas Art*, San Antonio Museum of Art
1990 *Northwest x Southwest: Painted Fictions*, Palm Springs Desert Museum, California; Yellowstone Art Center, Billings, Montana; Western Washington University, Bellingham, Washington; Sarah Campbell Blaffer Gallery, University of Houston
1990 *Tradition and Innovation: A Museum Celebration of Texas Art*, Museum of Fine Arts, Houston
1990 *Texas Figurative Drawings*, Dallas Museum of Art
1990 *Alternative Situations for Contemporary Printmaking*, The Print Club, Philadelphia
1989 *Now/Then/Again*, Dallas Museum of Art
1988 *Art for the Museum: A Legacy*, Art Museum of Southeast Texas, Beaumont
1988 *20th Century Art in the Museum Collection: Direction and Diversity*, Museum of Fine Arts, Houston
1988 *Master Drawings, 1977–1987: From Cézanne to Johns*, Janie C Lee Master Drawings, New York
1987 *Emerging Artists, 1978–1986: Selections from the Exxon Series*, Guggenheim Museum, New York
1987 *Third Coast Review: A Look at Art in Texas*, Aspen Art Museum, Aspen, Colorado
1986 *Amnesty International Exhibition*, DiverseWorks, Houston
1986 *Forum*, Edward Totah Gallery, Zurich
1986 *Cinq x Cinq*, Stedman/Hubbard Gallery, Paris
1985 *Texas Currents*, San Antonio Art Institute
1985 *Fresh Paint: The Houston School*, Museum of Fine Arts, Houston; PS1, Long Island City, New York
1983 *Southern Fictions*, Contemporary Arts Museum, Houston
1983 *New Orleans Triennial*, New Orleans Museum of Art
1982 *New Art from a New City*, Frankurter Kunsteverein, Frankfurt, Germany
1982 *Art from Houston in Norway*, Stavanger Museum, Oslo
1981 *Four Painters*, Contemporary Arts Museum, Houston
1981 *19 Artists: Emergent Americans*, Guggenheim Museum, New York
1980 *Texas Invitational*, Contemporary Arts Center, New Orleans
1978 *Fire!*, Contemporary Arts Museum, Houston
1974 *8th Annual National Drawing Show*, Corpus Christi
1973 *Ball State 19th Annual Drawing and Small Sculpture Show*, Muncie, Indiana

**Selected Public Collections**

Dallas Museum of Art
Solomon R Guggenheim Museum, New York
The Menil Collection, Houston
Museum of Fine Arts, Houston
San Antonio Museum of Art
Yale University Art Gallery, New Haven

## Earl Staley

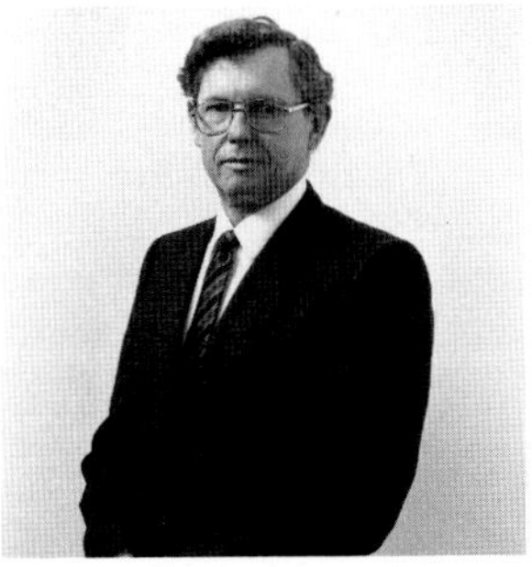

*Earl Staley, 1985. Courtesy of Moody Gallery, Houston.*

1938 Born in Oak Park, Illinois
Lives in Houston, Texas

**Education and Awards**

1960 Illinois Wesleyan University, Bloomington, BFA
1963 University of Arkansas, MFA
1975 National Endowment for the Arts, Individual Artists Grant
1978 National Endowment for the Arts, Individual Artists Grant
1982 Prix de Rome, American Academy in Rome
1985 National Endowment for the Arts, Individual Artists Grant

**Selected Solo Exhibitions**

1993 *New Paintings*, Moody Gallery, Houston
1990 *Paintings and Ceramics, 1976–1990: The Influence of Mexico*, Art Gallery, The University of Texas at San Antonio
1990 *Mexican Variations*, Galveston Art Center, Galveston
1990 *Recent Paintings: Volcanoes and Portraits*, Moody Gallery, Houston
1988 *Earl Staley Designs for "Faust"*, La Jolla Museum of Modern Art, California
1987 *Landscapes, Mythologies & Portraits*, Texas Gallery, Houston
1985 *Arriverderci Roma*, Watson/de Nagy & Co, Houston
1985 *Myth, Symbol Dream Landscapes/ Seascapes*, Carancahua Gallery, Corpus Christi
1985 *The Opera Faust*, Watson/de Nagy Gallery, Houston
1984 *Earl Staley: Skulls & Skeletons*, The Art Center, Waco
1984 The American Academy in Rome, Italy
1983 *Earl Staley: 1973–1983*, Contemporary Arts Museum, Houston
1983 The New Museum of Contemporary Art, New York
1983 Phyllis Kind Gallery, Chicago
1983 Watson/de Nagy & Co, Houston
1982 *Mediterranean Sketches*, Sewall Art Gallery, Rice University, Houston
1980 *The Big Bend*, Watson/de Nagy & Co, Houston
1980 *Earl Staley Mythologies*, Contemporary Arts Museum, Houston
1980 *A Print Retrospective*, Little Egypt Enterprises, Houston
1977 Art Museum of South Texas, Corpus Christi
1977 Stephen F Austin University, Nacogdoches, Texas
1974 Sarah Campbell Blaffer Gallery, University of Houston
1974 Texas Gallery, Houston
1972 David Gallery, Houston
1970 Meredith Long & Co, Houston
1968 Cedar Rapids Art Center, Iowa
1968 Louisiana Gallery, Houston
1966 Downstairs Gallery, St Louis, Missouri
1964 St James Episcopal Church, Milwaukee
1964 St Louis Junior College, Missouri

**Selected Group Exhibitions**

1992 *Printmaking in Texas: The 1980s*, Laguna Gloria Art Museum, Austin
1990 *Tradition and Innovation: A Museum Celebration of Texas Art*, Museum of Fine Arts, Houston
1990 *New Art of the West*, Eiteljorg Museum, Indianapolis, Indiana
1990 *Northwest x Southwest: Painted Fictions*, Palm Springs Desert Museum, California; Yellowstone Art Center, Billings, Montana; Western Washington State University, Bellingham, Washington; Sarah Campbell Blaffer Gallery, University of Houston
1989 *Texas Realism*, Art Museum of Southeast Texas, Beaumont
1989 *ROARR! The Prehistoric in Contemporary Art*, New York State Museum, Albany
1988 *Texas Arists Working in New York*, 5959 Broadway Gallery, New York
1988 *Elemental Visions/Personal Landscapes*, Art Museum of South Texas, Corpus Christi
1987 *Modern Myths/Classical Renewal*, Boise Gallery of Art, Idaho; Yellowstone Art Center, Billings, Montana; Washington State University, Pullman; Mills College, Oakland California; Whatcom Museum of Art and

History, Bellingham, Washington
1987 *Boundless Realism*, The Rockwell Museum, Corning, New York
1986 *The Texas Landscape*, Museum of Fine Arts, Houston
1986 *Second Sights, San Francisco Biennial*, San Francisco Museum of Modern Art
1985 *Fresh Paint: The Houston School*, Museum of Fine Arts, Houston; PS1, Long Island City, New York
1985 *Works on Paper: Eleven Houston Artists*, Museum of Fine Arts, Houston
1985 *Staged Stages*, Sarah Campbell Blaffer Gallery, University of Houston
1984 *Paradise Lost/Paradise Regained: American Vision of the New Decade*, American Pavilion, Venice Biennale
1983 *New Art from a New City*, Salzburger Kunstverein, Salzburg, Austria
1983 *Southern Fictions*, Contemporary Arts Museum, Houston
1983 *Texas Images and Visions*, Archer M Huntington Art Gallery, University of Texas, Austin; Art Museum of South Texas, Corpus Christi; Amarillo Art Center, Amarillo
1982 American Academy in Rome, Italy
1982 *Art from Houston in Norway*, Stavanger Kunstforeninig, Norway
1982 *Beast: Animal Imagery in Recent Painting*, Institute for Art & Urban Resources, PS1, Long Island City, New York
1982 *Texas on Paper*, Contemporary Arts Museum, Houston; University of Colorado, Boulder; Abilene Christian University, Texas; Tyler Museum of Art, Texas; Hallwalls, Buffalo, New York; University of Arizona Art Museum, Tucson; Amarillo Art Center, Texas
1982 *A Sense of Spirit*, Lawndale Annex, University of Houston, Houston
1981 *Directions 1981*, Hirshhorn Museum and Sculpture Garden, Washington DC
1981 *Two Views of Houston*, San Antonio Art Institute
1980 *New Orleans Triennial*, New Orleans Museum of Art
1979 *Fire!*, Contemporary Arts Museum, Houston
1979 *Made in Texas*, Archer M Huntington Gallery, University of Texas, Austin
1978 *Bad Painting*, The New Museum, New York
1978 *Cowboys, Indians & Settlers*, The Art Center, Newport Harbor, California
1977 *TEX/LAX: Texas in LA*, Union Gallery, California State University, Los Angeles
1975 *1975 Biennial Exhibition: Contemporary American Art*, Whitney Museum of American Art, New York
1975 *North, East, West, South and Middle*, Moore College of Art, Philadelphia,; Pratt Graphics Center, New York; Corcoran Gallery of Art, Washington DC; Fort Worth Art Museum; La Jolla Museum of Contemporary Art
1975 *Five Painters: Dallas/Houston*, Southern Methodist University, Dallas
1974 *Abstract Painting and Sculpture in Houston*, Museum of Fine Arts, Houston
1973 *Private Works*, Contemporary Arts Museum, Houston
1966 *Print Invitational*, Lindenwood College, St Charles, and Carlton College, Northfield, Minnesota
1965 National Academy of Design, New York

**Selected Public Collections and Commissions**

Brown & Root, Houston
Chase Manhattan Bank, New York
Continental Insurance, San Antonio
Dallas Museum of Art
Dannheisser Foundation, New York
*Faust*, 1984 Production by the Houston Grand Opera
First National Bank of Chicago
Frito-Lay Inc, Dallas
Modern Art Museum of Fort Worth
Museum of Fine Arts, Houston
The New Museum of Contemporary Art, New York
Prudential Insurance Co, Newark, New Jersey
San Antonio Museum of Art

## Richard Stout

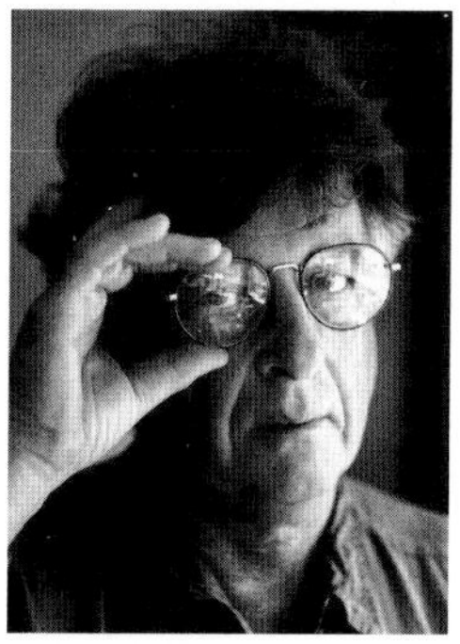

*Richard Stout, 1993. Photograph: Casey Williams. Courtesy of the artist.*

1934 Born in Beaumont, Texas
Lives in Houston, Texas

**Education and Awards**

1952–53 Art Academy of Cincinnati, Ohio
1957 The School of the Art Institute of Chicago, BFA
1968 Yaddo Residency Fellowship, Saratoga Springs, New York
1969 University of Texas, Austin, MFA
1976 Museum of Fine Arts, Houston, Travel Grant

**Selected Solo Exhibitions**

1994 *Recent Paintings*, Davis/McClain Gallery, Houston
1991 William A Graham Gallery, Houston
1989 William A Graham Gallery, Houston
1987 William A Graham Gallery, Houston
1985 Meredith Long & Co, Houston
1980 Meredith Long & Co, Houston
1979 Meredith Long & Co, Houston
1978 Meredith Long & Co, Houston
1977 Meredith Long & Co, Houston
1976 Meredith Long & Co, Houston
1975 Meredith Long & Co, Houston
1983 Touchstone Gallery, New York
1980 Jurgen Schwinebraden, Berlin
1975 Contemporary Arts Museum, Houston
1973 Tyler Museum of Art, Tyler, Texas
1971 Marion Koogler McNay Art Institute, San Antonio
1968 Yaddo, Saratoga Springs, New York
1968 Marion Koogler McNay Art Institute, San Antonio
1964 Kansas City Art Institute, Missouri
1961 Beaumont Art Museum, Texas
1959 New Arts Gallery, Houston
1958 Beaumont Art Museum

**Selected Group Exhibitions**

1993 *Conventional Forms/Insiduous Visions*, Alfred C Glassell School of Art, Houston
1992 *Island Inspired*, Galveston Art Center, Galveston
1989 *Texas Figurative Art*, Art Museum of Southeast Texas, Beaumont
1989 *The Food Show*, Grand Central Galleries, New York
1988 McNay Museum of Art, San Antonio
1988 *Drawn from Life*, Sewall Art Gallery, Rice University, Houston
1986 *The Texas Landscape, 1900–1986*, Museum of Fine Arts, Houston
1985 *Fresh Paint: The Houston School*, Museum of Fine Arts, Houston; PS1, Long Island City, New York
1985 *Works on Paper*, Museum of Fine Arts, Houston
1983 *New Art from a New City*, Frankfurter Kunsteverein, Frankfurt, Germany
1983 New Orleans Triennial, New Orleans Museum of Art
1982 *Art from Houston in Norway*, Stavanger Kunstforening
1981 Galleria de Arti Pellegrino, Bologna, Italy
1980 *Man and the Environment*, International Graphic Portfolio, Jurgen Schweinebraden, East Berlin
1980 *Eros*, Julius Hummel Kunsthandlung, Vienna
1979 Achenbach & Kimmerchi, Dusseldorf
1977 International Art Fair, Cologne, W Germany
1977 *Texas Twenty*, Nave Museum, Victoria, Texas
1975 *Five Painters*, Southern Methodist University, Dallas
1974 *Abstract Painting in Houston*, Museum of Fine Arts, Houston
1974 *Three Americans*, Texas Fine Arts Association; traveled across Texas and Mexico
1971 *The Other Coast*, California State University, Long Beach
1968 *Contemporary American Art*, US Department of Commerce, toured Australia
1968 *The Sphere of Art in Texas*, Hemisfair, San Antonio
1966 *100 Contemporary American Drawings*, Museum of the University of Michigan, Ann Arbor
1964 *The Festival of the Bible in the Arts*, Temple Emmanuel, Houston
1964 *Texas Painting and Sculpture Annual*, Witte Museum, San Antonio
1960 *Fifth International Hallmark Art Award*, Wildenstein Gallery, New York
1960 The American Provinceton Exhibition, Provinceton, Massachusetts

1960 Delgado Museum of Art Annual Exhibition, New Orleans
1960 New Arts Gallery, Houston
1959 New Arts Gallery, Houston
1958 New Arts Gallery, Houston
1957 Denver Museum of Art Annual Exhibition
1955–78 Beaumont Art Museum Tri-State Annual
1951–52 Beaumont Art League

**Selected Public Collections**

Archer M Huntington Art Gallery, Austin
Art Museum of Southeast Texas, Beaumont
Butler Institute of Art, Youngstown, Ohio
Dallas Museum of Art
Kuperstitch Kabinet, Museum of Art, Dresden
Marion Koogler McNay Museum, San Antonio
The Menil Collection, Houston
Museum of Fine Arts, Houston
University of Houston

## James Surls

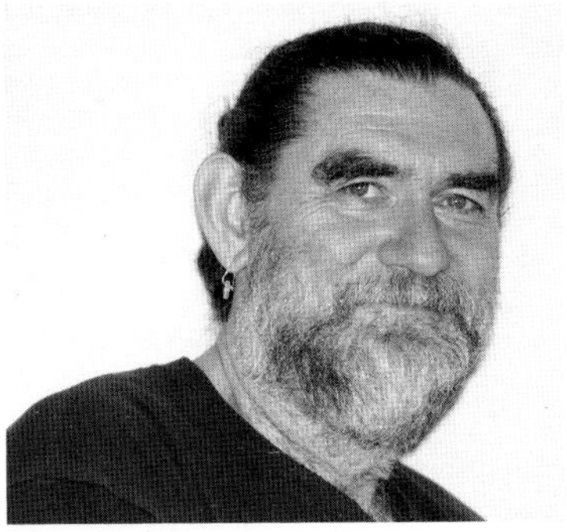

*James Surls, 1993. Photograph: Charmaine Locke. Courtesy of the artist.*

1943 Born in Terrell, Texas
Lives in Splendora, Texas

**Education and Awards**

1965 Sam Houston State College, Huntsville, Texas, BS
1969 Cranbrook Academy of Art, Bloomfield Hills, Maine, MFA

**Selected Solo Exhibitions**

1994 Marlborough Gallery, New York
1991 *Looking Out: Sculpture, Drawings and Prints by James Surls*, Contemporary Museum, Honolulu, Hawaii
1989 *Look and Listen*, Hiram Butler Gallery, Houston
1988 *James Surls: Crossing Over*, LA Louver Gallery, Venice, California
1987 *James Surls: Recent Sculpture*, Cranbrook Academy of Art Museum, Bloomfield Hills, Maine
1987 *New Work*, Pittsburgh Center for the Arts, Pennsylvania; Allan Frumkin Gallery, New York
1986 *James Surls: Drawings, 1980–85*, Allan Frumkin Gallery, New York
1986 *James Surls: Drawings*, Hiram Butler Gallery, Houston
1985 *James Surls: New Work*, LA Louver Gallery, Venice
1984 *Visions: James Surls, 1974–1984*, Dallas Museum of Art; La Jolla Museum of Contemporary Art, California; Seattle Art Museum; University of Oklahoma Art Museum
1984 *Sculpture and Drawings by James Surls*, Honolulu Academy of Art, Hawaii; Delahunty Gallery, Dallas
1982 *CURRENTS 16: James Surls*, St Louis Art Museum, Missouri
1982 *James Surls: Sculpture & Drawings*, Akron Art Museum, Ohio
1981 Daniel Weinberg Gallery, San Francisco
1981 Delahunty Gallery, Dallas
1980 *James Surls: New Sculpture*, Allan Frumkin Gallery, New York
1979 Delahunty Gallery, Dallas
1977 *James Surls: Recent Drawings*, Contemporary Arts Museum, Houston
1977 *James Surls, Sculpture*, Delahunty Gallery, Dallas
1975 *James Surls, Sculptor*, Contemporary Arts Museum, Houston
1974 *James Surls*, Tyler Museum of Art, Tyler, Texas
1974 Delahunty Gallery, Dallas

**Selected Group Exhibitions**

1993 *Virgil Grotfeldt, Joe Havel and James Surls*, Hiram Butler Gallery, Houston
1992 *The National Drawing Invitational*, Arkansas Arts Center, Little Rock
1991 *Sticks and Stones*, Katonah Museum of Art, Katonah, New York
1991 *Retrieving the Elemental Form*, Schmidt Bingham Gallery, New York; Lakeview Museum of Arts and Science, Peoria, Illinois; Fresno Art Museum, California
1991 *Image and Likeness*, Whitney Museum of American Art, Downtown, New York; and Stamford, Connecticut
1990 *Word and Image: American Art, 1960–1990*, Milwaukee Art Museum, Wisconsin
1989 *The Boat Show: Fantastic Vessels, Fictional Voyages*, Renwick Gallery, Washington DC
1988 *Contemporary Art From Texas*, Groninger Museum, The Netherlands
1988 *One + One: Collaborations by Artists and Writers*, Alfred C Glassell School of Art, Houston
1987 *Structure to Resemblance*, Albright-Knox Art Gallery, Buffalo, New York
1987 *Sculptors on Paper: New Work*, Madison Art Canter, Wisconsin; Pittsburgh Center for the Arts, Pennsylvania; Kalamazoo Institute of Arts, Michigan; The Sheldon Memorial Art Gallery, Lincoln, Nebraska
1986 *75th American Exhibition*, The Art Institute of Chicago
1986 *A Sense of Place: Contemporary Southern Art*, Minneapolis, Minnesota
1986 *America: Art and the West*, Art Gallery of Western Australia, Perth; Art Gallery of New South Wales, Sydney
1985 *Whitney Biennial*, Whitney Museum of American Art, New York
1985 *Works in Wood: A Survey of Contemporary Sculpture*, Monterey Peninsula Museum, California
1984 *American Art Since 1970: Painting, Sculpture and Drawings from the Collection of the Whitney Museum of American Art*, Whitney Museum, New York; La Jolla Museum of Contemporary Art; Museo Rufino Tamayo, Mexico City; North Carolina Museum of Art
1983 *A Century of Modern Sculpture: 1882–1982*, Museum of Fine Arts, Houston
1983 *Minimalism to Expressionism: Painting and Sculpture since 1965 from the Permanent Collection*, Whitney Museum of American Art, New York
1982 *A Sense Spirit*, Lawndale Art and Performance Center, Houston
1982 *20 American Artists: Sculpture 1982*, San Francisco Museum of Modern Art
1982 *Art From Houston in Norway*, Stavanger Kunstforening, Stavanger
1981 *The First Annual Abilene Outdoor Sculpture Exhibit*, Abilene Cultural Affairs Council, Texas
1980 *The Eleventh International Sculpture Conference*, International Sculpture Center, Washington DC
1980 *Fine Art for Federal Buildings, 1972–1979*, National Collection of Fine Arts, Smithsonian Institution, Washington DC
1979 *Whitney Biennial*, Whitney Museum of American Art, New York
1979 *Fire!*, Contemporary Arts Museum, Houston
1978 *Art of Texas*, The Renaissance Society, University of Chicago
1977 *Nine Artists: Theodoron Awards*, Guggenheim Museum, New York
1976 *The Permanent Collection: A 75th Anniversary Retrospective*, Fort Worth Art Museum, Texas
1975 *Exchange DFW/SFO*, Fort Worth Art Museum, San Francisco Museum of Modern Art
1975 *Texas Tough*, Witte Memorial Museum, San Antonio
1974 *12/Texas*, Contemporary Arts Museum, Houston

**Selected Public Collections**

Albright-Knox Gallery of Art, Buffalo
Centro Cultural/Arte Contemporáneo, Mexico City
Contemporary Arts Museum, Honolulu
Dallas Museum of Art
Solomon R Guggenheim Museum, New York
Los Angeles County Museum of Art
Marion Koogler McNay Art Museum, San Antonio
Memphis Brooks Museum, Memphis
Milwaukee Museum of Art
Modern Art Museum of Fort Worth
Museum of Fine Arts, Houston
Museum of Modern Art, New York
Nelson-Atkins Museum of Art, Kansas City, Missouri
San Antonio Museum of Art
San Francisco Museum of Modern Art
Stedelijk, Amsterdam
Whitney Museum of American Art

## Michael Tracy

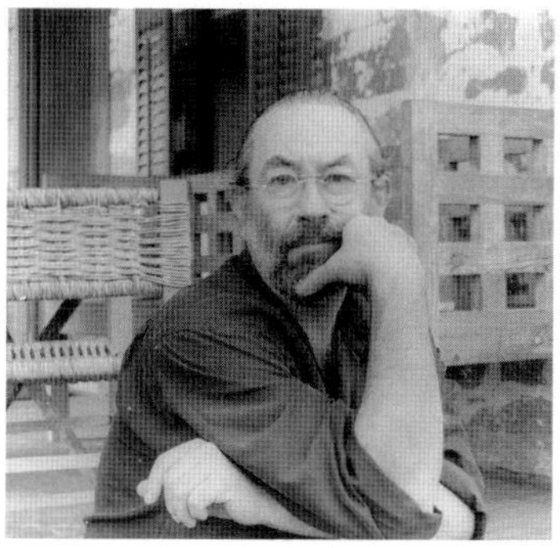

*Michael Tracy, 1993. Photograph: Henry Estrada. Courtesy of the artist and Henry Estrada.*

1943 Born in Bellevue, Ohio
Lives in San Ygnacio, Texas

**Education and Awards**

1964 St Edwards University, Austin, BA
1964–67 The Cleveland Institute of Art, Ohio
1969 University of Texas, Austin, MFA

**Selected Solo Exhibitions**

1993 *Cempazúchitl y Flores de Sangre*, Moody Gallery, Houston
1992 *Smoking Mirror*, Blue Star Art Space, San Antonio
1991 *Michael Tracy*, Zolla Lieberman Gallery, Chicago
1991 *Michael Tracy*, Daniel Weinberg Gallery, Santa Monica, California
1990 *The River Pierce: Sacrifice II, 13.4.90*, a ritual performance, San Ygnacio
1990 *The Rio Grande: My Berlin Wall*, Raab Gallery, Berlin
1990 *A Prayer for El Salvador*, McNamee Gallery, St Louis University, Missouri
1989 *Michael Tracy: Las Estaciones de la Cruz*, Centro Cultural/Arte Contemporáneo, Mexico City
1989 *New Work from the Templo Mayor Series*, Paule Anglim Gallery, San Francisco
1988 *Santuarios*, Nuevo Santander Museum, Laredo Junior College, Laredo, Texas
1987 *Terminal Privileges*, The Institute for Art and Urban Resources, Long Island City, New York; Everson Museum, Syracuse, New York; Center for Contemporary Art, Seattle; University of Southern California, Los Angeles, Ohio State University, Columbus; The Menil Collection, Houston
1986 *Michael Tracy in Situ*, Studio of Henry Estrada, San Ygnacio
1986 *Via Dolorosa a Nicaragua*, Studio of Eloy Tarcisio, Mexico City; Hiram Butler Gallery, Houston
1986 *Homenaje Rio Bravo del Norte*, Adair Margo Gallery, El Paso
1986 *Michael Tracy*, Zolla Lieberman Gallery, Chicago
1984 *Requiem Para los Olvidados*, Contemporary Arts Museum, Houston
1982 Mary Boone Gallery, New York
1980 Mary Boone Gallery, New York
1979 *Homenaje a México*, Galeria Pecanins, Mexico City
1972 *Michael Tracy/Six Paintings*, Art Museum of South Texas, Corpus Christi
1971 *Seven Gold Paintings*, Marion Koogler McNay Art Institute, San Antonio

**Selected Group Exhibitions**

1991 *After the Apocalypse: A Different Humanism*, Southeastern Center for Contemporary Art, Winston-Salem, North Carolina
1991 *The Bleeding Heart*, The Institute of Contemporary Art, Boston, Massachusetts; Contemporary Arts Museum, Houston; other venues
1989 *Revelations*, Aspen Art Museum, Colorado
1988 *Contemporary Art from Texas*, Groninger Museum, Groninger, The Netherlands
1986 *Other Gods, Containers of Belief*, Everson Museum of Art, Syracuse, New York
1986 *Seventy-Fifth American Exhibitions*, Art Institute of Chicago
1986 *Memento Mori*, Centro Cultural/Arte Contemporáneo, Mexico City
1986 *Monumental Drawing*, Brooklyn Museum, New York
1985 *Works on Paper: Eleven Houston Artists*, Museum of Fine Arts, Houston
1984 *Content: A Contemporary Focus, 1974–1984*, Hirshhorn Museum and Sculpture Garden, Washington DC
1983 *New Epiphanies*, University of Colorado, Colorado Spring; Ohio Foundation on the Arts, Columbus
1983 *New Art From a New City*, Salzburg Kunstverein, Austria
1983 *New Art*, Tate Gallery, London
1982 Venice Biennial, Italy
1979 *Photographie als/Kunst, Kunst als Photographie*, Tiroler Landesmuseum Ferdinandeum, Innsburck Austria
1974 *12/Texas*, Contemporary Arts Museum

**Selected Public Collections and Permanent Installations**

Art Museum of South Texas, Corpus Christi
Centro Cultural/Arte Contemporáneo, Mexico City
Dallas Museum of Art
Emmanuel Chapel, Corpus Christi Cathedral, 1985
Marion Koogler McNay Art Institute, San Antonio
The Menil Collection, Houston
Metropolitan Museum of Art, New York
San Antonio Museum of Art
Sagrario San Miguel Arcangel, Our Lady of Guadalupe Catholic Church, Alice, Texas, 1992

## Randy Twaddle

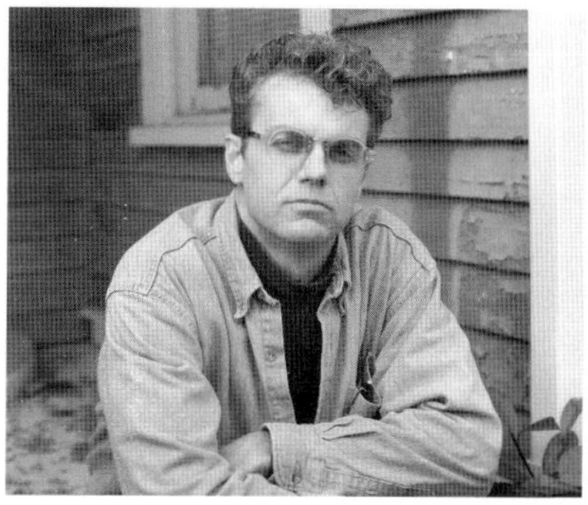

*Randy Twaddle, 1993. Courtesy of the artist.*

1957 Born in Elmo, Missouri
Lives in Houston, Texas

**Education and Awards**

1975–76 University of Missouri, Columbia
1980 Northwest Missouri State University, Maryville, BFA
1985 Art Matters, Performance Grant
1986 Anne Giles Kimbrough Award, Dallas Museum of Art
1987 National Endowment for the Arts, Artists Fellowship
1990 Awards in the Visual Arts 9, Winston-Salem

**Selected Solo Exhibitions**

1992 *Recent Drawings*, Moody Gallery, Houston
1992 *UPC Drawings*, Barry Whistler Gallery, Dallas
1991 *Recent Drawings: CHPL HL*, Stephen Writz Gallery, San Francisco
1991 *Recent Drawings*, Damon Brandt Gallery, New York
1991 *CHPL HL*, University of North Carolina, Chapel Hill
1990 *Recent Drawings*, Moody Gallery, Houston
1989 *New Drawings*, Barry Whistler Gallery
1989 *Carnival*, Damon Brandt Gallery, New York
1988 *Carnival*, DW Gallery, Dallas
1987 *Changing Nature: Recent Drawings and Prints*, Moody Gallery, Houston
1986 *Early Warning Systems*, Tyler Museum of Art, Tyler, Texas
1985 *Introductions '85*, Moody Gallery

**Selected Group Exhibitions**

1993 *Landscapes: Left to Right*, Landfall Press, Chicago
1993 *Darkness + Light*, Sarah Campbell Blaffer Gallery, University of Houston
1993 *Everpresent Moment*, Ringling School of Art and Design, Sarasota, Florida
1992 *Point of View: Landscapes from the Addison Collection*, Phillips Academy, Andover, Massachusetts
1991 *Recent Acquisitions of the Achenbach Foundation for Graphic Arts: Part Two, 1950–1991*, California Palace of the Legion of Honor, San Francisco
1991 *The State I'm In: Texas Artists at the DMA*, Dallas Museum of Art
1991 *A Sense of Place: Recent Acquisitions in Contemporary Texas Art*, San Antonio

Museum of Art
1990 *42nd Annual Purchase Exhibition*, American Academy and Institute of Arts and Letters, New York
1990 *Drawn to Scale*, Addison Gallery of American Art, Phillips Academy, Andover
1990 *Awards in the Visual Arts 9*, New Orleans Museum of Art; Southeastern Center for Contemporary Art, Winston-Salem, North Carolina
1990 *This Land: The State of Texas*, Lawndale Art & Performance Center, Houston
1990 *Tradition and Innovation: A Museum Celebration of Texas Art*, Museum of Fine Arts, Houston
1988 *Memory*, Center for Research in Contemporary Art, University of Texas, Arlington
1988 *The Texas Triennial*, Contemporary Art Museum, Houston; Texas A&M University, College Station; Art Museum of South Texas, Corpus Christi; Lubbock Fine Arts Center; San Angelo Museum of Fine Arts, Texas; Center for Research in Contemporary Art, Arlington; Bridge Center For Contemporary Art, El Paso
1987 *Third Coast Review: A Look at Art in Texas*, Aspen Art Museum, Colorado
1987 *Recent Drawings*, University of Texas, El Paso
1986 *Artists' Response to Architecture*, Nave Museum, Victoria, Texas
1986 *SPECTRUM: Drawn Out*, Corcoran Gallery of Art, Washington DC
1986 *Monumental Drawing*, Brooklyn Museum, New York
1986 New Orleans Triennial, New Orleans Museum of Art
1985 *The Artist's Eye*, Kimbell Art Museum, Fort Worth
1985 *One Up*, Lawndale Art & Performance Center, Houston
1984 *Four Texas Painters*, University of Illinois, Chicago
1984 *Patterns in Contemporary Art*, Laguna Gloria Art Museum, Austin

**Selected Public Collections**

Addison Gallery of American Art, Phillips Academy, Andover
Brooklyn Museum, Brooklyn
California Palace of the Legion of Honor, San Francisco
Dallas Museum of Art
Archer M Huntington Art Gallery, University of Texas, Austin
Modern Art Museum of Fort Worth
Museum of Fine Arts, Houston
New Orleans Museum of Art
Arthur M Sackler Museum, Harvard University, Cambridge
Tyler Museum of Art

## Dick Wray

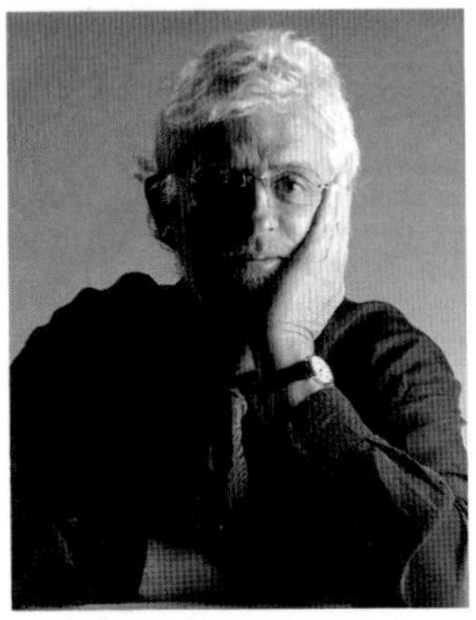

*Dick Wray, 1993. Photograph: Rob Ziebell. Courtesy of Art Industrial, Houston.*

1933 Born in Houston, Texas
Lives in Houston

**Education and Awards**

1955–58 University of Houston, School of Architecture
1958 Kunstakademie, Dusseldorf, Germany
1978 National Endowment for the Arts Individual Artists Fellowship

**Selected Solo Exhibitions**

1994 *Dick Wray: Paintings and Drawings*, Museum of East Texas, Lufkin
1993 *Xerography and Collages*, Moody Gallery, Houston
1991 *Recent Paintings*, Moody Gallery, Houston
1989 *Recent Paintings*, Galveston Arts Center, Galveston, Texas
1989 *Monotypes*, Cathleen Gallander/Susan Lang, New York
1986 *New Paintings*, Moody Gallery, Houston
1985 *Paintings and Monotypes*, Southwest Craft Center, San Antonio
1985 *Dick Wray: Paintings, 1975–1985*, Midtown Art Center, Houston
1984 Monotypes, Moody Gallery, Houston
1981 Paintings and Drawings, Moody Gallery, Houston
1979 Galveston Art Center, Galveston
1979 Roberto Molina Gallery, Houston
1978 Tyler Museum of Art, Tyler, Texas
1977 Lerner-Heller Gallery, New York
1977 *Paintings and Drawings*, Pelham-Van Stoffler Gallery, Houston
1975 Contemporary Arts Museum, Houston

**Selected Group Exhibitions**

1993 *Artists' Progress: Seven Houston Artists, 1943–1993*, Alfred C Glassell School of Art, Houston
1992 *New Texas Art*, Cheney Cowles Museum, Spokane, Washington; Boise Art Museum, Idaho
1992 *Singular and Plural*, Museum of Fine Arts, Houston
1991 *One Line: Drawings by Texas Artists*, Amarillo Art Center, Amarillo, Texas
1990 *Printmaking in Texas: The 1980s*, Modern Art Museum of Fort Worth, Texas; Laguna Gloria Art Museum, Austin
1990 *Tradition and Innovation: A Museum Celebration of Texas Art*, Museum of Fine Arts, Houston
1989 *Just Paint*, Blue Star Art Space, San Antonio
1989 *Drawing Conclusions*, Southwest Texas State University, San Marcos
1988 *Selected Prints: Shark's Incorporated*, Boulder Center for the Visual Arts, Boulder, Colorado
1987 *Third Coast Review*, Aspen Art Museum, Colorado
1987 *Line and Form: Contemporary Texas Figurative Drawing*, Art Museum of South Texas, Corpus Christi
1986 *Collaborators: Artists Working Together in Houston, 1969–1986*, Alfred C Glassell School of Art, Houston
1986 *Third Western States Exhibition*, The Brooklyn Museum, New York; New Orleans Contemporary Art Center; Colorado Springs Fine Arts Center; Art Museum of South Texas; other venues
1985 *American Abstraction: Four Currents*, Louis Meisel Gallery, New York
1985 *Sam Scott, Dick Wray: Paintings*, Nave Museum, Victoria, Texas
1985 *Works on Paper: Eleven Houston Artists*, Museum of Fine Arts, Houston
1985 *Fresh Paint: The Houston School*, Museum of Fine Arts, Houston; PS1, Long Island City, New York
1984 *Gateway Gallery Experience*, Dallas Museum of Art
1983 *New Art From a New City*, Salzburg Kunstverein, Austria
1982 *In Our Time: Houston's Contemporary Arts Museum, 1948–1982*, Contemporary Arts Museum, Houston
1981 *Two Views of Houston*, San Antonio Art Institute
1980 *Response*, Tyler Museum of Art, Texas
1977 *Texas Today: Three Exhibitions — Dick Wray Paintings*, Fort Worth Art Museum
1976 *The Texas 20 Best*, Nave Museum, Victoria
1974 *Abstract Painting and Sculpture*, Museum of Fine Arts, Houston
1971 *Texas Painting and Sculpture: The 20th Century*, California State University, Long Beach
1965 *100 Contemporary American Drawings*, University of Michigan, Ann Arbor
1964 Tamarind Lithography Workshop, Los Angeles
1962 *Southwest Painting and Sculpture Exhibition*, Museum of Fine Arts, Houston
1961 *Ways and Means*, Contemporary Arts Museum, Houston

**Selected Public Collections**

Albright-Knox Gallery of Art, Buffalo
Amarillo Art Center, Amarillo
Museum of Fine Arts, Houston
Museum of Modern Art, New York
National Gallery of Art, Washington DC
San Antonio Museum of Art
Southern Methodist University, Dallas
Witte Memorial Museum, San Antonio